INHERITING the NATIONS

McDougal & Associates
Servants of Christ and Stewards of the Mysteries of God

ENDORSEMENTS

I simply call him "Joe" or "Joe-Z." He is a friend, a brother, a co-worker, and a fellow servant in the service of our Lord Jesus Christ. I have known Joe for more than forty years and have travelled with him into many nations in Asia and North America. His favorite scripture, in Psalm 2:8, *"Ask of Me, and I will give you the nations for Your inheritance, and the ends of the earth for Your possession,"* speaks of his life journey and commitment to the call of God on his life. He believes and claims that every nation or country he set his foot on is his inheritance. He also never stops fighting for his possession, believing that God is not willing that any should perish, but that all should come to repentance. Joe is a real evangelist, a carrier of the Good News!

Joe's book is like a "written epistle" of an ordinary servant of God who did exploits in many mission fields in many nations of the world through a simple faith and all-out obedience to God's call. It is a road map of faith and obedience and a must-read for everyone who desire to experience who God is and what He can do with a person who is willing to give it all to Jesus that others might have the opportunity to hear about the love of God. Joe and Brenda are very dear friends to me and to my family.

Sonny Largado
International Director
Ethnos Asia Ministries International (EAMI)
Executive Director
Christ To Thailand Mission
Bangkok, Thailand

§

Inheriting the Nations has been written by a sincere servant of God, Joseph Zeyak, Jr. If you know Brother Joe, there is chance that, just like me, you will be captivated by other details of his life story that you didn't already know. If you don't know him personally, you'll be blessed with a sincere narrative that talks, not only about victories, but also about disappointments and mistakes.

I think that the story develops according to this Bible verse:

But you will receive power when the Holy Spirit comes upon you; and you'll be witnesses in Jerusalem, and in all Judea and Samaria, and to the ends of the earth.   Acts 1:8

Here you will read about a journey from a small American town to the unreached peoples of Southeast Asia, the Communist countries of the Far East, the remote places of South America, as well as other corners of the world. This is the story of a most ordinary man who has led a supernatural life through his following of God. I pray that the book will have the same impact on you, that as you personally become acquainted with Brother Joe, it will not only fill you with knowledge, but will extend a friendly hand, not just to share some sound doctrine, but also to impart an anointing for ministry. I wish you a pleasant reading and fellowship with the author.

Andrey Derkach
YWAM Eastern European Director

§

I have known Joseph Zeyak for more than forty years. From the first time I met him, I recognized that he had an apostolic calling on his life. I have listened to Joe over the years when he returned from his mission work, first in South America and then from other nations. His work in God's Kingdom has been calling the nations to gird up for spiritual war. His stories have been thrilling and astounding of how God has led him in difficult and often dangerous areas of the world.

Now, Joe has written his life adventures into a biographical record. His new book, *Inheriting the Nations*, details his incredible journey. His easy-to-read, breezy writing style is just like his thrilling storytelling.

I highly recommend this book to those interested in fulfilling Christ's Great Commission.

Pastor Phil Roland
Sheepfold Ministries
Sharon, Pennsylvania

§

I met Joe Zeyak in 1983 in Rio de Janeiro, Brazil, while we were there ministering at churches in several different Brazilian cities. It so happened that we were ministering at the Maranata Church where Joe was working at the time, and he drove us to the different Maranata churches in the city of Rio to minister. This was such a great blessing that the Lord provided.

I've known Joe now for forty years, and I can say he's a great and powerful brother in Christ. We have gone to several countries together. to proclaim the good news, and he has ministered many times in our church, Lighthouse Christian Fellowship here in Madera, California. This book actually comes off the pages and into the hearts of our people every time he ministers here.

I have proofread many pages of the book and have been abundantly blessed by it already. I believe it is going to be a Holy Ghost tool to bring men and women who are out there wondering what God is all about to find themselves in the very place that God has designed for them in His Kingdom. God is going to use this book and the life of Joe to thrill and fill God's people with the zeal and enthusiasm to activate the giftings God has distributed throughout His Body!

God Bless you and your ministry, Joe. What a great achievement you have accomplished for the Kingdom of God!

Bernard Morris, Senior Pastor (Semi retired)
Lighthouse Christian Fellowship
Madera, California

INHERITING the NATIONS

BY

JOSEPH ZEYAK JR.

Inheriting the Nations
Copyright © 2023, 2024, 2025 — Joseph Zeyak, Jr.
ALL RIGHTS RESERVED. No portion of this book may be reproduced in any form without the written permission of the author.

All Scripture references are from *The Holy Bible, New King James Version*, copyright © 1979, 1980, 1982, 1990 by Thomas Nelson, Inc., Nashville, Tennessee. Used by permission. All rights reserved.

Published by:

McDougal & Associates
www.thepublishedword.com

McDougal & Associates is dedicated to spreading the Gospel of the Lord Jesus Christ to as many people as possible in the shortest time possible.

ISBN 978-1-950398-78-2 Trade Paper
ISBN 978-1-950398-90-4 Case Laminate
ISBN 978-1-950398-91-1 eBook
4th Revision

Printed in the U.S., the U.K., Australia, and the UAE
For Worldwide Distribution

DEDICATION

My journey has been both wonderful and challenging. There have been times of great joy and times of great sorrow. There have been successes, and there have been failures, but through it all the Lord has given me grace to continue to be faithful. With the anointing He has given me, I have traveled the nations, raising up men and women—young and old—to be an army of warriors, prepared for war, expanding God's Kingdom everywhere they go.

I've had the privilege to minister and pray with many in Southeast Asia and other parts of the world that live in countries that are under heavy persecution, and yet they continue to be faithful to the Lord. To all of them and to the generations to come who are hungry and thirsty for the things of the Spirit, I dedicate this book.

ACKNOWLEDGMENTS

On October 14,1971 at 6:30 at night, I was lost, living in darkness, spiritually dead, living for my own desires. Then *Joan Koniszewski-Slish* told me over the phone that God wanted to come into my life and encouraged me to pray. God came, and my new life began because of her. Thank you, Joan.

A few years later, a college girl named *Lynn Thornton* gave me a book entitled *The Holy Spirit and You: A Guide to the Spirit Filled Life*[1] by Episcopal priest, Father Dennis Bennett and his wife Rita. Inspired by that, I received the baptism with the Holy Spirit and begin to operate in the gifts of the Spirit. Thank you, Lynn.

While I was in seminary, *Rev. Greg Fitch* used to say to all of us. "If you don't go into all the world and preach the Gospel, you're disobeying the Word of God." I wasn't interested in being a missionary, but I became one partly because of him. Thank you, Greg.

On my first mission trip, I went to Ecuador, and there I met *Rev. Harold McDougal*. I knew nothing about missions, but he made a place for me and encouraged me. Four decades later, I connected with him again, and he became the editor and publisher of this book. Thank you, Harold.

---

1. Newberry, Florida (Bridge-Logos: 1971)

I had thought many times about writing a book but never did. Then, in 2022, while visiting a friend in Ohio, I met *Pastor Joel Dickson and his wife Dina*. Dina told me she thought God wanted me to write a book. I told her I had thought about it, but I had a problem called "procrastination." She took my hands that day and prayed for me. A few weeks later I began to write because of her encouragement and prayer. Thank you, Dina.

My wife, *Brenda,* has walked with me now for thirty-five years, accompanying me to many of the nations of the world. We have encouraged many and given what the Lord has given to us—both as a couple and as individuals. Thank you, Brenda.

My friend, *Sandi Mahlow*, with her Photoshop skills, helped me design my book cover.

There are *many others* in the nations of the world that have allowed me to walk with them in their nations and made a place for me to share the things the Lord has taught me. The names are too many to mention. You'll meet some of them as you read about my journey.

> Ask of Me, and I will give You
> The nations for Your inheritance,
> And the ends of the earth
> for Your possession.
>
> —Psalm 2:8

CONTENTS

    Excerpt from Caitlin Ann 13
    About the Cover... 15
    Introduction... 19

1. A Young Man Encounters God... 25
2. The Promise of the Father 33
3. Prayer in the Spirit... 48
4. God Moving in the Workplace 55
5. God's Call... 61
6. "Ask of Me".. 71
7. Walking in the Footsteps of Martyrs.. 77
8. God's Guidance through Ordinary People 89
9. Life and Ministry on a Brazilian Fazenda 95
10. The Lord's Financial Blessings.. 103
11. Japan, a Country of Two Worlds.. 110
12. A Vision to Deliver Bread to the Family 117
13. The Medical Mission Force of Nepal 121
14. No Place Like India 126
15. Kenya, Africa 131
16. Entering the Stone Age 139
17. The Power of Friendship 151
18. Love and Sacrifice 167
19. The Angelic Host of the Invisible World............................... 174
20. Around the World in Four Months.. 187

21.	We Continue Around the World	201
22.	The Karen Tribal People of Burma	206
23.	Those of Whom the World Was Not Worthy	210
24.	Betrayal—the Making of a Leader	242
25.	To Love Again	253
26.	The Power of a Hug	266
27.	Jehovah-Rapha, the Lord Who Heals	281
28.	Religious Strongholds	295
29.	Tsunami in Asia	305
30.	Training and Traveling in Southeast Asia	312
31.	Bibles into China	326
32.	The God Who Delivers Us	336
33.	Encountering the Master	340
34.	The Healing Power of Joy	346
35.	The Roar of the Lion of the Tribe of Judah	355
36.	Seasons of Change	364
37.	A Vision for Central Asia	376
38.	Expressions of Heaven in Russia	393
39.	The Sword of the Lord	408
40.	Descending into Darkness	417
41.	The Rooms of My Heart	426
42.	Passing the Mantle of War	440
43.	They Called Me Father	456
44.	Preparing for War	463
45.	Religion or Relationship	475
	Suggested Reading	496
	Author Contact Page	497
	Golden Bowl Ministries	498

I BOARDED THE PLANE TO …
AND FACED THAT MOMENT I DREAD
EVERY TIME I RETURN TO THE MISSION FIELD,
THAT PAINFUL MOMENT OF TENSION BETWEEN
EXCITEMENT FOR THE ADVENTURE AHEAD
AND THE FEAR OF TERRITORY COMPLETELY UNKNOWN.
IT'S THE ACHE OF TURNING MY BACK ON MY LOVED ONES
AND EVERYTHING FAMILIAR,
WHILE TRYING TO BE STRONG ENOUGH TO RUN INTO MY DESTINY.
IT'S THE MOMENT WHEN I AM EXACTLY WHERE I'M SUPPOSED TO BE,
YET LOSS AND FEAR TRY TO TELL ME OTHERWISE
AND WHERE PIECES OF MYSELF ARE PAINFULLY SQUEEZED OUT OF ME,
MAKING ROOM FOR NEW CULTURES, NEW FRIENDS,
AND A NEW MISSION.

– CAITLIN ANN
FROM *BELIEVE AND BE LOVE*[1]

---

1. Self-Published: 2013. Used by permission

ABOUT THE COVER

I chose this cover photo for several reasons. The large mountain on the right is Mt. Ararat, and the smaller mountain to the left of it is known as Little Ararat. In the book of Genesis, we read:

Then the ark rested in the 7th month, the 7th day of the month, on the mountains of Ararat.   Genesis 8:4

Then God spoke to Noah, saying, "Go out of the ark, you and your wife, and your sons and your sons' wives with you. Bring out with you every living thing of all flesh that is with you: birds and cattle and every creeping thing that creeps on the earth, so that they may abound on the earth, and be fruitful and multiply on the earth."   Genesis 8:15-17

It was here, in this area of the world, which we now call Armenia, that new life would begin. Man and animals would multiply in the earth as God had intended from the beginning.

Unfortunately, the Ararat mountains no longer belong to Armenia. The land in that area was taken over by the Ottoman Empire, which is now modern-day Turkey, during the Armenian Genocide of 1915-1916. The Turkish government took over a large area of Armenia, and that included the area of the mountains of Ararat. Armenians were taken captive and forced to marry into Muslim families and convert to Islam. It is estimated that up to 1.5 million Armenians died during the mass killings and deportations by the Turks of the Ottoman Empire.

INHERITING THE NATIONS

The devastation of that era is still fresh in the hearts and minds of the Armenian people today. The present population of Armenia is 2.7 million. However, there are another 7.6 million Armenians living outside of Armenia. A large number of them live in Southern California.

The large castle-like structure on the right side of the photo is known as Artashat. What happened there in 301 AD changed the culture of Armenia. According to ancient tradition (supported by historical evidence), Christianity was preached in Armenia in the second half of the first century by two of the disciples of Jesus, Thaddeus and Bartholomew. They were both martyred there in Armenia.

Another Christian, later known as Saint Gregory, went to Armenia to proclaim the Gospel. The Armenian king, Tiridates, imprisoned Gregory in a dungeon in Artashat for many years. During that time, a group of Christian nuns, led by Saint Gayane, were fleeing persecution in Rome, and decided to go to Armenia. It is said that the king was attracted to one of the nuns, but she resisted him. In his anger, he had all of the nuns killed.

History states that after the king killed these Christian nuns, he developed an incurable mental illness. His sister told him that only Gregory, the preacher who was imprisoned in the dungeon, could cure him. By this time, Gregory had been in the dungeon for fifteen years and was presumed dead. The king sent for him, he was found still alive and was brought out from the dungeon. When Gregory prayed for King Tiridates, the king was healed, and his whole family converted to Christianity. All the pagan altars around Armenia were destroyed, except for one that remains partially standing today.

As a result of the king's conversion in 301 AD, he declared Christianity to be the official religion of Armenia. With the support of the royal family, Christianity spread quickly throughout Armenia, and within just a few centuries it permeated all aspects of Armenian life and culture. From Armenia, missionaries were sent out to other countries in the region.

I have visited the monastery in the photo numerous times. I stood in the dungeon where Gregory was imprisoned, and I looked over the walls at the majestic beauty of Mt. Ararat and the other nearby mountains. When the Lord looks at these mountains, He looks beyond them and sees a people living in darkness in the chains of Islam, and He is looking for someone who will go and preach the Gospel to them and break the chains of darkness for the people of Turkey.

INTRODUCTION

As I have journeyed with the Lord for more than fifty years now, I have often thought of writing a book. In the beginning, I kept a diary, but as I began to work in restricted countries, I discontinued that for security reasons. Through the years, I have worked in four major areas of the world—Brazil, Southeast Asia, Armenia, and Central Asia. I recently realized that my friends in one area didn't know much about the other areas I was working in. A book would be the only way to bring all my stories from these different areas together, hopefully in a format that would glorify the Lord and that would challenge those who would read it, maybe even those of the next generation.

I had a friend named Val who was an amazing worship leader. He would come to our home, and we would have soaking worship sessions. We would take the furniture out of our living room and tell people to bring blankets and pillows. Then we would lie on the floor for two or three hours as Val played his keyboard. There were no words, just music, and the presence of the Lord would come mightily. Those were amazing times. No one prayed for anyone; we just let the Lord speak personally to each of us. Often, some were hearing His loving voice for the first time. Tragically, when Val was only in his fifties, he developed a severe liver problem and died. Unfortunately, we had never recorded any of his music, so his ministry died with him. No one would ever hear his songs again.

INHERITING THE NATIONS

I have thought many times, "I'm not getting any younger, and I need to write a book." As noted in the acknowledgments, last year, on a trip to Ohio, I met a precious couple Pastor Joel Dickson and his wife Dina. We spent several hours sharing our stories with one another, and in the end, Dina asked me, "Have you ever thought of writing a book?"

I said to her, "I've thought about it many times, and I even thought of writing it during the covid crisis. I just have one problem. It's called 'procrastination.'"

She said, "I've never heard stories like yours, and I've never heard anyone tell them like you do. I think God wants you to write a book."

I asked her if she wanted to pray for me. She said yes. Then she took my hands and prayed. Her prayers did something, and I began to write a few weeks later, on June 17, 2022.

After I became a Christian, I began to read Christian books. Most of them were how-to books or testimonials of the glorious life following Jesus. I only recall two books that were different. One was about a pastor who had been embezzling funds from the church he was pastoring. He was eventually discovered and was tried in court. Instead of him being sent to prison, the judge, with the agreement of the church people, allowed him to remain the pastor. His only stipulation was that he pay back, from his salary, all the money he had taken. It was a true example of the mercy of God and the people of his congregation and of the restorative power of the Gospel.

The second book was filled with heartache and sacrifice. It was the life story of Adoniram Judson, the first missionary to leave America. His first wife died in Burma, the place of their calling, and, sadly, he lost two more wives during his lifetime. The truth is that ministry is not easy. It's hard. It's filled with heartache and joy, sacrifice and rewards, pain and pleasure. For those who minister in foreign countries, it can mean uncomfortable accommodations and strange food. But in all of these circumstances, the Lord receives glory through us, and Jesus receives the reward of His suffering.

It has taken more than a year, but this book you are about to read is my story, my journey, trying to follow the Lord to the best of my ability in the nations of the world. It is not a theological book, although I have devoted one chapter to talk about the gifts of the Holy Spirit.

Aside from this chapter, I have no intention of trying to write a book that theologically pleases everyone. I'm sure that there will be those who will totally disagree with my experiences, but that's okay. I'm not trying to change anybody's theology in this book. Probably, in the end, when my whole story is told, it's just about a young man who had an encounter with Jesus, got detoured sometimes, but tried to follow Him to the best of his ability.

It was not my intention to write a book filled with flowery language and intriguing stories, leaving the impression that the Christian life is easy. The truth is that this Christian walk is challenging and sacrificial. When I teach in Bible schools around the world and talk to leaders of many denominations, I always say, "This is not a picnic; it's a war!" Yes, this is a war for the souls of men and women in the nations of the world, souls that are locked in darkness. Part of my vision is to raise up warriors who will advance God's Kingdom everywhere they go.

In my own life, there have been times of great darkness and sorrow, times when I thought to myself, "I can't do this anymore." The truth is, however, that I have no choice. There is something burning in my heart that compels me onward. It is God's will, not mine. When I arrive in another country, I feel like I'm alive, and I feel like I'm doing what I was born to do.

INHERITING THE NATIONS

My journey into the nations of the world has taken me to many countries where Christians are seen as the enemy of the State, and persecution can range from very light to very extreme, in some cases, even death. Because of that, I have not used full names of the people I have encountered in those countries, to protect them from any repercussions of what I have written.

Paul said in Romans 1:11:

For I long to see you, that I may impart to you some spiritual gift, so that you may be established.

As of this writing, I've been to fifty nations of the world. I've tried my best to impart to others what the Lord has imparted to me. As the Holy Spirit has led me, I've tried to encourage and bless people every place I go. When the Lord called me to ministry, He gave me Psalm 2:8:

Ask of Me, and I will give You
The nations for Your inheritance,
And the ends of the earth for Your possession.

When I step into a nation for the first time, I realize that, along with my call, comes authority to do the works of Jesus and to glorify the Father, that Jesus might receive the reward of His suffering! I've tried my best, through His grace, to be faithful to the Lord and to my friends in the nations of the world.

Throughout this book I often use the phrase, "May Jesus receive the reward of His suffering." It was the early 1700s in Germany when John Leonard Dober and David Nitschman first heard about a needy island. They were at their Moravian Brethren Church on an ordinary Sunday morning, and the pastor was speaking about an island in the West Indies called St. Thomas, an island where there had never been a Gospel witness. He told of a British man who lived on an island. He was an atheist and slave owner and had about three thousand slaves. "All of these," the pastor said, "will live and die without a chance to ever hear of Jesus."

Deeply disturbed by what they heard that day, these two men, both in their early twenties, made a decision to go to this island place to reach those slaves with the Gospel. Their plan was to sell themselves into slavery so that they could be among the slaves. Imagine it! Selling themselves into slavery! These guys were not heading out on a short-term missions trip. No, they left to live and suffer as slaves, and they had no idea if they would ever come back again. As you can imagine, their families and friends, in large part, were all against this decision, and yet John and David prepared to go.

The story goes that these two young men arrived at the pier to board the ship, their families and friends all there to say goodbye, sure they would never see them again. The men boarded the ship and set out, and as the gap between the shore and the ship widened, the two men linked arms. One of them raised his hand and shouted across the gap these final words:

May the Lamb that was slain receive the reward of His suffering!

As you read my story, it is my prayer that the Lord will give you the vision and the grace to obey His calling for your life, so that through you, Jesus might receive the reward of His suffering!
This is my story.

Joseph Zeyak, Jr.

Chapter 1

A YOUNG MAN ENCOUNTERS GOD

Therefore, if anyone is in Christ, he is a new creation; old things have passed away; behold, all things have become new. 2 Corinthians 5:17

It was late August of 1971. When I returned home from work that evening and opened the door, I immediately noticed that most of the furniture was gone. I ran frantically through the house from room to room and found the same everywhere. All the rooms were nearly empty. I suddenly realized that my wife and two children were gone. Prior to that moment I'd had no clue that she would ever leave me.

I should have known. I was a young man (twenty-five at the time) living my own life, doing my own thing, and not accepting the responsibilities of fatherhood or marriage. What did I expect?

I immediately called my mother-in-law, knowing my wife would be there, but she hung up on me. I got back in the car and drove over there. Emotionally, I was totally out of control. I simply couldn't believe this was happening to me, that my wife had left and taken our children with her. To me, it seemed like the end of the world.

I frantically knocked on the door. I saw her inside, but at first, she wouldn't come out. Eventually she did, but she said it was over. She was never coming back. As much as I hated it, I had to turn and leave without her and my children and go home ... to what I wasn't sure. My life, for all intents and purposes, seemed to be over.

What happened after that moment is kind of a blur, but what I do remember is that I called a friend of mine named Frank. I'm not sure why I called Frank. There were many people closer to me that I could have called. Frank was the brother of an ex-girlfriend. Looking back, I realize that my calling him and not someone else was directed by the Lord. Frank immediately came over and sat with me, trying to comfort me and give me some practical advice. As the days unfolded, I talked with Frank many times.

I went to a doctor and got some medication to help me sleep, to help me function during the day, and to help me handle the anxiety and depression I was experiencing. I was working at the time for General Electric as a designer, and many times during the day, I would just stand at my drawing board and weep. Thankfully, I was in the very back of the room, and only two people could see what was going on with me.

Eventually I got the idea to go see a Catholic nun who had been a friend of both my grandfather and father. She was now ninety-two years old and had been seventy-five years in the convent. Surely she knew how to pray. Surely she would pray, God would hear her prayers, and my wife and children would come home to me. Every Friday I began to visit that nun, and every Friday she prayed for me. Still, my family didn't come home.

Months passed. On October 14, Frank and his wife Joan invited me to come to their house for dinner. Just before I was to leave to go there, I got a phone call from my wife. I don't remember exactly what she said, but I do remember that it left me very depressed, and I decided I couldn't go to dinner after all. I called to inform Frank and Joan of my change of plans.

Joan answered the phone and said she understood and that I could come another time. Then she asked me, "Why are you going to this nun?" I told her I was going there to have the nun pray so that God would answer her prayers and bring my wife back. "Well," she said, "why can't you just pray yourself?"

I said, "Because I don't feel worthy!"

A YOUNG MAN ENCOUNTERS GOD

Joan said, "You're *not* worthy, but the Lord wants to come into your life anyway." Then she added, "All you have to do is tell God that you're a sinner and you're sorry for your sins. Tell Him you believe Jesus Christ died on the cross for you *personally* and then ask Him to come into your life."

Knowing how important this was, Joan repeated it a second time. Then she concluded, "When you're feeling better, come up to see me. I have a Bible I want to give you."

"I can't read a Bible," I told her.

She said, "I have one you'll be able to understand."

I had been raised in a Catholic home in a middle-class family in upstate New York, had gone to church every Sunday and gone through all the religious ceremonies as I was growing up. Then, however, when I turned eighteen, I got a car and soon got involved in drag racing. The problem was the drag racing was on Sunday, so now I had to choose which was more important to me—drag racing or church. For an eighteen-year-old boy, drag racing was the priority. So, I left church and had never gone back. Even after my wife and I married, we never attended church services.

From my religious upbringing, I knew all the basics. I knew in theory that Jesus died for the sins of the world, but I had never once thought of Him dying for me *personally*. I wasn't against the church, but for me, religion was for Sunday, not for everyday life.

But where had this outlook gotten me? I had lived selfishly, and my lifestyle and bad choices had not only destroyed me; they had destroyed my wife and children. Now, as a consequence, I was alone, and I was filled with fear, confusion, and anxiety. I was able to function only with medications.

It was October 14, 1971 at 6:30 in the evening. I got down on my knees to pray for the first time in many years. Even as I prayed, I was filled with all sorts of negative emotions. I remembered what Joan had said, so I prayed, "God, I am a sinner, and I'm sorry for my sins! I believe Your Son Jesus Christ died on the cross for me personally! Please come into my life!" The moment I uttered those words, it was like a flash bulb had gone off. I looked around, but there was nothing. The windows in the room where I prayed were situated so that no light from the street could come in. What was it that I had seen?

I suddenly realized that all the fear, confusion, and depression I had been experiencing for months now had left, and in their place, a peace I had never before experienced filled me. Looking up, I saw all of my medications there on the bed and suddenly realized I would never need them again. And I didn't!

When I got up from my knees, I was filled with such peace and such excitement that words could not fully describe it. I didn't know any religious terms to describe what I had just experienced. I just knew that in that moment God had come into my life!

I got in my car and drove to Frank and Joan's house and, with great joy and excitement, told them what had just happened. That has been so long ago that I don't remember what else transpired that night except that Joan gave me a wonderful New Testament entitled *Good News for Modern Man*.[1] This would become my food for many months to come. Every waking moment I read it.

The day after this experience, I went to see my mother-in-law. I must be honest and say there was nobody I hated more than her. I felt that she had forced me into marrying her daughter, and I also felt that she was responsible for my wife leaving. For sure, she was the one who had moved my family out. I told her that I had committed my life to God and that I was confident He was going to bring her back to me. "That's good," my mother-in-law said, "but I'm not interested in God."

Over a period of months, I took other people to share the Gospel with her, but she would never accept Jesus. Her only brother had died in the war, and she blamed God for his death.

Just a few years ago now, almost fifty years after I first shared my experience with my mother-in-law, she was on her deathbed at her

---
1. New York, New York (American Bible Society: 1966)

son's home in Florida. A Christian lady was at her bedside trying to comfort her. She kept saying, "I'm not ready to die." The lady shared with her once again the love of the Father, and this time, ready to breathe her last breath on this earth, my mother-in-law accepted Jesus. Just a few minutes later, she went into eternity, into the loving arms of Jesus! Thank God!

Now back to Frank and Joan. Frank was a policeman who worked nights, so every evening I would call Joan and tell her what I had read in the Bible during the day. She never tried to explain things theologically to me. She just encouraged me to keep reading and seemed happy about what I was learning as I read the New Testament.

At work, things quickly changed. I was no longer weeping. Instead, I was telling everybody in sight about how God had come into my life. Some of my worker friends probably wished that I would have kept crying. Even on breaks, I would read the New Testament, and eventually some of those in the office who were Christians began to share their experiences with me. Prior to that, they had been what I call "silent Christians." One brother at work whose name was also Joe began to take me to Friday meetings at his Presbyterian church, and he bought me my first full Bible, a wonderful Scofield Reference Bible.

Although I had grown up in a religious home, we never read the Bible in those days. Only the priest could understand the Bible, or so we were told. Because of this, reading the Bible was a whole new experience for me. I began to share with everybody I knew that God had come into my life and what I was learning about Him.

I didn't know theologically how to explain what I had experienced. I just knew that inside I was different, and everything was changing. I was not the same person. My desires and dreams were changed.

Because I had been raised Catholic, I returned to the Catholic Church, and I continued to visit that lovely nun every Friday. As I continued to read the New Testament, I had many questions, so over

INHERITING THE NATIONS

time I spoke with two priests in my church, sharing with them what had happened to me and asking them if they had heard about what the Bible called in John 3 being "born again."

Eventually, I went to visit the home of the Monsignor who was over all the priests. I asked him how I could know if I was going to Heaven. He said, "Joe, the truth is that nobody can know for sure if they're going to Heaven or not." I picked up his Bible that was sitting on the edge of the desk, opened it to 1 John 5:13, and began to read:

These things I have written to you who believe in the name of the Son of God, that you may know that you have eternal life, and that you may continue to believe in the name of the Son of God.

"Every Sunday," I said to the Monsignor, "hundreds of people come to church here, and they're looking to you for the answer of how to go to Heaven. The truth is you don't know the way. I do, and I'll be praying for you." Then I got up and walked out. It was dark outside, but small lights lit up the sidewalk as I walked away from the Monsignor's home. I looked up to Heaven and said to God, "I'm never coming back here again." I needed to find a church that could help me understand the Bible more clearly.

I started going to church with my spiritual mom, Joan, and her husband Frank. At the time, they were attending a Wesleyan Methodist Church, which had a Wednesday night Bible study. I was there whenever the church was open and spent many hours with the pastor and his family at their home. I was hungry and thirsty for more. The pastor gave me books about John Wesley's life, and this formed some of my early theology. It also caused me to realize that God was calling me to walk in holiness.

I attended a couple of Methodist camp meetings, and they were amazingly powerful. One evangelist would open with prayer, and

A YOUNG MAN ENCOUNTERS GOD

the other evangelist would preach. Even while the one evangelist was praying, people were coming forward with tears of repentance and kneeling at the altar for prayer.

Eventually I saw the need for water baptism by immersion, so on March 26, 1972, I was baptized in water in the name of the Father, the Son, and the Holy Spirit, confessing my new faith in Jesus. It took place at the Balltown Wesleyan Methodist Church in New York, and I was baptized by Pastor Charles McCollum, Sr.

Inside me, there was now a burning fire to share my experience with everyone I knew every place I went. As a result, I saw many people come to the Lord. Although my understanding of biblical theology was still in its infant stages, the people who knew me saw that my life had dramatically changed. They could not deny that God had done a miracle in me. The power of my testimony was undeniable.

With my spiritual mom, Joan

Chapter 2

THE PROMISE OF THE FATHER

And being assembled together with them, He commanded them not to depart from Jerusalem, but to wait for the Promise of the Father, "which," He said, "you have heard from Me; for John truly baptized with water, but you shall be baptized with the Holy Spirit not many days from now." Acts 1:4-5

The transformation of my life was truly a work of God's grace. Nothing I had done in my former life could have earned the things the Lord was doing for me and through me. I had become what the Bible calls a new creature, old things had passed away, and all things had become new.

It was the deep desire of my heart for the Lord to bring reconciliation between me and my wife and children. Psalm 37 spoke to me in a powerful way, and I was convinced that the Lord would bring us back together for His glory.

I eventually enrolled my two sons in a Christian school near my home and began to attend the church that was connected to the school. It was a Community Church, and the pastors were great Bible teachers. I spent as much time as I could around the church. One day, when the janitor didn't come in because he was sick, I volunteered to clean all the bathrooms and the Sunday school rooms just so I could be there.

INHERITING THE NATIONS

My wife and I began to go out on dates together and to sometimes do things together with the children. I was encouraged to think that we would become a family that the Lord would do great things in and through. He had spoken to me many times, and my faith never wavered that we would be back together. I began to fast one day a week for my family and also just so that I could draw closer to the Lord. I continued that practice for many years. Once, I even fasted for forty days to attempt to get clarification on my marriage situation. At the time, we were legally separated, but neither of us was moving toward a full divorce.

While attending this new church, I met many new friends. One couple, Paul and Doris Morgan, became like a mother and father in the faith to me, and I spent many hours with them in their home. One evening, while we were sitting in their dining room, Doris said she wished they had a deck. I looked at the two windows at the end of the room and said, "Well, that would be very easy. We'd just have to remove those two windows, build in a patio door leading to the deck and then build the deck itself." She didn't think it would be easy, but the following week construction began, and they ended up with a beautiful deck that she still uses with great delight.

The Morgans' son had some physical problems, and we had heard there was a group called the Full Gospel Business Men's Fellowship that was having meetings in which people were being healed, so we decided to attend one of their meetings. For all of us, this was new territory. Someone shared a testimony, and then there was an altar call and people came forward to receive the Lord and get prayer for healing. It was during this altar call that I first heard what they called "speaking in tongues." It was a language, they said, that came from God, and the speaker didn't know the language. We had recorded the whole meeting, even the ministry time, so when we got home we listened to everything again. When we heard that new language being spoken, we laughed. It seemed so odd.

THE PROMISE OF THE FATHER

The Billy Graham Association was starting to use movies played in movie theaters as a tool of evangelism. Working with the local churches, they had a program to teach believers how to pray with someone who wanted to receive the Lord, and then you would complete a card with their name and address so that a local church could contact them for follow-up and discipleship.

Our church got involved in this, and my friend Paul decided to teach the program for other people in our church who wanted to counsel at the outreach. I was a fairly new Christian, but Paul wanted me to assist him in some way. I agreed because he was my close friend. However, on the day the course was supposed to be taught, Paul got sick and asked me to teach in his place. I wasn't really qualified to do this, but there was a book provided by the Billy Graham Association that I could follow. I didn't think it would be very hard.

Just prior to the class starting, someone came to me and said, "Margaret Barnhouse is here, and she would like to counsel at the movie."

I said, "Okay, tell her to come and join the class."

He said, "This is Margaret Barnhouse."

Being a new believer, I had no idea who Margaret Barnhouse was, so I repeated, "No problem, just tell her to come in and join the class." A little while later, an elderly woman very gracefully entered, sat down, and attended the whole class.

It wasn't until some time later that I learned that Margaret's husband had been Dr. Donald Barnhouse, the world-renowned theologian and Bible teacher, who often traveled with Billy Graham in his crusades. Pastor of Tenth Presbyterian Church in Philadelphia until his death in 1960, he had been one of the first to put Bible teaching on the radio with a program called "The Bible Answer Man," had founded *Eternity* magazine and the Evangelical Foundation.

INHERITING THE NATIONS

The Lord had brought me a great blessing in allowing me to become friends with Margaret. It turned out that she lived very near my home. Many times I went over to her house to help her move furniture or do some tasks she was no longer able to do. Then we would have tea together and talk about the things of the Lord and pray.

One day, when I was getting ready to leave Margaret's home, she gave me a gift. It was a four-volume commentary on the book of Romans written by Dr. Barnhouse himself. To know Margaret Barnhouse and to be able to spend time with her was one of the greatest blessings of my early Christian life.

One day, when she and I were talking about spiritual warfare, she told me a story about experiencing spiritual warfare personally. She was sitting in the front seat of an old car, which, at the time, had bench seats, so three people could sit in the front very easily. Dr. Barnhouse was on her left, driving, and on her right was Billy Graham. They were in the middle of a very heavy snowstorm on their way to a crusade. She said the storm and the winds were buffeting the car, and she couldn't help but think it was a spiritual war against what she called "two titans of the faith" as they were on their journey to share the Gospel.

When it finally came time to show the movie, which the Billy Graham Association had prepared to show in movie theaters as an outreach, some young college people had walked several miles in the rain to come and help us. After the meeting, Paul and I offered to give them a ride home. Over time, I developed a relationship with these young people, so I invited them one evening to my friend's house, to have a home-cooked meal, which is the delight of every college kid.

After dinner, we sat in the family room sharing our personal testimonies. One of the young ladies, a girl named Lynn, mentioned briefly that she spoke in tongues. I couldn't believe it. Although I had heard someone speak in tongues during the ministry time at the Full Gospel Business Men's Fellowship, I had never personally known anyone who had this gift. In all the churches I had attended and in all the books I had read, I had never heard about the gifts of the Spirit (other than hearing pastors teach that the gifts of the Spirit experienced by the early believers were not for our time.)

I don't recall anyone specifically teaching me anything *against* speaking in tongues, but for some reason I had concluded that this gift was not from God at all. It had to be from the devil. Now, sitting before me was a girl whom I knew had a deep commitment to the Lord, and she was saying she spoke in tongues. In my mind, I thought, "There are only two things that could be happening here. Either she is demon possessed, or my theology is wrong." Although I had been a believer for only three years, I was sure my theology could *not* be wrong. Therefore, this young lady must be demon possessed.

I went to visit the students at their school and spent quite a while with them. I was ready for a theological debate about the gift of tongues, but they didn't want to argue about it. They said they would accept me whether I believed in this gift or not. One of them said, "We just want to love you!" I was unprepared for this encounter with real love!

As noted in the acknowledgments, Lynn gave me a book entitled *The Holy Spirit and You: a Guide to the Spirit Filled Life,*[1] written by an Episcopal priest named Father Dennis Bennett and his wife Rita. His church in Seattle, Washington was having what they called "a visitation of the Spirit." By this, they meant that people were being filled with the Spirit and were operating in the gifts of the Spirit. They had, therefore, become known as "a Charismatic church." This was new terminology for me.

Although my inner life had been radically changed, I still had a hunger and a thirst for more, and deep in my spirit I knew that the Lord had more for me. Even to this day, more than fifty years later, I can see that one of the secrets of growing in the Lord is to stay hungry

---
1. Newberry, Florida (Bridge-Logos: 1971)

and thirsty, to never be satisfied, because the Lord always has more for us.

As I read the book Lynn gave me, I came to a better understanding of the gifts of the Spirit and to the belief that these gifts were still in operation today. I also concluded that although my salvation had been a powerful personal experience, the Bible spoke of another important experience, one that would prepare me for my destiny.

After Jesus was crucified, His disciples locked themselves in a room, fearing that they would be killed next. Then Jesus, in His resurrected body, walked through the wall and said to them, *"Peace be with you!"* (John 20:19). This, of course, filled them with great joy. Then He said it a second time and added a phrase: *"Peace be to you! As the Father has sent Me, I also send you"* (John 20:21). He then breathed on them and said, *"Receive the Holy Spirit"* (John 20:22). Theologically speaking, this was the first time the Holy Spirit had come to live and remain in a human body. This was their born-again experience.

Later, however, as recorded in the book of Acts, Jesus said to His disciples, *"Wait for the Promise of the Father"* (Acts 1:4). He had spent three years of His life living with these men. He had taught them to pray, and He had taught them to bring healing and deliverance to those in need. He showed them how to do it themselves, and then He gave them authority to do it, but all this preparation and experience was not enough. There was something else they needed in order to enter into their destiny to change the world.

Acts 1:4-5 reads:

And being assembled together with them, He commanded them not to depart from Jerusalem, but to wait for the Promise of the Father, "which," He said, "you have heard from Me; for John truly baptized with water, but you shall be baptized with the Holy Spirit not many days from now."

THE PROMISE OF THE FATHER

These were the same disciples Jesus had breathed on some days before. The Holy Spirit was already living inside of them, and yet now He was saying, *"Wait for the Promise of the Father!"* Then Acts 1:8 records more of Jesus' words. He said:

But you shall receive power when the Holy Spirit has come upon you; and you shall be witnesses to Me in Jerusalem, and in all Judea and Samaria, and to the end of the earth.

So the primary purpose of this experience, called here *"the Promise of the Father,"* was so that these early disciples could be witnesses for Christ wherever they went—both at home and in the other nations of the world. In my spirit, I knew this was for me. Over the years, I had seen many people come to the Lord as I shared my testimony, but I knew that there was more. I now came to the conclusion that this thing Jesus called *"the Promise of the Father,"* the baptism with the Holy Spirit, was for today and that, according to the Scriptures, it would give me the ability to speak in tongues and the power to be a greater witness.

Now I was at a crossroads. I knew this experience was for me, but my church didn't believe in it, and I didn't personally know anybody except Lynn and her college friends who had received the experience. But the Lord saw my heart.

I was offered an engineering job for GE out of town. It would pay a lot more, but it would involve traveling far from home. I would stay there through the week and then be able to come home on weekends. I went out and bought a new car and showed up for work on Monday.

The boss whom I had the phone interview with wasn't in when I arrived, so the person under him asked me where I had gone to college. I told him I had never gone to college. He asked me where I had gotten my engineering degree. I told him I had just worked my way up to becoming an engineer. I didn't actually have a degree. He said,

INHERITING THE NATIONS

"Well, how long have you been doing exhaust system design?" I had to answer truthfully, that I had never done exhaust system design. I was an architectural designer. A bit frustrated, the man finally said to me, "Well, just pick a desk there. The boss will be in in a little bit."

When the boss arrived, I saw the two of them talking. Instead of waiting, I went into the office and said, "Look, if there's been some kind of misunderstanding, and I can't do the job, that's not a problem. I can leave."

"No," the boss said, "we'll work this out." So I sat down at a desk for a job I was totally unqualified for. God had a plan.

When I left the factory that night, there was a long sidewalk against a high fence, and as I was walking along there the Lord spoke to me very clearly and said, "You're not going to leave this place until I do something *to* you and *through* you!"

At the time there were no personal computers or personal phones to carry, but I consulted what was known as the Yellow Pages, a much larger and more extensive printed version of what exists today. Back in my hotel room that night I opened the Yellow Pages to the section on churches and looked for Pentecostal churches. I found one and called the number listed. The pastor answered. I asked, "Do you have a mid-week service?"

"We sure do, brother!" he said.

I asked, "Do you believe in the baptism of the Holy Spirit?"

"We sure do, brother," he said!

"Well, my name is Joe," I said, "and I'm coming looking for it."

That Wednesday night, with a hunger and a thirst within me, I drove into the parking lot of what had been a house made into a church. I turned off my car and then started to pray. I prayed, "Lord, there are probably demon-possessed people in this church, but You know what I'm looking for, and I'm asking You to protect me. Your Word says, in Luke 11:11-13, that if we ask the Father for a fish, He will not give us a snake. He will give the Holy Spirit to those who ask.

That might sound like a crazy prayer, but it was where my heart was at the time. The churches I had attended did not believe that the gifts were in operation any longer. They believed that when you received Jesus as your personal Savior, you received everything, and there was no second experience. With a little fear, but with a great expectation, I walked into that simple little church.

I had arrived early, but there were already a few people on their knees between the pews praying, and I could hear very quietly a language being spoken that I didn't know. I sat on the very front row right in front of the pulpit, which was only a few feet in front of me. I was hungry and I was thirsty, and I was believing that the Lord would come and fill me and that, as a result, I, too, would have the ability to speak in tongues.

The pastor was a big guy with big hands, and he spoke with a very loud voice. It seemed that after every sentence, the people in the pews would shout out, "Hallelujah! Praise the Lord!" I had never experienced anything quite like this before. In the other churches I had attended in those days (back in the 1970s) we only said "Amen!" We never shouted out, "Hallelujah, praise the Lord!" and we never raised our hands. In fact, usually we worshipped sitting down. These people got to their feet and glorified God in earnest.

I don't remember much of what the pastor preached about that night. I do remember him saying, "I feel the Holy Ghost in here tonight!" and everybody shouted back, "Hallelujah! Amen!" He said, "I believe somebody is going to get the Holy Ghost here tonight!" And again, everyone responded, "Hallelujah! Amen!" Next he reached over the pulpit with his long arm and big hand, almost touching my nose, and declared, "Brother Joe is looking for the Holy Ghost!" And everyone shouted, "Hallelujah! Amen!"

INHERITING THE NATIONS

When an altar call was finally given, I quickly stood. I was ready for whatever the Lord had for me. Going to a Pentecostal church was super-radical for me, but I knew this was the place where I would meet the Lord in a new way, and He would satisfy the deep cry of my heart.

As I said, we almost never raised our hands in church. Probably the last time I had raised my hands was when I was a young teenager, and the police were after me. Now, as I stood there, two ladies came up. One lifted my left hand, and the other raised my right hand. The pastor laid his big hands on my forehead and began to shake my head back and forth as he prayed in English and then in tongues. As for me, there I was with my head going back and forth and saying, "Ah! Ah! Ah!"

I don't remember exactly how it finally ended, but I do remember that nothing of consequence happened that night, and I returned disappointed to my hotel room.

However, I felt a deep peace as I fell asleep that night, and I woke up with something stirring in my spirit. As fast as I could get the words out, I was saying, "Praise the Lord! Praise the Lord! Praise the Lord! Praise the Lord!" over and over again.

I fell back asleep, and when I awoke, I was again speaking as fast as I could, "Praise the Lord! Praise the Lord!" I went back to sleep again, and this continued throughout the night. I wasn't sure what was happening, but I knew I got something. The next day at work, under my breath, I kept repeating, "Praise the Lord! Praise the Lord!" as fast as I could speak.

That weekend I attended my Community Church, and after the service I saw a very close friend of mine in the back of the sanctuary. I quietly whispered to him, "Bill, I went to a Pentecostal church this week."

Bill answered me, "Joe, my whole family got baptized in the Holy Spirit, and you can't imagine what's going on in my house." He invited me to lunch, and afterward we sat in his office, and he shared with me what was going on with him and his family.

He told me he had been walking on a bridge one day and saw a stranger walking toward him. God gave him what he called "a word of knowledge" about the man. He stopped the man and told him, "I'm a Christian, and God told me this about you. Bill concluded, "Right there on the bridge the man repented and received Jesus."

I couldn't believe it. I said, "No way! How's that possible?"

He told me how he had prayed for people, and they had been instantly healed. Again, I couldn't believe it. This was like hearing stories from the book of Acts. In the churches that I had attended, we believed in healing and prayed for healing. Most of us had prayer cards with prayer requests on them, and every day, when we prayed, we would take those cards out and pray for the people on them. If you needed healing, we prayed for you, but most of those we prayed for died, and then we crossed their names off the list. We justified this by saying, "They got a better healing; they went on to Heaven." Praying for people and seeing them healed at that moment was not part of our theology at the time. I was entering a new level in my walk with the Lord.

Bill continued with many testimonies of what was going on with him and his family, and I just sat there thinking, "This is exactly like the book of Acts, and yet it's happening today." We finally ended in prayer and then Bill said to me, "Joe, the Lord showed me that you can speak in tongues right now; you're just not doing it." I protested that I was not stopping the Lord, but he said, "Joe, you don't understand. It's not the Lord. It's your spirit speaking. You have control of it."

Sure enough, 1 Corinthians 14:14 says:

For if I pray in a tongue, my spirit prays, but my understanding is unfruitful.

Verse 15 says:

INHERITING THE NATIONS

What is the conclusion then? I will pray with the spirit, and I will also pray with the understanding. I will sing with the spirit, and I will also sing with the understanding.

I had been thinking that a voice was going to take control of me and speak through me, but it wasn't that way at all. It was my spirit that had to do the speaking, and I was in control of it.

1 Corinthians 14:2 says:

For he who speaks in a tongue does not speak to men but to God, for no one understands him; however, in the spirit he speaks mysteries.

This new language was an intimate prayer language that was now available to me and would give me the ability to speak to my Father directly. I didn't *have to* speak in tongues, but I had the ability to pray in tongues if I wanted to. I soon began speaking in tongues.

When I returned to work the following week, I shared what had happened with one of my new Christian friends. His church was having a retreat that weekend, and he asked me if I would come and share about my experience of being baptized in the Holy Spirit. It was a great opportunity that blessed many people.

The Lord had told me, "You're not leaving here until I do something *to* you and *through* you!" He baptized me in the Holy Spirit and then He opened a door for me to speak at that church retreat. He had fulfilled His word to me. The following week my boss came to me and said, "I'm sorry, but this is just not working out. We're going to have to let you go on Friday."

I told him I fully understood. "No problem," I said, "I can leave now if you want me to."

"No," he said, "stay till Friday."

Now I had a problem. I had a new car with a car payment due in a few days, and I would soon have no job. I went to that Pentecostal church on Wednesday and got down to pray before the service and started to tell the Lord I needed a job. I never heard anything more clearly as I did that day. I barely got the whole prayer out of my mouth when the Lord said, "Don't worry! I have this!"

I didn't even look for a job. The following day I got a call from an engineering firm, saying, "We heard you're out of a job, and we want to offer you a job in your city for the same amount of money you're making now." Actually, the job was back at the General Electric factory where I had been when I received the Lord, and I was working for the same boss. I called him for an interview, but he said, "Joe, you don't need an interview. I'll see you Monday." I never did find out how that engineering firm knew I was out of work, but the Lord was faithful and provided for me more than I ever expected.

I was now back in my hometown among my friends, but most of them had not yet experienced the baptism of the Holy Spirit. A few of us started a home meeting where we prayed for one another and listened to messages that we got from a Charismatic tape library in California. My friend Bill led the group, but whenever it was time to pray for people he would ask me to lay hands on them and pray. I really didn't know what I was doing, but the Lord knew I needed the experience for what would come in my future.

One day in the lunchroom of the GE plant, a young lady named Doreen was in line with me to get our food. We didn't know each other, but she struck up a conversation by asking me how my weekend had gone, I answered, "It was great! I went through a really neat Bible study!"

After I had found a spot and sat down to eat, Doreen came over and asked if she could sit there too. I said, "Sure!" She asked me to tell her about the Bible study and then asked if she could go with me

INHERITING THE NATIONS

sometime. I was happy about that, and we made plans that I would meet her near her home and drive to the study. When the time came, we did as we had agreed.

Once we got to the place, I introduced Doreen to everyone. When the meeting got started, we had a time of worship and then listened to a cassette tape with a teaching about family. Afterward my friend Bill said, "Everyone, repeat this prayer after me," and he prayed what we call a "sinner's prayer," inviting Jesus to come into our hearts. The strange thing was: everyone there was already a Christian except Doreen. Next, Bill said, "Did anyone pray that prayer for the first time?" Doreen raised her hand, and everyone got excited and began to encourage her.

"Praise the Lord," one person said, "now you're a Christian."

I was embarrassed about this whole thing. To me, it seemed like an absolute setup of a young lady who didn't have a clue about Christianity. Now I had to drive Doreen home and explain to her what had just happened, and I wasn't sure what I would say.

As I was getting ready to pull out of the driveway, one of my friends knocked on the window. Doreen rolled down her window, and she said to her again, "Praise the Lord! Now you're a Christian!" Then she added, "See you next week."

As I was thinking about what to say, Doreen spoke first. She said, "You know, Joe, when I prayed that prayer, I could feel Jesus coming into my heart!" I couldn't believe what I was hearing! The Lord had seen Doreen's heart and had come to her as a result of that simple prayer. He is indeed a loving Father! How wonderful His promise of power!

Lynn and her husband

Chapter 3

PRAYER IN THE SPIRIT

Now concerning spiritual gifts, brethren, I do not want you to be ignorant. 1 Corinthians 12:1

Praying in the Spirit is one of the most powerful and intimate gifts the Holy Spirit desires to give us, but it is also one of the most misunderstood gifts of the Spirit. Some people, even devout Christians, don't believe that this gift is available for us today. Although I didn't pray in tongues when I was baptized with the Holy Spirit, I did start praying in tongues when this manifestation was explained to me clearly from the Bible.

As noted above, Paul wrote in the Corinthians: *"Now concerning spiritual gifts, brethren, I do not want you to be ignorant."* I must admit that even though I had a dramatic encounter with the Lord when He came into my life and I started sharing my testimony that resulted in some of my friends and fellow workers coming to Jesus, I knew nothing about the gifts of the Holy Spirit. The purpose of this book is to share my testimony, my experiences of walking with the Lord these fifty plus years. However, because I believe the ability to pray in the Spirit is so important, I'd like to also share some scriptures here that I hope will bring clarity to this precious gift.

It is important to understand that there are two types of tongues in the Bible. There is the gift of tongues spoken of in 1 Corinthians

PRAYER IN THE SPIRIT

12, when it lists the nine gifts that are given by the Holy Spirit. Then there is the ability to pray in tongues as a private language. The gift of tongues is to be used in the church and must be interpreted. Not everyone has this gift. It is sovereignly given by the Holy Spirit. Praying in tongues or prayer in the Spirit is a prayer language that is available to every believer.

Prayer, or simply worded, communication with the Father, has no equal here on this earth. Imagine such a wonderful gift: the ability to speak to the heavenly Father and then to be able to hear Him speaking back to us! Think back to the Garden of Eden when Adam walked with God in the cool of the day, as the book of Genesis records. From the very beginning, our heavenly Father desired a relationship with Adam, but because of sin, that relationship was broken, and Adam and Eve were driven out of the garden. Sinful man cannot approach a holy God!

Although it is not recorded, I can imagine how God's heart was broken. He had enjoyed creating this beautiful garden for Adam and Eve, and He had enjoyed walking with them and talking with them. But now sin had interrupted this vital communication. Adam and Eve would no longer hear the voice of God or feel His embrace. They would now wander in spiritual darkness, and they would pass this spiritual darkness down to coming generations. Today we continue to walk in that same darkness, unable to know the loving God Adam knew in the garden.

But God, because of His great love for His sons and daughters, prepared a sacrifice so that our sins could be atoned for, and so that we can once again experience an intimate relationship with the Father, just as Adam and Eve had experienced in the Garden. The crucifixion of Jesus, His blood poured out for our sins, and His resurrection have made available a relationship with the heavenly Father and an assurance of everlasting life to all those who believe and receive Jesus as their personal Savior. This relationship is a daily walk in which we become more and more like Jesus.

INHERITING THE NATIONS

As believers in Christ, we have good times and bad times. We go through trials and tribulations and also times of extreme joy. All of these life experiences form us into the very image of Jesus. Although we may not be perfect, somehow others begin to see Jesus in us.

However, even though, because of the sacrifice of Jesus, we can again approach and speak with our heavenly Father, the question remains: how do we pray? Even Jesus' disciples, when they saw Him praying, realized that they didn't really know how to pray.

> *Now it came to pass, as He [Jesus] was praying in a certain place, when He ceased, that one of His disciples said to Him, "Lord, teach us to pray, as John also taught his disciples."*   Luke 11:1

For those of us who have believed, the Holy Spirit now lives within us, and He can help us to pray. Paul wrote to the early Roman believers:

> *Likewise the Spirit also helps in our weaknesses. For we do not know what we should pray for as we ought, but the Spirit Himself makes intercession for us with groanings which cannot be uttered. Now He who searches the hearts knows what the mind of the Spirit is, because He makes intercession for the saints according to the will of God.*   Romans 8:26-27

The disciples of Jesus walked and talked with Him for three years. They lived and ate with Him. They saw Him heal sick people, and He gave them authority to heal too. It was a glorious time for them. Then, however, He was crucified, and their dreams were shattered. Fear overtook them. They thought, "They have killed Jesus; now they will come and kill us too." Then Jesus appeared to them:

> *Then, the same day at evening, being the first day of the week, when the doors were shut where the disciples were assembled, for fear of the*

PRAYER IN THE SPIRIT

Jews, Jesus came and stood in the midst, and said to them, "Peace be with you." When He had said this, He showed them His hands and His side. Then the disciples were glad when they saw the Lord.
So Jesus said to them again, "Peace to you! As the Father has sent Me, I also send you." And when He had said this, He breathed on them, and said to them, "Receive the Holy Spirit. If you forgive the sins of any, they are forgiven them; if you retain the sins of any, they are retained."
John 20:19-23

In the Old Testament, the Holy Spirit came upon certain people for a particular task, but when that task was completed, the Holy Spirit left. Now, for the first time, when Jesus breathed on His disciples, the Holy Spirit came to live within human beings, and He would never leave. They would not need to go to a certain building to approach God. Now they were living temples, because of the indwelling of the Holy Spirit.

Later, Jesus told them more:

And being assembled together with them, He commanded them not to depart from Jerusalem, but to wait for the Promise of the Father, "which," He said, "you have heard from Me; for John truly baptized with water, but you shall be baptized with the Holy Spirit not many days from now."
Acts 1:4-5

The primary reason for the Promise of the Father, which Jesus called "the baptism with the Holy Spirit," was to empower the disciples to take the Gospel to the ends of the earth. When the book of Acts, which is the history of the earliest church, recorded a person receiving the baptism of the Holy Spirit, other manifestations also came with the experience: tongues of fire sitting upon them, they began to prophesy, and they began to worship the Lord in a language they had not learned

INHERITING THE NATIONS

or spoken before. When you receive the baptism of the Holy Spirit, you receive the ability to pray in tongues as a personal prayer language.

Here are some statements and Bible verses on praying in tongues to think about and pray about:

- All believers have the ability to speak in tongues:

And these signs will follow those who believe: In My name they will cast out demons; they will speak with new tongues; they will take up serpents; and if they drink anything deadly, it will by no means hurt them; they will lay hands on the sick, and they will recover.

Mark 16:17-18

- This prayer language is for communication between your spirit and God:

For he who speaks in a tongue does not speak to men but to God, for no one understands him; however, in the spirit he speaks mysteries.

1 Corinthians 14:2

- This prayer language is for your personal edification:

He who speaks in a tongue edifies himself.   1 Corinthians 14:4

- Praying in the Spirit is not the Holy Spirit speaking, and it is also not your mind; it is your spirit praying directly to God:

For if I pray in a tongue, my spirit prays, but my understanding is unfruitful. What is the conclusion then? I will pray with the spirit, and I will also pray with the understanding. I will sing with the spirit, and I will also sing with the understanding. 1 Corinthians 14:14-15

PRAYER IN THE SPIRIT

Let the word of Christ dwell in you richly in all wisdom, teaching and admonishing one another in psalms and hymns and spiritual songs, singing with grace in your hearts to the Lord. Colossians 3:16

- Paul had this ability to speak in tongues:

I thank my God I speak with tongues more than you all.
1 Corinthians 14:18

- Praying in the Spirit builds up your faith:

But you, beloved, building yourselves up on your most holy faith, praying in the Holy Spirit. Jude 1:20

- Speaking in tongues is a prayer language:

Praying always with all prayer and supplication in the Spirit, being watchful to this end with all perseverance and supplication for all the saints. Ephesians 6:18

These scriptures above are about praying in tongues or praying in the Spirit, which I believe is available for every believer who has received the Promise of the Father. Other scriptures speak about another gift of tongues, as recorded in 1 Corinthians 12, where it lists the nine gifts of the Spirit given by the Holy Spirit as He desires. This gift of tongues and the gift of prophecy are to be used in the church to bless others. The gift of tongues in the church must be interpreted:

But he who prophesies speaks edification and exhortation and comfort to men. 1 Corinthians 14:3

INHERITING THE NATIONS

I wish you all spoke with tongues, but even more that you prophesied; for he who prophesies is greater than he who speaks with tongues, unless indeed he interprets, that the church may receive edification.
1 Corinthians 14:5

But the manifestation of the Spirit is given to each one for the profit of all.
1 Corinthians 12:7

Therefore let him who speaks in a tongue pray that he may interpret.
1 Corinthians 14:13

How is it then, brethren? Whenever you come together, each of you has a psalm, has a teaching, has a tongue, has a revelation, has an interpretation. Let all things be done for edification. If anyone speaks in a tongue, let there be two or at the most three, each in turn, and let one interpret
1 Corinthians 14:26-27

In conclusion, there is a gift of tongues that is a prayer language and is available to every believer who is baptized with the Holy Spirit, and there is a gift of tongues that is only given by the sovereign will of the Holy Spirit to be used in the church. That gift must be interpreted and must result in edification, exhortation, and comfort to others.

What a wonderful gift from God to His people!

Chapter 4

GOD MOVING IN THE WORK PLACE

And they [the disciples of Jesus] went out and preached everywhere, the Lord working with them and confirming the word through the accompanying signs.   Mark 16:20

In the early 1970s, I was working for an engineering firm and was sent on an assignment to do some drafting work for IBM. Because the job was out of town, I lived in a motel and came home on the weekends. On that job was a guy named Al. Al dressed and looked like a playboy and would party every night, but he still came to work every day. Although the two of us were total opposites, he and I became very close friends and sat next to each other at work.

One day we heard that a two-bedroom cabin on a lake was available for rent. It would be cheaper than a hotel, so Al and I moved in together. Living on the lake was great because Al had a small sailboat.

While Al was out bar-hopping one night, he met a girl who was separated from her husband and in the process of getting a divorce. They started dating, and one day she came by our cabin to go sailing with Al. While Al was getting the boat ready, she came inside and started talking with me. She told me she and her current husband were getting a divorce. She was glad, for she felt sure life would be so much easier when the divorce was final. I warned her that she would still feel the pain of it long afterward.

INHERITING THE NATIONS

The next day, when Al came to work, he told me that this lady wanted to know if I would come by her apartment some evening. She wanted to talk more with me about this subject. I accepted the invitation and went there one evening and spent some time talking with her and another young lady about the pains of divorce. I also took the opportunity to share with the lady about the Lord and His plan for her life. The Lord wonderfully touched her heart, she stopped dating Al, and was restored to her husband. She called me about a year later and told me that she and her husband were doing fine. They had moved to another state, and they had found a good church to attend there.

When Al and I had started living together in that cabin on the lake, everybody at work wondered what would happen. The playboy or the Jesus boy, who would win? I can't say for sure that Al received the Lord, but he saw the Lord working, and he became interested, so I bought him a Bible. The day Al walked into work with a Bible under his arm, everyone at work was shocked.

I left that job about a month after that. At least a marriage had been restored, and a playboy was now reading the Bible. The Lord was moving at that office, and I was moving on to another company, General Dynamics.

General Dynamics is an engineering and construction firm that works with the Defense Department. They were involved in building a model of the Trident nuclear submarine at a military base near my home, and they were looking for engineers. I was offered a job there and accepted.

It was a large construction site. A nuclear reactor was being installed in a model of a submarine so that servicemen from many places could come and learn how to operate a nuclear submarine. They would then go on to the company's shipyard on the oceanfront in Connecticut where they would be able to operate an actual submarine. It was very interesting to see this huge submarine being constructed. It was also a potential danger, so next to it was being built a three-story building filled with safety equipment in case the reactor ever exploded. I was working on the equipment in that building, but our office was a large mobile home near the sub. Every time I left the office, I had to wear a hard hat, which I had covered with stickers, all about Jesus. I was now on a new assignment to share the Gospel. I always tried to do my job well, but I also knew there would be people on the job looking for Jesus, even if they didn't yet know it.

Next to me worked a young man named Rick who was a Scientologist. At the time, Rick was living with his girlfriend Beth. Every day we would go back and forth talking about Christianity and Scientology, and then he would go home and tell Beth what I had said. One day he told me that he and Beth would like for me to come to dinner with them. I accepted and had a great time at their home. There wasn't much for me to say about the Lord because Rick had already told Beth everything I was saying to him during the day. She was ready, and that night after dinner she received the Lord!

Now Rick had a serious problem. During the day he was debating with me about the Bible, and then, when he got home at night, he had to debate Beth. He said one time when they were arguing about the Bible, she said to him, "Well, Joe said ..."

He picked up her Bible, said, "I don't care what Joe said," and threw the Bible across the room. Within a short time, Rick, too, had surrendered his life to the Lord, and he and Beth got married. God was moving on the construction site!

One Friday a coworker named Bob, who was sitting behind Rick and me, asked if he could talk to me privately. He told me that he had been lying in bed praying, and suddenly a presence and peace came all over him, and he wanted to know what I thought about it. I said, "Well, what were you praying?"

INHERITING THE NATIONS

He said, "Well, I heard you and Rick talking about how to receive Jesus, and so I just prayed and asked Jesus to come into my life, and this peace and presence came over me."

I said to him, "Congratulations, Bob, you just got saved. Praise the Lord!"

Over the weekend I began to think: "I should have warned Bob that when you get saved the enemy comes to try to discourage you and that he should be on guard." When he came to work on Monday, I told him, "Watch out for the enemy!"

He said, "You're too late! My wife told me this weekend that she wants a divorce." I don't remember the exact timing, but I visited their home shortly after that and had a long talk with Bob's wife. Unfortunately, her mind was set, and they ended up divorcing.

Bob, however, continued to walk with the Lord. Sometime later, he ran into his childhood sweetheart, who was also a Christian. Her father was a Methodist pastor. They ended up marrying, and Bob himself became a Methodist minister. God had saved him and called him to the ministry on a construction site.

A couple weeks after I started writing this book, a friend of mine who has a program that helps you search for people all over America found Bob's telephone number, and I called him. What a surprise and blessing it was for both of us! He said, "My wife and I always wondered 'where is Joe Zeyak?'"

We talked for a long time. He told me that he had worked with the Methodist Church until their mandatory retirement age of sixty, and during that time he had pastored several churches in the Vermont/New York area. I am looking forward to visiting him and his wife.

Whether it's on the job or sharing with your neighbor, there's nothing more powerful than our testimony. It's our personal story of how the Lord brought us out of darkness into His light, and every time we share it, there's a power, an anointing released through our words that allows the Father to draw more people into His family through Jesus.

GOD MOVING IN THE WORK PLACE

And they overcame him by the blood of the Lamb and by the word of their testimony, and they did not love their lives to the death.
                                                                Revelation 12:11

In early 1976 I read an article saying that Princess Margaret of England was going through a divorce. Because of my own situation, I thought about the pain and discouragement she was probably going through, so I decided to send her my testimony. I hand-wrote a two-page letter and sent it to her. A short time later, I got a thank-you note back from her lady in waiting. Never underestimate the power of your testimony.

Bob and Priscilla Hurd

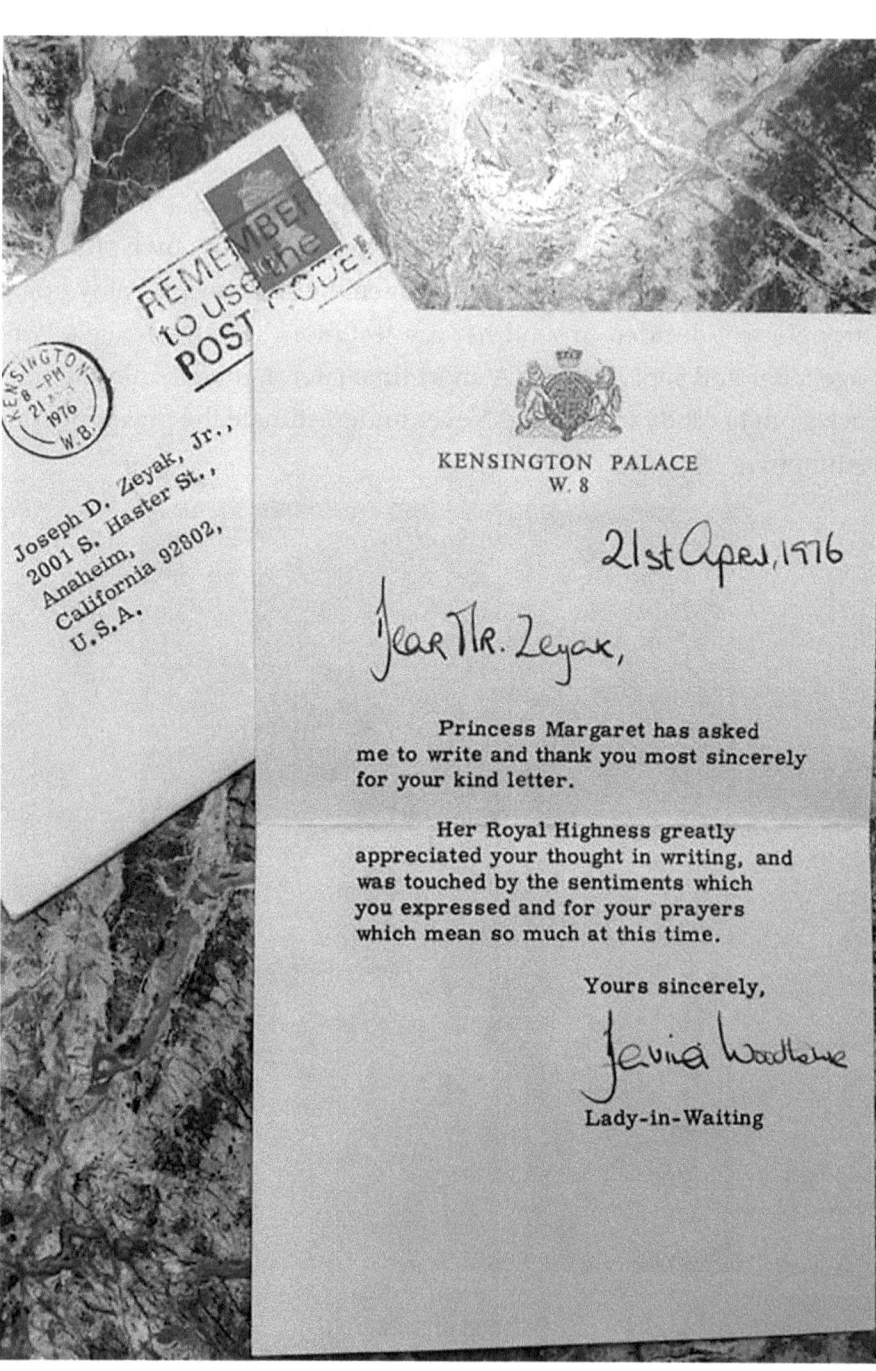

Chapter 5

GOD'S CALL

By faith Abraham obeyed when he was called to go out to the place which he would receive as an inheritance. And he went out, not knowing where he was going.   Hebrews 11:8

My job was going well, and the Lord was opening the doors to my wife's heart. When an evangelist came to town who had a great gift of healing, I invited her to go to the meeting. When I called her on the morning of the meeting, she started telling me that she had a hole in her tooth. The tooth was abscessed, and she was in a lot of pain. I understood and said, "That's okay. Maybe you can go another time."

To my surprise, she answered, "No, I'm still going." I was delighted!

The meeting packed out the Charismatic Lutheran Church that had invited the evangelist to town. He was a very humble guy and always pointed people to Jesus. There was a great time of worship, and then he got up to speak. He began, "Before I preach, I have realized that the Lord is already healing people here in this room. If the Lord is healing you now, stand up." To my shock, my wife stood up.

The evangelist called on her, and she testified that she had come to the meeting with a hole in her tooth and that the tooth had been abscessed. Now, she said, the hole was gone, and there was no more abscess and no more pain. I couldn't believe what she was saying. This was truly an amazing miracle that the Lord had done for her. I felt that

INHERITING THE NATIONS

this was just one more confirmation that the Lord was drawing my wife to Himself and that we would soon be back together as a family.

I continued to grow spiritually with the small group which had now become a small church. One brother named Tony held prayer meetings at his house almost around the clock it seemed. We would pray for hours, and some would prophesy. One night we all prayed for Tony. He was seated on a chair which we commonly called "the hot seat," and we laid hands on him and prayed. For the first time in my life, I felt that I had a prophetic word. It was for Tony.

As I stood in front of Tony, I began to prophesy that the Lord was going to open many doors for him. He would travel to many nations of the world proclaiming the Gospel. I was very excited with this, my first prophecy, for I felt that I had arrived at a new level of operating in the gifts of the Spirit. Then Tony looked up at me and said, "I don't think that prophecy was for me. I think it was for you!" I didn't know what to say. I had only been on an airplane once, and that was just a one-hour flight. I didn't know any foreign languages, and I didn't know anybody in any foreign country. Could it be possible that my first prophecy that I had been so excited about was wrong? Looking back on it now, I realize that Tony was correct. He eventually moved to Florida and is there to this day, while I have been around the world more times than I can remember, sharing the Gospel in some fifty nations of the world.

One evening, when I left the prayer meeting at Tony's house, I decided to stop by and see my wife because she was living nearby. I had always called before I went there, but because I was so close, I didn't call ahead this time. As I rang the doorbell, I looked in the window and saw her sitting on the couch with another man. She looked up in shock, came to the door, and then came outside to talk to me. I said, "What's going on? There's another man here. I thought we were going to get back together."

She answered, "Joe, I told you I was never coming back."

GOD'S CALL

This experience was so traumatic that I don't remember what else happened that evening. I just had to continue to trust that the Lord wanted us back together, and therefore I was determined to stand strong in faith. BUT things quickly got worse. Some days later I got a call from the boys' school saying that they had not come to school that day. Someone from the school had tried to call their home but found that the number was disconnected. I didn't know what to think.

I went to the home, but no one was there. I looked in the door and could see that the place was empty. My wife had done it again. She had moved without even telling me where she was going.

I called her mom, but she wouldn't tell me anything. It was a challenging time. No one seemed to know where my family was or at least no one would tell me. It was getting close to Christmas, and I didn't know what to do.

I had a great friend named Bill. He had worked with me on my first job when I was just eighteen and had gone on to become a drug dealer. Then, after I had received Jesus, I shared the Gospel with him, and he also become a believer. He had gotten married and moved to Arizona. When he heard that I was going to be alone at Christmas time, he invited me to come to Arizona and have Christmas with him and his wife. That sounded good to me, but all the flights were booked. When I told him, he said. "Fly to California. I know a great church there. We can attend their Christmas Eve service, then go to Disneyland, and then come back here to my home in Arizona." So I bought a ticket to fly from New York to Los Angeles, my first long flight.

As planned, on Christmas Eve, we attended a service at Melodyland Christian Center directly across from Disneyland. The church had bought an old theater building and turned it into a two-thousand-seat auditorium with its own seminary. In the mid-1970s, Melodyland was one of the main churches of the Charismatic Movement, and speakers from all over the world came there to minister.

INHERITING THE NATIONS

That Christmas Eve service was like nothing I had ever seen. The auditorium was full. The theater seats were arranged in a large circle with the pulpit area in the center. Speaking that night were several prominent Christian leaders. These were some of the men I had been listening to on cassette tape back in New York, and now here they were live before me.

That night a family was called to come forward to pray for their son who had some kind of disease, and they had prayer for healing. Then the pastor turned to the father and said, "Let me ask you something. Are you working right now?"

The young husband said, "No!"

The pastor then turned to the congregation and said, "It's Christmas Eve, and this young couple doesn't have any income. I want all of you to come down here and place an offering for them on the altar." Within a few minutes, the altar was piled with money. I had never seen anything like that in my life.

A neighbor friend of mine in New York named Bonnie had been led to the Lord by her brother, Jeff, whom I had led to the Lord. She and her two young daughters were now living in San Francisco. When I knew I was going to California, I called her and suggested that she meet us, to attend church with us on Christmas Eve and then go with us to Disneyland. I knew this would be exciting for her young daughters. In those days an airline ticket was only $29, so she flew in with her daughters, and we had a wonderful time at the church and a fun time together in Disneyland before they had to return home.

Then I traveled to Tucson, with Bill and his wife, and we did some fun things. One day, for instance, we went up beautiful Mount Lemmon, the highest point in the Santa Catalina Mountains. It was an amazing drive, with amazingly beautiful scenery. The vegetation changed from desert to finally snow on the very top of the mountains where there was a small ski lift.

GOD'S CALL

On the way up the mountain was a small rest area called Inspiration Point. When we stopped there, I took out my Bible and went to sit on the top of a picnic table and began to pray. The Lord spoke to my heart that day and said, "I want you to move to California and go to seminary at Melodyland." I don't recall this as an especially emotional time, but it was clear to me that God had spoken, and I was slowly learning that when He speaks we must obey.

After my visit with Bill and his family, I went back home, put my house up for sale, and gave notice at my work that I would be leaving. I still didn't know where my family was, but I knew what God had promised and felt that no matter where I lived, He would bring them to me. During that time, two different young ladies from the church I was attending had dreams that my wife had a child with another man but that she would leave him and return to me.

My younger brother Steve, who was not a Christian, decided to move with me to California. We packed up my car with everything we could, even his skis that we tied to the back bumper, and with my last paycheck for expense money, we left for California. We had no way of knowing exactly what to expect. I was just trying to walk in obedience to God.

In those days many apartments did not allow children. I kept looking until I finally found a two-bedroom apartment that did because I believed that one day my wife and children would join me there.

The Melodyland school was set up so that all the classes were in the evening, and I found an engineering job during the day with a medical company. I made very good money, and was able to meet many new friends, while studying under anointed men of God. It was a great time.

One friend I met was Randy, a young man who had grown up in California. Randy became my best friend, and we did many things together. We joined a ministry that showed movies on Friday nights at the church as a tool of evangelism and were even able to travel

INHERITING THE NATIONS

to other places with these Christian movies. This was extremely rewarding.

The head of this movie ministry was a brother named Greg, and Greg had one message: "Go into all the world, and preach the Gospel to every creature!" He said, "If you don't go, you're disobeying the Word of God." This was like a non-stop message coming from him. Neither I nor Randy were interested in going to other countries or other places. We were enjoying California life. Although I didn't yet have much of a vision for the future, I rather imagined that I would return to New York and work in some small church there.

Greg had become a close friend to both Randy and me, and we often did things together, but he would never stop preaching: "Go into all the world, and preach the Gospel to every creature. If you don't go, you're disobeying the Word of God." Eventually Randy and I couldn't take this anymore. We continued to work in the movie ministry but spent less and less time with Greg outside of that setting.

I didn't know exactly what the Lord was calling me to. I was just taking it one day at a time, working and attending classes in the evening. The church itself was very powerful, and their Sunday night services were over the top with speakers coming from all over the world. I was enjoying it. I certainly had no desire to go to some foreign mission field or to become what people called a "missionary."

My impression of missionaries was not a good one. I considered a missionary to be someone who couldn't do anything else, so he became a missionary. And (excuse me for saying so), I thought missionaries married women who were so homely that they could only marry a missionary. Clearly this was not my desire for the future. I was standing for my beautiful wife and family to return, as the Lord had promised me.

When Steve and I first moved to California, we looked up his godparents, who had also moved there. They had been our backyard

GOD'S CALL

neighbors and had attended the same Catholic Church we did. It was great to see them again after so many years and also to learn that they, too, had become believers. They were now teaching Sunday school, along with three other couples in the Catholic Church. They really loved the Lord but felt that they were not growing enough in their church, and they asked me if I would start a home Bible study for them. I did that, and we had wonderful times together studying the Bible and fellowshipping. Over the course of many months, all of those attending the study received the Promise of the Father and began to operate in the gifts of the Spirit. It was a very rewarding and powerful time.

In the second year of my classes at the seminary, I got to choose an elective, which meant I had a choice of several classes I could take that were not mandatory for my degree. When I saw that there was a class on missions, I thought that might be an easy one, so I decided to take it, even though I still did not have any desire to be a missionary myself. The teacher for this class was an ex-missionary from Japan and looked just like I expected a missionary to look. He wore his black hair in a flattop and had very thick black glasses, but there was something about him. There was a fire burning in him for the nations of the world, and his voice was like the Father speaking directly to me.

For that class, I was required to write a term paper on the biblical perspective on missions. It was through researching that paper that I came to realize that God's heart was not just for America. It was for all the nations of the world. The Holy Spirit was speaking to me, even though I didn't realize it at the time.

I don't remember the exact timing of things, but one night I was home alone. My friend Randy had spent the night there and had left a small world map on the bed. I taped it to the wall in front of my desk, and I would lay my hands on that map, asking the Lord to bless the missionaries out there in the nations of the world, even though I didn't know any of them personally.

INHERITING THE NATIONS

One night as I was praying (I don't remember about what), the Lord spoke very clearly deep into my spirit and said, "Will you give me your family for a world ministry?" I found that I could not answer Him. For several years now I had stood in faith for the restoration of my family. I had claimed scripture verses and believed that God had promised them to me personally. Now, it seemed that He was asking me to give up those promises He had given me.

Some may doubt that this was God speaking to me, but in my heart there was no such doubt. Still, I could not answer Him. I have never claimed to have the faith of Abraham, but at that moment I think I felt what Abraham felt when the Lord asked him to give up his only son, Isaac, the son of promise. Amazingly, without wavering, he went up that mountain to offer his son as a sacrifice.

Now the Lord was asking me, "All that I promised you, all that you dreamed about and prayed and fasted for, will you give them to me in exchange for a worldwide ministry?" For several days I could not answer Him. I wasn't looking for a ministry; I was waiting patiently for the restoration of my family and the fulfillment of God's promises to me. Finally, after three days, I got on my knees and with tears streaming down my face, I prayed, "Lord, You know whether my family will ever come back or not, but regardless, I am going to serve You the rest of my life. So, to the best of my ability, I give them to You."

There was no flash of light or overwhelming presence from the Lord. It was just a decision of my will to follow the Lord and obey His call for my life, no matter what the cost. I believe the Lord recorded my decision in Heaven that day and noted that I was willing to pay the cost to fulfill my destiny. This decision was not just for me; it was also for the people the Lord was calling me to, and it was so that Jesus might receive the reward of His suffering through me.

Several weeks later, Rev. Harry DeVries, an elderly missionary who had just come from Africa, came to speak at our mission's class

GOD'S CALL

and shared with all of us that he would be traveling to Ecuador on his next trip to the foreign field. I was led to invite him out to dinner because a friend of mine had a call to Africa, and I wanted to gather information for that friend. During our conversation that day, Harry asked me what my desires were and if I was at all interested in the mission field. I had to admit, "No, I'm just trying to get information about Africa for my friend."

Sometime later, however, while I was in prayer, the Lord spoke to me and said, "I want you to call Harry DeVries and tell him you'd like to travel with him." I still had some classes to finish for my degree, and I also had a very good paying job, "But," I thought "this might be interesting. I could learn something from this older brother, and then I could return and finish my schooling later."

I called Brother DeVries and told him what the Lord had said to me, and he was very excited about it. He said he would be driving down from his home in Washington State and suggested that he meet me in Arizona at my friend's home. From there, we could travel across America sharing in churches as we went. Then, in Florida, we would get a visa and go to Ecuador to attend a conference at a Pentecostal missionary training center he knew about there. That sounded good to me, so the dates were set.

I finished my term at seminary but didn't enroll in the next term. I quit my job and liquidated everything I had, giving up my apartment to a missionary friend who had just come off the foreign field. Harry DeVries had said to me, "Don't worry about money. As we travel across America, churches will give us offerings." So, I left California with only the amount of my last paycheck in my pocket. It was about $650. I was on my way to Arizona to meet Harry DeVries, and I thought I might be away two or three months.

Seeking God on Mount Lemmon in Arizona

Chapter 6

"ASK OF ME"

Ask of Me, and I will give You
The nations for Your inheritance,
And the ends of the earth for Your possession.   Psalm 2:8

It was Sunday, January 15, 1978, when I left California for Tucson to meet Harry DeVries and travel with him across America and then to Ecuador. Pam, a sister from the Bible study, had given me a scripture before I left. It was Psalm 67:1-2:

God be merciful to us and bless us,
And cause His face to shine upon us,
That Your way may be known on earth,
Your salvation among all nations.

Verse 7 says:

God shall bless us,
And all the ends of the earth shall fear Him.

I was very excited. God was going to do some great things on this trip. I was sure of it.

INHERITING THE NATIONS

I got to Tucson, but Harry DeVries had not arrived yet. Then, as I waited and waited, he still didn't come. In those days, there were no cellphones, so I couldn't just call him to ask what was going on. It was a trying time, to say the least.

Eventually, my friend Bill, acting like one of Job's comforters, began to suggest to me that I abandon the notion of going to Ecuador, and that I go back to California and finish my studies instead. I should never have dropped out of school in the first place, he said. I decided it was time to do some serious praying. As I was praying, the Lord gave me what would become my life verse: Psalm 2:8. God said that all I had to do was ask. It seemed clear to me that He was telling me to step out in faith and go on to Ecuador, even if I had to go by myself.

The following day a friend in California, who was getting my mail for me, received a letter from Harry DeVries saying that his car had broken down, and he couldn't call because he had lost the paper with my telephone number on it. He had spent all his money and was returning home to Washington State. He encouraged me to go on alone and gave me the address of a missionary in Ecuador, Harold McDougal. He said Harold had a Pentecostal training center outside the capital city and assured me that he would receive me and take care of me.

I mailed a long letter to Harold explaining who I was and giving details about my arrival. I also sent a Western Union telegram giving him my flight information and arrival time in Quito. I bought a one-way ticket to Ecuador going through Mexico City, where I would stop and get the visa needed to enter Ecuador. On January 21, after buying my ticket, I had just $150 left. I was to begin my first missionary journey by faith.

What I thought would be a trip of a few months, being mentored by the illustrious Harry DeVries, over the next ten years, became a trip to twenty nations, being led and taught by the Holy Spirit.

I came to realize after many years of ministry that it had not been about the seminary I had attended. It was about the church connected

"ASK OF ME"

to that seminary, and it was about the men and women of God who had come from many nations to speak at the Sunday night services at Melodyland. As I was sitting there in that anointed atmosphere, the Lord was planting in me a vision that could not be taught. It could only be imparted by the Father in Heaven.

One of my favorite Bible verses (and one that I try to put into practice every place I go) is what Paul said to the Roman believers:

> *I long to see you, that I may impart to you some spiritual gift, so that you may be established—that is, that I may be encouraged together with you by the mutual faith both of you and me.*   Romans 1:11-12

One commentary suggests that the phrase *"so that you may be established"* actually means "that you might come into your destiny." I was sure that was true, and also that I would be the beneficiary.

On January 27, 1978, I arrived in Quito, Ecuador. The signs in the airport were all in Spanish, as were the announcements over the loudspeakers. It was as if everybody was speaking in tongues, and I didn't have the interpretation. I was able to make my way through immigration, baggage claim, and customs, but when I exited the international terminal and looked around, no one seemed to be waiting for me. What should I do?

Eventually I made my way to the domestic terminal and found a phone book. To my horror, I realized that the address of the radio station my friend had given me was wrong, and the Western Union telegram I had sent to the radio station had no call letters. I was in a foreign country, and no one knew I was there, except the Lord. What now?

I had addressed the cable simply:

Rev. Harold McDougal
c/o Radio Station
Quito, Ecuador

INHERITING THE NATIONS

As I walked back toward the international terminal, I was thinking to myself that perhaps I could get a taxi and somehow explain to the driver that I wanted to go to the Pentecostal camp outside of the city. Would he know what I was talking about?

Then, before long, I saw what looked like an American man. He was holding up a crude sign, and it had my name on it. Praise God, it was Harold McDougal, coming to receive me. The letter I had sent detailing all about me didn't arrive until two months after I had been there. The telegram I had sent by Western Union had a very limited address. Fortunately, the deliveryman, seeing that it was addressed to a reverend, realized that it must be for the only Christian radio station in town and took it there. Then, someone from the radio station had taken the telegram out to the camp, about eighteen miles outside of the city. Harold had gotten the telegram and come directly to the airport, without knowing anything about me. Looking back, I realize that he was the first person to accept me when I was stepping into my calling for the nations.

The camp was beautifully situated in a valley with lush green grass all around and cabins and buildings of red brick that housed the students and guest speakers, as well as a large auditorium for meetings. Because I was a guest, I was given a private room with wonderful accommodations. I was treated very special. Immediately, I was given the opportunity to share the things I had learned in my journey with the Lord up to that point.

The camp, known as *Campamento Nueva Vida* (New Life Camp), was a training center where young men and women from all over Latin America were taught for several months and then sent out for a few months at a time for practical ministry training. When the time came to go out, Harold told me that Juan Coello, one of the camp leaders from Ecuador, and Sunamita, his Filipina wife, were inviting me to travel with them. She had been translating for me while I was there and therefore felt that it would be very easy for us to work together. Juan and Sunamita had no exact plans, they said, except going to the jungles of Ecuador. Wow! That sounded very exciting.

Harold preaching in the chapel of New Life Camp

CHAPTER 7

WALKING IN THE FOOTSTEPS OF MARTYRS

When He opened the fifth seal, I saw under the altar the souls of those who had been slain for the word of God and for the testimony which they held. And they cried with a loud voice, saying, "How long, O Lord, holy and true, until You judge and avenge our blood on those who dwell on the earth?" Then a white robe was given to each of them; and it was said to them that they should rest a little while longer, until both the number of their fellow servants and their brethren, who would be killed as they were, was completed. Revelation 6:9-11

Ecuador, as it turned out, was made up of three very distinct and different regions. First, there was the Coast, the lands bordering the Pacific Ocean. Because Ecuador sits at the equator (*ecuador* in Spanish), the coast is very tropical and hot. More than half of the population of the country lives in this region. The largest city in Ecuador, Guayaquil, is in this coastal region.

The second most populous region of the country is the Sierra, the lands that form part of the Andes Mountains. That's where the camp was located. Quito itself, the capital of Ecuador, sits at 9,350 feet above sea level.

The third region of the country, the Oriente (East), made up of the lands flowing down from the mountains to the east toward the

INHERITING THE NATIONS

Amazon River, is sparsely populated and still largely undeveloped. A part of that population is made up of primitive tribes. One of those tribes gained notoriety by killing five American missionaries. They are known as the Aucas, and unbeknownst to us, that was where we were headed.

In January of 1956, five evangelical missionaries attempted to take the Gospel for the first time to this tribal group living in the jungles of Ecuador. Unfortunately, the tribe was ruled by fear. Fearing these intruders, they killed them, and this became an international story. It was covered by leading newspapers and magazines like *Time*. Many Americans, inspired by the story of these five martyrs, decided to become missionaries and went to Bible school.

A young Auca girl named Dayuma had left the tribe some years prior to the killings and ended up living in Quito and marrying an Ecuadorian man. Sometime after the death of her husband, Dayuma decided to return to the tribe. At the same time, the wife of one of the slain missionaries and his sister had a deep desire to go to these tribal people, knowing well that they might also lose their lives. They were able to connect with Dayuma, and she safely brought them into the tribe and translated for them, and many Aucas became believers. These two America women, Elizabeth Elliot and Rachel Saint, lived among the Aucas for many years.

With no exact plans where we were going (the camp leadership had asked us to be led by the Spirit), Juan, Sunamita, and I purchased tickets to go to a city on the edge of the Ecuadorian jungle. The bus would leave late in the afternoon, so we decided to visit a pastor friend of theirs. While visiting him, we saw an article in a local newspaper about the Auca Indians and suddenly felt that this would be our mission—to find the Aucas.

After a very long bus ride (we slept on the bus), we got into a small boat and headed down the Rio Napo. We were now entering the primitive jungles of Ecuador. It was all very beautiful, and also very exciting.

After about an hour the boat pulled up at a small sandbar, and we were told this was where we should get out. There were, we were advised, steps cut into the cliff above us. We were to climb up those steps to a village that sat at the top. The people of that village would help us find the Aucas.

As the boat moved off into the distance, I looked up at the cliff before us and wondered what we would find at the top of those crude stairs. Here we were in the middle of the jungle, and our only transportation was quickly disappearing in the distance. We were there, but nobody knew we were there, nobody except the Lord!

At the top of the steps, sure enough, we saw several bamboo buildings and some smaller huts. As it turned out, the largest of the buildings was a school. Very soon, as the village people saw us, many of them came running out to meet us. This was a Quechua village.

The villagers spoke enough Spanish that it was no problem for Juan and Sunamita to communicate with them. We soon told them of our desire to find the Aucas, and they informed us that there was a man who traveled between their village and the Auca villages. He could take us there, they said, and he would be arriving in a few days. In the meantime, we were given accommodations to stay in.

My room was a small bamboo hut with little more than a bamboo bed. I spread some of my clothes out on it to make it more comfortable, but to me it was like sleeping on a pile of rocks. Welcome to the mission field!

There was a small church in the village, and we were invited to share the Gospel there each evening. There were a few light bulbs that were connected to a generator, but the generator had long since broken down, and the villagers had no way of repairing it, so each night we would set candles on the pulpit for light. This attracted bugs that bothered us while we were preaching. It was a very interesting time, to say the least. The village people were very accommodating and very interested to hear us share the Word of God.

One day a couple invited us to come to their hut for lunch. We accepted and followed them into the jungle to a large one-room bamboo hut. As we were seated, I noticed there was no food to be seen. After a time of conversation, the wife went outside and began to dig up some roots, which she then cooked like potatoes. She gathered some eggs from their chickens. Then she caught one of the chickens and killed it for our dinner. For drink, she found some lemons and made us some lemonade. What a memorable time!

Eventually, we met Pedro, the Ecuadorian man who lived between the two tribes, and he offered to guide us to the Aucas. We would leave early the next morning, he said, and it would be about a six-hour walk through the jungle. As it turned out, this was a walk that I was totally unprepared for.

We woke up late the next morning, so we were unable to have breakfast, other than a few bananas. We crossed the river by boat and then began our hike.

The jungle was muddy from recent rains, and the "path" we followed went up and down many slippery hills and crossed many small creeks. Where necessary, fallen logs were placed across the streams as our bridges. I was not in the best of shape, and every time we got to the top of a hill, my heart was beating so loudly I could hear it in my head. There were times when I thought to myself, "I can't do this!" Then I felt the Lord give me a revelation of Jesus carrying His cross to Calvary. Oh, the agony and the pain He must have suffered ... until finally someone came to carry the cross for Him. My agony was probably nothing compared to what He experienced.

After six hours of arduous hiking, we arrived at a large river. Pedro said he would be right back, and then he disappeared into the jungle.

WALKING IN THE FOOTSTEPS OF MARTYRS

As we sat there on the jungle floor, totally exhausted, I thought to myself, "Pedro has disappeared, and we are here in the middle of the Ecuadorian jungle, and nobody knows we're here, nobody but God!"

Before long, Pedro came back with a canoe that he had apparently hidden someplace upriver, and we got into it. "At least," I thought to myself, "the walk is over!"

We had travelled only a short distance when a heavy rain descended upon us. I rebuked the rain, and it stopped. Then, however, about twenty minutes later, it started raining again. I rebuked the rain a second time, and it stopped again. I thought, "Praise the Lord! We do have authority over nature." But a short time later, it started raining again, even harder. By this time, we were completely soaked, and I decided not to bother to rebuke the rain anymore.

Pedro informed us that before we reached the main village there was a hut for a family that lived alongside the river. We could stop there and find shelter from the rain. The man who lived in that hut was named Numuga, and when we saw him and his family, we had finally come face to face with some Aucas. I can't say positively, but I'm pretty sure that we were the first Charismatic or Pentecostal people to visit the Auca Indians. The other missionaries who had been involved with them through the years had been evangelicals.

After a time of talking and prayer with Numuga and his family and having something to drink and bananas to eat, Pedro informed us that it was time to go. I said, "It's still raining," but he insisted that we needed to leave. Soon enough it would be dark, and we had to reach the main village before nightfall. He now had two canoes for us with canvases to put over our heads because of the rain. It really didn't matter much because we were already totally soaked.

We finally arrived at the main village of the Aucas. This was where Pedro lived and had a small school for the local children. We were soaked and hungry, but we were now starting to live out our vision of

INHERITING THE NATIONS

contacting the Aucas deep in the jungles of Ecuador.

We changed into dry clothes and prepared ourselves for the first full meal with the Aucas. On that night, the main course was monkey stew.

We used Pedro's schoolroom to teach the Bible to anyone who was interested, and these were rewarding times. The leader of another Auca village, one even further into the jungle, came and heard us teach and invited us to come to his village too. I said I didn't think I had the energy to make another trip, but he said there was only one hill and then it would be easygoing to his village. He would send a couple men to guide us, so we said "okay."

It rained all night nonstop, so I thought our trip would surely be canceled, but the men came to guide us and seemed sure that the rain would eventually stop. With the rain still coming down lightly, we began our journey. In order to make it to the other village by nightfall, we had to go.

I had put on a T-shirt, a regular shirt, and a sweatshirt to keep me dry, but as we began our journey, the jungle was so hot and humid that within a short time, first, my sweatshirt, and then my regular shirt were off and tied around my waist. Because of the heavy rains, the trail was slippery the entire way. When we came to a small creek, we had to cross on a fallen log. Part of the way across, I slipped off and went into the creek. My powder-blue polyester pants were now almost completely covered with mud.

When we came to the one hill the chief had mentioned, it was like a mudslide. We literally had to link our arms together, and one of the Auca brothers would grab hold of a tree and pull the rest of us up to it. Then we went to the next tree and the next. It took quite some time for us to navigate that one "hill." It was more like a mountain.

After three hours of traveling, we came to a swift-flowing river. One of the Aucas waded into the river up to his waist and then turned and motioned for us to follow. I looked at Juan and Sunamita and thought to myself, "No way! There must be an easier way to cross this river." I looked up and down the river, but it was the same width all along and all running swiftly. There didn't seem to be any alternative. So we, too, waded in up to our waist, expecting that we were crossing at that point.

The Auca man leading us, however, didn't cross. Instead, he began to push his way upriver, against the raging current. It wasn't until we got to the village that we learned they normally walk on the riverbank, but because of the all-night rain, the river had overflowed its banks, all paths had disappeared, and the jungle was too thick to walk through. The only choice had been to walk in the water itself. Eventually the water level went down to our knees for the more than three hours we had to walk in it. When we finally exited the water, we had to hike two and a half more hours before reaching the village.

The village people treated us like family, immediately bringing us lemonade to drink, and peanuts, which they were harvesting, along with sweet fried bananas and eggs. The leader of this village was Kimo, the man who had married Dayuma, the lady who had brought the missionaries safely into the camp many years before. Kimo was also one of the Aucas who had killed the five missionaries.

Early in the mornings and in the evenings, we shared the Scriptures with them. Everyone seemed eager to learn more about the Bible. Because none of them could read or write, their knowledge was limited to what the missionaries had taught them.

From the first day we had arrived in the jungle we were given a drink called *chicha*. We didn't know what it was made from but were told that it was a traditional drink. In this village, for the first time, we saw how *chicha* was made. The main ingredient was the root of the yucca plant. It was first boiled and then mashed up into what looked like mashed potatoes. Usually, some fruit was added to it for flavor. Traditional *chicha* is fermented, but ours was fresh.

INHERITING THE NATIONS

The Auca men loved their *chicha* and would take it with them when they went on long hunts. We were told that they would add river water to make a drink that gave them the energy they needed to hunt. But what we were about to see was shocking!

After the yucca was mashed, four women sat around a huge bowl of it. They would take a portion of the substance, put it in their mouth, chew it for a while to make it even finer, and then spit it back into the bowl. They continued to do this until the mashed potato substance was very fine. When I saw how this drink was made, imagining that these women had never gotten close to a dentist's office in their lives, it was quite a revelation, one that took the joy out of drinking the *chicha* they so kindly offered.

Dayuma's brother was named Mincaye, and he was also one of the men who killed the five missionaries. Later, however, he had become a believer.

Mincaye had nine children, and whenever we sang songs, he was the song leader. One afternoon we traveled down river to visit his home and have a meal with him. Being a special guest, I was given the first serving. It was from a large metal bowl of turtle soup, which was very nice, but it had the claw of the turtle sticking up in it, and I was honored to receive it. I wasn't at all sure how to eat that claw. At just the right moment, a dog appeared next to me, I gave him the claw, and he quickly disappeared into the jungle with it. I was glad that my hosts didn't seem to notice.

Many years later, Mincaye was brought to America by Elizabeth Elliott's son, Steve, who was promoting an up-to-date movie about the Auca Indians called "End of the Spear." Steve and Mincaye were speaking at a large church near me, so I went, hoping to speak to Mincaye. After the service, I was able to approach him, but unfortunately, no one was there to translate for me. I had an idea. I had taken along a photo of the two of us together in the jungle. I just handed it to him. He looked at the picture and then looked back at me, then he looked at the picture again and looked back at me. Suddenly, a big smile came across his face, and we hugged for a long time. I read on the Internet a few years ago that he had passed away.

When the time came to leave Mincaye's home, Dayuma asked if we would like to see the beach where the missionaries were killed. We said yes. Another canoe-load of Auca men joined us to go there. The "beach" was actually just a small sandbar on the edge of the Curaray river. Although it was small, Nate Saint, a Missionary Aviation pilot, had been able to land and take off on that small strip of sand that he and his fellow missionaries called Palm Beach many times with his single-engine aircraft.

As I stood on the beach next to Dayuma to take a photo, I realized just how special this place was. On this very spot, five missionaries with a burning desire to share the Gospel with tribal people had paid the ultimate price. Their blood had been poured out on this beach, and now I was standing there with some of the Aucas whose salvation had been paid for, first by the blood of Jesus, but also by the blood of those men who had sacrificed all for the salvation of the Auca tribe. A little more than a month earlier I had been sitting in my comfortable apartment in California enjoying the good life, but now here I was standing in this almost-sacred place deep in the Ecuadorian jungle. Who was I that the Lord had allowed me to be in such a place? And what did this have to do with my calling and destiny?

The next day Kimo brought me back to Palm Beach and, with a large machete, began to clear the overgrown path to a tree under which the five missionaries' bodies had been buried. We stood there together, an Auca chief who had killed missionaries and I, a young missionary, and we prayed together.

A few days later, before beginning our journey out of the jungle, we baptized nine Aucas in the river not far from Palm Beach. It was a

INHERITING THE NATIONS

very moving experience. The chief and his wife had shown us incredible hospitality, having given us their hut, which had a mosquito net and a mattress, the only ones in the village. They had served us with good food and protected us, and as I walked away from the village, I couldn't hold back the tears. I don't believe I had ever received so much from people who had so little. I had, once again, seen the love of Jesus in action, this time in the jungles of Ecuador!

When we exited the jungle and came to a small village, I began to suffer from chills. Fortunately, we were able to stay at the home of a lovely couple who had been referred to us by another missionary. Seeing how I was shaking, they made me a bed in front of their fireplace and started a fire to keep me warm. For the next two days, I lay there shaking, with a high temperature, suffering first chills, then sweats. It seemed very probable that I had contracted malaria because of the many mosquito bites received in the jungle. However, very soon I got better and had no further complications from it.

We eventually got back to Campamento Nueva Vida and shared the exciting testimony of our time with the Auca Indians. Two weeks after we arrived back at the camp, Kimo, Dayuma, and a couple men from another tribe came to visit us there. It was a very special time. One day I took them to a "baño," a pool thermally heated by the surrounding volcanos. It had a large slide going into the water, and the Aucas really enjoyed that.

The following day we took a hike up a hill near the camp that had a large metal cross on top of it. Kimo and I climbed up to the top of the cross. The group was only able to stay for three days before returning to their homes in the jungle, but those three days were glorious. My favorite part was serving them as they had so graciously served us.

The story of the five missionary martyrs had become a best-selling book and movie. Their story and my trip to the Ecuadorian jungle to meet some of the Aucas played an important part in my future ministry. The fact that I was from a Charismatic seminary had closed many non-Pentecostal doors to me, but when I returned to the United States, many churches opened their doors to me. Among them were Baptists, Lutherans, Episcopalians, and others. I was invited to do television and radio programs to share my testimony of the trip into the jungles of Ecuador to share the Gospel and fellowship with the believers among the Auca tribe.

Juan and Sunamita with the Aucas

With Dayuma on Palm Beach

An Auca meeting with two translators, Sunamita into Spanish and Dayuma into Auca

Chapter 8

GOD'S GUIDANCE THROUGH ORDINARY PEOPLE

A man's heart plans his way,
But the LORD directs his steps.   Proverbs 16:9

While in seminary, I met an elderly couple who lived on a ten-thousand-acre ranch in southern Brazil. They and another couple who had a six-thousand-acre ranch there had a vision to make money to support missions. That area of Brazil was formerly used for coffee plantations, but because of a terrible fire in which many of the plantations had been destroyed, some, like my friends, turned to cattle for income. On the ten-thousand-acre ranch were two thousand head of cattle, and on the six-thousand-acre ranch were five hundred head of cattle. The rest of the land was replanted with coffee.

Across from the second ranch was a Bible school called Bethany. It was a very amazing place. My plan was to go from Ecuador to southern Brazil. I had a very limited budget and very little knowledge about how to go about it, but God did some amazing things on this journey, which shows that He is interested in even the little detail of our lives.

A missionary lady, Lois, was traveling from the camp in Ecuador to Guayaquil on the coast, so I flew with her. In Guayaquil the next day I attended a Foursquare church and then boarded a bus for a twenty-two-hour ride to Lima, Peru. Someone had given me the address of a

INHERITING THE NATIONS

pastor in Lima. He wasn't in town when I arrived, but his people welcomed me and gave me a place to sleep in their building.

The next day, I flew to La Paz, Bolivia, landing at the highest airport in the world at more than 13,000 feet. When I got off the plane, it was hard to breathe because the air was thinner at that altitude. During the day the temperature was quite comfortable, but whenever a cloud passed in front of the sun, I could immediately feel the temperature changing.

Lois had called some Wycliffe missionary friends stationed in La Paz, and they met me at the airport and took me to stay at the home of their Nazarene pastor. Sadly, the pastor's wife had recently left him, so he was very depressed. During my five days with him, we were able to have some good times together—praying, studying, and discussing the Bible.

The day before I left that pastor, we attended an evening Bible study, and there I met a missionary who lived in the next city, Cochabamba. Since I was going to Cochabamba, he arranged for his wife to receive me there.

I got a ticket on what was called a "ferro bus." It looked like a bus but ran on railroad tracks. The ferro bus had two cars—one first class and one regular. I traveled first class, but their first class was nothing like first class by American standards.

The city of La Paz lies along the big bowl-shaped crater of a long-extinct volcano. The ferro bus climbed its way out of the crater onto what is called the Altiplano, or high plain, and we were on our way to Cochabamba.

The trip was somewhat boring because the terrain was fairly flat with a few small hills to be traversed. Along the way, however, many of the local people used the railroad right-of-way as a path to get from place to place. As we approached, people scattered in all directions to get off the tracks.

Unfortunately, one man didn't get off the tracks in time. Fortunately, the train had a guard on the front in case it hit an animal. That guard pushed the animal away. In this case, it was a man. Although he wasn't killed in the process, he was injured. The train stopped, he was loaded on the back of the second car and taken to the city for medical care. Once in a while, I could hear him screaming in pain.

At another point in the journey, out my window I saw a massive lake. To this day, I can't figure out what lake that was, but it seemed like it was entirely filled with pink flamingos. What an amazing sight! I assumed it was migration time. We arrived at our destination, and my missionary friend's wife, Faith, gave me a room for the night.

The next morning was Easter, and I went with Faith to a Nazarene church. When I entered, the pastor saw that I was new and asked me to share a testimony. At least that was what I understood. It soon became clear that I hadn't understood very clearly. I got up and gave my testimony when I was introduced. Then, during the worship service, a boy standing next to me said, "He just announced that you will be giving the message today about the resurrection." The pastor was turning the whole service over to me.

At dinner that night, I met a Baptist missionary from Argentina named Hugo. Hugo insisted that God was only moving in the traditional church. Not realizing that I was a Charismatic, he said the Charismatic Movement was satanic. By that time I had come to realize that some people were simply not open to change. Sure that nothing I could tell him would change his mind, I sadly left him to his beliefs. It was becoming clearer and clearer to me that just the opposite was true. Traditional churches were growing at a snail's pace, while Spirit-filled churches were flourishing.

Another missionary named Daniel took me to the airport that night. He introduced me to a lady he knew who was going on my flight to Santa Cruz. Her name was Mrs. Cortez. She and I sat together and talked a lot about the Lord. When we arrived, she ordered a taxi and dropped me at a home where there was a Bible study. I don't remember how I knew these people, but the meeting was all in Spanish, and no one understood or spoke English.

During the meeting, the phone rang. It was Mrs. Cortez calling to make sure I was okay and to ask if I needed anything translated. She told the people of that household that I needed to catch a train at 6:00 AM the next morning. On that train, I met two men who would be used by the Lord to help me on my journey.

One more train ride would take me across the Bolivia/Brazil border to city called Campo Grande. It was hot in the train, with no air-conditioning, so the man next to me had the window open all night, and black dust from the engine covered us. I tried to communicate with him, but he only spoke a few words of English. I was able to explain to him that I was a missionary. As we neared our destination, I bowed my head and prayed, "Lord, You have to help me. I'm not sure how to make the next connection."

When I looked up from my prayer, a man in a white shirt and white pants was coming into our car. He began passing out pieces of paper to everyone in sight. When he got to us, the man next to me apparently told him I was a missionary. The man turned to me and started speaking perfect English. He, too, was a missionary, and he was passing out Gospel tracts to everyone on the train. I told him my situation, and he said, "No problem! When you exit the train, just look for me, and I'll have my daughter help you make your connection." The Lord was continuing to guide me through His people.

The daughter helped me to purchase a ticket that would take me to a town called Londrina. Then she took me to a snack bar near where the buses would be loading and showed me the gate my bus would be leaving from.

As I sat down, I once again saw the two men who had been on the train with me. They looked at my ticket and then said, "This bus is leaving now!" Apparently the gate had changed. As they looked up,

GOD'S GUIDANCE THROUGH ORDINARY PEOPLE

the bus was starting to pull away. One of the men ran and stopped the bus. He told the driver I was supposed to be on that bus, and I was able to board. Once again, the Lord had used ordinary people to help me on my way.

The bus stopped around noontime at a little restaurant to allow us to get some lunch. I was now in Brazil, the local language was Portuguese, and no one seemed to be speaking English. I sat down at one of the small tables. I didn't know what or how to order, but soon a waitress came and began filling my table with small plates. There were vegetables, meat, and fruit on them. I saw that this was what the bus driver was eating, so I just started eating too. "What might a meal like this cost?" I wondered. When the bill came, I couldn't believe my eyes. It was only $3.00. Praise the Lord!

In Londrina, I would have to buy one more ticket to get to my destination, a town called Umuarama. The name, I was told, meant "where friends meet." An older lady saw my frustration when I couldn't communicate with the ticket agent, and she came to my rescue. She helped me get the ticket, and then we went together to sit where the buses would be leaving.

For some reason, we thought my bus wouldn't be leaving for quite a while, so I bought some hotdogs and drinks, and we sat down near the buses to enjoy our snack. As we were eating, she looked up and said, "Hey, this bus is the same number as your bus!"

The driver had just closed the door, but when she got up and went to the door, he opened it, and they talked. She came back and said to me, "This is your bus, and it's leaving now." They loaded my bag, and I said thank you to the lady. I later wondered if she might have been an angel. I couldn't say for sure, but I knew that the Lord had helped me.

I arrived at the Umuarama bus station at 3:30 AM, and the town was dark. There were no streetlights, just one dim light at the bus station. There was also no pavement, just red dirt roads. The bus station was tiny, a wooden structure painted blue with a doorway but no door. As I stepped off the bus into the dark, I was wondering, "What do I do now?" I must have looked lost because a man picked up my bag and walked me down the street to a very small hotel. It was closed, but he kept knocking on the door until someone answered, and I got a room for the night.

The next day I took a taxi to the only Christian bookstore in town. It was the only address I had. The owner of the bookstore knew my friends and decided to drive me out to the ranch, about fifteen miles from town on dirt roads through coffee fields and other fields filled with grazing cattle.

It had been eighteen days since I had left Ecuador, and I had traveled through Ecuador, Peru, Bolivia and Brazil, sharing the Gospel whenever the Lord opened doors for me. I was now sitting with Morrey and Verna Sands and their son-in-law George. We had met in California before I had any interest in being a missionary, but God knew my future and had connected me with them for His purposes. Now I was with them on their ten-thousand-acre cattle ranch in southern Brazil. It seemed surreal.

I had traveled many miles, on many different types of transportation, through four countries, and all along the way the Lord had people guiding me safely to my destination. For me, those days were very special. I was able to see the Lord's hand lovingly guiding me through other people, and He was teaching me to hear His voice, preparing me for my destiny.

Chapter 9

LIFE AND MINISTRY ON A BRAZILIAN FAZENDA

The humble He guides in justice,
And the humble He teaches His way.   Psalm 25:9

I remember an incident that happened when I was five years old like it was today. We had been living on my grandparents two-hundred-acre farm. One day, my uncle arrived with a very large moving van. Before long, everything we owned was loaded onto that truck, and it was time to go. We were moving to the suburbs.

I wasn't at all happy about this turn of events. I loved the farm. I remember sitting between two massive trees crying. My father came, leaned down, picked me up, and put me in the front seat of the truck between himself and my uncle. We were moving to a new development with brand new houses to begin a new life.

When I was a teenager, I went back to the farm every summer to work. It was a lot of fun driving tractors, plowing fields, putting up thousands of bales of hay and stacking them in the hot barns, milking cows, and collecting eggs. The farm had many types of animals, even race horses, which my grandfather was very proud of. When I was older, I lost money on one of those horses at the track with my grandfather. Looking back, it was a great time of building character and building my physical body. Nowadays, it would be called "slave labor."

INHERITING THE NATIONS

Now I was on a ranch again, this time in Brazil. After an early breakfast, horses, already saddled, were brought up for me and George, the son-in-law who oversaw the everyday workings of the ranch. The days differed, but it was always hard work. It was also fun spending time with George in his various activities.

George had built a small chapel on the ranch, and in the evenings we had services there. Sometimes there were just a handful of people, and sometimes there were many. The first night I was at the church I spoke about the baptism of the Holy Spirit and five people came forward to receive. Even local pastors and missionaries would sometimes come to the services.

As I noted in an earlier chapter, the second ranch had a Bible school across the street from it called Bethany. It was full of students and always busy with different activities and classes. I was invited to speak there on many occasions.

After being there awhile, I developed a very bad sore throat, so I went into town and got some medication. Verna made a drink for me, put it in the refrigerator and told me to drink it throughout the day. At one point, I began to feel a little uneasy in their home. For some reason, there seemed to be some tension in the air, and I couldn't figure out exactly what it meant. The next day, when Morrey and I were working around the ranch, I asked him if I had done anything to offend them. He assured me that would never happen.

A couple days later, everyone went into town to get supplies, and I was left behind with Verna because of my sore throat. Somehow the two of us struck up a conversation about being teachable, and she asked me: "Are you really teachable?" Of course, I said yes, without having any idea what was coming next. I don't know how long Verna talked that day. It seemed like an eternity, as she told me that I was nothing like Jesus. Then the truth about what I had done to offend them came out.

LIFE AND MINISTRY ON A BRAZILIAN FAZENDA

They couldn't believe that I would have gone to their refrigerator and taken something out without first asking permission. Even their sons wouldn't do that, Verna said. I explained to her, "You made that drink for me and told me to drink it during the day." Plus, I had bought some food when we were in town, and it was also in their fridge. But that didn't matter at all. According to their custom, I should have asked permission to open the refrigerator.

I explained to Verna that I had asked Morrey if I had done anything to offend them and he said no. She explained that he was too embarrassed to tell me the truth, and she made me promise never to tell him about our conversation. If I did, she said, "You will never be welcome here again."

This incident taught me a great missionary lesson. I have stayed in many homes across the world in my more than forty years of ministry, and whenever my hosts say, "Make yourself at home," I always remember this story of the refrigerator in Brazil. Sometimes, when people say, "Make yourself at home," it comes with exceptions to the rule.

Many pastors came by the ranch during my stay, and this opened opportunities for me to speak in a couple churches in town. I was even invited to go over to Asunción, Paraguay and speak at an Anglican church there. In the process, I was able to encourage some missionaries who were working there in Paraguay.

Because of that first trip to Paraguay, on future trips to Brazil I often travelled through Paraguay and spent some days there with the missionaries before going on to Brazil.

Over the years I returned to the ranch several times. One time I took four young people from a church in Rio de Janeiro to minister at the ranch and at some churches in the nearby town. One night, on the way back to the ranch, the red dirt was thick mud because it had rained all day. I was driving as fast as I could so we wouldn't get stuck in the mud, but it wasn't fast enough. The car ended up stuck in the middle of the road with mud up to the bumpers. We had to get out of the car, we men in our suits, the ladies with long dresses, and walk several miles in the mud. Our only light was from the moon. By the time we reached the ranch, our shoes and clothes were covered with that red mud.

During one long holiday weekend in Brazil, two young guys and two young ladies from the nearest town came out to stay at the ranch. One of the guys was a good friend of George, and George had invited them. George had built a very nice swimming pool there on the ranch, something I don't suppose anyone else in that small country town had. It was a great treat for these young people to visit the ranch, go swimming, and just relax.

One of the young ladies, a girl named Nadie, was very pretty, single, and had a good job at a local bank. The problem was that only one of the group spoke English, and that was George's friend. All of my conversations with each of them had to be translated by him. One day he said to me, "Nadie wants to kiss you." Shocked, I said, "No, I can't do that."

Looking back on it, I don't know why I said no that day. I was single, and she was single, but we didn't kiss. What did result was a long conversation about my life and ministry and my commitment to the Lord, and I explained in detail what it meant to be a Christian. After that weekend these young people came out to the ranch several more times during my stay there, and I remember praying with Nadie on several occasions. I felt that she could be wonderfully used by the Lord to share the Gospel with many in that small town.

I can't remember how many times I visited the ranch. On one occasion when I was there, somebody came out to the ranch to give us some bad news. Nadie had a motorcycle that she rode to work every day. One day she took a route she was unfamiliar with. She failed to see a speed bump in time to slow down. When she hit that bump, she was thrown from her bike and killed.

LIFE AND MINISTRY ON A BRAZILIAN FAZENDA

It was hard for me to understand how someone so young and with such great potential could be killed like that. I spent quite a while praying after hearing that sad news. It has been so long ago that I don't remember the details, but as I prayed the Lord showed me an angel that came to Nadie's lifeless body, picked up her spirit, and took her to Heaven.

The day I was preparing to board a bus to leave town, someone called my name. I turned to see, and it was Nadie's sister, a local dentist I visited on occasion. We talked for a while, and I explained to her that I was leaving for another city. She pleaded with me to stay a few more days. She wanted me to come to her home to meet with all of Nadie's relatives. She said it had been very hard on them all losing Nadie. I decided to cancel my bus ticket and go home with her that day.

That evening all of Nadie's relatives came to her sister's home, and I was able to share the Gospel with them. When I told them about the vision I'd had of Nadie being taken up to Heaven by an angel, they were greatly encouraged. I took time to pray for each of them personally. This was a detour from my schedule, but it was ordained by God to share His love with an entire family.

Before I left, I went to the cemetery with Nadie's sister to visit the grave. I was surprised to find that it had a very tall tombstone with glass and metal doors on the front of it which opened to a small altar. On the altar was a picture of Nadie, a picture I had taken of her one day when she visited the ranch.

Nadie was only in her late twenties, and now she was gone. She had heard my testimony, I had shared the Gospel with her, and she was ready to go to Heaven. As a result of her death, all her relatives heard the Gospel through me. And yet, on my bus trip out of town, I wept. Sometimes it's difficult to understand why bad things happen. We just have to trust the Lord that He works all things according to the council of His will and for our good.

INHERITING THE NATIONS

I have a lot of great memories of my times on the ranch, but I guess the strongest memory would be learning that the Lord has a way of humbling us through other people, for He wants us to remain teachable.

With Nadie's family

On a Brazilian fazenda

SOUTH AMERICA

Chapter 10

THE LORD'S FINANCIAL BLESSINGS

Command those who are rich in this present age not to be haughty, nor to trust in uncertain riches but in the living God, who gives us richly all things to enjoy. Let them do good, that they be rich in good works, ready to give, willing to share.   1 Timothy 6:17-18

After an exciting five months in South America, I arrived in Albany, New York on May 23, 1978 to visit my family. The following day I received a call from Ken, a friend in California, inviting me to go to Japan with him. His parents were missionaries there, and he was born there and had grown up there. I told him I didn't have the money, but I was interested in going. He offered to go ahead and buy the tickets if I could pay him back when I got to California.

I spent the next several weeks in New York, Pennsylvania, and Ohio, speaking in churches, at home groups, and even on the radio. Most of the time I shared my testimony of what had been happening on the mission field and always ended by challenging people to pursue God's plan for *their* life. I always stressed that their life was important to the Lord too, and also for the people who were waiting to hear the Gospel through them. I met many wonderful people and ministered in churches that over the years I would return to whenever I had the opportunity to be in America. However, my focus was turning to the nations.

INHERITING THE NATIONS

Psalm 2:8, *"Ask of me, and I will give you the nations for Your inheritance and the ends of the earth for Your possession,"* which the Lord had given me when He commissioned me into the ministry in Arizona, was now becoming a reality!

When I finally arrived in California on June 18, I only had a few days for the Lord to supply the money I would need for the trip to Japan. My friend had paid for the tickets with a check, and I needed to pay him back before the flight.

Another friend of mine, Joe Andrews, was handling my mail and my finances. He suggested that I sell my car because I was traveling so much that I didn't really need it. That would pay for my trip. I didn't have any objections, but I felt in my spirit that the Lord wanted to do a miracle, something that would glorify Him. I knew for sure that He wanted me to go; I just didn't know how the finances would come.

Because of Joe's persistence, we went to a car dealership to sell the car, but were unable to do so because the car had been originally purchased in New York State and I would need special papers from the New York Motor Vehicle Department to sell the car in California. Once that option was closed, I still felt in my spirit that God was going to do a miracle.

On Thursday mornings, Melodyland Christian Center, my home church, always had what they called a miracle service. It was a time of worship and testimony and then prayer for the sick. I attended and the pastor called me up to share a short testimony about my travels. When I finished speaking, Pastor Cecil Pumphrey told me to sit in the front row because he was sure people would want to come by and give me money after the service. Two ladies came. One gave me $5. The other lady gave me a penny, telling me to put it in my Bible, and it would bring me luck.

Pastor Cecil invited me to breakfast, and while we were eating at a restaurant, Pastor Ralph Wilkerson, the head pastor, came in and joined us. During our conversation, he invited me to be on television

THE LORD'S FINANCIAL BLESSINGS

that evening to share my testimony. I told him I couldn't because I was leaving for Japan. He asked about my flight schedule, and after I told him, he insisted that there would be time for me to be on the television program first and still get to the airport on time. So, I said, "Okay!"

That afternoon, while I was packing, a friend of mine, Danny Chavez, came by and gave me $20 and twenty rolls of film for my camera. So now, I had $25, twenty rolls of film, and a penny, but in my spirit I knew the Lord was going to supply what was lacking. The nations were mine for the asking because of Psalm 2:8. It was my responsibility to ask and to go, and it was the Lord's responsibility to supply the needed finances. I didn't have any fear or anxiety. I knew He would somehow be glorified.

With my bags packed for the airport, we left to be on the television program at the church. No one knew of my financial situation except my friend Joe who handled my money. Even my friend who was expecting me to pay him that night didn't know that I didn't yet have the money for the trip.

The fellowship hall of the church was set up like a dining room with a few tables, and the TV program was called "Let's Get Acquainted." As he had promised, Pastor Wilkerson had me on first, and I shared my testimony about being with the Auca Indians in Ecuador. When I finished, he asked me, "Where are you going next?" I looked at my watch and said, "In three minutes I'm leaving for the airport. We're flying to Japan tonight!"

Some people believe that you must first make a positive confession for the Lord to move, but I've never really believed that. I believe you must first hear from the Lord, and when He tells you something, then you can begin to proclaim what He has told you. I wasn't making a positive confession out of fear or some theology. I was just saying what I knew in my heart God was going to do. He had told me I was going to Japan, so I was going.

INHERITING THE NATIONS

Pastor Wilkerson reached inside his coat pocket, took out his wallet, and said, "I've never done this before on this TV program, but I want to give you $100.00, and I want people all around this set to give you something too." Three minutes later, I went out the door with a handful of money, more than I would need for the trip. As we drove to the airport, my friend Joe was weeping. "I can't believe what just happened," he said.

When we got to the airport ticket counter, the agent on duty informed us that the tickets had been cancelled because they were paid for with a check that had insufficient funds. I said, "How much are the tickets?" When she told me, I took out my money and paid cash for both tickets.

I handed the tickets and passports to my friend to hold, and we walked toward the gate where the plane would board. Once at the gate, I said to him, "Where are the tickets?"

"You have them," he said.

I said, "No, I gave them to you."

He thought for a moment and then realized that when we had left the ticket counter, he had gone out to a phone booth in front of the airport while I and my friends went up to the gate. He had left the tickets and passports in the phone booth. Frantically, we went back to the phone booth, but there were no tickets or passports there. Next, we went back to the ticket counter. Praise the Lord, someone had found the tickets and passports and turned them in at the ticket counter. A short time later, we were boarding our flight, China Airlines Flight 007, for Japan.

I wrote that testimony in a newsletter that I send out, and it struck a chord. For years people would say to me, "I remember that time you left for the airport with not enough money for the tickets, but God supplied." Yes, God supplied, and therefore He was glorified! I could have sold my car and had enough money for the trip, and people would

THE LORD'S FINANCIAL BLESSINGS

have said, "Wow! Joe really made a sacrifice for this trip." But the Lord didn't want me to get the glory. He wanted to be glorified.

In preparation for writing this book, I was looking through a diary I kept for the first several years of my ministry. I had written there that I was traveling from India to Kenya and had a one-way ticket and only $15 in my pocket. After a couple days there, I only had $1.50 left. When I told a young missionary I was staying with about my finances, he rebuked me and told me it was wrong for me to come to Africa with so little money. I told him the Lord had supplied in the past, and He would supply again. A couple days later my brother contacted me from California and told me he had sold my car. This gave me the money I needed for my final ticket back to America.

This is not about me; it's about the Lord! It's about hearing His voice, doing what He tells us to do, and proclaiming what He says He's going to do! Then He is glorified, that Jesus might receive the reward of His suffering!

During the first eight years of my ministry, I traveled entirely by faith. I had no monthly supporters and most of the time just purchased a one-way ticket to the country I was going to. Often, I arrived there with little or no money in my pocket, but the Lord was always faithful to supply what I needed to obey His calling and pursue my destiny.

I was an American missionary, but the Lord was using people in other countries to supply my needs, both physically and financially. Sadly, most American and European missionaries have taught people in foreign countries that when it comes to money, God only supplies in America or Europe. This has robbed the people of the blessing of seeing the Lord supply financially in *their* country.

One time, when I was in Malaysia, I spoke at a church, and they gave me a $300 offering. I decided to give $30 of that to the young Malaysian missionary I had been staying with for the past few days. As I was getting on the train to return to Thailand, I handed him an envelope with the $30 in it, but at the same time he handed me an envelope. When I sat down on the train and opened the envelope, I found that it contained $300. The young Malaysian missionary had given me ten times what I had given him.

I have so many stories of the Lord supplying financially that I could write an entire book on nothing but that subject. I will share more of them in later chapters.

In the eighth year of my ministry, I was invited to speak at a church in Morton, Mississippi. It was a small town that didn't even have any stop lights in it. At the time, Morton was known as the chicken capital of America. The people were super-friendly in Morton, and through the years I returned there many times. On the first visit, I spoke at a small Baptist Church which had probably somewhere around a hundred members. Although I wasn't seeking financial backers, they made a pledge to send me $400 a month, a great blessing at the time. That was the first time I began to receive monthly support.

Being interviewed on TV at Melodyland Church

Chapter 11

JAPAN, A COUNTRY OF TWO WORLDS

For the kingdom of God is not in word but in power.
1 Corinthians 4:20

When I got off the plane in Japan, it was the first time in my life I understood what spiritual oppression was. It felt like an undersized helmet had been placed over my head. When someone is raised in such an atmosphere, it becomes normal to them, and they don't even realize that there are demonic forces controlling the atmosphere. It wasn't until years later I learned that most Japanese people testify that when someone dies, they see some kind of spirit leaving their body. The spiritual world is powerful in Japan, and it continues to hold the great majority of the people there in darkness, blinding them to the truth of the Gospel.

Several years later I was on a train by myself in Tokyo. I was the only foreigner. As I stood there looking around the train car, the veil of the spiritual realm opened to me, and I saw a demon sitting next to every single Japanese person on the train. At the same time, I found the Japanese people to be friendly, courteous, honest, and very hospitable.

As an example, when my friend and I arrived that first time, we had more suitcases than we could carry at one time, and we had to take a couple train rides to reach our final destination. We took some of our bags a distance, then left them there in the subway with hundreds, if not thousands, of people passing by them. Then we walked back and got the other bags we had left behind and brought them up to that spot. We had to do that many times before we arrived at our next train. I was very worried that the bags would be stolen within seconds of setting them down and leaving them, but my friend, having been raised there in Japan, knew that a Japanese person would never steal someone else's bag. Thinking about it now, I don't know any other country in the world where you could trust people as much as you can trust the Japanese.

In Japan, you also never have to worry about getting lost. You can just ask directions from someone, and they will most likely turn around and take you to where you need to go or, at least, get you to a place where you can see your destination.

Still, Japan is a hard place for missionaries. I'm not sure about the present, but for a long time there were more missionaries in Japan than in any country of the world, and the cost of living there was one of the highest in the world. Even now (in 2023), Japan ranks in the top ten most expensive countries to live.

Many of the Christian missionaries in Japan have been there for decades, but the Christian population is still less than five percent. One must ask the question: considering the number of missionaries in Japan for such a long time, and the massive financial investments for them to live there and do the work of a missionary, where is the fruit? Why do the people still live in darkness? Why cannot these kind people experience the love of the heavenly Father?

I've been to Japan many times and met many missionaries, as well as many Japanese believers. These missionaries are dedicated people of prayer and they love the Japanese people. You cannot question their dedication and commitment to Japan and its people. But where is the fruit?

INHERITING THE NATIONS

In the mid 1980s, I was in Switzerland ministering and had the privilege of meeting a Swiss man who had been a missionary in India for fifty years. When you do the math, that means he started working in India in the mid 1930s. I've been to India many times, but I can't imagine what it must have been like when he first went there. When I travel there, I only spend a few weeks at a time training Christian leaders, and to say it's challenging is to put it mildly. For sure this brother had made amazing sacrifices to be there during those fifty years. I'm sure he was a man of prayer and great love for the people, or he could never have stayed that long. He had heard about me and heard that I was operating in spiritual gifts, so he wanted to question me about those giftings.

With great sadness, he told me that he had been in India for fifty years and didn't have a single convert to show for it. Why no converts? I have heard some say that people go to the mission field just to sow seeds. I'm sorry, but I cannot accept that! Jesus said in Matthew 28:19-20:

Go therefore and make disciples of all the nations, baptizing them in the name of the Father and of the Son and of the Holy Spirit, teaching them to observe all things that I have commanded you; and lo, I am with you always, even to the end of the age.

I'm not an expert on Christian growth, but my personal experience tells me that with all the efforts of the mission forces in the world, Christianity is losing, and Islam is growing at a faster rate. What is missing?

As we noted in an earlier chapter, Jesus spent three years living with and training His disciples. He took them out with Him as He ministered. He showed them how to pray, and how to deliver and heal people. Then He gave them authority to do it themselves. But, as we have seen, all of this was not enough. There was one more thing they needed.

JAPAN, A COUNTRY OF TWO WORLDS

In Acts 1:4-5, Jesus commanded His disciples not to depart from Jerusalem before receiving enablement from the Spirit:

And being assembled together with them, He commanded them not to depart from Jerusalem, but to wait for the Promise of the Father, "which," He said, "you have heard from Me; for John truly baptized with water, but you shall be baptized with the Holy Spirit not many days from now."

Far too many of the Christians of the world, including missionaries, have no idea what Jesus was talking about when He said, *"Wait for the Promise of the Father."* It is not my intention to write a theological book, nor to debate theology. I'm just trying to share the story of my journey into the nations of the world, as the Holy Spirit has led me, in hopes that those of you who are reading my story will get a vision of what the Lord is calling *you* to do. This is something no one else can do except you.

The Lord opened many special doors for me in Japan, and I met wonderful people who became friends for a long time. One such couple was Captain Don and Donna Carter. They were stationed at an Air Force Base in Japan where he was a medic. I was scheduled to have a meeting at a home on the base at 3:30 one afternoon, but somehow I got mixed up and thought it was at 6 PM. So, I arrived late, but Don and Donna came even later.

Four of us and myself sat at the kitchen table, and Donna pushed a white envelope across the table to me and said, "Tell me your testimony." That was the beginning of a long relationship, as they moved to military bases in California and Texas over the following year. Their friendship was special to me, and the Lord used them to open many doors of ministry and avenues of financial support for me. It all began in Japan.

INHERITING THE NATIONS

Just recently I was able to reconnect with Don and Donna. It was very special talking to them. They are retired now and live in Florida. I'm hoping I can visit them one day to reminisce about our times in Japan.

I met another couple, Don and Ruth Maddox, who had an interesting ministry. They lived in a very fancy hotel called the New Otani Tokyo. The hotel had a very beautiful garden with a Japanese tea house, and there they held Christian services every day for anyone who wanted to come and hear Christian teachings and receive prayer. Even though they lived in luxury, they were humble people, filled with compassion and love. You could see Jesus in them.

While I was in Japan, I was invited to speak at the Women's Aglow meeting, where I met a lady whose nickname was Mimi. Her husband was a bass player in what was the number one rock band of that time in the 1980s. His name was Steve Fox, and the name of the band was Godiego. Steve invited me to be backstage with him when they were singing in the Budokan, a 14,000-seat stadium built for the 1964 Olympics. The place was packed.

We have arrived before the doors were open to the general public. We entered on the main floor, and Steve showed me that on every seat he had placed a full-color four-page newspaper all about his life and testimony. In every concert, the band members would take time to share something personal about their life. That night, when it was Steve's turn to speak between songs, he said, "My name is Steve Fox." Of course everyone knew because they had been chanting his name. He was the most popular one of the group and got the most fan mail.

Steve continued, "I'm the one who put that paper on your seat because the most important thing for me is for you to come to know Jesus Christ as your personal Savior!" The people at that concert probably had never gone to church or heard the Gospel, but now they were hearing about Jesus from one of the most famous rock stars in Japan.

And they would take home with them the four-page paper that would clearly lay out God's plan for *their* life. There is no telling how many people were touched and saved by Steve's testimony.

During the many times I have been to Japan, the churches and believers there have been a great financial blessing to me. Their generosity gave me the resources necessary to travel into other Asian countries where offerings were very seldom given.

Japan is a country of two worlds, a spirit world and a physical world. Still today, oppressive spirits rule the country and control the people. The Scriptures clearly show us that there is a spiritual war going on, but for some reason very few seminaries offer classes on spiritual warfare. For more than twenty years now I have been teaching on spiritual warfare to leaders in Southeast Asia, for ten years in the DTS Classes of Youth With A Mission in Armenia, and more recently in Russia and Central Asia.

After many years of observation of the mission fields around the world, it is my personal belief that until the mission forces experience the Promise of the Father, understand spiritual warfare, and operate in the power of the Holy Spirit, they will not accomplish the Lord's perfect and complete will for the lost in the nations of the world.

With Don and Donna Carter

Chapter 12

A VISION TO DELIVER BREAD TO THE FAMILY

Therefore those who were scattered went everywhere preaching the word.   Acts 8:4

In the fall of 1978, I made my first trip to the amazing city of Hong King. As we neared the island, out the windows of the airplane I could see the tall buildings of the city. The plane made several tight turns, as it wound its way between buildings and then to the short runway at Kai Tak Airport. When we finally stopped, the plane was just a short distance from the waters of Victoria Harbor.

Originally part of China, Hong Kong was, at that time, controlled by Great Britain through a ninety-nine-year lease (which expired in 1997). All the luxuries of the free world were enjoyed by the people who lived there in Hong Kong, but not very far away, bordered by a small waterway and high fences, were people who had been living in darkness for the nearly thirty years since Mao Zedong had brought Communism to China. These were like two different worlds that could only be totally understood by traveling between them. Until December of 1978, that was impossible for most of the world. China was tightly shuttered, but that was about to end.

This first trip for me to Hong Kong would only last four days, but it connected me with people who are still friends of mine today and

INHERITING THE NATIONS

played an important part in my calling and destiny. During those few days, I connected with a few missionaries, spoke at a Bible school, and shared at a church on my last night. That church was pastored by Rev. Dennis, a man of prayer and vision, who had a fire that burned in his heart for the people living across the border in Communist China. His church was made up mostly of young people who burned with that same fire. They had long been praying and were just waiting for the day they could physically cross that border. When it happened, they fully intended to carry the Bread of Life to those on the other side.

Since that first trip, I have been to Hong Kong more times than I can remember, but one picture is embedded deeply in my memory. I had arrived at the church one evening and was walking past Pastor Dennis' office. The lower part of the wall was solid, but the upper half was all glass, so you could see inside. At first glance, it looked like no one was there, but then I looked down. There, on his face before God, was Pastor Dennis, crying out for souls. I don't know how many years he had prayed like that because I had just met him, but the exciting thing was that within just a few months his prayers would be answered. The doors of Communist China would open to tourists, diplomats, and businessmen, and the pastor and his people would cross the border many times carrying the Bread of Life and fulfilling part of their destiny.

In the coming years, believers from many nations were shuttled through that church, prayed for, equipped with suitcases filled with Chinese language Bibles, and sent on their way as tourists visiting China. Once they arrived on the other side, drops were arranged with representatives of the underground church in China, and the Bibles thus reached their intended targets.

How many people died during those early years under Communism is not really known. It is probably a number beyond imagination. How the Chinese Church suffered during this time also cannot be totally

A VISION TO DELIVER BREAD TO THE FAMILY

understood. But in all of it, the Lord was working. Believers had been forced to go underground and to hold secret meetings. Their Bibles had been confiscated, but they began to write down what they could from memory. Persecution had scattered Christians to cities all over China, but the Lord gave them strategies to preach the Gospel every place they went. In the darkness and suffering, the Chinese Church was growing.

On that first visit, I made a point of traveling one day with some young people to the border with China, and there I looked across for the first time. We prayed for the Chinese Church that day and for our brothers and sisters who were on the other side of those metal fences topped with barbed wire. Pastor Dennis and his church people had been praying for years, we prayed, and the God of Heaven, El Roi, the God who sees, the God who stores our prayers in golden bowls, El Shama, the God who hears, heard those prayers. He had also heard the prayers coming up to His throne from the people inside China, and the time was now at hand.

For my part, I had other countries to visit at that time, but I would soon be returning to take part in the unimaginable joy of putting a Bible into someone's hand that hadn't had one in thirty years. They would just look at it and weep or sometimes kiss it. It was an experience that reached deep into my soul and was embedded forever in my mind and emotions.

Although prayers had been continually going up for years for China to open, no one knew the exact time it would happen. For sure, the Lord was storing up the prayers of His saints for China in His golden bowls. Soon those bowls would be full, and the answer to those prayers would come.

It was 1978, two years after Mao Zedong died, that the doors of Communist China began to open, and tourists were eager to visit this country that had been closed to the outside world for so long. The day would come soon when I, too, would enter China as one of those

INHERITING THE NATIONS

tourists to deliver the precious Word of God to Chinese believers. God had answered prayer so that Jesus might receive the reward of His suffering.

In December of that year, China opened to the outside world. Now the Church that had been refined in the fires of persecution would be revealed in all her glory to the outside world, and those who had prayed for the day they could carry in the precious Bread, the Bible, would finally see their prayers and their dreams become reality.

Bibles for China

Chapter 13

THE MEDICAL MISSION FORCE OF NEPAL

The mountains quake before Him,
The hills melt,
And the earth heaves at His presence,
Yes, the world and all who dwell in it.   Nahum 1:5

While still living in New York, I had met a couple (Tom and Cynthia), who were missionary doctors in the mountains of Nepal, a country made famous because of the Himalayan mountains and, in particular, Mount Everest, the highest mountain in the world. Tom and Cynthia had told me that if I ever got to that region to please come and visit their mission hospital. I now felt led to do that.

After checking the airline routes from Hong Kong to Kathmandu, the capitol of Nepal, I decided that the best route was to go through Bangkok, Thailand. I would have a one-day stopover there.

In Bangkok, I stayed at the YMCA, often frequented by missionaries and local Christians. While I was there, I got a chance to meet some wonderful people who were committed to that Buddhist nation and were doing whatever they could to bless the Thai people. At the time, I had no idea that Thailand would become a main focus for my future destiny (more about that in another chapter). The next day, I flew to Kathmandu.

INHERITING THE NATIONS

Nepal was a Hindu country that did not allow missionary evangelism, but people like my friends who were doctors were able to stay there to do medical work. They also used this opportunity to share the Gospel whenever they could.

The hospital was located high in the mountains, but the group they worked with had an office in the capitol, and they gave me a room for the night. I was to wait for a young man who delivered mail to the hospital and then trek up with him.

There at the mission office, I learned that just two weeks before, seventeen Nepali believers had been imprisoned for converting to Christianity. I also learned that more than six hundred locals had become Christians and been baptized that year. As it turned out, Tom was in town, so we spent an afternoon together and made plans for me to go to the mountain hospital.

I spent the next few days meeting Nepali believers and attending a few Bible studies in the evenings. The final evening, several brothers decided to walk me back to the mission base because the streets were very dark with no streetlights. As we were walking along, suddenly something struck me hard in the chest. It turned out to be nothing more than a cow walking in the middle of the road in the dark. Cows are sacred in Hindu countries and, therefore, are permitted to roam the streets and sleep wherever they want.

The next morning my journey to the mission hospital began, accompanied by the young man responsible for delivering the mail. First, we took a five-hour bus ride and then a four-hour walk through rice fields. These turned out to be very slippery because it had recently rained. Every once in a while, I would slip and fall to the ground. The ground, however, seemed to be swarming with leeches. Each time I got back up, I had to examine myself all over for leeches and pull them off so that they couldn't burrow deep into my skin. They did make my hands bleed. They even got into my shoes. When I took them off later, my feet were bleeding.

THE MEDICAL MISSION FORCE OF NEPAL

When we were unable to reach our destination by 7:00 PM, it began to get dark. My guide knew of a home nearby where we could spend the night, so we stopped there. Interestingly, he didn't speak any English and neither did the people we were staying with. So much for communication. Our hosts fixed us something to eat and served it to us as we sat on the dirt floor of their home. I was thankful to the Lord that there was only one candle, so I couldn't tell what we were eating.

The home only had one bed, and our hosts now insisted that I sleep on it. I was somewhat reluctant because it was a bamboo bed that was attached directly to the wall and had just two thin legs supporting it. The real problem came when they handed me that only candle, and I suddenly saw that the wall of the hut was covered with various kinds of living creatures. When these came down the wall, there was only one place for them to go, and that was onto the bed. I tried all kinds of hand motions to indicate that I did not want to take the only bed in the house, but they insisted, so I had no choice. Needless to say, I didn't sleep very well that night.

The next morning, we were on the trail again by 5:00 AM. At times, the trail literally followed the edge of the mountain, and we were getting higher and higher. As we came around one particular corner, I was startled to see that the clouds were below us. It was a beautiful sight. In the distance, I could see the snow-covered Himalayan mountains. That picture is still embedded in my mind.

After a four-hour walk, we arrived at the mission hospital. I was only able to spend four days there, but it was a fruitful time. I shared the Word in small meetings with the hospital staff and with Nepalis interested in the baptism of the Holy Spirit.

When I returned to Kathmandu, I shared in a couple more meetings. On my final night, I attended a home group led by a sister from Singapore. She had been working with this group for several years. I was very impressed with her. She was deeply committed and very anointed by the Lord. I learned later that her father was the pastor of a big church in Singapore, but she had chosen to obey the Lord's calling for her in this Hindu stronghold rather than live in the luxury of Singapore.

My time in these countries was short, but I did my best to encourage the mission force in whatever way I could with the anointing and wisdom I carried at the time. These early trips were just a small glimpse of the strongholds in Nepal that kept the people in darkness, unable to see the light of the Gospel, just a chance to spy out the land. Years later I would return to Nepal and other countries in the region, carrying new insights into the Spirit world and our spiritual weapons of war.

It wasn't long before I was on a mission to raise up an army of men and women with an anointing for war, anointed men and women who could go forth and break down the strongholds of the enemy in the nations of the world, that Jesus might receive the reward of His suffering!

A Nepali home group

Walking above the clouds in Nepal

Chapter 14

NO PLACE LIKE INDIA

The people who sat in darkness have seen a great light,
And upon those who sat in the region and shadow of death
Light has dawned.   Matthew 4:16

My next destination was Kenya in East Africa, but I had a two-day stopover in Bombay, India. They say that first impressions are lasting ones, and that was very true for me when it came to my first time in India. The weather there was always hot and humid, and the air was filled with the smells of incense.

I took a taxi to a hotel I had reserved, but when I got there, they informed me they had no reservation in my name. As luck would have it, they were also full—except for a suite that would have cost me three times what I expected to pay. I left there and went to two other hotels that were full, finally finding one that was small but clean and only cost $12 a night. Of course, there was no air-conditioning, only a fan.

It was late evening by this time, and I was tired, thirsty, and needed to rest. They brought me a large glass bottle of water. When I asked if it was okay to drink, they assured me that it was. Please remember: if you ever go to India, never drink the water unless it's in a sealed container, even if they tell you it's okay to drink.

Late in the night I woke up with my stomach totally bloated and in extreme pain from the contaminated water. The next morning I checked out of that hotel and found a Christian guest house. After that experience I was always cautious about drinking water in India.

I had a reminder of this experience a few years ago when traveling in Northeast India. I had been there for a pastors' conference and was getting ready to leave for the airport. After I packed my bags, I brushed my teeth for the last time, cautiously using only bottled water. But then, at the last second, I rinsed my brush off with the tap water and made one last swipe of my mouth with the toothbrush. Big mistake!

When I boarded my flight, I was happy to learn that I was being upgraded to Business Class for free. I was excited to enjoy the nice meals they would serve on my long flight back to California, but soon the water from my toothbrush reached my stomach, it became bloated, and I spent the rest of the time in Business Class running back and forth to the bathroom, never able to enjoy the nice meals.

Back to that first trip, after checking into the guest house, I decided to look around the city. After all, it was my first time in India. I thought maybe some tea would settle my stomach. I found an outdoor cafe and sat down to order. A man sitting in the cafe struck up a conversation, and later, when I was ready to leave, he walked along with me, explaining as we went some aspects of the city.

At one point, we came to the entrance of a cemetery where a Hindu cremation was taking place. I asked if it would be offensive if I took some photos, and he assured me that it was okay. We then walked further into the cemetery through a small doorway, and he explained to me that this area was where poor children were buried. As we turned to go back out that doorway, two large men were blocking our way. I was a little frightened and unsure of what to do. Then another of the men asked if I would like to give a donation to help the poor with their burials. He was sitting at a nearby table with a book, and he asked how much I would like to give. I told him I only had fifty Indian rupees to last me until I left the country. He wanted it all, but he finally settled for forty, I handed it over, and the two men blocking the doorway stepped aside. I left the cemetery feeling violated.

Then, I could not believe it when the man who had taken me there caught up with me and asked if I would give him a gift as well. I showed him my fist and said, "If you don't get away from me, I'm going to give you this."

He said, "How about the pen you have there? Will you give me that?" I continued to show him my fist, and he finally realized I was serious and walked away. All in all, it was a very frightening and unnerving experience for me, but I have been back to India more times than I can remember since, almost always in the northeast area. When I arrive there, I always say, "Lord, what am I doing here again?" But then, when I meet the friends I've developed there over the years and see the hunger and thirst in them for the things of the Lord, I invariably say, "Okay, Lord, Your will be done."

Another reason India is so difficult for me, along with a few other countries in the region, is that I don't like spicy foods, and I don't like curry. This creates a serious problem for me. They curry and spice everything. The only difference is in the degree of hotness.

On my final night in India on that first trip, there was a Baptist fellowship meeting on the rooftop patio of the guest house where I was staying, and I was asked to share something about my travels. It was a good group and a refreshing time of fellowship. That night I met two young ladies who were also traveling around the same time as me, so we went to the airport together. After helping them check in, I went to check in at my airline, only to find that the flight time had been changed. We wouldn't be leaving for another nine hours. Also my reservation had not been confirmed, so I would only be able to fly if there was an extra seat after everyone had boarded. I rebuked the enemy who was trying to block my travel to Africa.

NO PLACE LIKE INDIA

While waiting for my flight that day, I met a Hindu man who told me he was trusting Jesus to save him and that he read the Bible every day. When I opened my bag for something, he noticed that I had some anointing oil in there and asked if I would pray for him. I anointed him with oil for divine encounters, and we had a precious time of fellowship.

When I was finally able to board my flight headed to Nairobi, I had a one-way ticket and $15 in my pocket. It was time for the Lord to do a financial miracle.

In a village in NE India

An Indian street scene

Teaching in India

Chapter 15

KENYA, AFRICA

The people who sat in darkness have seen a great light,
And upon those who sat in the region and shadow of death
Light has dawned. Matthew 4:16

As I noted early on, every year the church in California would have a conference and invite leaders from all over the world to speak. It was in those conferences that God began to put a vision for the world within me, and one of the frequent speakers was a missionary working in Kenya. His name was Bud Sickler, and he and his wife, along with her twin sister and her husband, had been in West Africa for many years. The sister and her husband worked primarily in Uganda, ... that is until Idi Amin began his reign of terror there. Bud and his wife worked in Kenya and three other surrounding countries. Their main church was on the coast of Kenya in Mombasa. Over the years, they had planted more than a thousand churches under the covering of The Pentecostal Evangelical Fellowship of Africa.

Although Bud had what many would consider great success, I remember him saying to me one day that tribalism was the curse of Africa. Even though people were turning to the Lord, they often did not enjoy true fellowship with the rest of the Body of Christ if they happened to belong to another tribe.

The $15 that I arrived with quickly dwindled, and before long I found myself with just $1.50. Then I remembered that the Lord had

INHERITING THE NATIONS

told me to give an offering to a young lady who had translated for me in Japan, and I hadn't done it. "Maybe that disobedience was blocking the flow of God's provision," I thought. I confessed this to a young missionary I was staying with, and we prayed together about it. Then I made arrangements to mail some money to that young lady in Japan. A few days later, my brother contacted me and told me that he had sold my car and was putting $2,000 into my bank account. This was enough for me to buy a return ticket to America and still have the money I needed for the couple of months I would be preaching in Kenya. Praise the Lord!

Today there are many different teachings on giving and receiving. Some believe that everything we receive from the Lord is because of His grace. I believe that the Lord also calls us to obedience, and when He tells us to do something, we must obey. If we fail to obey, there are consequences, not only for us, but also for those we are called to bring the Gospel to. And those are eternal consequences!

Several years ago, our church was sending a team of young people to Uganda on a mission trip. Each member of the team would have to raise his or her own money. At the same time, I was getting ready to go to two countries in Central Asia, and my trip would require $5,000. When a friend of mine gave me $100, immediately the Lord spoke to me to give that money to one of the young men going with the Uganda team. I looked at him, with my years of experience of being a missionary, and thought to myself, "This kid is not a missionary, and he has nothing to offer. I'm keeping my $100."

I had been scheduled to leave in three weeks, and a group of intercessors who pray for me were praying for the Lord's provision. I was also praying, but the days we're getting shorter, and no money was coming in. That $100 was all I had received for my trip. It was now two weeks until travel time, and I still only had that initial $100. I decided that I had better start fasting, and I did, but still no more money came in.

KENYA, AFRICA

A little more than a week before I was scheduled to travel, I attended a home group for the first time, and across from me was sitting that young man the Lord had spoken to me to give the $100 to. Again, with all the wisdom I have gathered in the years of ministry, I looked him over, and again came to the same conclusion: he had nothing to offer. Why should I give the only funds I had for my own trip to him?

Anther thing that turned me off to that young man was the fact that he had brought a vegetarian soup to the potluck dinner that night, and I was a meat eater. Another legitimate reason not to support him. But when we are looking to the Lord to answer any kind of prayer, we must obey what He's telling us. He was telling me to give my $100 to the young man, and my not doing that constituted disobedience to the Lord. My problem wasn't the devil blocking the money or God not responding to my prayer. My problem was my disobedience. All the praying and fasting in the world cannot replace obedience.

Before I left the meeting that night, I asked two of my friends to pray for me. I said, "I think the Lord is telling me to do something, and I'm not doing it. Please pray that I'll be obedient."

The next day I went to the church office and gave the church secretary the $100, asking her to make sure it got to the intended target and that the gift remained anonymous. Two days later, somebody gave me $2000. This was a Thursday, and in order to remain on schedule, I would have to fly out the following Thursday, one week from then. Sunday morning, during church, I told my friend who had originally given me the $100 what had happened. He rejoiced and said, "Well, here's another $100." Now, I had $2,100, but I need $5,000. I was to leave in five days, and I was still $2,900 short of my goal.

I had been obedient to what the Lord told me to do, and now the rest was up to Him. When I was about to leave the church, I saw some of the young people from the Uganda team. I approached one of the young ladies and asked how she was doing with raising finances. She just answered, "I'm trusting the Lord!"

I gave her the $100 my friend had just given me and said, "Here, this will help you." She was excited and thankful.

On my way home, I felt the devil speak to me. He said, "God didn't tell you to give that money, and you only gave it because she was a pretty girl. God is not going to bless you."

I replied, "The Lord doesn't always have to tell me when to give. If I see a need, there is no problem with blessing people." And I rebuked the devil.

Not long after I got home that day, a couple pulled up in my front yard. I went out to greet them and invite them in. "We can't stay," they said, "we have other appointments. We just wanted to give you this envelope for your trip. " I took the envelope, thanked them, and they left.

When I opened the envelope, I saw what looked like a check for $300. I thought to myself, "Praise the Lord! The money is coming in." Then I put on my glasses to look at the check more closely and was amazed to see, not two zeros but three. It was a check for $3,000. Now I really praised the Lord! That Thursday I flew to Central Asia with the money I needed for the trip!

I could tell many similar experiences. I firmly believe with all my heart that when it comes to finances for the ministry, the Lord requires obedience to what He's calling us to do, and disobedience can have serious consequences, for us and for those we are called to minister to.

Matthew 21:28-31 records the story of a man who had two sons. He went to the first and said, "Son, go work today in my vineyard." At first, that son refused to go, but afterward he regretted his decision and went. Then the man went to the second son and said the same thing. This son answered that he would go, but he didn't. Jesus concluded, *"Which of the two did the will of his father?"* (verse 31). Obedience is everything.

KENYA, AFRICA

One day at a prayer meeting in a pastor's house, a brother said, "I believe the Lord is telling me that He has a very great ministry for Brother Joe in the future, big, like some of the great men of Christian history." At the time, I had been in full-time ministry for less than a year, I didn't have a lot of experience, and I hadn't developed the ability to see into the future, for myself or others. All I was doing was trying to obey the verse God gave me when He called me into the ministry.

Again that verse was Psalm 2:8:

Ask of Me, and I will give You
The nations for Your inheritance,
And the ends of the earth for Your possession.

I never questioned this promise. I was just trying to walk it out, one country at a time. I hadn't yet seen the fullness of my destiny. It soon became apparent that seeing the fulfilment of this promise would require a life of prayer on my part.

As I spent time in prayer with several missionaries privately and in prayer groups, the Lord convicted me that I needed to pray more on my own. Deep inside, I knew the Lord had more for me and that it would require me to pray more, not to earn something from Him, but just because prayer is a basic requirement for ministry.

Jesus' life was filled with prayer:

Now it came to pass in those days that He went out to the mountain to pray, and continued all night in prayer to God.   Luke 6:12

I am convinced that much of my success, if I can use that word, is due to the faithful prayers of others, people who pray for me every day, and I am very thankful for them.

INHERITING THE NATIONS

I was in Kenya that first time for three and a half weeks, and the Lord was faithful to open many doors for ministry. I spoke in churches, to home groups, and traveled to the Ugandan border to speak at a three-day outdoor crusade near Lake Victoria.

In Kenya I met a seventy-nine-year-old lady from America named Sister Princic. At sixty, she had decided to become a missionary, but no mission organization would accept her. In the end, she went to Kenya on her own by faith. She had a burning desire to minister to prostitutes. One afternoon, when I was having lunch with her, a prostitute came in the restaurant to ask her for some Gospel booklets. I remembered this because it was October 14, 1978, my spiritual birthday. Seven years before I had been living in darkness, filled with fear, confusion, and hopelessness, but the Lord had come and transformed my life for His glory! Now I was in Africa preaching the Gospel and met a prostitute who had the same glorious experience.

That morning, in the prayer meeting, I spoke, and thirty people came forward to receive the Lord. In the evening, another brother spoke on healing and then said, "Brother Joe will now pray for the sick." More than a hundred people lined up for prayer. The pastor and I anointed them with oil and prayed, and many gave testimonies to being healed. It was a great birthday gift from the Lord. I only wish that my spiritual mom, Joan, could have been there to see how the Lord was using her son.

While I was in Africa, I had the desire to go to a safari park, but my time was so filled with almost daily meetings that it proved impossible. However, when I left the meetings in the western part of the nation, to return to Nairobi, I saw many animals alongside the road. There were zebras, giraffes, antelope, and monkeys. When we reached the outskirts of Nairobi, I saw a sight I can never forget. Near the road was a massive dump for city trash, and walking among the trash looking for anything they could eat were giant buzzards. I couldn't believe how tall they were. They looked scary.

KENYA, AFRICA

I stayed in a Christian guest house for two nights before flying out to London, where I would catch a flight back to Los Angeles. The guest house was nice and only cost $7.33. The amazing thing was that this included three full meals.

On my final night in Nairobi, there was a church service at the guesthouse, and I was asked to speak. In that meeting I met a brother from Ohio. He needed a room for the night, and, since I had a double room, I offered for him to stay with me. That night we knelt together by my bed and prayed for a long time. The Lord's presence came, and it seemed as if we had touched Heaven. I still remember it to this day as one of the most powerful times I've ever had in prayer.

The next day I boarded an Ethiopian Airlines flight for London, with quick stopovers in Addis Ababa, Ethiopia and Cairo, Egypt. As the plane climbed out of the Cairo airport, I could see the pyramids in the desert and was able to take a quick photo out the window.

After landing in London, I went to a travel agent to buy a ticket to return to the U.S. In those days, there was a discount airline called the Freddie Laker Sky Train, one of the first discount airlines flying out of Europe. I was able to purchase a ticket from an airport outside of London to Los Angeles for only $168. God is so good!

When I arrived in Los Angeles, I had traveled around the entire world for the first time. There would be many more such trips in my future. I had ministered in eleven countries in more meetings than I could count or remember. The Lord had supplied the finances I needed, healed me when I got sick, and lead me in miraculous ways.

I had never wanted to be a missionary, but now I had new desires to preach the Gospel in all the nations of the world, to carry God's love to the hopeless, to bring light to people living in darkness, that He might be glorified, and that Jesus might receive the reward of His suffering!

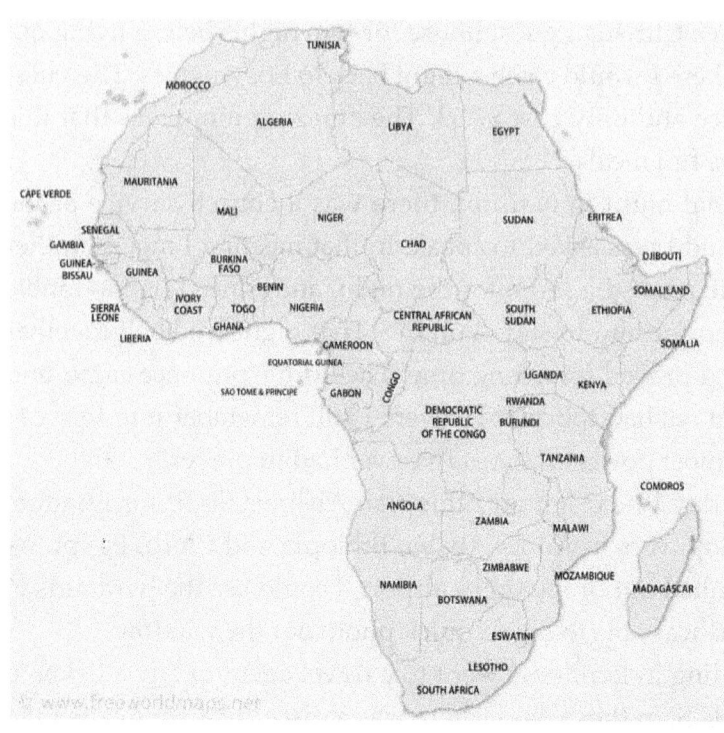

My first missionary offering in Kenya

Chapter 16

ENTERING THE STONE AGE

For the word of God is living and powerful, and sharper than any two-edged sword, piercing even to the division of soul and spirit, end of the joints and marrow, and as a discerner of the thoughts and the intents of the heart.   Hebrews 4:12

All scripture is given by inspiration of God, and is profitable for doctrine, for reproof, for correction, for instruction in righteousness, that the man of God may be complete, thoroughly equipped for every good work.
                                                              2 Timothy 3:16-17

In 1979, it was now my turn to cross the border from Hong Kong into China. I was about to see what this long-sealed country and its people were like, and more importantly, to carry in Bibles, the precious Word of God that for so long had been denied to believers under the reign of Mao.

Taking Bibles into China at the time was illegal, and if you were caught you never knew exactly what would happen. Sometimes Chinese custom authorities just took the Bibles out of your suitcase and let you go on in. At other times, they would send you back. Then there were times when they would let you take out of your suitcase what you needed and then put a seal on that suitcase, not allowing you to open it inside the country. They also put a note in your passport that alerted immigration on the way out to make sure the seal had not been broken. In this way, whatever you tried to bring in illegally was going back out with you. With time and the development of new security measures, it became more and more difficult to take Bibles and other Christian materials into China.

In the earliest days, the only way to go into China was on a tour package. Everything was taken care of—travel, hotels, food, and the activities the Communist Party wanted to show you. Transportation could be one of three ways—by airplane, by boat up the Pearl River, or by train. Because everything was taken care of by the tour company, once you checked your suitcases in Hong Kong, you wouldn't see them again until you got to your hotel. Then, they would be waiting for you in your room.

The church in Hong Kong had access to Chinese language Bibles, and more importantly, they had contacts in the underground church in China, where believers desperately needed Bibles. Because we knew our suitcases would not be checked or opened, we filled them with as many Bibles as possible and only the bare minimum of clothes we would need for the trip.

If we went by train, it didn't take long to reach the border of Communist China. There we had to exit the train and go through Chinese Immigration. Our passports were checked for the proper visas. Then we got back on the train, which was now parked on the Chinese side of the border, and continued our journey.

Once we were over the border, most of the landscapes we saw were green fields where all kinds of produce were grown. Canton, our first stop, was a very simple city in those days. The highest buildings were only three or four stories. Much of the population lived in apartment-style housing, and the hotels were very plain and simple. The only canned drinks available were water, beer, and an orange soda called Pearl River Orange.

ENTERING THE STONE AGE

Every hotel floor had a small counter manned by young Chinese ladies responsible for taking care of whatever needs the tourists on that flood had. The only problem was that these ladies didn't speak any English. One day I went to the desk on my floor. I told the ladies I was an American, but they didn't understand. Then I said, "California," but they didn't understand. Next I said, "Disneyland," but they still didn't understand. I finally drew a picture of a mouse.

Suddenly, one young lady's face lit up, and she said in English, "Mouse?"

I said, "Yes."

Then she asked, "In the room?" With that, I gave up trying to tell them where I was from. This was the last generation born under Mao, and they knew nothing of the outside world.

On that first trip, I was sharing a room with another brother, who was also carrying a suitcase full of Bibles. When we entered the room assigned to us, there sat the two suitcases at the bottom of our beds. They had never been opened.

I remember, as if it were today, opening the curtains of that hotel room and peering out with great curiosity. Before me was another world. It seemed that I had gone back in time and was visiting the Stone Age.

For one thing, the city and its people were void of color. Everyone was dressed similarly, either in dark blue or black. Very rarely we saw a lady dressed in beige. The houses, likewise were unadorned.

There were very few automobiles in the streets. Hordes of people, some on bicycles, filled those streets and slowed movement. Coming from America, it was hard to believe that a place like that still existed in 1979.

Because we were on an organized tour, our time was very controlled. Our Communist-appointed guides took us to restaurants to eat, occasionally to acrobatic performances, a Chinese opera, or sometimes to a museum.

INHERITING THE NATIONS

After dark, when we had returned to our hotel rooms, young people from the church in Hong Kong would meet us, take charge of the Bibles, and deliver them to the local believers. In those early days, we never made personal contact with the Chinese believers ourselves. It was too dangerous for their sake. If they even spoke with a foreigner, they could be arrested and harshly questioned by Chinese police.

That year, one church was allowed to open in the city, but it was more of a symbolic thing, to show the world that Communist China had freedom of religion (which, of course, was not true). The real Church in China, a dynamic, prayerful group of people, was underground, meeting in secret, unable to obtain Bibles unless foreigners like me brought them in.

Because the Bibles we brought in had already been delivered, the next day the teenage girl who had been the go-between for the Bibles told us it would be safe for us to visit that official church, so we sent. It was in a very old building, which had probably housed a church before Mao's days, and it was filled mostly with old people. Not a single Bible could be seen.

When the service ended, the streets were packed with people leaving. We noticed two young ladies outside and decided to talk to them. Our friend from Hong Kong was able to translate. As we talked with these Chinese ladies, they told us they had never heard the name of Jesus before, and they didn't know what a church was. But, when they heard that one had opened, they came to see what it was all about. We had a few Chinese New Testaments in our pockets, so we gave them each one, and we prayed with them. Our Hong Kong friend gave them her address, in case they had any further questions. About a month later, one of those girls (Ping was her Chinese name) wrote our friend to say that she had become a believer and was now connected with an underground church near her home.

ENTERING THE STONE AGE

In the future, I would make many more trips into China to deliver Bibles. I believe that I probably personally delivered about three thousand Bibles, plus other Christian materials. Ping, who was growing in the Lord and very active with the underground church, always helped us during these trips. When things became a little freer, she would even arrange for us to have dinner with some of the local believers at a restaurant. It was a very special time.

The other girl we met that first day was Ping's cousin. Eventually, they both moved to America. I remember meeting them in New York City, where the cousin had moved with her family. We visited the Empire State Building together.

Ping moved to California, where she opened a travel agency. She is still a very close friend to this day. The underground church that she was discipled in is filled with people of prayer, many rising before dawn and praying for two or three hours before they go to work. They are a people formed in the fires of persecution and committed to Jesus, ready to die for their faith. One day Ping told me that she had not been able to find Chinese believers like that in California, and my heart went out to her.

Over the years, I've been to China more times than I can remember. I want to mention a wonderful story about Manchuria. On one trip to China, I and another brother had filled our luggage with as many Bibles as we could safely carry on our short train ride from Hong Kong to Guangzhou (formerly known as Canton). Later that first evening, we met some Chinese believers who came to receive the Bibles we had safely gotten across the border.

The next day I received a call from one of the leaders of the underground church who had heard that I was in town. He was hoping he could get some Bibles from me. He told me that a brother from a church in Manchuria had traveled for many days to Guangzhou, having heard that Bibles were available there. He had been at the pastor's house for almost two weeks, but they had only found two Bibles for him to take back to his people. Sadly, I had to inform him that all of our Bibles had already been delivered.

Then I remembered that other believers were coming to Guangzhou that night by plane. I told him I would see if it would be possible to get Bibles from them and arranged for him to call me later that night. When he called, I was happy to inform him that I had some Bibles, and we made plans to meet at the local train station, a safe place because many people would be gathered waiting for their trains.

The pastor arrived on his bicycle and quickly began to tie the bag of Bibles I handed him onto the front carrier of the bike. As he did so, he shared with me the promise of Isaiah 65:24:

It shall come to pass
That before they call, I will answer;
And while they are still speaking, I will hear.

The Lord knew that the man would be coming down from Manchuria looking for Bibles, and He knew we would be coming in from Hong Kong bringing the needed Bibles.

After securing the Bibles, the pastor started to hug us and say goodbye, but I remembered there were more. I said, "Wait! This bag my friend is sitting on is also filled with Bibles for you!" My friend began to weep and quoted Ephesians 3:20:

Now to Him who is able to do exceedingly abundantly above all that
we ask or think, according to the power that works in us.

With tears in his eyes, the pastor tied the second bag onto the back of his bike and rode off into the night. My friend and I stood there weeping, realizing that we just had been part of a great miracle.

ENTERING THE STONE AGE

The next day those two bags of Bibles would begin their journey to Manchuria in Northeast China for the believers who were so hungry and thirsty for the Word of God.

As noted earlier, Mao had done everything he could to divide families and had sent them to difficult places to live, but God was actually moving an army of people into position, people empowered with His Word. Many of them had memorized the Scriptures prior to their Bibles being taken from them. The paper Bibles had been taken, but the living Bibles were inside of them, and everywhere they went they took the Word of God, and revival followed, as they shared and lived out the Word of God.

After opening to the West, China began to change very quickly, and many Chinese cities are more modern than American cities today. One day I spoke with an American businessman in the airport. He was just returning home from visiting one of the factories his company had built in China. He told me that every major American corporation has factories in China, and they are using the most advanced technologies. Another businessman told me that his company had a factory that only made paperclips. It was a big factory and had dorms attached to it where workers lived. This is apparently now very common in China. He told me that one day the Chinese government officials had come and notified them that they were taking over the factory and that all foreigners must leave. I asked him what they did, and he said, "We just went down the road and built another factory."

During all the trips I made into China with Bibles I never got caught ... that is until one particular trip. This time, there were several of us together. Immigration procedures had changed, and now you had to present your luggage for inspection at the border. Usually, they would just let you go through, seeing you were a foreigner. They seemed to be more concerned with the Chinese bringing forbidden items back home.

INHERITING THE NATIONS

On this particular day, our bags were full of Bibles and very heavy. I was at the back of the group. One couple from the Philippines had already been cleared through without a problem, but then I saw that the wife was struggling with a big heavy suitcase. One of the guards noticed it too, called her back and opened the bag. It was full of Bibles, and so now they checked the rest of us more thoroughly, and they found our Bibles. What would happen to us?

They ordered us to take out the clothes we needed, and then they put a round metal seal on the zipper handles of the bags so that they could not be opened without breaking the seals. We arrived safely at our hotel with bags full of Bibles, but they were sealed.

Most soft bags, ours included, have a zipper pocket on the outside which allows you to put last-minute items or magazines into it without unlocking the whole suitcase. We unzipped that pocket and cut the suitcase inside the pocket so we could take out all the Bibles. Now, however, we had another problem. The suitcase was way too light. This would create a problem with Immigration when we exited the country. One of my friends came up with an idea. We went out to the garden, which had a brick wall around it, and we broke off some of the bricks and put them in our suitcase so it would weigh what it had with the Bibles in it. When we arrived at Immigration, they saw that the seal was unbroken, and they lifted the suitcase and saw that it was heavy, so we were allowed to clear Immigration with no problems. Praise the Lord! Many times, when we remembered this story, we laughed and said that we had a ministry of smuggling Bibles into China and smuggling bricks out.

Ministering in countries that have restrictions on Christianity can be very challenging and requires the Lord to do miraculous things, to open doors that are closed in the natural. One thing is certain: There are still countries today where people don't have access to the Bible, and the Lord wants to put Bibles in their hands. Therefore, He is always

ENTERING THE STONE AGE

looking for someone who will make the sacrifice and trust Him for creative ways to deliver Bibles to those who still live under persecution. I've been in many countries where, if the Lord had not delivered me, I could have ended up in jail or worse. The local Christians I was with could also have been put in prison.

One of my close friends was involved in a plan called Project Pearl. The plan was to buy a barge, assemble a million Bibles in the Chinese language, wrap them in waterproof packaging, then have twenty missionaries take them on the barge up the Pearl River to Southeast China. There local believers would be waiting on the beach for this precious cargo to be delivered. It happened on June 18, 1981, and a book entitled *Project Pearl: The One Million Smuggled Bibles that Changed China*[1] is available that tells the complete story. It is well worth the read.

Most Christians in America, me included, have many Bibles, in many different versions. Now, with the Internet, you can access dozens of versions of the Bible right from your phone, computer, or tablet. It seems unbelievable, but there are still Christians in some countries who cannot and do not own a Bible.

Several years later a group of us were on the China-Tibet border to teach leaders in a secret location. We had planned to spend a couple days with them, sharing the Word, praying, and fellowshipping. Among them was a young man who had been a Tibetan monk. He had been a believer in Christ only nine months when we met him, but he was already leading an underground house church that had sixty-five members. The most amazing thing was that he also did not own a Bible himself. None was available in his tribal language. He'd had an encounter with Jesus that delivered him from Tibetan Buddhism and gave him the power and the anointing to lead others to Jesus, even without a Bible.

Looking back on my own life, I never read a Bible in my youth, but as I noted in earlier chapters, my spiritual mom, Joan, told me the Lord

---
1. By Brother David with Paul Hattaway, Arroyo Grande, California (Monarch Books: 2007)

wanted to come into your life. I told her I didn't feel worthy, and she said, "You're *not* worthy, but He still wants to come into your life." And praise the Lord, He did!

Why does God choose people like me? Why does God call a girl out of Buddhism and prepare her for a destiny that she could never imagine? How could God use a man who was a Tibetan monk to bring salvation to sixty-five people when he didn't even own a Bible of his own? These are the mysteries of the Gospel.

> *For you see your calling, brethren, that not many wise according to the flesh, not many mighty, not many noble, are called. But God has chosen the foolish things of the world to put to shame the wise, and God has chosen the weak things of the world to put to shame the things which are mighty; and the base things of the world and the things which are despised God has chosen, and the things which are not, to bring to nothing the things that are, that no flesh should glory in His presence.*
> 1 Corinthians 1:26-29

With Kathy and her cousin

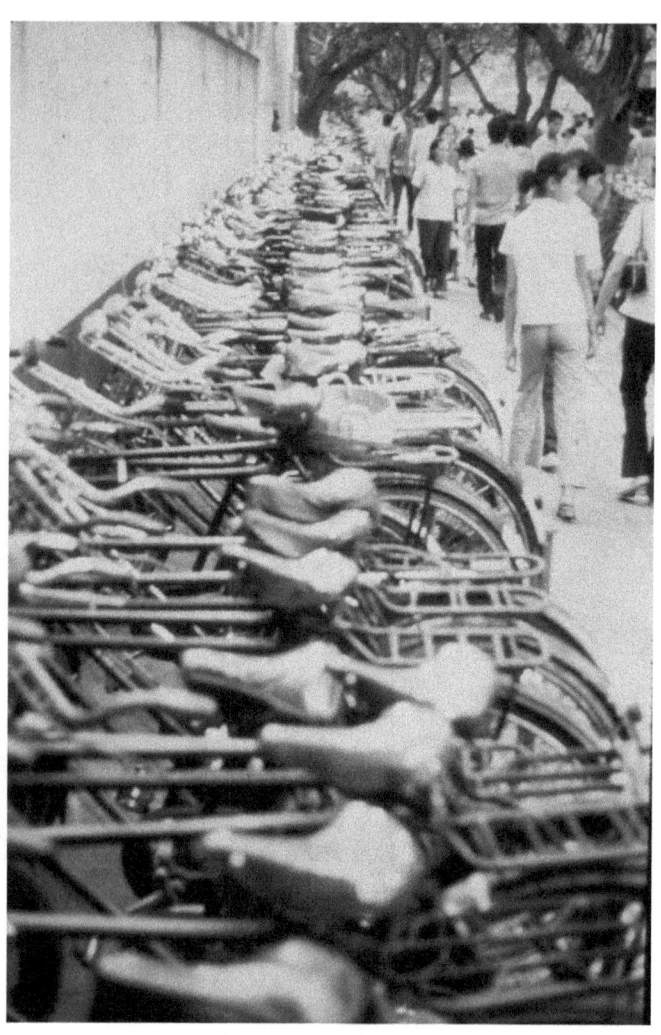

China was another world

Chapter 17

THE POWER OF FRIENDSHIP

He who walks with wise men will be wise,
But the companion of fools will be destroyed.   Proverbs 13:20

A friend loves at all times,
And a brother is born for adversity.   Proverbs 17:17

As iron sharpens iron,
So a man sharpens the countenance of his friend.   Proverbs 27:17

I believe with all my heart that each one of us is unique, each one of us is hand-made by the Master Himself to fulfill a destiny that only he or she can fulfill. There are people you and I are called to love, embrace, and touch with the healing power of Jesus. It might be in our neighborhood, our city, or our nation. But I also know that in pursuing our destiny, there's a cost. There are sacrifices to be made. Unfortunately, some people are not willing to make the sacrifices necessary to fulfill their destiny, and through them, affect the destiny of others.

In my journey with the Lord for more than fifty years now (more than forty of those years in ministry) I've had some wonderful times, but I've also had challenging times and lonely times. The Lord knows all things. He is El Roi, the God who sees me. He sees what we need and fulfills that need, many times through other people.

INHERITING THE NATIONS

David had a great army, but the Scriptures say he had three men who were known as *"mighty men."* These excelled above the rest of his warriors (see 2 Samuel 23:8-12). In my journey with the Lord, there have been at least three people the Lord has used to open wonderful doors to me to proclaim God's Word, to sharpen me, and help me to manifest God's glory. They are Pastor Paulo Brito of Rio de Janeiro, Brazil, Brother Sonny in Bangkok, Thailand, and Andrey in Rostov, Russia. I will not use the family name of these two to protect their work inside dangerous nations, but I do want to give them special mention.

PASTOR PAULO BRITO

I the early 1980s, I was invited to go to Rio to teach in a Charismatic Methodist Church. A missionary friend of mine named Robert Curry had lived in southern Brazil for many years and had traveled to many cities of Brazil preaching the Gospel. He had told this Methodist Church about me, and I was invited there to preach.

I got a room in an Anglican church that had a window that looked right out toward the Corcovado, the giant statue of Jesus on the mountain of Rio. The Methodist Church itself had something more than a hundred members, and they were burning with the fire of the Holy Spirit. The Promise of the Father had come to these hungry people, and each meeting with them was an experience of His presence.

My friend Robert also encouraged me to visit a Pentecostal group that had special meetings on Wednesday night in the center of the city in a newspaper building auditorium. One Wednesday night, my interpreter from the Methodist Church and I went to visit this group called The Maranatha Evangelical Missionary Association (*Maranata* in Portuguese). The auditorium was overflowing with people, and they were standing all around the walls.

As we entered the building, some deacons asked who I was. My translator handed them my card and told them I was just visiting and

THE POWER OF FRIENDSHIP

didn't want to say anything. We were escorted up to the first row, where people moved to make room for us to sit, and my card was given to Pastor Paulo, who was on the stage.

Pastor Paulo read the card and then asked, "Who is this Joseph Zeyak?" I raised my hand.

"What is this note?" he then asked. "You're just visiting, and you don't want to say anything? Get up here. You're preaching tonight!"

No one knew me in that room except my translator, but God knew my heart. That was the beginning of a lifelong friendship with Pastor Paulo. We felt a special bond from the very first day. We had similar personalities. We both loved to minister, but we also loved practical jokes. We seemed to be a perfect fit for each other.

Maranata Church had been started by Paulo's parents, Dr. Acyoli and Zenilda Brito. Dr. Acyoli was an elder in the very beautiful Presbyterian Cathedral in the center of Rio. He was also a doctor and a man of wealth and prestige. One day he and his wife went to another city to visit his brother, whom we hadn't seen in quite some time. When the brother opened the door, he started yelling uncontrollably and ran off down the street. Somehow he had become demon possessed. This was so unsettling for Dr. Acyoli that when he and his wife returned to Rio, he decided he would never go back to church. He felt that if there was a God, He wouldn't have allowed this terrible thing to happen to his brother.

Zenilda tried to reason with her husband. "Acyoli, you're an elder in the Presbyterian Church, but we don't pray much, and we don't read the Bible much, so we can't really blame God." This caused the doctor to decide, "If there is a God, then I must find Him!" That was a formula for success. The Bible declares:

> *And you will seek Me and find Me, when you search for Me with all your heart.*   Jeremiah 29:13

INHERITING THE NATIONS

The Lord heard the cry of Dr. Acyoli's heart and baptized him in the Holy Spirit. Now, with this new fire burning in his heart, he and his wife started a home Bible study. This quickly exploded when people heard that a doctor was preaching the Bible and praying for the sick. Maranata Church was born there in the living room of their home.

Paulo, their son, was a doctor too, but he was also a composer, singer, and pianist. He had no real desire to preach the Gospel. Some years later, however, Dr. Acyoli suffered a stroke and was no longer able to preach. Paulo and his wife, Claudete, now came alongside Paulo's mother to care for the spiritual needs of Maranata.

When I started going there, even though Dr. Acyoli could not speak enough to preach, he was still praying for the sick. I knelt next to him, placed his hand on sick people for healing, the Lord would touch them through him, and they were healed. I eventually moved into an apartment connected to Paulo's medical practice and began to spend more time with him and Claudete.

The church was growing, and Pastor Paulo had a desire to build a retreat center. He had heard about some property available outside of Rio, so we went there together one day to look at it. On a narrow dirt road was a rough-looking stone wall. We climbed up on it and looked over. Before us was a small house in a large field of tall green grass. Together we dreamed a dream that day. Today there is a massive complex on that site with air-conditioned rooms, a wedding chapel, two large auditoriums for meetings, a soccer field, a beautiful lake filled with fish, and a large kitchen. Churches from all around the area rent the center to have their church camps. Our dream became a reality.

Pastor Paulo and I loved practical jokes. For instance, I used to say to him, "I love you, Paulo. Not a lot, but I love you!"

In response, he would get very close to my face and say, "Joe, I love you very much." Then he would laugh because he knew he had disarmed me. Somehow, in those joyful moments, the Lord was beginning to teach me what real love was all about. What a great brother he was and is!

BROTHER SONNY

I described in an earlier chapter how, on my first trip out of the country, I went to Quito, Ecuador, and eventually travelled into the Amazon jungle with Juan and Sunamita Coello, to encounter the Auca Indians. Because Sunamita is a Filipina, they decided to visit the Philippines, and while they were there, they invited me to come to visit them and minister.

I was staying with an American missionary couple in Metro Manila, when a young Filipino brother named Sonny stopped by to say hello to them. He was on his way to the airport, for he was working as a missionary with his base in Bangkok, Thailand. I told him I had a friend from seminary who was a third generation missionary in Thailand and that I planned to visit him at some point. He gave me his card and invited us to visit his office. It was a very short encounter, probably less than thirty minutes, but it was the beginning of a relationship that would take us together to thirteen countries in Southeast Asia, sharing the Gospel and training Christian leaders.

Sonny was born on a small island in the Philippines. I can imagine the Lord looking down from His throne that day, seeing that baby boy and dreaming what he would be like if He filled him with fire, vision, and humility, if He gave him a servant's heart, willing to prefer others above himself, if He gave him the ability to see destiny in others before they could see it in themselves, if He gave him a heart willing to sacrifice everything for one person. He could then entrust him with the hearts of leaders in many of nations of the world. And that's exactly what happened. The Lord decided to use Sonny in a very special way for His glory, and I was often blessed to tag along.

INHERITING THE NATIONS

We were in Hong Kong together on July 1, 1997, the evening when the ninety-nine-year lease the British had held on that colony was coming to an end. China would take political control of the territory the very next day. Television cameras showed Communist Chinese troops in trucks sitting at the border, and many in Hong Kong feared that the night would end with people being killed for their Christian faith. Christians were praying.

Our plan was to visit a Christian family outside of the city I had worked with for many years smuggling Bibles into China. Then we would attend an all-night prayer meeting at the church that had supplied us with Bibles through the years. On the day after the Communist China takeover, we had planned to take a train and go into China to see what was going on there as a result of the takeover. (I share the details of this important evening in China and Hong Kong history in Chapter 36 "Seasons of Change."

In 2018, Sonny and I, along with some believers from Australia and New Zealand, went to Vietnam to train leaders. It had to be done in a secret location because it was illegal. We had two rooms where the leaders were gathered, and we would go back and forth between the rooms teaching for three days.

Prior to going to Vietnam, the Lord had told me, "You're going to have a foot washing." The day passed, however, and there didn't seem to be a correct time to do it. Before I knew it, it was Friday night, and the meetings for the day were over. In the morning, we would gather all the leaders together for a devotional word by a brother from New Zealand, and then we had to leave. I said to the Lord, "I thought You told me there was going to be a foot washing, but the opportunity has not opened."

That next morning, our friend had finished the devotional word and was praying a final prayer when the Lord spoke to me and said, "Now is the time!"

THE POWER OF FRIENDSHIP

As my friend was praying, I whispered in his ear, "I want to say something when you finish praying."

He finished and then said, "Brother Joe wants to say something before we close."

We were in Vietnam, and in that room were men and women from both North Vietnam and South Vietnam, During the war, they had been enemies and had tried to kill each other. A brother from the South said he had loaded bombs onto the American B-52 bombers. A brother from the North had lost a leg in the war and had to use an artificial leg. Former enemies had become brothers and sisters because the blood of Jesus had been poured out for them. They were now leaders of underground churches in Vietnam, and under their leadership were many thousands of members.

I shared how each of them had different giftings and callings, but that I wanted to talk to them for just a few minutes about their greatest calling—to be a servant. I shared with them how Jesus, the King of Kings and Lord of Lords, had knelt down and washed the feet of His disciples:

After that, He poured water into a basin and began to wash the disciple's feet, and to wipe them with a towel with which He was girded.
                                                                John 13:5

I said, "I don't have what I really want. All I have is this little washcloth and a cup of water, but I want to pass it around, and I want you to wash one another's feet." My friends quickly got more glasses and more little towels, and we began to wash each other's feet. What I can say is that there are no words to fully express what happened in that room that day. The presence of the Lord was so thick you could feel it, and men and women alike began to weep from deep down in their souls, as they washed one another's feet. It was a holy moment, a time that none of us would ever forget.

INHERITING THE NATIONS

Just a few years ago, one of the leaders who was in that meeting said to me, "We had never washed each other's feet until you showed us how to do it in that meeting. Since then, occasionally, in the secret home churches in Vietnam, we wash each other's feet." Disobedience is not an option. We must obey the Master, not just for our sake, but also for others. My obedience that day is still affecting churches in Vietnam today.

Every February Brother Sonny conducts a three-day missions conference in Bangkok to which he brings workers from all the different countries we are involved with, and they share what has been going on in their countries. They are so thankful for the Christians who are praying for them and supporting the ministry from all over the world.

The three days are filled with teachings, testimonies, and fellowship and are always amazing. It has been my honor to be one of the speakers at several of the conferences. In 2013, Pastor Paulo and his son, Paulo Jr., came to the conference, and it was a great joy for me to finally have these two men of God meet. This was an answer to a prayer of my heart.

After the conference, the four of us traveled to southern Thailand to visit a ministry which had a home group totally made up of Brazilians. They were so excited to meet with Pastor Paulo and have him share and pray for them. It was a very special time.

The following day we visited an orphanage that was part of a church pastored by Fred and Dianne Doell. They had been friends with Sonny and me for many years, and I had preached in their church several times. While we were visiting the orphanage, we were out in the backyard talking, and Pastor Paulo knelt in front of Diane and asked her to pray for him. When she laid her hands on him, he began to weep uncontrollably as he shared about the heaviness of ministry that he felt upon his life. It was a precious time as he opened his soul.

THE POWER OF FRIENDSHIP

Hopefully my two great friends, Brother Sonny and Pastor Paulo, will be together again, but this time it will be in Rio, where Brother Sonny can share the visions of his heart with Pastor Paulo's members at Maranata Church.

BROTHER ANDREY

Andrey is a Russian. He had been the director of the Youth With A Mission (also known as YWAM) base in Yerevan, Armenia for many years when I met him. He had traveled around the United States, sharing his vision with a missionary friend of mine and had come to my house on two separate occasions to share with my friends who had a heart for missions. On his third visit, he invited me to go to Armenia to speak with the YWAM Frontier Missions Class about spiritual warfare.

Youth With A Mission is an organization that is working in more than a hundred countries and has several hundred bases around the world where they train mostly young people to get involved in missions. Their entry program, known as Discipleship Training School, or DTS, is a course which involves three months of teaching, followed by two months of outreach to various nations around the world. They assist existing churches of many denominations and have many creative programs for street evangelism. Some bases are also involved in social work, particularly in the poorer areas.

Being with Andrey is like being with a history book. His knowledge of world history is amazing. He has even taught me things about America that I never knew before. Whenever I'm with him, he always makes time to take me around Armenia to visit the many monasteries that are an important part of the Armenian Christian history. One monastery was built exclusively for prayer, twenty-four hours a day, seven days a week.

INHERITING THE NATIONS

Andrey is also an amazing photographer. Several times he and I came upon old abandoned Russian factories in Armenia that were closed after the fall of the USSR. Investigating them and taking photos was always exciting. On some occasions, security guards either stopped us from entering or made us leave.

Brother Andrey introduced me to many Christian leaders over the years that have opened their churches and fellowships to me and have become wonderful friends. I can honestly say that, for me, my travels there have been more about the relationships I've developed than about ministering in their churches.

There are many things I could say about my relationship with Andrey, but one thing about him that sticks out in my mind happened just after the graduation of the first class I taught. The base facility was small at that time. It had just a few rooms, one, an office, another, a bedroom for two young ladies who lived at the base, a teaching room, and a kitchen. The graduation was attended by many pastors, family, and friends of the students, and was a time of celebration and wonderful Armenian food.

After everyone had left, I was talking with the two ladies who lived there. Then I walked down the hall and passed by the kitchen. As I looked in, I saw a long counter piled high with all the dishes, glasses, and silverware from the party. It was going to be a massive job to wash and dry all of that, and in that room working away was just one person doing it all—Andrey. That night I saw the living definition of a servant!

Andrey could have asked any one of the students to help with the dishes, and they would have gladly helped. He probably thought it was their night to celebrate, and so he didn't ask any of them to help. He also didn't ask *me* for help, but I stepped in, took a towel, and began to dry the dishes as he washed them. We enjoyed our time of fellowship together.

THE POWER OF FRIENDSHIP

I don't know how many years Andrey was in Armenia as head of the YWAM base, but while he was there, he met and married an Iranian girl named Marline. Marline had come from Iran with an older brother to plant a church called The People of God in Armenia. She was and is an amazing singer and worship leader and teaches courses on worship in DTS and at local churches.

In time, Andrey and his family left Armenia and returned to Russia, where he became the base leader of YWAM in the city if Rostov. Eventually he turned that base over to Brother Nick, and Andrey is now serving as the Eastern European Director for YWAM.

Paulo, Sonny, and Andrey—these three men—have been used by the Lord to guide me into my destiny among the nations. Pastor Paulo opened his heart and churches (now thirteen churches with eight thousand members) to me when I was single. I used to stay in Brazil six months at a time, traveling to many cities and churches. After I remarried, my wife and I used to go once a year to minister in Maranata. Sonny has allowed me to travel and minister with him in thirteen countries of South East Asia multiple times and teach in his Bible schools in Thailand and Myanmar since 1978. Prior to covid, I was in Asia four or five times a year. Andrey opened Armenia and Russia for me and helped me develop a vision for Central Asia, principally in Kyrgyzstan and Uzbekistan. There is a saying: If you want to go fast, go alone; if you want to go far, go with others.

PASTORS BERNIE AND LINDA MORRIS

When I talk about the power of friendship, I need to mention a family that has been very special in my life. Truth is there have been many, and I don't want to minimize any of them. The Lord has blessed me with more friends that I really can mention in this book, but I feel like I must mention this family.

Sometime in the early 1980s I was working with Pastor Paulo in Rio, and two couples came from California and shared at Maranata Church one Sunday morning. One of the couples was Pastor Bernie and Linda Morris. During the week I took the four of them around Rio to tourist sites and to do some shopping, which resulted in a friendship that is continuing more than forty years later.

After their visit to Brazil, I spoke in their church in California and Pastor Bernie traveled with me to four countries in Asia, one of them to smuggle Bibles into China. I don't remember exactly how it happened, but in the 1990s, when I stopped international ministry for a while and had a construction business, I lost track of them. Then, by the grace of God and the power of Facebook, I reconnected with him several years ago. They invited me to come and speak at their church and to come a few days early just for fellowship and to catch up on the years we had not seen each other.

They have four daughters, all Christians and married to Christians, and several Christian grandchildren. The four girls came over to see me as if I was a long-lost friend. We sat in the family room while one daughter, Amy, who writes Christian songs, played the large grand piano and all of the girls sang. It was like a personal concert just for me, and words cannot describe how special that made me feel. I know that there is probably not a perfect family in the world, but I'm sure the Morris family is the closest to perfection there is. I can't imagine Heaven being any different than being with this family.

One of the daughters, Tonya, always comes up to me and tells me what a blessing I am and how wonderful I am. She says so many positive things that I get embarrassed, but that's just who she is. She's a real blessing. All the girls and their husbands have been a blessing to me every time I've been there.

THE POWER OF FRIENDSHIP

Pastor Linda and her daughter, Amy, traveled one time to Thailand and then on to Sir Lanka for a women's conference organized by Sonny's wife Dahlia. Amy led worship, and they both shared in the teachings. I was told that they were a great blessing to everyone there.

Every year in March, their church, Lighthouse Christian Fellowship, celebrates missions. Every Sunday they bring in a different missionary they support. For the last several years they have invited me to be one of the speakers and have been financially generous with me, which has allowed me to continue my ministry work. Whenever I go there, I stay in their home. I am grateful for them, for the members of their church, for their prayers and their financial support and for being able to share my vision with them. They are so receptive and have even invited some of my overseas friends to minister there too. For me, even if I had never spoken at the church or received an offering from them, just to sit and talk with Pastors Bernie and Linda in their home by their fireplace on a cool morning just does something to my soul. I so love them, and I know they love me. There's really nobody like the entire Morris family in the world. They are a gift from the Father, from His heart to mine.

This year Pastor Bernie and Linda passed the senior pastorship over to their son-in-law, Pastor Stoney, and his wife, Amy, their youngest daughter.

With Sonny and Pastor Paulo

Brother Andrey and Marlin

Pastors Bernard and Linda Morris and their daughters

Pastor Stony and Amy

Chapter 18

LOVE AND SACRIFICE

But he who prophesies speaks edification and exhortation and comfort to men.   1 Corinthians 14:3

And the spirits of the prophets are subject to the prophets. For God is not the author of confusion, but of peace, as in all churches of the saints.   1 Corinthians 14:32-33

In the early 1980s, some drastic changes were coming to my life and ministry. I had been around the world once, and was now back in Rio, working with Pastor Paulo at Maranata Church. We had become close friends and were laboring together for the Gospel in Brazil. The Lord was blessing me, I had great favor with the people, and they were hungry for the things of the Spirit. It was a great season of my life.

It had now been ten years since my wife had left, and I had lost all contact with her and my children. I had tried my best to find them, but it had not happened. I was doing my best to try to follow the leading of the Holy Spirit and really enjoyed working with Pastor Paulo. He knew about my past and encouraged me to move forward with my personal life. One day he introduced me to his personal secretary. Her name was Elizabeth, and she was a pretty girl, she loved the Lord, and seemed to have a servant's heart. But I wasn't interested in girls at the moment. I had one focus: I was preaching the Gospel, and I had no time for anything else.

INHERITING THE NATIONS

Pastor Paulo invited me to be one of the speakers at a youth camp. It was a very powerful time. Many Brazilian young people were seeking the baptism of the Holy Spirit. One evening, after I had preached and given an altar call, the altar was full of young people crying out to the Lord. Then a demonic scream came from one of the young men, and it disturbed the prayer at the altar. He was quickly taken out, so someone could pray for him in another location. We continued to pray, and the Holy Spirit was moving. Many were being baptized with the Spirit and speaking in tongues for the first time. We prayed for almost an hour, and it was very powerful.

When the altar prayer ended, someone came to me and said, "Pastor Joe, can you come and help us pray for the demon possessed boy. We can't seem to get him delivered."

I thought to myself, "No problem. I am the man. Didn't he see how powerfully the Lord was moving at the altar. Delivering this boy would be no problem for me. I am the man of power!"

Three men had been praying for the boy, but they were still having a struggle to constrain him physically, and a large crowd had gathered around to watch and pray. I walked up to the boy and spoke in English, commanding the demon to come out in the name of Jesus. Everyone was watching Pastor Joe, the man of power, but nothing happened.

Then I thought to myself, "We are in Brazil. The demon probably doesn't understand English. So, in the limited Portuguese I knew at the time, I commanded the demon to come out in the name of Jesus. Everyone was watching, but nothing happened.

Then I thought to myself, "Okay, I'll speak in tongues." As everyone watched, I stood before the boy speaking in tongues. Still, nothing happened.

Just then, some of the crowd parted, and through the opening came Elizabeth, the church secretary. She walked up to the boy, raised her hands in the air, and a wave of power fell upon those close to her. I felt it too. In fact, it almost knocked me over. She said, "I worship You,

LOVE AND SACRIFICE

Lord," and then she prayed about a five-second prayer, the boy was totally set free, and she turned and walked back out through the crowd.

I couldn't believe what had just happened. Where did she get that kind of power? I learned an important lesson that day. During the altar call the Lord had been moving and using me and others to pray with power and signs following, but between that altar call and the moment I stood before that demon possessed boy a deadly thing called "pride" had intervened. I had thought because God was using me so powerfully that I was the man, but I couldn't deliver the young man from this demon. Why? Because pride had taken over, and God resists the proud. It is always important to remember that it's all about Him, not about us. We must remain humble when He uses us and give Him all the glory.

God resists the proud
But gives grace to the humble.   James 4:6

When the meetings at the camp had finally ended, and we returned to the city, I was still thinking about the power I had seen manifested through Elizabeth. I decided that I must talk with her and discover why she had such power. What was her secret?

I told Pastor Paulo of my desire to meet Elizabeth to find out what her secret was, and he was overjoyed, thinking that I would finally be personally interested in her. I assured him that I just wanted to know how she had so much power and that I was not interested in finding a girlfriend. He just kept smiling and saying, "No problem, Joe. I will arrange a meeting with her." And he did. He arranged for himself, his wife, and me to go to dinner at Elizabeth's home. The plan was for me to meet her at her work downtown and ride home with her. Pastor Paulo and Claudete would arrive a little later.

I arrived at Elizabeth's office a short time before closing, and we took the elevator down to an area where buses waited to take workers to the various zones of the city. She lived in Ipanema, and her bus was across the street. As we started to cross the street, Elizabeth reached out and took my hand. At that very second, my heart was captured by her touch, and I felt surely this was the girl I was to marry.

Until that moment, I'd had no desire to ever remarry or to even date. I was dedicated to the Lord and the ministry, and there was no time for a relationship that would lead to marriage. Elizabeth changed all that with just one simple touch.

Elizabeth lived with her mother, three sisters, and a brother in a small apartment one block from the famous Ipanema Beach. Pastor Paulo and Claudete arrived, and we had dinner, a time of fellowship, and prayer. Elizabeth and her loved ones seemed like a wonderful family. Over the next few months, she and I spent more time together. I learned she only had one secret to her power; it was her prayer life. Because she loved the Lord, she was dedicated to prayer.

As we spent more time together, we eventually talked of marriage and traveling the world together. One of her sisters was getting married in a ceremony that would take place in Pastor Paulo's church. Another of my friends, Pastor Silvio, from another city, was part of the ceremony. He got up to say a few words prior to the appearance of the bride and her bridesmaids, Elizabeth among them. He announced before the whole congregation what an honor it was to be part of the wedding of "Pastor Joe's sister-in-law."

Pastor Paulo quickly corrected this. "No," he said, "Joe and Elizabeth are not married."

"I know," Pastor Silvio replied," but I'm talking by faith."

After the wedding, everybody was congratulating Elizabeth on her marriage to Pastor Joe, even though it wasn't true.

Even though it had been ten years since my wife left, neither of us had filed divorce papers. Now I wanted to remarry. I returned to New York, hired a lawyer, and obtained a divorce document, so I would be legally free. When I returned to Brazil, Pastor Paulo invited me to become a pastor on the staff of Maranata. I would have my own apartment, a car, a salary, would be working with a church that was seeing many people saved in every service, and I would be marrying a lovely Brazilian girl. It appeared that this was going to be the most wonderful season of my life and ministry.

I drove Elizabeth home one night and then went to walk alone on the beach to pray. As I was praying, the spirit realm opened, and I saw multitudes of people from different cultures calling me and motioning with their hands for me to come to them. I instantly knew I could not stay indefinitely in Brazil. Although I loved Brazil and its people, my call was to the nations.

Family ties in Brazil are very strong, and when I told Elizabeth what the Lord had shown me, she struggled with the thought of leaving Brazil. At the same time, two of her sisters discovered that I had been married before, and they became totally against us getting married. Before long, things started to get ugly.

One day Elizabeth called me to say she needed to talk to me and wanted to come by my apartment. When she arrived, two other ladies were with her. One of them was supposedly a prophetess. Two pastors from Maranata were with me at the time. Before long, the "prophetess" announced that it was not God's will for Elizabeth to marry me, that I had a raging spirit inside me that I needed to be delivered from, and God had just wanted Elizabeth to see that and help me get free. There were even rumors circulating later that I was working for the CIA.

I must be honest and say that if this had happened to me at a later season in my life, I would have rebuked the prophetess and sent her out the front door with the right foot of fellowship. But I was in love, and I trusted Elizabeth. Surely, she must know that this was a false prophecy.

I stood in front of Elizabeth and said, "If you want to pray for me, go ahead and pray." But the "prophetess" reached in front of her, touched me, and prayed, announcing that I was now free. Then the ladies walked out the door, Elizabeth among them.

Just like that, it was over between us, and I was left numb and confused. One of the pastors who were with me said, "Don't worry about it! God will vindicate you." But now Elizabeth and her whole family left the church and eventually formed their own family church. She was a wonderful women of God, but she had been deceived by a false prophetess, and this was due, in part, to wrong teachings that had circulated in Brazil about the gifts of the Spirit. It is sad to say that Elizabeth never married, and she and her family still remain in those wrong teachings today.

In the Brazilian culture, women took a back seat. When any woman was empowered by prophecy, it elevated her and created the danger that she might think herself infallible. Their elevation was sometimes to their own destruction. The Brazilians believed that when a prophet or prophetess spoke, it was God speaking, not the person. They never judged prophecy. I had spoken with Elizabeth about this during our times together, but she insisted that you could never judge a prophetess. When she spoke, it was God speaking. For many years, I wanted to write a book addressing this problem, but was concerned that I might be operating out of the wrong spirit because of my painful personal experience with this false prophetess.

Soon after all of this happened, I went into a deep depression, and although Pastor Paulo encouraged me to stay for a while until I felt emotionally better, I felt that I needed to return to America. My Brazilian visa was about to expire anyway, and I didn't want to ask for an extension. I made immediate plans to return to New York.

Prior to leaving Rio, I went to Elizabeth's home to apologize to her and her family for any pain I may have caused them and asked them to forgive me. I loved her and she loved me, but she had to obey what she thought was the Lord's word. Because of wrong teaching about prophecy, she was unable to discern that the prophecy was false. I never saw her or any of her family again.

I returned to New York broken physically, emotionally, and spiritually. I spent a couple months at my brother's farm trying to build myself up physically. I then went to Christ for the Nations, a Bible school in Texas, to spend some time to build myself back up spiritually. I remember saying to the Lord at the time that I had to have more power or giftings to return to the nations of the world and to be victorious over the spiritual attacks that were sure to come.

Chapter 19

THE ANGELIC HOST OF THE INVISIBLE WORLD

*The angel of the Lord encamps all around those who fear Him,
And delivers them.*   Psalm 34:7

I know there will be those who may not agree with my theology here, but, again, this was not meant to be a theological book. This is the story of my journey with the Lord pursuing the destiny that He called me to. When I was in seminary, we would spend hours in theological discussions. Looking back, I can see that this was an exercise in futility. I can honestly say that in all my years of ministry I have never used one thing that I learned in seminary. I think the Lord had me there because it was attached to a ten-thousand-member church where speakers from all over the world came every Sunday night. As I sat there, the Lord was planting a vision in my spirit. Vision is something that cannot be taught in the classroom; it must be imparted by the Holy Spirit. But it can also be nurtured by the testimonies of men and women who labor in the nations of the world.

Every Christian believes in angels, but when you have an actual experience with angels, it seems that some Christians try to discredit it. Angels are mentioned 108 times in the Old Testament and 165 times in the New Testament, so they're real. This is my personal story about my experiences with angels and the spiritual realm.

THE ANGELIC HOST OF THE INVISIBLE WORLD

I returned to Brazil two years after the spiritual attack of the false prophetess. I had been in Asia, teaching in Japan and Burma and traveling into China on two trips, smuggling Bibles. It was now time for the Lord to answer the cry of my heart and to bring me into a new gifting that would take me deeper into my destiny with Him. I had prayed and told the Lord that I simply had to have more power or giftings to return to the nations of the world, to be victorious over the inevitable spiritual attacks.

A missionary friend of mine told me that sixty-five percent of the people that go to the mission field only stay for one term and never go back. They have physical problems, problems with the food and the culture, and personal conflicts with other missionaries that discourage them, so they don't return to their calling or destiny. They don't seem to realize that all these things are spiritual attacks planned by the enemy to detour them. They go back home and lead a good Christian life, attending church and reading the Bible, but never fulfilling their calling and never taking the Gospel to the people the Lord ordained them for. What happens? The missionary loses, the people they were called to lose, and Satan wins. In my opinion, the average missionary has little or no understanding of spiritual warfare.

I have believed, and still do, that if you're hungry and thirsty for the things of the Lord, He always has more for you. He takes us deeper and deeper into the things of the Spirit and closer to His heart. He has prepared our destiny, and He knows what we need to do to fulfill it.

When I went back to Brazil, I received an invitation from Pastor Jairo to visit his church in Salvador, Bahia. He was an engineer, but he also pastored a church that was being visited by the Holy Spirit in a special way. Angels were appearing in the church. Some people saw them, and some heard their movement but did not see them. Others could smell an aroma when the angels were present. The spirit realm had opened over this church. Pastor Jairo did not see angels himself,

INHERITING THE NATIONS

but the Lord gave him wisdom about what was happening and led him to scripture verses to validate the experiences.

Pastor Jairo worked at his engineering job during the day, so during the day I would be with the church members who were having these experiences. They would share with me what was going on, we would spend a lot of time praying, and every day I continually asked them, "But how do you see the angels?"

Their answer was always, "You just look!" I didn't see anything, but I believed it was possible, and I was hungry for whatever the Lord had for me.

During the evening, Pastor Jairo and I would go over my questions and search the Scriptures to bring biblical context to what was going on. I spent almost two weeks there, and it was very rewarding spiritually. His people laid hands on me and prayed for me every day. Still, by the time I had to leave, I had not seen any angels.

I concluded that at least part of this was a manifestation of the gift of discerning of spirits. This gift allows you to understand if something is of God, the devil, or the human spirit. As with most of the gifts, this gift can operate differently in different people. In this case, some people saw, others heard, and others smelled a heavenly aroma when the angels were present.

We know that there is a spiritual realm. We live in the physical realm, but all around us is a spiritual realm, and it is separated from the physical world by a thin invisible veil. I had a pastor friend from the Philippines who died and went to Heaven for two days and then came back. I'll say more about him in another chapter. One thing he said was that when his spirit came out of his body, he passed through what appeared to be a thin veil, like the negative of a photo, and then he was in the spirit realm.

In 2 Kings 6, the servant of Elisha went out one morning and saw that enemies had surrounded the city. He went to Elisha and said, *"What shall we do?"* (verse 15).

THE ANGELIC HOST OF THE INVISIBLE WORLD

Elisha answered, *"Do not fear, for those who are with us are more than those who are with them"* (verse 16). I can imagine that the servant must have counted Elisha and himself and saw that there were only two of them. Then he looked out and began to count the enemy, and they were too many to number. He must have thought to himself, "Elisha doesn't understand math very well."

Then Elisha prayed, *"Lord, I pray, open his eyes that he may see"* (verse 17). The Lord heard that prayer:

Then the Lord opened the eyes of the young man, and he saw. And behold, the mountain was full of horses and chariots of fire all around Elisha.   2 Kings 6:17

Because of the prayer of Elisha, the spirit realm opened to his servant.

I left Pastor Jairo's church and traveled south to Sao Paulo, the second largest city in the world. My longtime friend, Pastor Silvio, had a church and a small Bible school outside the city, and one of their great strengths was prayer. Sometimes they gathered and prayed all night. One evening I went with Pastor Silvio to the hospital to pray for one of his members. I don't remember why the man was in the hospital. Pastor Silvio stood next to the man and laid hands on him and began to pray. I stood at the bottom of the bed, and for the first time the spirit realm opened to me, and I saw an angel standing on the other side of the bed. I tested him and then asked, "Why are you here?"

He answered, "I have been sent by the Father to bring this man home."

We left the hospital, and when we got into the car, I told Pastor Silvio what I had just seen. It was opposite of what he had been praying, but sure enough, that evening the man died. What the angel told me had been true.

INHERITING THE NATIONS

It appears that the disciples in the book of Acts were aware of the spiritual realm, and it's my personal belief that they communicated with angels. This seemed normal for the early Christians as they walked in the Spirit.

> *Are they not all ministering spirits [angels] sent forth to minister for those who will inherit salvation?*   Hebrews 1:14

In Acts 12, Peter had been put in prison, but the church was praying for him. Then an angel came and rescued him from the prison. He didn't even realize it was an angel until he was outside the prison. Then the angel disappeared.

> *And when Peter had come to himself, he said, "Now I know for certain that the Lord has sent His angel and has delivered me from the hand of Herod and from all the expectations of the Jewish people.* Acts 12:11

In verse 12, Peter went to the house of Mary, where everyone had gathered to pray for him. In verses 13 and 14, he knocked on the door, and a girl came to the door. She recognized his voice and was so happy to hear from him that she didn't open the door. Instead, she ran and announced to the others that Peter was at the door. Their reaction is described in verse 16:

> *But they said to her, "You are beside yourself!" Yet she kept insisting it was so. So, they said, "It is his angel."*   Acts 12:16

Most Christians have never seen this verse or they try to explain it away, but it's very simple. These believers had been praying all night for Peter, and now there was a knock at the door. In their unbelief of their prayers being answered, they probably thought that Peter had been killed and his personal angel had come to inform them of his martyrdom before he returned to the Father.

In Matthew 3, Jesus was baptized in water by John the Baptist, the Holy Spirit came upon Him, and the Father spoke from Heaven saying, *"This is my beloved Son, in whom I am well pleased."*

In Matthew 4, the Holy Spirit took Jesus into the wilderness to be tempted by the devil, and He was there for forty days and forty nights fasting. He became very hungry, and then the devil came to tempt Him.

Then the devil left Him, and behold, angels came and ministered to Him.
                                                                Matthew 4:11

The Father can send angels to rescue us just like He rescued Peter from the prison. He can send angels to minister to us physically and spiritually, as He did with Jesus in the wilderness. He can send angels to battle for us, as happened many times in the Old Testament. The Father has an angelic army standing at His command, just waiting to come and help us in our time of need.

One year, I was in Tokyo with Pastor Jairo and two other brothers. We had been to four countries in Asia and were now ready to go back home. Because we had so much luggage, we took two different taxis to go to a hotel where we would get the airport bus. When we arrived, I got out and went into the hotel to ask when the bus would arrive at the airport, while everyone else loaded our suitcases on the bus. When I came back out to the bus, I asked my friend where my handbag was. Then we realized that it had been left in the taxi, which was now roaming the streets of Tokyo with a new customer. In that bag were our passports and tickets.

I decided I would stay behind and try to call the taxi company, while the rest of them took the bus to the airport. I would meet them at the airport later. But Pastor Jairo was led to pray. He prayed, "Lord, send out an angel and bring that bag back to us." In a few short moments, a taxi pulled up next to the bus to drop a customer off, and my friend Jeff said, "Hey, there's the taxi, and your bag is in the back window." That taxi had gone out into Tokyo and picked up a customer who needed to come to that hotel. They hadn't even noticed that my bag was in the back window. The Lord had sent an angel to get my bag with the tickets, passports, and money in it, because Pastor Jairo had prayed and believed. I hadn't thought about it until I was writing this book, but maybe that other customer was an angel. It's possible.

A Japanese man sitting on the bus was observing everything that was going on, and he commented, "I can't believe you guys were so calm about your bag being lost." Then the bag came back, and he was amazed, and we got to share the Lord with him.

Pastor Greg, the brother who, back in our seminary days, was telling everyone they had to go into all the world and preach the Gospel, and if they didn't, they were disobedient to the Word of God, planted a church in Geneva, Switzerland and invited me to come there to teach about angels. One day he took me to the old part of the city to see a beautiful church that had been pastored by John Calvin during the Reformation. Because of my experiences in looking into the spiritual realm, I believed that there was an angel assigned to every church and if you could speak to that angel, you could understand the assignment of the Lord for that church. Prior to us going there, Pastor Greg had not told me anything about the church. We entered and sat down in one of the pews to pray. As I was praying, the spiritual realm opened to me, and I saw an angel standing on the right side of the altar. When I tested him, he turned totally black, and the Holy Spirit spoke to me and said, "This is a counterfeit angel. My angel left here a long time ago." When I told Pastor Greg what I had seen, he said, "You're correct. There hasn't been a church service here in many years. This building is only used as a concert hall.

THE ANGELIC HOST OF THE INVISIBLE WORLD

You might say, "What is the purpose of seeing into the spiritual realm and talking with an angel?" The simplest answer is "to bless and encourage people in their walk with the Lord!" In my journey, I have prayed for more people than I can remember, the spiritual realm has opened, and I have seen an angel with them that was associated with their gifts and talents. When I pray for anyone, I tell them what I see and then I say, "What do you think?" This gives them the opportunity to accept or reject what I have seen. Every person I have prayed for, except one brother, has confirmed what I've seen and was greatly encouraged.

The one brother who disagreed with me was at a Foursquare church in California. He told me he was an evangelist, but I didn't see any angel with him that had anything to do with evangelism. I believe all of us are intended to share the Gospel with other people, and it might be possible that he was obeying that but that he was not in the office of an evangelist (which would have been indicated by an angel). I told him, "I can only say what I saw," but I encouraged him to keep evangelizing.

I spoke at a Pentecostal church in New York and shared my testimony about angels. Later, I was invited to come and speak at one of their home groups. I didn't know anyone at the group. They had only heard me one time at their church, but they were curious about angels and hungry for the things of the Spirit. I prayed for one lady named Judy, the spirit realm opened, and I saw an angel next to her that had a large bag. He was taking things out to give to people. I had never seen anything like this before, so it was very strange to me. Since that was what I saw, I told everyone exactly as I had seen it, They all began to laugh, and then someone said, "We call her the bag lady. Inside her purse is everything you could imagine. She's always taking things out and giving them to people." It was exactly what I had seen in the spirit realm. To be honest, this was very funny, but it greatly encouraged her

INHERITING THE NATIONS

when she realized there was an angel sent by the Lord to assist her with her gift of blessing people.

I spoke at another church in New York led by Pastor Bob Hulett. I had spoken there many times before, so he trusted me to talk about angels. However, at the end, he got up and said to the congregation, "I have to be honest and say I wasn't sure about Joe speaking about angels. Now, however, I want to testify that the whole time he was speaking the spiritual realm opened to me, and I saw an angel standing on the platform with him."

The apostle Paul, in 1 Corinthians 14:12, said:

Even so you, since you are zealous for spiritual gifts, let it be for the edification of the church, that you seek to excel.

We are called to be a blessing to others. That's what the gifts of the Spirit are for—to bless, encourage, and demonstrate God's love.

I believe the Lord has given each of us gifts and talents to bless others and to glorify Him. Each one of us is different. There is no one like you, and you have spiritual things inside you that people of other nations are waiting for. Their salvation and eternal destiny is in your hands and depends on your obedience to the call of God upon your life.

The Lord can do things without us, but for some reason, He has chosen not to. He has decided to use us to share His glorious Gospel with other people, to bring His healing touch, His love and embrace to the hopeless people of the world. When we know what our gifts are, we are then able to understand why the Father created us, and we can find joy and satisfaction in our lives.

Pastor Rick Warren wrote his famous book entitled *The Purpose Driven Life*,[1] and it has sold millions of copies. Why? Because people are searching for meaning in life. They don't understand why the Lord

---
1. (Grand Rapids , MI, Zondervan Publishing: 2012)

THE ANGELIC HOST OF THE INVISIBLE WORLD

created them. When they see His calling and embrace it, life takes on a whole new meaning, for them and for the people they will touch.

One day I was in my garage putting clothes in the washing machine. Through the corner of my eye, I caught some movement. I looked to the doorway and saw that an angel had stepped into the garage. The presence of the angel was so strong that I got on my knees and didn't look up, but I heard him say, "The Lord is your Fortress and your Provider!" Later I found this scripture:

> *After these things the word of the LORD came to Abram in a vision, saying, "Do not be afraid, Abram. I am your shield, your exceedingly great reward."* Genesis 15:1

When there were no other words from the angel, I finally looked up, and he was gone. When I shared this story in a meeting in Bangkok, one of my friends said, "Did you bow down to the angel?"

"No," I said, "I bowed down to the washing machine," and everyone laughed. We're not called to worship angels. Jesus is the Master, and there is no one else worthy of worship and praise.

The apostle John, in Revelation 5, was taken up into Heaven, and in verses 11 and 12 he said:

> *Then I looked, and I heard the voice of many angels around the throne, the living creatures, and the elders; and the number of them was ten thousand times ten thousand, and thousands of thousands, saying with a loud voice:*

> *"Worthy is the Lamb who was slain*
> *To receive power and riches and wisdom,*
> *And strength and honor and glory and blessing!"*

INHERITING THE NATIONS

Writing this chapter made me think about what Jesus said:

Most assuredly, I say to you, the Son can do nothing of Himself, but what He sees the Father do; for whatever He does, the Son also does in like manner. John 5:19

God is Spirit, and those who worship Him must worship in spirit and truth. John 4:24

Jesus only did what He saw the Father do while He was in human form and living on this Earth, so He had to have access to the spiritual realm to see what the Father was doing. That same ability to access the spiritual realm is also available to us today through the power of the Holy Spirit.

Paul wrote:

I know a man in Christ who fourteen years ago—whether in the body I do not know, or whether out of the body I do not know, God knows—such a one was caught up to the third heaven. 2 Corinthians 12:2

John wrote:

I was in the Spirit on the Lords Day, and I heard behind me a loud voice as of a trumpet. Revelation 1:10

Immediately I was in the Spirit; and behold, a throne set in heaven, and One sat on the throne. Revelation 4:2

The Bible shows that both Paul and John were taken up to Heaven. John not only saw in the spiritual realm; he also entered the spiritual realm. It has always interested me to read what the apostle John said:

THE ANGELIC HOST OF THE INVISIBLE WORLD

"I was in the Spirit on the Lord's day." What does it mean to be "in the Spirit"? Sometimes you go to a meeting and people say, "Wow, the Spirit was really moving!" But what does that really mean? Is it some tingling sensation that comes over your body? Do you feel heat all over you when someone prays for you for healing? Do you fall when someone prays for you because the presence of the Lord is so strong? To be honest, I don't have the complete answer to that question, but deep in my spirit, I feel that there is much more to being "in the Spirit" than most of us, myself included, are presently experiencing. I cannot say that I have had the experience of being taken up into Heaven, but I have heard the testimonies of those who have experienced Heaven, and I believe deep in my spirit that Heaven is available to us, as believers, as we draw close to the Father.

Just like the Shulamite woman in the book of Song of Solomon was desiring intimacy with her lover, I believe the Lord desires us to be closer to Him. He wants to draw us unto a place where our hearts are captivated by Him, where we desire to feel the kisses of His lips and the embrace of His strong arms, a place where if He chooses, we can be caught up into the third Heaven. In this place, we will see Him in all His glory, surrounded by a hosts of spiritual beings and angels worshiping Him and bowing down before Him.

Chapter 20

AROUND THE WORLD IN FOUR MONTHS

And they sang a new song, saying:

"You are worthy to take the scroll,
And to open its seals;
For You were slain,
And have redeemed us to God by Your blood
Out of every tribe and tongue and people and nation."   Revelation 5:9

In late May of 1985, I was planning a fourteen-country trip with two of my friends—Jeff and Tim. Jeff and I would leave California and fly to Europe, where we would meet Tim and travel together to ten countries. Then Jeff and I would fly together to Asia where we would meet two pastors and travel with them to four more countries before completing our round-the-world trip back to California in August.

Such a trip was expensive, but while I was making the plans that May, I received more money in one month than I had received in all of 1984. This would relieve me of any financial stress, so I could be free to focus on the trip. This was important, for the trip would be taking us into Eastern Europe to countries that were opposed to Christianity.

Jeff and I flew to London because, in those days, there were travel agencies known as "bucket shops," where you could find low airfares.

INHERITING THE NATIONS

There was no Internet in those days. In the evening we attended St. James Church in London, where they were having a Bible marathon, reading the entire Bible straight through without stopping.

After a couple days in London, we boarded a flight for Geneva, Switzerland, to connect with Pastor Greg, our friend from Bible school days. He had recently planted a church there in Geneva.

As the plane was flying over France, the spirit realm opened to me, and I saw a large black demon dressed in armor standing in the air. It is very possible that it was a territorial spirit ruling that area of France. We arrived safely in Geneva and spoke in a couple churches there. Then we drove over to France to speak in a French church (it was only about a thirty-minute drive from Geneva.) Those countries are so close together that one day we had breakfast in Switzerland, lunch in France, and dinner in Italy.

As I was speaking at the church in France, the spirit realm opened to me, and an angel told me that the Lord wanted a worship center that, through worship, would bring down the darkness over France. We returned to Switzerland that night, and as we were crossing the border, I felt a lightness in my spirit. There appears to be a spiritual heaviness over France.

We received a telephone call from Tim, who had arrived in Germany and was trying to buy a car that we would use on our trip into the Eastern Bloc. He finally bought a yellow 1974 Mercedes-Benz for $650, and we made plans to meet in Salzburg, Austria. We were going there to meet up with a young lady named Marcelene whom I had met at a Bible study in California. Since she was going to be in Salzburg at the same time we planned to go through there, she was going to see if she could set up some home meetings for us with her friends.

The night before we left Geneva, we met with a brother named Nocoli. He was a taxi driver. He was from Romania, and his father was a pastor there in Romania of an underground home church. Nocoli was able to give us information on how to connect with his father.

AROUND THE WORLD IN FOUR MONTHS

The next morning Jeff and I went to the train station to catch a train to Salzburg. Unfortunately, we missed our train by three minutes, so we took the next one two hours later. The ride through the mountains of Switzerland was breathtaking, but at the next station we missed our connection and had to stay overnight in a hotel.

We finally arrived in Salzburg and connected with my friend Marcelene, and a short time later Tim arrived from Germany with our car. The four of us drove down to the center of the city to get something to eat. I can still see it in my mind's eye. We parked by a bridge outside of what I guess would be called the old city, or maybe the center of the city. It had walls all around it, and as the sun was setting, it looked majestic. In the center of it, high up on a hill, was a fortress, where, in wartime, people would flee for safety. Next to where we parked was a street vendor selling bratwurst sandwiches. Of course we had to have one, and they were delicious.

Whenever I think of Salzburg, I think of that view at night. Maybe it was the friendships, the food, or just the first look at the city, or possibly all three. Salzburg became one of my favorite cities in the world. It was in that part of the city, behind the walls, where the famous composer Mozart was born, and one day we had the opportunity to visit his home.

We were in Salzburg a couple days and met with several people in home meetings. In one of them, I spoke about inner healing or healing of memories and had an opportunity to pray for several people.

As we were organizing the car and getting ready to leave, the spirit realm opened, and I saw an angel standing by the car covered with armor. I felt this was a sign from the Lord that His angel would be protecting us on our journey.

When we arrived at the border of Hungary, guards were opening the trunks of cars and checking them very carefully. The line was long, so Tim decided to get out and use the restroom that was before the guard shack. He came back very quickly but didn't say anything right then to me and Jeff. We decided to go use the restroom too. The door to the restroom had a high threshold, so you had to step down into it. But we didn't step in because the entire floor was flooded up to the threshold and feces was floating across the water. When we got back to the car, Tim was bent over laughing because he knew what we had just seen. Welcome to a country controlled by Communism.

As we were sitting there, waiting for our turn to be inspected by the border guards, the muffler fell off our car. Tim got out and threw it in the trunk, but now our car sounded like a race car. When it was finally our turn to be inspected, we pulled up to the guard stand, but all the guards suddenly walked away, and we drove through without stopping. Praise the Lord!

We arrived in Budapest without any hotel reservations, so we went to a government reservation center that got you a room in people's homes. We got a room for the three of us in a private home with a couple that had one child, and it only cost us $12 for two days stay.

The next day we found a Baptist church and decided to attend. However, when we sat down, we realized that the service was just ending. A young lady came up to us, told us that there was a Pentecostal church down the road, and took us there. The people were friendly and invited us to come back and share in the evening service. We invited the couple we were staying with to go to church with us, and they did. A young lady who translated for us told us that the church had a lot of freedom. However, they were not allowed to evangelize on the streets.

The next four days we spent in Yugoslavia. We spent a couple days of that time with the relatives of a Christian sister from California. The husband was a doctor, and his wife stayed home during the day, but she didn't speak any English. One day we understood that she was making lunch for us, but we couldn't figure out what she was making. She was mixing water and flour and making a dough and then cutting it into strips. We finally realized she was making egg noodles to cook a pasta meal for us. It was a blessing.

We eventually went and stayed one night in Belgrade, the capital of Yugoslavia at the time. We stayed in a hotel called the Moscow Hotel and downstairs was a room where a band was playing. The room was filled with very small round tables that two or three people could sit at comfortably. The band had a violin and big stand-up bass, but the music was different and relaxing. The only problem was everybody was smoking. At the table next to us was a lady who was holding her cigarette up with her arm on the table. Her smoke was drifting over our table directly in front of Jeff, and it was really bothering him. He finally couldn't take it anymore, but what should we do? We were in a Communist country and were the only foreigners in the room, white Americans. Jeff reached over, took the lady's hand, pulled it down onto the table and said, "I don't mind if you smoke, but I don't want to smoke your smoke." I couldn't believe he had done that. Shocked, I stood up, turned around, and walked out. Tim came out of few seconds later. When Jeff finally came out, he said, "What's the problem?" The problem was we could have been in big trouble.

On June 22, 1985, we arrived at the Romanian border. The guards were friendly but very thorough in checking our car. We were overflowing with food because we had learned that food was very scarce in those days in Romania. The guards didn't question it. We were now in a country where religious persecution was extreme.

We arrived in Timisoara, just inside the western border of Romania with Yugoslavia. Nocoli, the taxi driver in Switzerland, had told us that his father lived in this city. He said that when we arrived, there would be railroad tracks. We should hide our car somewhere in that area and then walk down the tracks until we came to a small village. That was where his father lived.

INHERITING THE NATIONS

There was no building on that road except one by the railroad tracks, so we parked our car behind it and began walking down the tracks. We eventually came to an area where there was a group of houses, but we didn't know which house was the father's. All of them were very old and poor looking, with wooden outhouses in the backyards. There were no streets, only grass.

Suddenly, the spiritual realm opened, and I saw an angel pointing at one of the houses. We walked up to it and knocked on the door. Some young people answered. Sure enough, it was Nicoli's father's home. Tim went with some of the family, brought our car, and they hid it in a barn near their home. We spent a couple days in that area visiting several homes, spending a lot of time in prayer and praying for one another. It was a precious time.

Next, we traveled five hours in a northeast direction to a city called Cluj-Napoca. When Tim had been in Germany trying to find a car, someone had told him about this city and given him the name of a pastor of a Pentecostal church there. As it turned out, they were not having a regular church service; they were just having a prayer meeting when we got there. However, it was standing room only. There were several hundred people in that room. We all shared about healing and then began to pray for the people. It was almost like being at a rock concert. The room was so full that the people lifted Tim and passed him from shoulder to shoulder till he could get to another area of the room to pray for people. These people were very hungry and thirsty for the things of the Spirit.

The next day, before leaving, we walked around the town a bit. I went in a grocery store, but every shelf was empty, except for a few jars of green beans, and they had mold in the jars. Later that day I saw a white truck back up to that store, and there was a line of people all the way around the block waiting to buy whatever was in that truck. We spoke to some of the people. They said they didn't know what was in the truck, but at least it was some type of food. When they started to unload the truck, we saw that the cargo looked like a long stick of soft salami. Everyone in the line was buying one. It was so sad to see what Communism had done to that country, at one time considered the breadbasket of Eastern Europe. We had lunch with several pastors and their families and then had a time of prayer before we left for another city.

We had been invited to stay and speak in four more churches, and looking back, we probably should have stayed. But we were trying to maintain a tight schedule because we had a long way yet to travel.

The money in Romania was called Leu, and the official rate of exchange at the time was 13 Lei (the plural of Leu) for $1, but you could sell your dollars on the street for 55 Leu each. We changed the money on the street and got local currency to continue our journey.

We eventually arrived in Bucharest, the capital of Romania, and got a hotel for the night. The food we had been eating for the past several days was rather sub-standard, and I was looking forward to a nice sandwich. In the hotel, a good sandwich cost $14.00, but we bought some anyway.

In the hotel lobby, I noticed that there were two-liter bottles of soda from America—Coca-Cola, Sprite, and others. The entire time we had been in Romania, there was only one type of soda available to drink. It was called Quick Cola. You had to pay for it, drink it right there, and then hand the bottle back. You couldn't keep the bottle. At one stand a girl was selling their cola, and we wanted to buy the bottle for a souvenir. She wouldn't sell it to us. We offered her $5, and she said no. We even came up to $20, but she refused to sell the bottle. So, when I saw the Coca-Cola for sale in the hotel lobby in a two-liter bottle, I was interested in buying it. The cost was $3, and that was a lot of money at the time. But I figured, "Let's do it." In my wallet I had currency from France, Italy, Switzerland, and the U.S. I decided, because I had so many French Francs left, that I would pay in French money. But I made a mistake and confused my Swiss Francs with French Francs. The next day, when we were at a hotel on the Black Sea, I was counting my money and realized that I had just paid $30 for that bottle of soda, not $3. The boy behind the counter hadn't said anything. It was one of the very few times I confused my currencies overseas.

As we were traveling south to the Bulgarian border, the map we had showed that the main road would be much longer than just going straight on a secondary road, so we decided on the secondary road. We were noticing some very large signs on the road, but they were in a language we couldn't read. Every once in a while, we would see a person waving to us to go back, but we just kept going straight because we knew it was only a short distance to the border. We eventually arrived at a very small town, and now everyone was motioning for us to go back, but we didn't. Within minutes, we found ourselves at a dead end in the parking lot of a military base.

Before we could turn around, two guards came out with guns. We tried to explain that we didn't know we were entering a military zone, and they were about to let us turn around. Then, a third military man came out and asked to see our passports. He said, "Americans?" In the end, everything turned out okay, and they let us turn around. Tim even traded a hat that he was wearing for a small military pin from one of the guards.

We got turned around, but now the problem was that we had to go all the way back and then take the long road the map was showing we should have been on all along in order to arrive at the Bulgarian border. We eventually got there.

This crossing posed a major problem. Because our car could be sold in Bulgaria for a massive amount of money, the officials didn't want us to enter the country with it. We were at the border for several hours discussing the matter before they finally agreed to make a notation in our passports that we had the car and had to have it in our possession when we crossed into Turkey. There was a very high demand for Mercedes vehicles and Mercedes parts, so they wanted to make sure we didn't sell the car in Bulgaria. The worst part was this: because of the car, they would only give us a transit visa. This meant that we could not make any stops inside the country. We had to drive straight through to Turkey.

Tim's family had come from Sofia, Bulgaria, and we had been hoping to go there and possibly find some distant relatives, but we now drove straight through, as our visa required us to do, and arrived in Istanbul, Turkey. We were very tired and hoping to get some extra sleep. However, early in the morning the Muslim mosque began to broadcast morning prayer over their loudspeakers.

In downtown Istanbul stands a massive structure. When it was originally built in the sixth century, it was a Christian church known as St. Sofia or Hagia Sophia, and it was where the Emperor worshipped. For almost a thousand years that church was the center of Christian worship for the believers in Turkey. Then, in 1453, it was remodeled and became a mosque. In 1935 the Turkish president made it into a museum, but in 2020, President Recep Tayyip Erdogan, in a controversial decision, converted the building back into a mosque, and it is now Turkey's number one tourist site. What was built as a Christian church, where prayers went up daily to the God who sits on the throne of Heaven. is now devoted to Islamic prayers. That was very sad for us to see.

We headed for Greece with the intention of visiting some of the cities of Christian history. We visited an archaeological dig in Philippi, a museum in Thessaloniki, and a museum in Berea. Acts 17:11 speaks about the Berean believers and says:

> *These were more fair-minded than those in Thessalonica, in that they received the word with all readiness, and searched the Scriptures daily to find out whether these things were so.*

INHERITING THE NATIONS

I opened my Bible and, while leaning on an ancient stone column, read that scripture. We longed to be as fair-minded as the noble Bereans.

After driving all day through winding mountainous roads, we arrived on the northwest coast of Greece. As we came over the last mountain, below us was a very small town called Igoumenitsa. From there, cars and trucks transporting goods to and from Western Europe would load onto huge ferries for a ten-hour ride to the shores of Italy. We spent the night in the town. Then, at 6:30 the next morning, our yellow Mercedes was loaded onto the ferry to cross the Ionian Sea.

About two hundred miles into our journey, we saw the coast of Albania, the only country in the world at that time whose official religion was Atheism. There was no evidence of any Christian church in those days. We raised our hands and prayed for that country and for any believers who might be in hiding there. We arrived in Italy at 5:00 in the evening.

Over the next five days, we were tourists in Italy. We visited sites around Rome, including the Vatican. As we were entering St. Peters Basilica through a massive door crowded with people going in and out, I heard someone say, "Pastor Joe." It was one of the deacons from Maranata Church in Brazil. He was in Rome on business and had come to see the church, but when he sat down in one of the pews, he fell asleep. He had just awakened and was going out the door as we were coming in. He became our free personal tour guide for the day, and then we had dinner together.

He knew the area well and took us all over the Vatican, even up into the very top of the dome over the Basilica, the tallest dome in the world. In those days, that wasn't part of any tour, but he knew how to get up there. Now you have to pay to go up there. The view of the Vatican area and the skyline of Rome was amazing from that dome. We also visited the catacombs where the early Christians hid during times of persecution.

AROUND THE WORLD IN FOUR MONTHS

After leaving Rome, we traveled to Florence, Italy to meet up with Pastor Greg and his outreach team. We joined them for street meetings, and it was a fruitful time.

We traveled north and stopped in Pisa to see the famous Leaning Tower of Pisa, and then on to Genoa, where we had dinner on the Mediterranean Sea. The next day we visited Torino to see the church that houses the famous Shroud of Turin. Some believe it is the burial cloth of Jesus. I'm not sure, but it was an amazing display.

Late in the evening of July 10 we arrived back at our starting point in Geneva, Switzerland, at Pastor Greg's home. We stayed there a few days sharing testimonies and showing the videos we had taken on our journey.

Pastor Greg was a big believer in street ministry, and many of his members had come to know the Lord through that outreach. One evening we walked with them up a narrow street lined with restaurants. People were seated outdoors right up to the edge of the street. Greg said, "This is amazing! These people have paid good money to come here, eat, and hear us preach the Gospel." In his street meetings, a few of his people would play guitars and sing songs. Then Greg would stand up and give a short Gospel message. As soon as he did that, people would begin to react, and they would then talk to people one-on-one. That particular night one man stood up, held up a big mug of beer, and shouted, "This is my God." We took that as our cue to approach individual tables and start sharing the Gospel with anyone who would listen. It was powerful!

I sat down at a table that had a few men and was sharing the Gospel. Somehow, in the course of the discussion, I made the comment that those who refused to accept Jesus were going to Hell. No one at the table that I remember objected to that, but when I returned to the street, one man came up to me a little bit upset and said, "Did you tell my friend he was going to Hell?"

INHERITING THE NATIONS

I replied, "I didn't say that to him. I told him that if he didn't accept Jesus he was going to Hell. Do you know Jesus?" And we got into a long conversation. To me, there is nothing more exhilarating than interacting with people on the street and sharing the Gospel.

Our days of traveling around Europe in our yellow Mercedes were coming to an end. How many miles we traveled in total I don't know, but we had traversed eight countries, some of them Communist, some Muslim, and some Catholic. Each had varying measures of freedom. We had worshipped with and taken physical food to the brothers in Romania and spiritual food to others in many countries on this trip. We had shared our life and given out what the Lord had given us in the Spirit.

In parts of the journey, we saw the places of Christian history, where the original disciples of Jesus had walked in proclaiming the Gospel to the nations. However, the greatest experience was seeing the living Church, the Body of Christ, living under varied conditions and sometimes under great oppression, walking in the grace that the Lord had given them to experience His love and His provision.

I returned to some of these countries in later years, but to others I would never go back again. I would only have in my heart and mind the believers I encountered during this season of my life, until that final day, by God's grace, when we will all bow before the throne of Heaven and worship Him who is worthy of all praise.

On July 14, 1985, we said goodbye to Tim and the yellow Mercedes. He was returning to Germany, where he would sell the car before returning to California. Greg, Judy (his wife), and their boys would continue for some years to grow the living Church in Geneva. Jeff and I flew back to London, where we caught a connecting flight to Thailand, to continue our journey in five Asian countries.

Tim with the Mercedes

A Romanian food line

Chapter 21

WE CONTINUE AROUND THE WORLD

And He said to them, go into all the world and preach the gospel to every creature.   Mark 16:15

After a short stop in London, Jeff and I took a plane to Thailand to continue our around-the-world journey. There we connected with Bob Charters, a friend and missionary in that country. I had met Bob first at a missions meeting in California. He had also been a student at Melodyland School of Theology. The room where the teachings were held had a world map on the wall that was really a massive piece of wallpaper. Bob and I had not yet met, but we both ended up standing before that map. I pointed to Albany, New York and said, "I was born here." Bob reached a long way across the map, pointed to Thailand, and said, "I was born here."

I couldn't believe it. I said, "Really?"

He said, "Yes" and started telling me his story. His grandparents were missionaries in Thailand, and his grandmother was one of the first persons to translate many of the old hymns into the Thai language. Bob's father was from Ireland, and his mother was from America. They also became missionaries in Thailand, so Bob was born there. As a result of that encounter before the world map, Bob and I became friends and traveled around Thailand together ministering during my many trips to that country.

INHERITING THE NATIONS

Bob, Jeff, and I now traveled around southern Thailand sharing the Gospel in various churches. If my memory serves me correctly, Christ for the Nations Institute, a Bible school based in Dallas, Texas, was starting a school in southern Thailand. The leader was Dr. Harold Rentz. Jeff had been a student in Dallas, and I had spoken there many times, so we both knew Dr. Rentz. The school would be starting its first classes the following week, so Dr. Rentz asked me to be the speaker for five days.

The property that the school was on was surrounded by many palm trees, and on one side was the Andaman Sea. It was a beautiful place and a wonderful time of ministry and fellowship.

After my class that first day of, several of us piled into a pickup truck to go into town and get something to eat. I set my Bible, which had all my notes for the week inside it, on the roof of the truck while I let someone else get in the front seat. When we took off, some of the students who were sitting in the back of the truck started yelling. We stopped. My Bible had flown off the roof and was in the middle of the road, quite a distance back. I walked back to retrieve it, but a young boy had already picked it up and he handed it to me. It was in three different pieces and the cover was completely torn off, but my notes were not in it. I looked over to the side of the road and saw a man mowing grass. At that very moment, he was shredding all my notes for the week with his mower. I don't remember what I preached that week, but I assume that the Lord wanted me to rely more on the Holy Spirit and less on my notes that were now tiny pieces of white paper mixed with grass on the side of the road.

We returned to Bangkok, had some time of ministry and fellowship with Brother Sonny, then Jeff, Bob, and I flew to Hong Kong. There we would meet up with Pastor Jairo from Brazil and Pastor Bernie from California.

I mentioned Pastor Jairo in an earlier chapter where I talked about angels. It was in his church in Salvador, Brazil where people were seeing and interacting with angels. As I have noted, Pastor Bernie was over a church in California. I had met him and his wife and another couple in Rio de Janeiro, Brazil back in the early 1980s and had preached in their church prior to inviting him to Asia. Now we were five, and our goal was to take Bibles into China for the underground church.

We spent a couple days in Hong Kong and then went to Pastor Dennis' church to pack as many Bibles as we could possibly carry into our suitcases. The next morning, we boarded a bus that would take us across the border to our hotel in China.

As noted in earlier chapters, taking Bibles across the border where it is illegal is always an experience. There is an acceleration of your emotions when you're packing the Bibles, there's a lot of praying, and when you near the border where you have to clear Immigration with your suitcases, your adrenaline starts to run high. Underneath your breath, you're praying, and if you get through without the Bibles being detected and/or confiscated, there's a feeling of excitement and joy, knowing that they will go to people who have long lived under oppression and persecution. On this trip, all five of us got through with our Bibles undetected, and later that night Chinese young people would deliver them to the underground church. Mission accomplished! Praise the Lord!

On one trip, some of us were caught. At the time, the official policy was to confiscate the Bibles from our suitcases and backpacks. The Communist guard on duty removed the Bibles from my suitcase and piled them beside it. As he began to take Bibles from someone else's suitcase, I could see that he was very preoccupied with it, so I took the opportunity to put the Bibles piled in front of me back in the suitcase. I closed it and walked away, free to deliver the Bibles to those who needed them most.

On the trip in question, we all returned to Hong Kong after a successful delivery in China, Bob returned to Thailand, and the rest of us

INHERITING THE NATIONS

flew to South Korea to attend a church growth conference. The conference was held at Yoido Full Gospel Church in Seoul, which at that time was the largest church in the world. In 2021, it had a weekly attendance of about 800,000. Next to the church sanctuary was what looked like a skyscraper, but it was the administrative building with a finely-tuned group of people who kept this mega-church functioning and growing.

The church has thousands of home groups of ten to fifteen in each group, and they are run by lay-people. Outside the city, in the mountains, was what they called Prayer Mountain. There was only one large building with forests all around it where people would go to pray. Prayers ascended to the very throne of the Father twenty-four hours a day.

They also had what they called "prayer caves." These were only large enough for one person. It was a private place where a person could go and spend days praying and fasting. Pastor Cho said that whenever someone in the leadership was having a problem, he would tell them to go to Prayer Mountain and fast and pray until the Lord told them what to do to resolve the problem. He was devoted to prayer with a do-or-die desperation. He said, "When we apply God's Word in our lives and experience God's promises, we are empowered by God." Pastor Cho also claimed that the churches in Europe were empty because they had betrayed the Holy Spirit.

Because Pastor Jairo and Pastor Bernie both had planted churches and were senior pastors, they were very interested in attending this conference to get some ideas on how to grow their churches. We attended all the meetings, and then early one morning rode on several chartered buses to Prayer Mountain, where we had a teaching about prayer and then spent the rest of the day praying in the forest.

We returned from Prayer Mountain to the city late that evening, and the next morning Bob flew back to Thailand, and the four of us flew to Japan. Our stay in Japan would only be a few days. We got rooms at

WE CONTINUE AROUND THE WORLD

a Christian guesthouse in Tokyo. I had been there many times, but it was the first time for my friends, so we spent a lot of time just touring around, looking at many of the things the Japanese culture has to offer.

I decided to take my friends out to a home church pastored by two missionary friends of mine, Ken and Lila. We shared at their church, prayed for people, encouraged one another, and had a wonderful time of fellowship. Since Ken and Lila had been missionaries there for several decades, they had many interesting testimonies.

A day or two later, the four of us took two taxis to a hotel where we would board a bus to the airport. That day was one of the most amazing days in all of my years of ministry. My handbag with all the tickets and passports, plus my money, got left in the taxi. We needed a miracle, and the Lord gave us that miracle! You can read about this miracle in Chapter 19, "The Angelic Host of the Invisible World."

We flew back to Los Angeles. Jeff and I had been to fourteen countries during the last four months and had traveled completely around the world. We were now home. Pastor Bernie would have a short flight to his home in central California, and Pastor Jairo would take another overnight flight to arrive home in Brazil.

As I noted in earlier chapters, while I was in the School of Theology, Pastor Greg would always quote to us Mark 16:15 and tell us that if we didn't go into all the world sharing the Gospel, we were disobeying the Word of God. Jeff and I had been doing our best to follow that scripture during this round-the-world trip.

CHAPTER 22

THE KAREN TRIBAL PEOPLE OF BURMA

These all died in faith, not having received the promises, but having seen them afar off or assured of them, embraced them and confessed that they were strangers and pilgrims upon the earth. Hebrews 11:13

In February of 1812, Adoniram and Ann Judson, the first missionaries from America, began their journey by boat to India and, eventually, Burma. In Burma they encountered a people group called the Karen. The Karen legends spoke of a man who would come on a ship, have a book, and that book would show the way to Heaven. Adoniram was that man, and he landed on the shores of Burma to share the Gospel with a people who lived under the darkness of Buddhism.

Some biographies say that Adoniram's original desire was to go to India but that a storm diverted the ship, and it ended up on the shores of Burma. Others say that he went to India for a season and then on to Burma, which became his life work. I'm not sure which is true. However, I do know that this man poured himself into evangelizing men and women and then discipling his converts, which eventually led him to translate the first Bible into the Burmese language. Interestingly, this translation is still the most widely used and preferred Bible in Burma more than two hundred years later.

THE KAREN TRIBAL PEOPLE OF BURMA

Adoniram had arrived in Burma in 1813 without knowing a single word of the Burmese language, but by December of 1832 he had printed three thousand copies of the New Testament in Burmese, and, in 1834, he completed the translation work on the Old Testament.

The Karen were among those evangelized, but because Burma was a Buddhist stronghold, they suffered severe persecution. In 1988, due to heavy persecution by the Burmese government, many Karen fled to the border of Thailand, where it is estimated that more than one hundred thousand of them still live in nine refugee camps. Some have lived there all their life and never been outside of the camps. Some live in the forest areas, but must of them move on when any Burmese military comes into their area.

My story with the Karen began in 1982. Three friends and myself loaded Burmese Bibles into a white van in Thailand and headed to the Burmese border. There we loaded our van onto a small wooden platform called a car carrier, but it only held one vehicle at a time. We crossed a river and then drove into the Burmese forest. Eventually we came to a sign that read: BORDER OF THE KAREN STATE. Next to that sign the road was blocked by a gate made from a large tree limb, and guarding it was a very young boy dressed in green military garb. His feet were bare, but he held a military rifle in his hands. We were entering a small military camp, but since our arrival was expected, the young soldier opened the gate for us.

We were warmly greeted by the Karen, and soldiers came to help us unload our boxes of Bibles. As we looked around, all the structures were made from bamboo and had dirt floors. There was only a bamboo-type rug for us to sit on. We were escorted into the hut of the head military man in charge of the camp. My friend was acquainted with him. He was the one who had requested the Bibles. On the outside of his hut was a large banner that said:

IN GOD WE TRUST!

INHERITING THE NATIONS

And there was a Bible verse:

He who does not love does not know God, for God is love.   1 John 4:8

As we were sitting with this man, he told us that it was his desire for every one of his soldiers to have a Bible. I don't remember a lot of what was discussed in the hut that day, but I do remember that we had a precious time of prayer with him. He was a man of God who had to lead his people in real war and also in a spiritual war, a war for their survival as Christians, against the Burmese military and the Buddhist spirits that control the jungles of Burma.

The temperature in the jungle was very hot and humid, so a few young Karen ladies brought water from a nearby creek for us to pour over ourselves so that we could cool down before beginning our journey back to Bangkok.

A few weeks later, I crossed the river again in a different area of the jungle, this time to teach among the Karen for a week with another brother. Again, all the buildings were made of bamboo, and we slept on very thin mats on a bamboo floor in the hot, humid jungle and bathed in the river at the edge of the camp. The meetings were well attended. To be honest, this was probably because there was nothing else to do in the camp. For us, it was great to share the Bible and pray for people.

Around the outer perimeter of our teaching area were what seemed like young boys, even one girl, all with military rifles ready to protect their people if the Burmese military came into the camp. Several months later that village came under a rocket attack. Some Karens were killed, and everything was destroyed. Those who got out alive were now forced to move on to another area of the jungle and build another village or cross over the river and move into a refugee camp in Thailand for greater safety.

Many of the Karen are still believers, and they love the Lord with all their heart. When preachers or teachers come to their camp, there are always wonderful meetings. There is even a Bible school in one of the camps, even though the Karen life is hard and their future uncertain. Through the years, there have been promises of giving the Karen people their own land again inside Burma, but these promises always come with conditions from a political leadership that is mostly run by military men.

The purpose of my book is not to be political but to tell my story and allow you somehow to see what I've seen, that you might experience the Lord's heart for these people. I've been in the Karen camps several times over the years, and it has been an honor.

Hebrews 1:38 talks about a people, of whom the world was not worthy. They wandered in deserts and mountains or hid in dens and caves of the earth. The Karen people wander in the mountains and jungles of Burma, trying to survive, trying to live another day. Their only hope is their Savior, whom they love and worship.

CHAPTER 23

THOSE OF WHOM THE WORLD WAS NOT WORTHY

Women received their dead raised to life again. Others were tortured, not accepting deliverance, that they might obtain a better resurrection. Still others had trials of mockings and scourgings, yes, and of chains and imprisonment. They were stoned, they were sawn in two, were tempted, were slain with the sword. They wandered about in sheepskins and goatskins, being destitute, afflicted, tormented—OF WHOM THE WORLD WAS NOT WORTHY. They wandered in deserts and mountains, in dens and caves of the earth.

Hebrews 11:35-38, Emphasis Mine

Hebrews 11 could be divided into two parts. The first part talks about those who heard God's voice and did something by faith, and the second part talks about those who did not receive their promise. The average American Christian has no concept of how the rest of the world lives. Most of us get up every morning to go to work and earn a decent salary. Others work from home, and some are retired and get up and try to decide what they should do that day for fun. Tragically, many in our world get up with one thing on their mind—where and how they can get enough food to live another day, and they have to walk long distances just to get enough water for their basic needs.

Then there is another group of people. These are called Christians, believers, followers of Jesus—different names in different countries. All of them have had a personal experience with the heavenly Father and have accepted Jesus Christ as their personal Savior. In some countries, if they express their faith in Jesus, they will be killed by their non-Christian neighbors or even their own family. It is considered a disgrace to the family when they choose to serve another god. In some areas of Southeast Asia, the houses of Christians are often burned by their neighbors or local authorities, and their churches are torn down. Other believers are put in prison for many years and are forced to exist in horrible conditions. Many are physically beaten because of their faith. This is what the second part of the book of Hebrews is referring to. The only difference is that these things are also happening today in the twenty-first century.

There are many men and women of God preaching the Gospel in the nations of the world today, and why the Lord chose me to be one of them, only He knows. There are many who are richer, smarter, better educated, more eloquent of speech, possibly even more spiritual. If I had to list my own qualifications, I would say that I'm hungry and thirsty for the things of the Spirit, I love people, and I've tried to remain faithful to what the Lord tells me to do. Maybe it's just because of His mercy. I'm not sure, but since He came into my life in 1971, He has allowed me to share His love in fifty countries around the world.

I have made mistakes and failed Him numerous times, and there have been times when I didn't trust Him as I should have, and times when I didn't love as He loves, but I've done my best to repent and follow the voice of the Holy Spirit. It has been my greatest honor to have met, prayed with, and ministered to brothers and sisters like the ones mentioned here in the second part of the book of Hebrews. I always wonder, "Who am I to speak to them or pray for them?" I cannot sufficiently answer that question.

INHERITING THE NATIONS

Many of my years of ministry have been spent working with my friend Sonny through a base in Bangkok, and there is no way to count the number of times I have been there for ministry or traveling through Bangkok en route to some other country in Southeast Asia with Sonny. This chapter is a small glimpse into the lives of some of the men and women we have encountered and served in the restricted nations of Asia, men and women of whom the world is not worthy. For the protection of these Christians, I will not be using their real names.

NORTHEAST INDIA-NAGALAND

I should explain a little about this area. If you look at a map of India, there is the main area and then, on the eastern part, there's a small area that goes up over Bangladesh and then upward in a northeasterly direction. When the British ruled India, these were seven independent nations with their own kings and royal families. When the British left, however, they made no provision for these seven nations, so the Indian military went into that area, exiled all the royalty, and took the entire area as part of India. There are still a lot of Indian military in the area. We refer to this area as the Seven Sisters, and Nagaland is one of them. It is also famous for the ghost peppers, the hottest chili peppers in the world.

While we were having a pastors' conference in Nagaland, one pastor asked if we would come and pray for his father who was in his nineties and his mother who was in her eighties. We met her as she was just coming back from working all day in the fields. I asked if we could hear a little of the father's testimony before we prayed for him. He told us that he had not been able to read or write but was a member of a Baptist Church back in the 1950s and 60s. Later, the Holy Spirit sovereignly came upon the group, and the people were filled with the Spirit, began to speak in tongues, received healing, and operated in the gifts of the Spirit. Because of this move of the Holy Spirit, Nagaland became ninety-nine percent Christian and was the only area of India that had no Hindu temples.

As the pastor's father continued to share his testimony with us, he said that one day he was in the church, and the Holy Spirit fell upon him. When he went home, even though he couldn't read or write, he picked up a Bible and started reading it for the first time. The Lord began to visit him and give him revelations about the Scriptures, and soon people, even pastors, began to come to his home to hear what the Lord was revealing to him.

At that point, my friend Sonny turned to me and said, "Are you ready to pray, Joe?"

I said, "Me, pray? Are you crazy?" I knelt in front of the elder brother, put his hand on my head, and said he needed to pray for us. He prayed for me, for Sonny, and for two other leaders from Canada who were with us. Before we left, we did pray for the man and his wife. I learned later from his son that it was a common manifestation among them that when someone was filled with the Holy Spirit who had not been able to read or write, they received the ability to read the Bible. When unbelievers saw this, they realized that it had to be from God, so this became one of the reasons so many were turning to the Lord.

That revival was so long ago that the new generations know nothing about the amazing move of God in those days and have turned to sex and drugs. Now it is estimated that the Christian population in Nagaland is down to only about fifty percent. One positive thing is that most Christians are very evangelistic and continue to preach the Gospel with signs and wonders. This is true in Nagaland and in the other regions of the Seven Sisters as well. Nagaland has made a commitments to send a large missionary force into mother nations

§

INHERITING THE NATIONS

I was invited to preach at a church in Nagaland, and a young lady named R translated for me. It was quite a large church with lot of members, and we had a good meeting. Later, when I was in a taxi with R, going back to meet my friends who had been speaking at other churches, I asked her what she did for a living. I had assumed that she was a member of that church. As it turned out, she was a missionary to the furthest area of Northeast India on the China border, in a place called Arunachal Pradesh. She said the living conditions there were very bad. In the winter, it was very cold, and many of the people still lived in bamboo houses. Many times, she said, they would fast for several days because there was no food ... until the military dropped sacks of rice from helicopters.

The first time R had gone there, she was with another young lady, but the conditions were so harsh that the other lady didn't stay. I asked her if the mission board had not warned them about what it was like before they went. She said they did, but she wanted to go where the Gospel had never been preached. I sat in that taxi thinking, "This young lady is more committed than I am, and she translated for me. I should be translating for her."

§

Pastor A invited Sonny and me to come and teach a group of Baptist pastors in West Bengal. Sonny is a real master at training leaders and has some amazing teachings that challenge them to come up to new levels of ministry. I don't remember what I was teaching about, but on the second day I decided to speak about the gifts of the Spirit, particularly prophecy and the word of knowledge. I used 1 Corinthians 12 as my foundation and said, "I'm going to demonstrate how to prophesy, and then you're all going to prophesy to one another." Understand that these were all Baptist pastors. Some of them had been baptized in the Holy Spirit, but most had received no teaching about the gifts of the Spirit.

THOSE OF WHOM THE WORLD WAS NOT WORTHY

One brother, who had been sitting near the front the day before with his arms folded, kept his arms folded the entire time. I called him up to pray for him. I instructed the pastors that I was just going be quiet and see what the Lord showed me or spoke to me. I took the brother by the hand and just stood there quietly. In my mind, all I could see was him sitting there with his arms folded. I finally said, "The only thing I'm seeing is you sitting there with your arms so tightly folded." I shook his arms and said, "Relax! Relax!" In that moment, he started weeping uncontrollably. I hugged him, prayed for him, and he went to his seat.

Soon my translator said to me, "Look at him." I looked over, and his face was glowing. He had a big smile on his face, his arms were no longer folded, and he just looked relaxed and peaceful.

I prayed for two more people. Unfortunately, I don't remember anything about the second person, but the third person was a lady. As soon as I touched her, she started to fall. I put my arm out and said, "Don't fall," and held her so she couldn't. I don't remember the word I gave her, but it really spoke to her. Then I turned to the pastors and said, "Okay, I want you to find a partner now, and you're going to give each other a word. I don't want you to pray. I just want you to hold hands, and be quiet. Then the Holy Spirit will speak to you and give you a word."

After a little while, I said, "Okay, give the word to your partner." The Lord was faithful, and everyone had a word except two. I walked over to one of the pastors and said, "Listen, and a word will come." I touched his ear and said, "Hear!" and he received a word immediately. I did the same with the other brother, and he, too, received a word. Pastor A told me the next day that many of the pastors hadn't slept all night. They stayed up talking about what had happened. Most of them had never seen prophecy or the word of knowledge in operation. They invited me to come back and teach more about the gifts of the Spirit. Unfortunately, my schedule has not permitted me to go.

§

INHERITING THE NATIONS

Sonny was invited to speak for two days at a large graduation ceremony for a theological school. He invited me and a pastor from the Philippines to join him, along with Pastor G from Nagaland. During the break times and in the evening after the meetings ended, Pastor G and I decided to walk around and pray for people, giving prophetic words as we were led.

We anointed the people with oil, laid hands on them, and prayed for those who were responsible for serving the food. We went into the kitchen and prayed for the cooks. We prayed for everybody we could find who was unable to attend the meetings. They were all very grateful, and the Lord was faithful in allowing us to give encouraging words and prayers.

Late one evening we were praying outside the area where the ladies were supposed to be sleeping, but when they heard us, they came out and wanted us to pray over them. One young lady opened her heart to us, confessing her sins and asking us to pray that the Lord would forgive her and give her victory over them.

During the first day of that ceremony, a government official who was a believer came with his bodyguards to the meeting. We took him into a private room, and several of us laid hands on him and prophesied.

N.E. INDIA-ARUNACHAL PRADESH

Arunachal Pradesh is another of the Seven Sisters of the northeast, and its northern border is with Tibet. In telling my stories of traveling, this one always has to be told.

We were invited to this area to teach at a leadership conference. Sometimes accommodations are challenging when you are on the mission field. When I was younger, living in the jungles of Ecuador was okay, but now that I'm older, it's a little more difficult. I usually don't mind where we stay, but the one condition I have is I must have a hot shower.

THOSE OF WHOM THE WORLD WAS NOT WORTHY

Because of problems with a visa getting into this area, we arrived late and had to quickly check into our hotel and then go directly to the meeting. When Brother Sonny advised me that the hotel didn't have hot water, I couldn't believe it. Then he said they had a device that heated water in a bucket, and we could use it to heat some water for a shower. The device was a metal coil that plugged into an electrical outlet. You would suspend that coil from a piece of wood straddling the rim of the bucket, and it would heat the water. No problem!

We went on to the meetings, had a great time, and later had dinner before returning to the hotel. Sonny and our friend from India had one room, and they had given me my own room. These were basically one-star rooms, but that was not a problem. I don't remember what we paid, but it was cheap. That night I put the heating coil into the bucket and plugged it in to prepare my hot water. I was looking forward to a nice hot shower after a long day of driving on dusty roads and then preaching quite late.

I entered the bathroom wearing only what I was born with, no clothes. I stuck my hand into the water to see if it was getting hot, not realizing that the coil was hooked up to a 220-volt outlet. My whole body began to shake like I was sitting in an electric chair. When I finally got my hand out of the bucket, my body was still tingling. I eventually unplugged the device and took a nice hot shower.

My bed was a large one, and I expected it to be fairly comfortable. However, when I got into it, two of the legs broke, and the bed came crashing down. This was unacceptable. I put my clothes on and went over and knocked on Sonny's door.

As I walked in, I noticed that their rug was rather squishy under my feet. It was completely soaked. Sonny told me that every time they flushed the toilet, the rug got wet. Apparently the sewer line ran under the rug and was broken. We needed a different hotel.

INHERITING THE NATIONS

The next day, while we were teaching, we sent a brother out to find us a better hotel. Sadly, when he returned, he informed us that the hotel we were in was the best one in town. At least it makes for an interesting story.

But the story doesn't end there. When I was in Armenia many years later, I met two pastors who had gone to that same city in Arunachal Pradesh and stayed at the same hotel. When I told them of my experience at that hotel, they had their own experience to relate. They said that the sheets were so dirty they requested fresh ones. Then, when the new sheets arrived, they were dirtier than the sheets they already had. We all had a good laugh about our adventures.

Recently, wile reviewing this chapter, I was talking to Sonny, and he reminded me of some things I had overlooked. As I have mentioned before, I have a lot of problems with Indian food. It's too spicy for me, and I don't like curry. That leaves me with a serious problem in several countries. Because our hotel was less than satisfactory, you can imagine how the food was there. It was a real challenge for me. Sonny reminded me that during the five days we were there, I ate forty-eight eggs. The meetings were the important part. They were well attended by leaders who were hungry for the Word of God, and so it was a real pleasure to give to them what the Lord had given to us.

The interior of the church had recently been painted white and had dark wooden trim and looked very beautiful. There was also a white concrete wall around the church property. But on the street side of that wall were piles of garbage where cows and dogs came to eat. It was so disgusting that one day, when I got up to preach, I decided to address the issue.

I said how beautiful the church looked but how horrible it was to have a garbage pile right in front of it. This was a bad testimony for a church, I said, and I challenged everyone to get up right that moment, go outside, and clean it all up. Thankfully, everyone participated in the cleanup. Sonny reminded me that all the men leaders had been dressed in suits and ties that day.

Our final meetings in Arunachal Pradesh were in the afternoon. The last meeting is always a time for personal ministry. We lay hands on the people, pray for them for an importation, and sometimes have a prophetic word for them. We want everyone to be encouraged and edified during their last time together.

After that meeting, the pastor took us to a small outdoor crusade that was being held in the area, and all of us on the team had a chance to share an encouraging word. The seating was very interesting. Instead of chairs, there were just small tree trunks for the people to sit on.

After we had shared in the meeting, the pastor took us to his home. He had planned for us to have a special home-cooked Indian meal before we left for our night flight back to Bangkok. As we entered his home, there was a massive table covered with dozens of plates with different types of Indian food. If you like Indian food, you would think you had entered Heaven. For me, it was quite the opposite. I thought to myself, "What is on this table?" As I looked toward the kitchen doorway, there were three women standing in the doorway looking at us. I could only imagine they had probably worked hard all day preparing this special meal. For me, it was time to pray. I didn't want to offend anyone, but I also did not want to eat anything on that table.

I cried out to the Lord, "Lord, help me," and, praise the Lord, He answered my prayer. Within a very short time, the power went out, all the lights went off, and the room was left in total darkness. Quickly our host got a few candles and put them on the table, but it did little to light up the room. It was an answer to prayer. I put some rice on my plate, and then went to sit in a very dark corner so that no one could see what I was or was not eating. Thank God for His mercy upon me. The lights never came back on the whole time we were in that dining room.

INHERITING THE NATIONS

After dinner we prayed for the pastor and for the ladies who had worked all day to prepare the meal. Then we left for the airport.

BHUTAN

On the northwestern side of the Seven Sisters is the mountainous nation of Bhutan. The official religion in Bhutan is Tibetan Buddhism, practiced by about seventy-five percent of the people. Freedom of religion is guaranteed by the king, but Bhutan's National Assembly banned the open practice of non-Buddhist and non-Hindu religions by resolutions passed in 1969 and 1979. Because of these resolutions, being a Christian in Bhutan can be very challenging.

The only way to enter Bhutan is on a tourist visa, which is very expensive. At the time of this writing, it costs $350.00 a day to get a visa for visiting Bhutan. Physically, Bhutan is a paradise. The rivers are crystal clear, and the mountains are majestic. Those who love trekking find it ideal. There is even a special hotel in a very concealed area where only the super-rich of the world go for vacation.

We were speaking at a pastors' conference for a few days in a church, and on the last day, we visited the host pastor's home for lunch. After we had eaten, the pastor told us that one of the other pastors, a man who lived in a small mountainous village, had to leave to take the bus home and wouldn't be attending the afternoon meeting. We decided to pray for him for his safety. We prayed, and as he was preparing to leave, Brother Rudy from Australia said to me, "I just had a vision of him, and in the vision, he was leaving the ministry."

I suggested that we tell the pastor what he had seen and pray again, and we did. It wasn't until the next day that the host pastor told us that the other pastor had come to the meetings just to turn in his resignation. Then, however, when my friend from Australia had told him about the vision, he realized that it was the Lord, changed his mind, and decided to recommit himself and remain in the ministry.

THOSE OF WHOM THE WORLD WAS NOT WORTHY

A prophetic word, a word of knowledge, a vision, or a dream can be a powerful thing to encourage people and help them to make the proper decisions for their life.

I'm sure it's not easy being a pastor in Bhutan, especially in an isolated area, but the Lord saw this man's heart. Since he was needed in that area, the Lord had sent a brother from Australia to encourage him to keep the faith and run the race until the final day.

In 2011 I was invited to minister at a youth conference in Bhutan. I decided to invite a friend of mine, Ed West, who has a real heart for youth, to go with me. Two other young people from Singapore also joined us—Moses and his then girlfriend, Ewan. They are now a married couple with two precious children.

The only way to describe Ed is to say "he is over the top" when it comes to praying for people. He is a man of power and prayer and really blessed a lot of young people during those meetings. I will be telling more about Ed in Chapter 34.

Moses and Ewan work with the youth in their church in Singapore, and they, too, really impacted the youth during our meetings. Moses is continuing to minister to the youth in Singapore and also taking ministry teams to other countries in Southeast Asia.

The final night of those meetings, everyone wanted prayer and so we decided to have what we call a "prayer tunnel." We make two lines of the people who will be doing the praying. We face each other and allow the people who want prayer to walk between us. It is a very powerful method that allows everyone to get prayer and even prophetic words as they walk through the tunnel.

PAKISTAN

There are many stories of the Lord visiting Muslims in dreams. One member of the Taliban who oversaw the local Taliban Internet site, had a young daughter with a heart problem. One night he had a dream. He saw a man in white standing over his daughter. He woke up in fear and ran to his daughter's room. There stood the man he had seen. He was standing over the daughter, touching her heart with his hand. As the man rushed into the room, the other man disappeared.

The daughter said, "Daddy, why did you scare him?"

The father said, "Who was that?"

She answered, "That was Jesus. He touched my heart and told me I was healed."

The father took his daughter to a hospital for an examination. Sure enough, her heart was healed, and she had no more heart problems. This father posted the testimony on the Taliban website. About ninety minutes later, it was taken down. He estimates that many thousands had probably already read the entire testimony.

§

Several of us from the Bangkok base were invited to an Anglican church in Pakistan. I was in Bangkok at the time, and so I applied for a visa at the Pakistani Embassy in Bangkok but was denied. My friends made plans to go without me.

The church in Pakistan was built like a rectangle and has an open courtyard in the middle. One week before my friends were scheduled to travel there, the children of that church had gotten out of Sunday school and were playing in the courtyard when a young Afghan boy with bombs strapped to his body under his coat walked into the courtyard and blew himself up, killing many of the children. Hearing the explosion, the adults rushed out into the courtyard. At that moment, another young Afghan boy came into the courtyard and blew himself up. In all, more than two hundred people died in that courtyard that day. The team from Bangkok arrived the following week.

You can imagine the grief, sorrow, and anger that filled the people's minds over what had happened in that courtyard. "Where was God when the bombers came in?" "We need to find out who is responsible for this atrocity and bring them to justice." There were many questions to my friends, but there could be no answers. They could not alleviate the pain in these people's souls. They decided that all they could do was worship the Lord, and so they began to pray and worship. They all concluded, during worship, that they had to forgive the bombers and pray for those responsible for these deaths.

Across the border of Pakistan in Afghanistan is a school with two hundred students being trained as suicide bombers. The church in Pakistan was praying, and God was listening to their prayers. He was moving in that school in Afghanistan upon the three leaders who had planned the bombing. The Lord appeared to them in dreams, but they were not telling each other. Then, one day, one of them asked, "Do you men have anything to tell me?"

The others responded by saying, "Well, do you have anything to tell us?" They finally confessed to one another that Jesus had appeared to them in their dreams, and they all became believers in Jesus.

You might say, "How do you know that?" The reason I know is that the three Taliban leaders came across the border to the Anglican church and confessed that they were the ones who had planned the bombing, that they had become Christians, and had come to ask forgiveness. They knew that the Pakistani police were looking for them, and they were ready to go to jail, but first they needed forgiveness. This is the amazing power of the Gospel in action!

The believers in the Anglican church had already been forgiving them and praying for them, and now here they stood before them, also believers in Jesus, asking for forgiveness. They forgave them and decided not to call the police. Then the Taliban brothers asked for a favor. They said, "We must go back and preach to our fellow Taliban, but we know that if we do, we will be killed, and our families will be killed. We're asking if you would take our wives and children and protect them here in Pakistan." The Anglican believers accepted this responsibility, received the families, and the three Taliban returned to Afghanistan to preach the Gospel. I learned from some friends recently that they have already planted five churches among the Taliban in Afghanistan.

VIETNAM

I remember well my first trip to Saigon when it was still part of South Vietnam. It was later renamed Ho Chi Minh City after the Vietnam War ended and North Vietnam overran the South. As I walked around that city, I wondered, "Why was there so much war here?" First, there had been war with the French and then, later, with the Americans, and millions had died. There was no great city to conquer. There was no gold or silver mines or oil fields to possess. Why was there so much death in this country? Then I felt the Lord opening my eyes, and I saw something more precious than gold and silver, something greater than cities to conquer. It was the souls of men and women, people with dreams and destinies who were now eliminated by war.

The Vietnamese people are very friendly, the food is delicious, and it's a wonderful place to visit … if you're a tourist, but that's not my calling. We were there to encourage and empower the Christian believers, and they were hungry and thirsty for the things of the Spirit.

In the north of Vietnam and reaching into Laos live a tribal people called the Hmong. During the Vietnam War, the CIA recruited these people to attack the North Vietnamese supply lines, so when the war was over, the Hmong were greatly persecuted by the new Communist regime.

In the highlands of the north, the government supplied the Hmong with small transistor radios so they could broadcast Communist propaganda to them. What the authorities didn't know was that this small radio also picked up a Christian station from the Philippines that was broadcasting the Gospel.[1] As a result, revival came to the Hmong. It is

---

1. Thank God for FEBC, the Far East Broadcasting Corporation, that sends the Gospel into many sur-

estimated that between 100,0000 and 200,000 Hmong became believers. What the devil had meant for evil God turned around for His glory.

It's difficult to say if there is religious freedom in Vietnam. The constitution says there is, but a lot depends on the local government, which most often is anti-Christian. Permits are required to have any sort of religious function, and most of the time the local government will not issue the proper permits. Therefore, many meetings still take place in secret, and there is still a great need for Bibles that must be smuggled in from other countries.

Just this week I was talking to Pastor B, one of the leaders in Vietnam, and when I told him I was writing a book, he reminded me of my first trip there, when Sonny and I met him and another pastor. In the evening I invited them, with some other pastors, to go to an American all-you-can-eat buffet that I saw advertised in a tourist booklet. There were probably about eight of us. Most of the pastors had never been in a fancy hotel, and they had never seen a buffet. We ordered drinks and then proceeded to go up to the buffet line and get our food.

In the process, I looked back and noticed that several of the pastors were still sitting at the table, not coming up. Pastor B went back and talked to them. He told me they said that most of their members didn't have much food, and they felt it would be wrong to spend money and eat that much food when their members had so little. Pastor B explained to them that this was a gift that Joe wanted to give them, and for him it was not a lot of money. They finally understood and enjoyed their first American all-you-can-eat buffet. Pastor B told me on the phone just the other day that he remembers they were eating so much they had to keep loosening their belts.

§

Pastor B told me about a water baptism they had planned for two hundred people at a lake outside of the city. The people had all arrived,

---

rounding nations. FEBC broadcasts are heard in 145 languages and 50 countries around the world aired from 260 stations and transmitters, totaling 1,571 hours of programming a day.

and then they received a phone call informing them that the police had somehow learned about the baptism and were coming to arrest the leaders. Pastor B told everyone to quickly get in the water, and then he said, "In the name of the Father, Son, and the Holy Spirit, I baptize you all." Then he commanded them all to go under the water. Before they came up from the water, he ran to his car and escaped. When the police arrived, all they saw was people enjoying a day at the beach.

§

In a village outside of the city, government officials sent people to tear down a small Christian church. When the believers rebuilt it, the government officials were furious. The police chief came on his motor scooter to the church and announced to the pastor, "As long as I'm police chief, there will be no Christian churches in this village." He got on his scooter to leave, and as he drove over the railroad tracks, he failed to see an approaching train. It hit him, and he died. The church is still standing.

§

A pastor from a very poor area was arrested and brought to the police station where he was questioned by the chief. This police chief, in front of some of his officers, made a deal with the pastor. He said, "If you can convince me that there is a God, you can have your church in this town. But, if you can't, the church must be torn down."

The pastor answered, "I'm just a poor uneducated pastor, and I don't have the proper vocabulary to convince you that there is a God. But one thing I know: one second after you breathe your last breath you will know there is a God." They all laughed and sent the pastor on his way. That night the chief and some of his men were in a local bar, celebrating and drinking a lot, when suddenly the chief had a heart attack and died. The other officers remembered what the poor pastor had said, and they never bothered him again.

§

THOSE OF WHOM THE WORLD WAS NOT WORTHY

The mayor of a Vietnamese city died, and his wife was heartbroken. She was a believer and she went to a local pastor, Pastor L, and asked if he would come and pray for her husband. The pastor went to the city morgue with her, but when the body was brought out, he looked at it and said, "Okay, put him back." He didn't pray.

The next day Pastor L came back again, and the body was once again brought out. Again he looked at it, and then said, "Okay, put him back." Many in the coroner's office began to wonder what was going on with this pastor. Why didn't he pray?

Pastor L came back on the third day. By now the mayor's wife and other family members and friends had gathered, and they wondered what this pastor was doing. This time he prayed, and the God of Heaven, who hears and answers prayer, heard his plea, and the mayor, who had been dead now for three days, came back to life and became a believer like his wife.

Afterward, the people asked the pastor why he hadn't prayed on the first day or the second day. "Well," he said, "in the Bible, Jesus raised Lazarus from the dead on the third day, and even Jesus was in the grave for three days before He was resurrected. That's why I had to wait three days." Sometimes simple prayers from believers with little education are very powerful!

LAOS

Laos is a Socialistic country, but its government is Communist, and because of that, they are very hostile to Christianity and most extreme when it comes to persecution. I know many first-hand stories that I don't feel I can share in this book because it would jeopardize too many of my friends who live in Laos. I will just share two stories about people I've met personally, and I think they will be okay to tell.

INHERITING THE NATIONS

One family had been meeting with a group of about two hundred believers in a private meeting in their home until the police found out about it and were continually harassing them. One Christmas Eve, they cut the pastors throat and left him to die on the main road of their village. Three months later I was in a conference in Bangkok. At the end of the meeting, we began to pray for people. Near me stood this man's widow with her hands raised high in the air, worshiping the Lord. It made me think of Hebrews 13:15:

Therefore by Him [Jesus] let us continually offer the sacrifice of praise to God, that is, the fruit of our lips, giving thanks to His name.

As I looked at this woman with her hands raised to God in worship, I was seeing the ultimate definition of the sacrifice of praise. Her husband had been killed by the police, so there was no one to complain to. They were the law in Laos. Now she had young children to raise by herself, and what about the church, the believers who had looked to her and her husband for their spiritual growth? What would happen to them? What should she do now?

I have over seventy thousand photos stored in my computer, but I chose twelve of my favorites to put around a world map on the wall of my office. One of them is the picture of this woman with her hands raised to Heaven, offering up the sacrifice of praise.

I know she is a woman of prayer, so I'm sure she had many days struggling with the Lord about what she should do now that her husband was dead. She must have counted the cost and decided to make the sacrifice. In the end, she became the leader of the church that, eventually, under her leadership, grew from two hundred to five thousand members. I believe it's the largest church in Laos at the present time.

Whenever I'm in Southeast Asia and I see this woman, I always bow my head and ask her to lay hands on me and pray for me. She probably thinks I'm a little crazy, but I know there's an anointing upon her life that I don't have, and I know that when she prays, the Lord can impart things into my spirit that will help me in my journey toward my destiny.

§

Pastor L and his wife had a small underground church in Laos. He was also a government worker. One day the police came, and he was arrested and sentenced to serve thirteen years in prison. His wife also took over the leadership of the church.

Because this brother was a government worker and had become a Christian, the authorities decided to make an example of him and be very harsh. He was placed in solitary confinement many times, where he was only given a handful of rice each day. When he was in a normal cell with the general population, he shared the Gospel, and many prisoners became Christians. Some of them, when they were released from prison, joined his wife's church. Under her leadership, the church grew to three thousand members, all while her husband was in prison for his faith.

I met this precious man shortly after he was released from prison, and I asked him, "Brother, what was it like in prison?"

He said, "Joe, it was depressing, especially when I was in solitary confinement. Sometimes I would cry all day long. During some of those days, a man in white would appear in the dark cell, and His glory would light up the cell. Other times, when I could worship, angels would appear, and their presence would illuminate the cell." What more needs to be said?

CHINA

The testimonies of the believers in China are like the stories in the book of Acts. Persecution under the Communist regime has only strengthened and purified the believers, the majority of whom still gather in secret home groups. Most believers in those home groups pray for two to three hours before going to work in the morning. It is estimated that forty thousand people a day convert to Christianity in China.

To make themselves look good before the world, the Chinese government proclaims that they are printing and distributing Bibles inside China. The truth is they cannot print enough Bibles to meet the demand, and if you get a government Bible, you must give all your personal information. So, then they know where you live and that you are a Christian. There is still a massive need to smuggle Bibles to the underground churches in China.

Christian evangelists are daily traveling the cities and villages of China proclaiming the Gospel. It is estimated that eighty percent of them are women. The astounding growth of Christianity in China, particularly, in the underground home groups, is attributed to many things.

Here are five things that Chinese believers are ready to do <u>anytime or anywhere</u>:

1. **Pray:** Most get up before daybreak and pray two to three hours.
2. **Testify:** At a bus station right next to a police station, some young Chinese ladies decided to preach. They knew they were in danger of being arrested, but they did it anyway. Sure enough, they were arrested and beaten. Thankfully, they were eventually released.
3. **Suffer for Jesus:** A pastor's daughter was jailed and beaten. In the same cell with her was a young lady who had committed murder. Nobody else was willing to associate with her, but even though the pastor's daughter was in pain from her beating, she reached out to that young lady with God's love, and the murderer received the Lord. Witnessing this, all the other ladies in that cell became believers too.

THOSE OF WHOM THE WORLD WAS NOT WORTHY

4. **Flee or Disappear:** Sometimes believers have to be ready to run from the police and hide until things cool off.
5. **Die for Jesus:** No one knows for sure the actual number of the Chinese martyrs, but there were many.

§

Two young Chinese women traveled to thirteen villages in a year. When they arrived at a village, they would ask, "What is the main problem here?" In one village they were told that at the end of the street was a demon-possessed man. Whenever anyone walked near his house, he would come out and beat them up. The two women began to pray.

I don't know how long they prayed. I'm assuming they prayed until the Lord told them, "Now is the time." With many people from the village watching, they walked down to the demon-possessed man's home. When he saw them, he ran out, enraged, to attack them. Then, however, he mysteriously fell on his knees in front of them. They prayed, and he was delivered and saved. The result was that the entire village accepted Jesus. In all of the thirteen villages they went to, the results were the same. In each of the villages, everyone came to Christ.

§

A believer saw many people working in the fields to harvest the crops. Just then, a dark rain cloud threatened to prevent them from completing the harvest. Then he saw a large machine appear, and it was able to finish the harvest before the rain came. He realized that the large machine represented unity, so he did his best to bring unity among the Christian believers and leaders. Because of that unity, sixty million people were saved in that area of China.

§

One Christian man was sentenced to a hard labor camp, where his job was to break up rocks every day, and he did that for many years. When he finally got out, the Lord gave him a vision to carve a cave out of a mountain. He did this, and the cave he carved out became a secret training center for believers. What he had suffered in the labor camp the Lord used for His glory.

§

One Chinese brother was sent to prison, and his assigned job was to clean the feces and urine out of a hole that was six feet by six feet and six feet deep. He had to do that every day. He said that he loved that job, first, because he didn't have to be in the cell that was overcrowded with prisoners. Second, it smelled so bad that the guards wouldn't come near him. This allowed him to be alone all day, and he could sing to the Lord and quote scriptures. He said that smelly hole became his fragrant garden where the Lord would come and speak and minister to him. Many years later, when he was released from prison, he made the statement that he now missed the intimate times he'd had in that secret garden with the Lord.

§

There are many hard labor camps in China today. The Communist authorities call them "reeducation centers." Many of them are in western China, where the people group known as Uyghurs live. Most of the Uyghurs are Muslims, and they have carried out terrorist attacks around China. Many believe the government built these reeducation camps specifically for the Uyghurs, but many Uyghurs are Christians. Some have been in those "reeducation camps" for a very long time, and if they are expected of being Christians, they may never be released. I personally know a Christian missionary couple who lived in China among the Uyghurs for fourteen years and have many wonderful testimonies of their conversions.

One couple had a fruit farm. Because they were Christians, the husband was taken away by the police during the night to one of these "reeducation camps," and he has never been seen since. The only reason we know he's still in there is that some people who got out reported that he was still there.

After he was taken away, the authorities also shut the water off to their farm. "You're Christian," the family was told, "so let your God take care of your farm." The wife became totally discouraged. Her husband was in prison, and now there was no water to produce crops. She abandoned the farm and moved to the city. When harvest time came, she received a communication from one of her neighbors. They were asking why she hadn't come to harvest her fruit. She told the messenger that the water supply had been cut off, so there wouldn't be any fruit. "Oh, but there is a lot of fruit," she was told. She now returned to the farm to see what was happening. Somehow, miraculously, the trees were being watered from an underground source, and she was able to harvest the fruit and sell it in the city for a good price.

§

In China, there is a maximum-security prison for those who receive life sentences, and no one gets out of that prison alive. A pastor was sentenced to this prison. When he arrived, he was beaten by the guards until he was unconscious and then thrown into a cell. When he finally regained consciousness, he was lying on the floor, and many faces were standing over him, looking down at him, asking who he was. He explained that he was a Christian pastor. They told him the whole time he was unconscious there had been a light coming down from the ceiling moving up and down his body. He shared the Gospel, and everyone in that cell received Jesus.

When he began to teach his cellmates Christian songs, the guards were so upset that they took him out of the cell, beat him unconscious again, and threw him into a different cell. The same thing happened this time. When he regained consciousness, many cellmates were looking down on him, and they told the same story. They had seen a light that came down from the ceiling and was moving up and down his body as he lay there unconscious. He shared the Gospel with that

INHERITING THE NATIONS

group of men, all of them received Jesus, and he taught them Christian songs too.

This happened over and over until he had been beaten and thrown into every cell and had led every prisoner to Jesus and taught them Christian songs. The guards became so upset with him that they threw him out of the prison. That man, to my knowledge, is the only one who has ever come out of that particular prison alive.

I can imagine that the Lord looked down from Heaven, saw the prison filled with men who were on their way to Hell and would never experience the love of the Father in Heaven. They had no hope of ever getting out of that prison, so He sent someone to share the Gospel with them and show them the way to receive forgiveness, peace, and eternal life. God had seen a pastor He could trust to go to prison, take the beatings, and still share the love of the Father, so that all those prisoners could one day feel the embrace of the Father in Heaven.

§

Four of us traveled to Shangri La, China, which is located near the Burma/Tibet border. We got two hotel rooms. In one of them, we planned to secretly teach ten Tibetan believers who had come over the border for this purpose. We were with them for three intense days, sharing the Bible and praying with them. Some of them sat on the beds, and others sat on the floor.

The first day I was teaching, I just stood in front of the dresser sharing some of the stories from the Bible. I don't remember exactly what I was teaching, but I do remember that I was using the story of Noah. As I looked into their eyes, it appeared to me that they didn't understand a thing I was saying. Then I realized that they have never read a Bible and had never heard of Noah. Everything I was saying to these young, but hungry believers, was brand new to them.

One brother had been a Tibetan monk and had only been a believer for nine months, but he already had sixty-five people he was teaching in an underground church. The amazing thing was he didn't even own a Bible, for there was no Bible available in his dialect. Before we left that place, we made a commitment to find Bibles for him.

BURMA, NOW CALLED MYANMAR

Myanmar, formerly known as Burma, is a very unique and challenging country, the largest in mainland Southeast Asia. It is a Buddhist stronghold that has trapped the majority of its people in darkness. Mandalay, where we have a Bible school, is a place where many of the Burmese people come to worship powerful Buddhist deities.

The northeast corner of the country is known as the Golden Triangle. It is where Myanmar, Thailand, and Loas come together. The majority of the opium in the world comes out of this area. Opium is given freely to all teenagers by the Burmese military to enslave and neutralize the younger generation, and the sale of these drugs fuels the military government.

We have a yearly conference in Bangkok to which we bring leaders from the thirteen countries we are working in. One year a pastor from Myanmar was speaking. With tears, he shared how his son had become a drug addict and asked for prayer. We laid hands on him and prayed for the family and his son. Praise the Lord, the following year he testified that his son got free and was now leading a drug-rehab center in their city.

Surprisingly, some North Koreans, trying to escape their own ills at home, end up in Myanmar. There are many people, believers and non-believers alike, who are trying to escape from North Korea. Most of them go to China or Mongolia and eventually make their way down into the countries of Southeast Asia. There they can apply for political asylum and eventually go to some other country where they can start a better life.

A pastor I know in Myanmar was helping a group of believers who were assisting North Koreans. One of the Burmese believers was caught and put in jail. He admitted what he had been doing, but he also told the police that Pastor M was helping the North Koreans as well. So they went and arrested him too. He was sentenced to twelve months in prison. He couldn't believe what was happening and was complaining to the Lord for not protecting him from the police. He was also very angry with his friend who had told the police what he was doing. He was eventually put into a prison cell with twenty-five other men. These men were rejoicing and told him that he was an answer to their prayers. They had all become believers and we're praying that the Lord would send them someone who could help them grow in their new-found faith.

Pastor M was truly an answer to their prayers, even though he wasn't happy about being in prison. Now, he changed his attitude and poured himself into these men, teaching them the Bible and helping them to learn Christian songs of worship. This became a very rewarding time for him.

When the twelve-month sentence was finally ending, Pastor M asked the other men to pray for him because he would be leaving prison and returning to his church. They refused to pray. "No," they said, "we need you here. We cannot give you our blessing to leave." The pastor promised that he would not forget them. He would send others from his church to continue to teach them. Eventually, they relented and blessed him. The Lord had seen their hearts and knew that they were hungry for the Word of God, so He had sent His servant, Pastor M, to feed them.

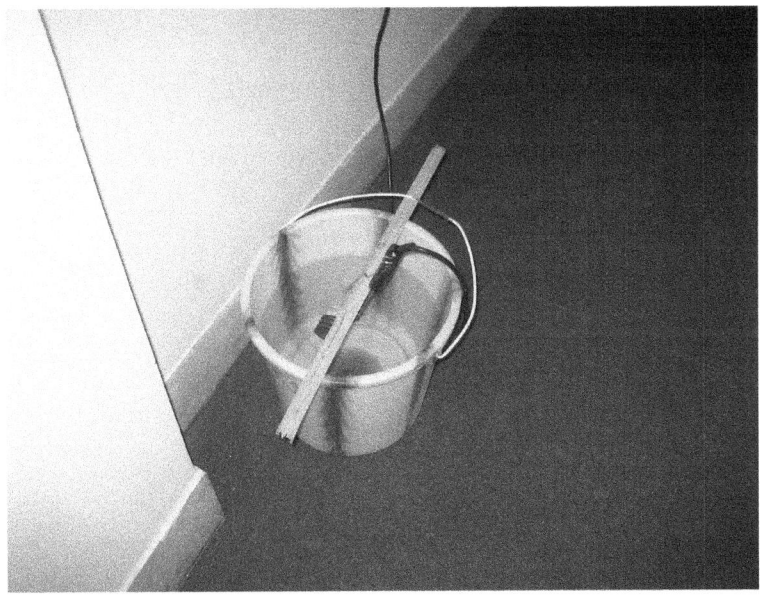

The one-star hotel in NE India

A hot shower?

In Bhutan with my friend Rudy from Australia

Praying over the waters of Bhutan

A fire tunnel in Bhutan

Nagaland, a pastor and his father who received the ability to read the Bible when he was baptized in the Holy Spirit

Teaching in China

Teaching leaders in Pakistan

CHAPTER 24

BETRAYAL—THE MAKING OF A LEADER

And while He was still speaking, behold, a multitude; and he who was called Judas, one of the twelve, went before him and drew near to Jesus to kiss Him. But Jesus said to him, "Judas, are you betraying the Son of Man with a kiss?"   Luke 22:47-48

This is one of the chapters I dreaded writing, but it's part of my story, an important part. Many times, when I speak to leadership, I tell this story. Why? Because if you are to be a leader, you can be sure betrayal will come your way. I believe it is part of the process in the making of a leader.

Whenever I was home in California, I spent a lot of time with a couple named Bob and Pat. Bob was a scientist at the Jet Propulsion Laboratory in Pasadena. Later, he became a teacher at Melodyland High School. Pat was involved in many types of ministries and always had some type of Christian meeting going on in their home. Whenever guest speakers were in the area, she invited them to come, where many of us from different type of churches in the area gathered to hear them. These were powerful times of teaching, ministry, and prayer and created a more intimate environment to know great men and women of God. Because people came from different churches, it was also a place to meet new brothers and sisters, and many great friendships were developed in that home.

I had not dated since my experience in Brazil with the false prophetess, but at one of these meetings, I met a young lady named Candace, and eventually invited her to go with me to a church in the mountains an hour from my home. The two pastors of that church and their wives had become my closest friends, so whenever I was in town, I went there for fellowship with them and to speak in their church.

The head pastor of that church had gone to seminary with me, and the assistant pastor was his brother-in-law. Over the years, I had developed an incredible bond with these two couples. I would do anything for them, and they would do anything for me. It was a very special relationship, so I was excited to introduce them to Candace, so that they could get to know her, and she could get to know them.

This was the first time Candace and I had done anything together. It was a Friday night service, and we were excited to see what God would do. The worship and the time of ministry were great as always, and we stayed awhile afterward fellowshipping with my friends.

I was still traveling overseas, but whenever I was home after that, Candace and I did things together. We seemed to have a lot in common, and eventually we began to talk about marriage. I even took her back to New York once when I was ministering there, so that she could meet some of my friends. She stayed in my brother's home so she could get to know some of my family. Everyone loved her, and I was excited about our relationship. Candace loved the Lord, and I sensed that overseas we would complement each other and be a blessing in many nations. I eventually came to the conclusion that it was time for us to marry.

I realize that there are always two sides to every story, so I want to be honest and say this is my side of the story. In my eyes, I loved Candace, and she loved me, and so marriage was the logical next step. I also need to reemphasize that the two pastor friends and their wives I mentioned were amazing Christians, and we enjoyed deep fellowship together. Again, I loved them, and they loved me.

INHERITING THE NATIONS

The assistant pastor worked very near my fiancee, so he stopped by a few times to have lunch with her. There was nothing secret about this. She always told me about it.

I can't remember the exact time frame from when Candace and I met to when tragedy struck our relationship. The bottom line is this: my friend, the assistant pastor, left the church, he left his wife and children, and he ran away with Candace. Words cannot describe the depth of pain this betrayal caused me. The man had a beautiful wife, two wonderful children, and was helping pastor a wonderful church. Why did he have to steal my fiancee? For more than two months, I would go to bed every night thinking, "How can I kill him and not go to jail?" Then I would get out of bed, get on my knees, and pray, "Lord, I will to forgive him." Then I would get back in bed and think, "How could I kill him and still go to Heaven?" Every night, night after night, week after week, this went on. It was tormenting. He had been one of my best friends. How could he do this to me?

King David lamented about the betrayal of a friend in Psalm 55:12-14:

> *For it is not an enemy who reproaches me;*
> *Then I could bear it.*
> *Nor is it one who hates me who has exalted himself against me;*
> *Then I could hide from him.*
> *But it was you, a man my equal,*
> *My companion and my acquaintance.*
> *We took sweet counsel together,*
> *And walked to the house of God in the throng.*

It's my observation and personal experience that real betrayal can only come from someone close to you.

Eventually, a pastor friend and his wife invited me to come and stay with them for a while at their home in North Carolina. I went, in hopes that they could help me, and I could find peace in my soul once again.

One night, as I was getting ready for bed, I had a demonic visitation. I was sitting on the edge of the bed when the spirit realm opened, and there stood within a couple feet of me a big, black, hairy demon. He was very scary looking, and I knew he had come to kill me. Just as he lunged at me, an angel appeared and killed him. Then the spirit realm closed.

Near this couple's home was a large Christian ministry, and one night we went there to attend the service. I don't remember many details about the message, but the speaker was talking about forgiveness. He said, "This offense will become one of two things in your life. If you don't forgive, it will become your tombstone, the death of your dreams and visions, the death of your ministry and destiny, and possibly your physical death. If you do forgive, it will become a stepping-stone," and he drew a verbal picture of steps going upward. "These," he said, "are stepping-stones into your destiny."

Then he told the story of the betrayal of Jesus. Jesus had poured His life into twelve men. He lived, ate, and slept with them for three years. He showed them how to minister and then He gave them authority to minister themselves. He poured into them everything He had, to prepare them for their destinies, and yet one of them betrayed Him. Jesus, the King of Kings and the Lord of Lords, washed the feet of His disciples, and among them was Judas, the one who would betray His Master.

The night came, and Judas, with a group of guards, drew near and kissed Jesus. It was a kiss of betrayal and the agreed-upon sign that this was the Man the soldiers should take. The truth, however, is that this betrayal would move Jesus into His destiny. The cross and

INHERITING THE NATIONS

His crucifixion on it would pay for your sins and mine. The betrayal of Jesus would bring the salvation of multitudes of people from many nations.

That night in North Carolina, when the message was over, the preacher gave an altar call, and I went forward. I laid down my pain, my broken heart, the anger, the bitterness, the girl I wanted to marry, and I forgave my best friend for stealing her. It was done! I was free! Praise the Lord!

I must be honest and say that although forgiving him brought me freedom, the devil continued to attack me. Now I began to question myself. What had I done wrong that allowed my fiancee to be stolen from me? Was I the guilty one, not him? Was I even worthy to be in ministry? The questions continued to bombard my mind to the point that I felt I needed to step down from international ministry.

For the next several years, I stopped ministering. I got counsel from several pastors, continued to go to church, read my Bible, and prayed. The enemy had convinced me that I was no longer worthy to be in the Master's service.

When I left North Carolina, I decided to go to my hometown, Albany, New York, and stay with my brother and his family, to recover and rethink my future. My brother had a small farm there, and I helped him do things around the farm, to get physically in shape again. He built a special bedroom for me there, where I could have privacy. Although I had forgiven the betrayer and was free from bitterness, I still missed Candace very much and couldn't envision going forward without her. This caused me to slip into a deep depression with eventual thoughts of suicide.

My brother and his family were not believers, and I thought to myself: "If I commit suicide in their home, when they find me, they'll question my Christianity and probably never become believers themselves." Somehow I had to put this terrible thought of suicide out of my mind.

A friend of mine from California was continually calling to check up on me, and I eventually confessed to him that I had been having thoughts of suicide, but knew that I couldn't do it in my brother's home. This man was a worship leader at that time at the Eagle's Nest Ministries, and he called his Pastor, Gary Greenwald, and told him what was going on with me. Pastor Gary immediately called me and told me I needed to get back to California where I could be among friends, and he invited me to come spend some time with him. I knew he was right.

I flew back to California, and for the next two or three weeks, I spent every moment with Pastor Gary, except when I slept at the home of a friend of mine. I was at every church service, every business meeting, we ate together and prayed together, laughed together, and even went to the movies together for relaxation. I hadn't been to a movie since I became a Christian, not because I thought it was wrong; I just didn't have time for movies. Pastor Gary was a very creative person, and he loved to go to movies, and I enjoyed going with him.

The mental and emotional healing I needed came by just spending time with a friend, someone who cared for me, not because of my ministry, but just because he cared. I'm not sure where I would be today if Pastor Gary had not reached out to me. I owe him an eternal debt.

I started attending his church regularly, and eventually an elder in the church, John Zahn, offered me a room in his home where I could stay for free. I started doing a few jobs for my brother Steve, because I had to start earning money to live. Other people saw my work and asked if I would do things for them. It all eventually resulted in me starting a tile contracting business. It was hard work, but the money was good, and I think I can honestly say that on every job I shared the Gospel with my customers.

I was leading a good Christian life, going to church, and blessing other people financially, but it wasn't enough. Why? Because I had

INHERITING THE NATIONS

left my calling and destiny and, in doing that, I had also robbed other people I was destined to share the Gospel with in other nations. Worst, the fire that had long been in my heart for the nations of the world had been extinguished by the guilt and shame of my betrayal.

One night I attended church with a friend of mine. At a certain part of the service, the pastor said, "There is someone here tonight who was in full-time ministry, but you left the ministry, and the Lord is wanting you to return. Who is that?" A few people went forward. One by one, he asked them, "Were you in full-time ministry?"

Each one answered, "No, just part-time."

Then my friend began to poke me and say, "It's you."

I said, "No it's not."

The pastor continued his call. "You were in full-time ministry. Who are you?"

Again, my friend said, "It's you." Then he waved at the pastor and pointed to me.

The pastor looked at me and said, "Is it you?"

I finally admitted it was probably me, and he began to prophesy and pray for me. Unfortunately, I don't remember much of what was said that night except this: "The Lord wants you to get your bags packed. It's time to return to ministry." I knew that was a word from the Lord, and yet at the time I didn't do anything to respond to that prophetic word.

Then one day I was reading the book of Jonah. In chapter 1, the Lord told Jonah to go to Nineveh and to cry against that city, for its wickedness had come up before Him. But Jonah disobeyed and fled from the presence of the Lord. He found a ship going to Tarshish. Then, it says in verse 3:

But Jonah arose to flee to Tarshish from the presence of the LORD. He went down to Joppa, and found a ship going to Tarshish; so HE PAID

*THE FARE, and went down into it, to go with them to Tarshish from the presence of the L*ORD. (Emphasis Mine)

He paid the fare. In other words, there is always a price to pay when we disobey the divine call upon our lives. We lose the gift of God's presence and intimacy with the Master, and the people we were destined to go to also lose. They will never hear the glorious Gospel from our lips, they will never feel the healing touch of our hands, and their eternal destiny is sealed by our disobedience. Yes, there is always a price to pay when we disobey the Master's voice, a BIG price!

I don't fully understand the theology of what I'm about say, but it seems that God allows some of us to disobey Him, to enjoy the pleasures of sin for a season, to do what we want to do, not His will, but our own. However, it seems that some callings are far too important for that. They matter for the Kingdom, and it seems that the Lord looks down from Heaven and says, "Enough is enough! You will not run from Me any longer! You will obey Me!"

It's at those times that the Master, who sees all things, begins to bring correction and discipline that cause us to return to Him and our destiny. We return to His will and abandon our own. His loving arms reach out to us, and we come back to His presence.

In the book of Jonah, the Lord prepared a great fish to bring Jonah back to his calling, and for three days the Bible says he was in the belly of that great fish. There Jonah called upon the Lord. I'm sure it was painful there, and it was a place of great darkness, but the Lord was working in the darkness with Jonah, and He can work in our darkness too.

As I was reading Jonah 3:1-2, the Lord of Heaven stood up and loudly spoke to me:

*Now the word of the L*ORD *came to Jonah the second time, saying, "Arise, go to Nineveh ... ."*

INHERITING THE NATIONS

God's call to me for ministry came a second time, and this time I returned to the ministry and to my calling to the nations of the world. I remember that He also said to me, "I never told you to leave the ministry!" I was chastened and repentant.

Some years later, I don't remember the time span, I got a call from Candace, the lady I had planned to marry. She wanted to see me. We went out to dinner together, and she asked me to forgive her and tried to explain what was going on in her heart and emotions during that time that had caused it all. I forgave her, and we ended up having a wonderful dinner together.

After that night, I saw Candace in many meetings, and we always greeted one another. Interestingly enough, she was always alone. My ex-friend, her husband, was never with her, and I never saw him again. I heard that they adopted a daughter. Sadly, I recently heard that, after thirty years of marriage, they had divorced.

I said early on in the book that it is not meant to be a theological book. It is my story of trying to walk out the will of God for my life. Clearly, sometimes I failed, but God always forgave me and called me back, giving me another chance to fulfill my destiny for His glory.

I have had the privilege of standing before hundreds of leaders in many nations of the world, many of them who live under very oppressive situations. They have sacrificed and suffered much more than I, and many times I have questioned myself: "Who am I to stand before such men and women of faith?"

I know from experience that there's a price to pay when the Lord calls you to be a leader. You will have to sacrifice many things to come into the fullness of what He has for you, and sadly, not everyone is willing to pay that price. Therefore, they miss out on fulfilling their destiny, not only for themselves, but also the destiny of those to whom they were called to minister and bring the salvation message, that they might be saved.

Again, it is my personal belief that betrayal is part of the plan of God for the making of every leader. I can say from personal experience that it is very painful, and it will cut your heart deeply. It may even shake your faith, and may even cause you to question God. It is my prayer for those reading this book, my story, that the Lord would give you the grace to respond with love and forgiveness when you receive the Judas kiss of betrayal. May your betrayal not become your tombstone; may it become your stepping-stone up into your final destiny.

THE SADDEST THING ABOUT BETRAYAL IS THAT IT NEVER COMES FROM YOUR ENEMIES. IT COMES FROM FRIENDS AND LOVED ONES.

Chapter 25

TO LOVE AGAIN

*He who finds a wife finds a good thing,
And obtains favor from the LORD.* Proverbs 18:22

The effects of betrayal affected me deeply, causing me to make the decision to discontinue international ministry for a season. Through a series of circumstances, I started that tile contracting business. There wasn't a lot of work, but at least I was doing something. In time, better doors opened, and I began working with interior designers on high-end jobs. I became part of the church that Pastor Gary led. It was a great church where the Holy Spirit was moving. There I made many new friends. Looking back, however, I realize that I had lost my vision and passion for my calling to the nations of the world.

While attending church there, I noticed a young lady in the service every week. I sent one of my friends over to sit with her to find out her name. Her name was Brenda. Once I had her name, I went to the finance department, where a friend of mine was working, and found out the address where she lived. Once I had the address, I drove by to see what kind of place Brenda was living in. This was kind of useless because I later learned that she was just renting a room from a friend.

I was staying with two friends at the time, John and Annette, and we decided to have a barbecue at their house where we would invite a few couples and Brenda. The idea was that because everyone else was in couples, Brenda and I would end up pairing off together.

Prior to the barbecue, Pastor Gary and I traveled to Florida for some meetings he was speaking at, we missed our return flight, and as a result, missed the barbecue. Several weeks later we scheduled another barbecue, and I finally got to get acquainted with Brenda. I eventually learned that she was living with those friends. Because she had come out of a very abusive marriage, she was very unsure what the future would bring. We began to spend more time together and eventually began to date and think about marriage.

Pastor Gary understood the pain the both of us had come out of, so he advised us to get some marriage counseling and to not think about marriage for at least a year. We took his advice, continued in the church, and continued to make new friends.

One evening, Brenda and I were at the May Company, a local department store here in California, looking at engagement rings. We didn't have enough money to buy a diamond ring, so we were looking at the artificial diamonds. Brenda turned and said to me, "Did you even ask me to marry you?"

I said, "Yes, didn't I ask you?" We bought the ring, got engaged, and set a marriage date. Two of our friends knew of our financial situation and gave us the money to buy two beautiful Christian wedding bands. It was a real blessing.

We got married at the end of the church service one Sunday and had a reception in our friend's backyard. It was the hottest day ever recorded for our city.

We had planned a one-day stay at a resort hotel in Palm Springs, California for our honeymoon. On the way driving there, we were opening the cards we had received and counting up how much money we had. One person had added a second day at the hotel, to extend our honeymoon over the weekend. We didn't have much money, but we were both ready to love again.

I believed in Brenda, she loved and trusted me, and healing was coming to both of us. We both had a gift of hospitality, so together we were a great team. The Lord blessed us and many through us, so it was a great season in our lives.

We were both working, but for several years we lived in an apartment. Brenda really wanted to have a house that we could call home, but even to those making good money buying a home in Southern California is a real challenge. We didn't even have enough money for a down payment. We began to pray that God would open the way for us to get a home. One day, when we were sitting with some of Brenda's relatives, they mentioned that her father had sold his home, and the money was just sitting in a bank because he had moved into a small condominium. They suggested that we ask him for a loan. We did that, offering him more interest than the bank was giving, and he gladly loaned us the money for a down payment.

To be honest, I wasn't really interested in a home, but Brenda was. She had prayed for the Lord to give her a sign of what was the right house. She said it had to have a red rose bush in the front yard. The wife of her boss had passed away, he eventually met another woman, and they planned to get married and wanted to sell her house. He took Brenda over to see it one day, and she immediately fell in love with it. When they were leaving, Brenda noticed that the front yard had several rose bushes in it, but, since it wasn't the right time of year, there was no color to be seen. She asked the owner what color the rose bushes were, and the lady replied, "Crimson red." In that moment, Brenda knew this was her home.

That night, when I came home from work, Brenda was excited and told me she had found the perfect home. We went right over to see it, and we made an offer on it. About a month later, with her father's money for the down payment, we were able to get the needed bank mortgage. We did some major remodeling for a month, but finally moved into our own home.

INHERITING THE NATIONS

I don't remember the exact timing, but as I mentioned in the preceding chapters, the Lord spoke to me through the story of Jonah, and I heard His call to me the second time to return to international ministry. I was making very good money at the time, so I didn't need a financial support base. Brenda and I began to travel three times a year out of the country, once to Brazil and twice to Asia. We usually traveled together, but on a couple occasions, she traveled without me to Asia. She was anointed and a woman of prayer, with an amazing gift of encouragement. Every place we went, everyone loved her, some even more than they loved me.

Before Brenda and I met, she had traveled to Hong Kong to smuggle Bibles into China, so she was a perfect fit for the ministry in Bangkok. On her trip into China, she and two other ladies were supposed to deliver their bags of Bibles to a locker where they would be picked up by the local Chinese believers. In those days, however, things were very primitive, and they got lost and didn't know how to find the lockers or to get to their hotel. They prayed and then noticed a man down the road pointing a different way. When they finally got on that road, they realized where they were and where they were going and were now able to reach their destination. When they turned to thank the man, he had disappeared. They thought later that he must have been an angel.

One year we traveled with three of our friends to attend a missions conference in Thailand, then afterward went on to Burma and Vietnam. We carried many Bibles into Vietnam. One day in Vietnam we had planned to teach young people all day and into the evening, but we were informed that police were watching the area. We arrived at the church building prior to the light of dawn so we would not be detected by the police.

One of the friends with us was named Pilar. She loved the Lord and was a great intercessor, but she didn't feel confident doing anything else but pray. Our lunch was prepared on the top floor of the building in the open air. Fortunately, it had a covering over it to shade us from the hot Vietnamese sun. At one point, I looked around at all the young people, and in another area, there sat Pilar on a small stool with dozens of young people around her, listening to everything she had to say. I don't know what she was telling them, but they were totally captivated by her. When we finally left, many of them wanted a kiss from Pilar. She had made their day, having touched them with the love of Jesus.

Security was very tight in Vietnam in that season, and the church was under heavy persecution. One day we were with some Christian brothers who were going to take us to lunch. We started walking and came to an area that was filled with the large shipping containers you see on the back of tractor trailers. I was a little upset, wondering what we were doing in that container yard and not going to a restaurant. Then one of the containers was opened, and there was a large table with chairs set around it. We were informed that it would have been too dangerous for us to go to a public restaurant, so they had arranged for food to be brought to this container yard. One of those containers became our personal restaurant, where we didn't have to worry about the police coming and all of us having dinner in jail.

I don't know how many countries Brenda and I have been to together. I lost count. There was a time when we went to Brazil almost every year, plus we have traveled together to many of the countries of Southeast Asia.

Brenda has an amazing gift of encouraging others. Sometimes it's just a handwritten note sent in the mail or a special gift. Some time ago she started making what she called a "Happee Packet." This was comprised of encouraging pictures, poems, and scriptures that she would gather and put in plastic inserts and then tie them all together with beautiful ribbons. These were always sent at just the right time to the right person who needed encouragement. She eventually decided to put them into three-ring binders, which meant more pages with more

INHERITING THE NATIONS

thoughts. Most of the pages would surely be personalized for the individual they were going to. A friend of Brenda's gave her some binders that were four inches or more thick. She reserved these for special occasions and special people.

Once, when we were preparing to go to Thailand, Brenda decided to make one of these special binders for a missionary friend named Barb. Barb didn't have much time to get out because she was raising five or six children and homeschooling them all. It was a big job and took most of her time. Brenda decided to make her the "Mega-Happee Book." It was very thick and very heavy. When we were ready to travel, I said, "I'm not carrying that book. If you want to take it, you'll have to carry it." She did, and it was an amazing blessing to Barb.

Barb decided to give some of the special pages in the book to other missionaries who needed encouragement, and this became like a mini ministry for her. Eventually, the other ladies wanted to know who the lady was who had made this book; they wanted to meet her. On one trip to Thailand, Brenda traveled alone to the central part of the country to meet and minister to the group of women who had been encouraged by the Happee Book she made for Barb.

When I bought my first printer, my son gave me some advice, informing me that paper and ink were expensive, but I wouldn't be using that much. He had no idea the amount of paper and ink used in making Brenda's Happee Books. We have three printers now, and when she gets inspired, they can all be going at one time. I always complained about the cost of the ink, but that was about to change.

While I was away once on a missionary trip, Brenda attended the church of some friends of ours, and there she met a precious lady who appeared to need some encouragement. Later she asked our friends about the lady. They admitted she could use some encouragement but said she was a great Christian and a great friend. Brenda felt led to send the lady a small Happee Packet. Because she lived quite far away,

Brenda put the Happee Packet in a large plain envelope, took it to the Post Office, and mailed it. The day that package arrived in the lady's mailbox, she had said goodbye to her husband and children and left home with a gun in her purse, planning to commit suicide that very day. As she passed by the mailbox, she noticed the large envelope, so she took it out and put it in the car. She sat in her car with the Happee Packet in its envelope and her gun nearby. Her plan was to drive out into the desert and kill herself.

Before killing herself, she decided to open the envelope, and when she did, she began to read the encouraging things Brenda had been led to put there. That day, instead of ending her life, she recommitted herself to the Lord and put her trust for the future in His hands. Brenda's Happee Packet had made all the difference.

Sometime later, this lady sent Brenda a beautiful framed picture of a woman entitled: A WOMAN OF VALOR. On the back of it she had written a little note:

> "To Brenda, a mighty woman of valor: Thank you for being a willing vessel of God to save my life (literally) and build my faith in Christ Jesus, and for being a beautiful friend, and a true gift from our Father!" Shalom, Bev

Brenda is always ready to share the Gospel and extend the compassion of Jesus to others. Once, when we were in Brazil for a couple weeks of ministry, on one of the final nights, Pastor Paulo gathered all of his leaders and their wives and asked Brenda to share with them whatever was on her heart. We had all gathered on the open-air rooftop of an apartment in Rio de Janeiro. It was a beautiful night, and there sat the leaders of the Maranata churches, which now numbered more than eight thousand members.

INHERITING THE NATIONS

As I described in an earlier chapter, the church was formed after Pastor Paulo's father was baptized with the Holy Spirit and began to pray for the sick and share the Gospel in his home. Through the years, in my opinion, the church had become less Pentecostal and more evangelical, with less emphasis on the things of the Spirit. That night Brenda decided to share her testimony of how she had been baptized with the Holy Spirit and what a change it had made in her Christian life. After she spoke, there were several questions, which ended up with some very fruitful discussion about the things of the Spirit. Several pastors confessed that even though they were leading a Pentecostal church, they had not taught about the baptism of the Holy Spirit for years, and they decided that it was time they did so and that they would even have special meetings for those hungry and thirsty for the Holy Spirit.

As I write this in 2022, it appears to me that the young people of Maranata are getting on fire for the things of the Spirit. Hopefully, this will bring the church back to its original calling, where there will be more salvations, more healings, and more baptisms with the Spirit so that Jesus might receive the reward of His suffering!

As of this writing, I continue in international ministry. Brenda was women's pastor at a local church for a season. She has monthly women's meetings in our home, which she started eighteen years ago. She also continues to encourage people through her Happee Books.

Unfortunately, because of her commitment to the local church and also having some responsibilities to assist in raising our grandchildren, she has not been able to travel to Central Asia with me. Both she and I have what I would call a gift of hospitality. We continually have people at our home for barbecues and fellowship. Our home is a place where people can feel secure and be encouraged in the Lord. Brenda is continually buying signs with scriptures or positive things on them and posting them around the house. If you're not a Christian and you come to our home and read all the signs, you're probably going to receive the Lord before you leave.

Because both Brenda and I have strong personalities, there have been many challenges in our journey together, but the Lord has been faithful, and His grace has been sufficient for us.

On our wedding day

Opening our wedding gifts

My son Ken, his wife Cindy and their sons

My son Joseph III and his wife, Tammy

Chapter 26

THE POWER OF A HUG

Whom have I in heaven but You?
And there is none upon earth that I desire besides You. Psalm 73:25

ONE DAY SOMEONE IS GOING TO HUG YOU SO TIGHT THAT ALL OF YOUR BROKEN PIECES WILL STICK BACK TOGETHER!

I read an article recently about the importance of being held, embraced with the heart. The article stated that the average length of a hug is about three seconds, but researchers have found that if a hug lasts twenty seconds or more, there are definite therapeutic effects on the body and the mind. A sincere embrace, it is said, produces a hormone called oxytocin, and this substance has many benefits for our physical and mental health. It helps us to relax and feel safe and calms our fears and anxieties.

The article went on to say that hugs strengthen the immune system. The gentle pressure on the sternum and the emotional charge this creates activates the solar plexus. This, in turn, stimulates the thymus gland, which regulates and balances the body's production of white blood cells, which keep you healthy and disease free.

Brenda and I attended a small home meeting where a man, whom I believe, was in the office of a prophet, would be speaking and praying for people. He didn't know us, but I was a close friend of his brother-in

THE POWER OF A HUG

-law and knew that this man was a real servant of the Lord. I'm not a person who needs a prophetic word. I know who I am and what my calling is, but it's nice to get a word occasionally, especially from someone who doesn't know you.

When it came time for prayer, I asked the man if he would pray for my wife and me because we were scheduled to go to Vietnam. Knowing the anointing he operated under, I expected that the clouds would open, angels would fill the room, and he would have a ten-minute prophecy over us (just something simple like that). He laid his hands very lightly on our foreheads, as we stood there with our eyes closed and our hands extended, and he prayed, "Lord, may they feel the kiss of Heaven." He didn't say anything else. I was waiting and thinking, "And what else?" But he didn't say anything else.

When I finally looked up, he was gone. He was at the back of the room praying for someone else. I thought, "What kind of prayer was that? Forget him We're going to Vietnam."

I'd like to tell you that I was so spiritual that night that the Lord visited me and gave me incredible revelations on that little prayer, but He didn't. And it did not come two days later, or even two months later, but two whole years later. One day I was reading the Song of Solomon:

> *Let him kiss me with the kisses of his mouth—*
> *For your love is better than wine.*
> *Because of the fragrance of your good ointments,*
> *Your name is ointment poured forth;*
> *Therefore the virgins love you.*   Song of Solomon 1:2-3

It was as if the Lord was knocking on my head, saying, "Hello! Hello! Joe, are you in there? Do you hear Me?" I realized what I had thought was a crazy prayer two years earlier from the prophet was really a cry from the heart of the Father, calling me to a place I knew nothing about. He was calling me into an intimacy with Him that I had never experienced. I knew about love, preached about love, and even quoted the scriptures about love, but God was calling me to a place of love that would totally capture my heart.

I knew the Lord was calling me deeper into Himself, but how do you go to someplace you've never been and you don't know where it is? I began to teach more in my meetings about love and intimacy and even created a syllabus to teach on the subject. I hadn't arrived where I knew the Lord was calling me to, but at least I was getting closer to His heart, so that I could testify in my teachings as to where I was in my journey into His love. I also realized that the power of a physical hug could impart things that our words could not, so I changed the way I ministered at the end of a message.

I was in Armenia preaching in a church for the first time on the Wednesday before Easter Sunday, and I spoke about God's love. The church had about a hundred people in attendance. At the end of my message, I said, "I don't want to pray for anybody; I just want to hug you. If you want a hug, come up." No one came forward.

I could imagine what they were thinking: "Who is this guy? His first time in our church and he wants to hug us?"

After a short period of inactivity, several children lined up. I got on my knees and started to hug them. Then everyone in the congregation got up and lined up behind the children, and I hugged every one of them. Some wept in my arms.

The following Sunday was Easter, and I was invited back to preach. Before the preaching, a lady came to me. She said, "When I was growing up, my father never told me he loved me. He died several months ago, and on his deathbed, he still didn't tell me he loved me. The result was that I had a very painful hole in my heart. I had gotten prayer from the elders and the pastors, but nothing happened. Then, last Wednesday, when you hugged me, Jesus healed that hole in my heart."

THE POWER OF A HUG

That's the healing power of a hug. Praise the Lord!

One of the most powerful things that happened to me personally in relationship to a hug happened in Sir Lanka. We had been traveling around Sir Lanka ministering in different churches, escorted by Pastor L, when we started to have some car troubles. We stopped at a mechanic shop, and all of my friends went in to talk to the mechanic. While I was waiting, I noticed a homeless lady across the street from us. She was the only homeless person I had seen in all of Sir Lanka. I decided I wanted to get a photo of her, but you just can't walk up and stick a camera in someone's face. That would be very rude (even though Americans have a reputation for rudeness).

I decided to hide my camera on my chest with my hands and just walk by her. Then I would turn quickly, take the picture, and walk back to our vehicle. I covered my camera and calmly walked by where she sat on the ground with her belongings—probably everything she owned. I readied my camera and turned, but to my surprise, she had gotten up, and when I turned, she was about five inches from my face. She was a dirty, smelly beggar, but I felt compelled to put my arms around her, and I hugged her for a long, long time.

When I finally stopped hugging this woman, she stepped back a little, pointed to herself and said, "Picture? Picture?" She sat down among all her stuff, and I took her picture. Then I gave her some money. I later wondered: when was the last time someone, anyone, had paid attention to her? When was the last time she felt she had value, the last time she felt the embrace and the love of another human being? She probably sat in that same spot every day, and no doubt most people walked on by, never even glancing at her. I would have loved to talk to her, but I didn't know her language. I can only hope that somehow the Lord touched her through my hug. I know that hug changed me. I have more than seventy thousand photos on my computer. I chose fifteen of them to put up on the wall of my office, surrounding the world map.

INHERITING THE NATIONS

One of those photos is the one I took of that homeless lady in Sri Lanka that day.

One evening, Brenda and I were going into a hospital to pray for a friend recently diagnosed with cancer. The area around the front door of the hospital had a flower planter, and on it was sitting a person. I say *person* because I couldn't tell if it was a man or a woman. On closer observation, I could tell that it was a young girl. She had every color you could possibly imagine in her hair. On her ears, she had five or six sets of pierced earrings going up both sides. She also had a ring in her nose and one in her lip. She had on a black motorcycle jacket with a large chain hanging down from it. She was scary looking. Brenda, who tends to be much bolder than I, said to me, "Let's pray for her."

I objected. "No," I said, "we've got to get into the hospital and pray for this man who has cancer." I took her by the hand, and together we walked on into the hospital, heading toward the elevators.

Then, for some reason, we looked back, and there was the girl walking behind us. Brenda decided to disobey me, broke away from my hand, and went to the girl and said, "Do you need a hug?" As Brenda embraced her, the girl started to cry uncontrollably. It turned out that her twenty-one-year-old friend was in the hospital dying.

In the hospital room of our friend was another man. His wife was standing beside his bed. They were so close she could hear everything we were saying. When we finally finished talking and praying with our friend, the lady came over and said, "I heard you praying. Are you a Christian?"

I said, "Yes, I'm a missionary."

She said, "My husband, Frank, is not going to live much longer, and he doesn't know the Lord. I really would appreciate it if you could pray for him."

I went to Frank's bedside. I asked him if he went to church, and he said, "Sometimes." I asked him if he knew the Lord, and he said, "Yes."

"According to your wife, you don't know the Lord," I responded.

His head went down, and he said, "Well, not really."

"Frank," I said, it seems that you don't have much time left. The Lord loves you and wants to come into your life. It's time. Are you ready to pray and receive Him now?"

He said, "Yes," then repeated a prayer after me, asking Jesus to come into his life.

Sometimes you have time to share the Gospel in detail with people, and sometimes you don't. In these cases, you just tell them that God loves them. Very often you can let the Lord embrace them through your arms. This is the power of a hug!

I was in Vietnam with two pastor friends of mine from Brazil and a pastor from California. The pastor from California was there to give a theological study to a group of about thirty Vietnamese pastors, and my two Brazilian friends and I would be teaching in a church at a secret location about spiritual warfare for three days. One day Pastor David from Brazil briefly shared his testimony, which I had never heard before. When he got saved in Brazil, it was in a small home Bible study with people who were very interested in missions. They had a map of Southeast Asia, and in every meeting he would pray for Thailand and Vietnam. He never dreamed that he would ever travel out of Brazil, but he had a heart to pray for those countries. The week before, we had been in a conference in Thailand, and now on this day too, he was physically standing on the place that he had prayed for many times. His dream had become reality.

I have twelve PowerPoints, teachings about Spiritual Warfare, that I use at Bible schools and at Youth With A Mission bases, so I was well prepared for this subject. The first morning I gave an introduction about what spiritual warfare was and shared many testimonies of my own experiences in the nations of the world. Then we took a lunch break. During the break, a pastor, who was a professor in two Bible schools, went to the head pastor and asked, "What is with this speaker? I came here to listen to a theological talk on spiritual warfare, but he's only giving testimonies. When is he going to start teaching the Bible?" I didn't learn about his criticism of my teachings until later that night. It probably would not have mattered to me, but I did notice that all morning he sat there with his arms folded.

After lunch, I turned on my PowerPoint presentation, but I felt the Holy Spirit say to me, "Talk about the power of a hug." This was not in my notes, but I felt I could quickly talk about it and then get back to my PowerPoint outline. I began to speak about God's love and the embrace of the heavenly Father, giving testimony of my encounter with the Father. The entire time this man sat there with his arms folded.

When I finally finished speaking, I said to the people, "I have two friends with me from Brazil. I want them to come up, and if you want to feel a hug from the Father, come up to the altar, and I'm going to have them hug you and kiss you." I had not told my friends prior to the altar call what I was going to do. Everyone came forward for a hug and kiss, all except the theology professor.

After the worship leader got a hug and kiss, he took his guitar and quietly played while we continue to minister to the people. Some began to weep as they were being hugged. Others ended up on their knees worshiping the Lord. It was a powerful time.

Just before we ended the prayer time, Pastor David from Brazil came to me. He was moved. He had never seen anything like it. As we were talking, I noticed the professor still sitting in the back with his arms folded. He was the only one who had not come forward. I told Pastor David to go back and hug him. When he went back there, the professor resisted him. Finally Pastor David knelt in front of him, took the professor's hand, put it on his own head, and asked the pastor to pray for him. This act of humility broke the professor, and he started to cry. He not only embraced Pastor David; when David tried to get up, the professor kept embracing him. Love, humility, and the embrace of the heavenly Father broke through to this professor. It was a victorious time.

In Brazil, especially in Pentecostal churches, it's very common to hug people, but one night after ministry time, we were talking, and Pastor David said, "You know ... hugging is a part of life in my church. I hug everybody, and I even kiss most people. But here in Vietnam, when we were hugging people, it was somehow different. It seemed as if I could feel the Lord hugging through me!"

I believe that people everywhere, Christian and non-Christian alike, are hungry for real love, which can only happen when they experience the embrace of the Father's arms, usually through us.

We finished our teachings at the church in Vietnam, my friend finished his theological teachings with the pastors, and we would be leaving the following day. The head pastor came to me and said, "I'd like for you and your friends to come and talk to my pastors for about an hour, but I want to warn you that they are not emotional. They will not cry when you pray for them."

I said, "I don't really care if they cry or not. We would love to pray for them." Then I said to my two Brazilian minister friends, "We have forty-five minutes to turn off their heads and turn on their hearts."

I talked that day about God's love and about the power of a hug and shared the story in the Song of Solomon, where the Shulamite woman desired the kisses of His lips. I said, "This is what I'd like to do. I want you to experience the kiss and embrace of the heavenly Father, so I have my two Brazilian friends here to hug you and kiss you." I told them that Pastor Bob and I would anoint them with oil, and then one of my pastor friends from Brazil would hug and kiss them. My goal was for them to experience the love of the Father in a deeper way than they had ever experienced it before.

These pastors love the Lord with all their hearts and were totally committed to the ministry. Most of their churches were underground churches, illegal in the eyes of the government, but in those churches, under their leadership, were many thousands of members.

As the pastors came forward, Pastor Bob and I anointed their foreheads with oil and prayed a short prayer. Then they went on to receive a hug and a kiss from my Brazilian friends. As we were anointing them, some started weeping the minute we put oil on their foreheads. Others wept uncontrollably as my friends hugged and kissed them. Some were so overcome with the love and presence of the Lord that they fell to the ground. It was a precious time, and the lead pastor, my friend, through his own tears said to us, "I can't believe what I'm seeing." His own brother was so overcome he lay on the ground for quite some time.

For me, it's not about whether you cry or even have an emotional experience. It is my heart's desire that deep within your soul and spirit, you experience the overwhelming love of your heavenly Father.

When I teach at the Youth With A Mission bases in several countries, usually most of the students are under thirty. Every morning I try to greet them with a hug and sometimes even during the day. A couple years ago I was teaching at the YWAM base in Armenia. Some weeks prior to leaving home, I had received some very bad news that deeply affected me both emotionally and spiritually. But even though it was so devastating and overwhelming, I didn't immediately recognize it as a spiritual attack. It was so powerful that many times during the day I would weep uncontrollably. It got so bad that Brenda wanted me to cancel my scheduled trip, but I couldn't. I felt the need to be faithful. That's part of my makeup. If I make a commitment, I will always follow through on it. To make a long story short, the Lord came, visited me, and set me free. I went to Armenia and had the most powerful three weeks of ministry I'd ever had in my entire life. I'll tell more about that spiritual attack in a later chapter.

Even though the trip ended as my most powerful trip, it was very challenging. The bad news I had received before leaving was only

THE POWER OF A HUG

multiplied when I got to Armenia and learned that two of my friends had left their callings. They were still believers, but they had left the plan of God for their life. This was so overwhelming for me that there were nights when I lay in bed at the base weeping, trying to understand what had happened to these believers who had extraordinary callings on their lives. They had been destined to change nations, but they were now detoured by the devil.

Looking back on my time in Armenia during that season and thinking about the power of a hug, I realized that as I was hugging the students, it was helping me too. Somehow it was reaching down into my emotions, into the pain that my soul was experiencing, and bringing healing. None of the students realized the emotional pain I was suffering, but the Lord knew. He wrapped His arms around me, through them, giving me the strength to minister at the base and in the churches around Armenia. I don't think I could have fully succeeded without their hugs.

It's hard to single out one person, but there was one young lady in particular. Her name was Dina, she was from Russia and was probably still in her twenties. Her father had been one of my students in 2019, and is now a missionary to South Africa. Dina was full of life and energy and was always smiling. When she talked, it was with a laugh that made you laugh, and she was a hugger. I so enjoyed joking with her while giving and receiving hugs.

As I'm writing this chapter, Dina is leading a team in a Muslim country. Her text to me yesterday told me that she announced that they were going to pray for healing on the streets, and people were lined up waiting to get prayer. If I were younger, I would like to be just like Dina.

During the last few years, the world has experienced this strange virus called covid. This has affected every nation, and many people died. One of the most devastating effects of the virus was fear, which resulted in the wearing of masks, maintaining a social distance of six feet from other people, not going to church, but having church over Zoom on the computer. In the process, the ability to experience a hug from another human being was lost for that season, and losing the power of a hug was straight from the very pit of Hell.

In some areas of Southeast Asia, particularly in Thailand and Cambodia, parents tell their daughters, "Don't allow any man to hug you," but at the same time, Thai and Cambodian parents are selling their sons and daughters into prostitution in big cities like Bangkok and the beach cities, to financially support their family. They will tell you it's all part of their culture, but the more I think about it, it really is a curse, a curse of Buddhism, that robs them of the power of a healthy, life-giving hug from the heavenly Father through the arms of other believers.

During my latest trip to Armenia, my friend Aram, who is the leader of YWAM there and usually translates for me, said, "You have hugged many people during our ministry times. However, you have never hugged me." I gave him a big hug.

I don't know of any seminary or Bible school in the world that has a course on the power of a hug. I don't know any book that you can buy that teaches how you can allow the Lord to hug people through you. There is a good chance, as you're reading this chapter, that it is the first time you have ever even thought that the heavenly Father wants to hug people through you and that He wants to hug you through the arms of other people. I've said it before, and I'll say it again, people—Christians and non-Christians alike—are hungry for real love. Many times, as we are on this journey called life, we have encounters with people that last only a few minutes, and you don't really have time to present the Gospel effectively. However, there is always time to hug someone and pray that they will feel the love of the heavenly Father through your embrace.

Sometimes we just need a hug. A hug where someone wraps their arms around you so tight and reminds you that everything will be okay.

The Sri Lankan beggar I hugged

Did you know that a twenty-second hug releases the bonding hormone and neurotransmitter oxytocin, which is a natural antidepressant.

Anastasia in India

Lucine, an Armenian hugger

Lucine in the Congo

Chapter 27

JEHOVAH-RAPHA, THE LORD WHO HEALS

And Jesus went about all Galilee, teaching in their synagogues, preaching the gospel of the kingdom, and healing all kinds of sickness and all kinds of disease among the people.   Matthew 4:23

We are a spirit that has a soul and that lives in a body. This is how God made us. He created a garden and every living thing, and then He created Adam:

And the LORD God formed a man of the dust of the ground, and he breathed into his nostrils the breath of life and man became a living being.

Genesis 2:7

The LORD God took the man and put him in the garden of Eden to tend and keep it.   Genesis 2:15

And the LORD God commanded the man, saying, "Of every tree of the garden you may freely eat; but of the tree of the knowledge of good and evil you shall not eat, for in the day that you eat of it you shall surely die."   Genesis 2:16-17

INHERITING THE NATIONS

Then the Lord God put Adam into a deep sleep, took out one of his ribs, and, from it, made woman and brought her to Adam. Together they enjoyed fellowship with one another and with the Lord God in the beautiful garden He had created for Himself and for them. The Lord then came in the cool of the day and walked and talked with them.

Imagine what this must have been like. Maybe He even took their hands, just like an earthly father takes the hand of a young son or daughter, and they walk along together, conversing. Adam and Eve had a unique relationship with the Lord God. They could see Him physically, and they could touch His hands and feel His embrace.

Genesis 3 tells the sad story of the consequences of them disobeying the Lord God. Eve became deceived by Satan and ate the fruit of the tree that God had commanded them not to eat. Then she went to Adam, offered it to him, and he also ate the fruit. At that moment, fear entered their lives, and they tried to hide from the Lord God.

God had told Adam. "The day you eat of it, you will surely die." His body was still alive and functioning, his soul, which involves the mind, will, intellect, and motions, were still controlling him, but something had happened to his spirit. He would no longer enjoy intimacy with the Father who loved him so deeply. Verse 24 records:

So He drove out the man; and He placed cherubim at the east of the garden of Eden, and a flaming sword which turned every way, to guard the way to the tree of life.

I can imagine that the Father's heart was broken. His son and daughter had disobeyed Him, and this brought a loss of intimacy with Him. They would now learn to love the things of the world, instead of loving the Father. They would no longer experience the plan of God for their life. Their destiny was now detoured by Satan. But Jehovah-Rapha, the Lord who heals, had a plan to restore man back to

JEHOVAH-RAPHA, THE LORD WHO HEALS

fellowship with Himself.

The sin of Adam and Eve had consequences, but it also had a penalty, and that penalty could only be paid by the shedding of blood. It had to be a pure, sinless blood, an eternal blood. There would have to be a sacrifice made in which blood was poured out to pay the penalty for the sin of all mankind. The Lord God, in His deep love for mankind, decided on the sacrifice. He would sacrifice His only Son:

> *For God so loved the world that He gave his only begotten son, that whoever believes in Him should not perish but have eternal life. For God did not send His Son into the world to condemn the world, but that the world through Him might be saved.* John 3:16-17

Jesus came, not only to pay for our sin, but also that we might be restored to the Father and once again enjoy intimacy with Him. Jesus came that we might be whole—body, soul, and spirit:

> *Now may the God of peace Himself sanctify you completely; and may your whole spirit, soul, and body be preserved blameless at the coming of our Lord Jesus Christ.* 1 Thessalonians 5:23

The Lord God put our sin, its consequences, and its penalty upon His only Son. Why? Because He loved us, and He wanted, once again, to have the relationship with us that He'd had with Adam and Eve in the garden.

The crucifixion, death, and resurrection of Jesus assures us of eternal life, but they also provide for our physical and emotional healing:

> *Surely He has borne our griefs*
> *And carried our sorrows;*
> *Yet we esteemed Him stricken,*

INHERITING THE NATIONS

Smitten by God, and afflicted.
But He was wounded for our transgressions,
He was bruised for our iniquities;
The chastisement for our peace was upon Him,
And by His stripes we are healed.   Isaiah 53:4-5

After Jesus was baptized by John the Baptist, the Holy Spirit came upon Him and the Father spoke from Heaven, *"This is My beloved Son, in whom I am well pleased"* (Matthew 3:17). Then the Spirit took Jesus out to the desert where He would encounter Satan and defeat him by quoting the Scriptures. After this encounter, Jesus went back to Nazareth, went into the synagogue, opened the book of Isaiah, and read these words:

The Spirit of the Lord is upon Me,
Because He has anointed Me
To preach the gospel to the poor;
He has sent Me to heal the brokenhearted,
To proclaim liberty to the captives
And recovery of sight to the blind,
To set at liberty those who are oppressed;
To proclaim the acceptable year of the Lord.   Luke 4:18-19

Then Jesus closed the book and sat down. Then, in Luke 4:21, He began to say to them, *"Today this scripture is fulfilled in your hearing."* I am a witness to His power. On October 14, 1971, at 6:30 at night, the Lord came into my life, and all depression, anxiety, fear, and confusion miraculously stopped. I looked up and saw my medications and knew I would never need them again. Maybe it was an emotional healing, some type of deliverance, or the results of the Holy Spirit coming to live inside of me. I'm not totally sure. All I know is that a deep peace came over me.

JEHOVAH-RAPHA, THE LORD WHO HEALS

I believe that healing is biblical, that Jesus healed sick people in His day, that He gave His disciples authority to heal the sick, and that this authority has been handed down to us as believers. We are commanded in John 16 to go into all the world and preach the Gospel. Then it says that one of the signs that will follow us is that we will lay hands on the sick, and they will recover.

As I said earlier in Chapter 2, in my early years of walking with the Lord, while attending evangelical churches, I believed in praying for the sick, and I was taught early on to write down prayer requests for those in need on a small card and keep it in my Bible to continuously pray for them. However, I can't say I saw any instantaneous healings like those recorded in the Bible. When we prayed for someone to be healed and they died, we would say, "Thank the Lord, they got a better healing." I know there are many who will disagree with me, but I no longer see death as healing. The extreme suffering that someone has gone through is over, they are in the arms of the Father, and that is wonderful, but it's not healing.

I had a friend named Polly come to me one day in the church I was attending. She loved to play tennis, but arthritis had so overwhelmed her shoulder that she could no longer play. She couldn't even lift her right arm. When she told us about her situation, I mentioned to her that I had heard that massive doses of vitamin C would saturate the joints and possibly bring healing. I remember her look of shock or bewilderment when I said that. She responded, "I thought you were a man of God and that you would pray for me."

I must admit that I didn't have faith for her healing, but I said, "Okay, if you can believe, we'll pray." She sat down and our friends and I put our hands on her and prayed. I must be honest and say I didn't believe anything was going to happen. It was almost like she had embarrassed me into praying for her. But the Father heard our prayers, He saw her desperation and her faith, and when we touched her, He touched her through us, and she raised her arm with no pain. Jehovah-Rapha had come. Polly returned to playing tennis, but now she had a testimony that Jehovah-Rapha still heals today.

Many years later I was at a Bible study in their home, and she testified that whenever she got depressed and started complaining to the Lord that He wasn't doing anything for her, she would hear His voice say to her, "Lift your arm." Then she would remember the day Jehovah-Rapha had touched her, and she would rejoice.

Some friends of mine invited me to go and pray for an elderly lady who was having trouble seeing because of a cataract. My son, who was not yet a teenager at the time, was with us. We talked a little while, and then it was time to pray. I turned to my son and said, "Ken, lay your hands on her eyes and pray." To be honest, I don't even know if he was a believer at the time. I only know that he prayed, God heard his prayer, and the lady's eyes were restored.

As noted in Chapter 2, a friend of mine named Paul Morgan had a son who had some serious physical problems, so Paul and I decided to visit some Full Gospel groups because we had heard that there was a strong emphasis in these groups on praying for the sick. It seemed to us that some things that were being taught were not biblical, but it caused us to look deeper into the Bible and to continue to pray for his son. Unfortunately, his son, who was only in his early twenties, died, but we continued to search the Scriptures even after this great loss. For me, this was a door that eventually led me to a Pentecostal church and to being baptized with the Holy Spirit.

Some years later, Paul's wife, Doris, ended up with the same physical problem. If my memory serves me correctly, it was a cancerous growth in the stomach area. She had surgery and then one treatment of chemotherapy. That first treatment, however, was extremely painful, so during her first follow-up appointment with her doctor, she informed him that she would rather die than take another treatment. As she was sitting there in his office, an audible voice spoke to her and said, "I will be with you, daughter." She told me that she'd been a Christian almost all her life, but when that voice came, it changed everything. She now didn't care if she lived or died from the cancer. God's voice had given her the assurance that He was with her, and she would one day be in Heaven with Him. Although she never had another treatment, the cancer was gone and never came back.

As I'm writing this book Doris is now in her nineties. She and Paul traveled with me to Brazil in the 1980s, and she was able to share her testimony of healing in several of the churches in Rio de Janeiro.

Sometime in the 1990s we lived in a small mountain town and attended a church with about fifty members. It was small enough that everybody knew everybody, and we always had great times of fellowship there. After church one day, we went to the pastor's home for lunch. There were not enough chairs for us all to sit around the table, so many of us were just sitting on the floor in a big circle. It was a fun time.

A lady who was visiting the church went to lunch with us that day. During lunch, she said, "I'd like prayer." Until this time, it had just been a time of talking with no prayer involved. She now told us, "I'm having a mastectomy on Wednesday. I have breast cancer." The room went silent. She had not told anybody about it before, and nobody knew what to even say. It was totally unexpected. I can't say really what happened that day. It was like something rose up in me, almost like an anger. I stood up, walked across the room, and was now standing in front of her. I pointed at her and said, "You are worthy." She put her head down.

I said to her, "Look at me." She looked up, and I said a second time, "You are worthy."

She looked down again, and again I said to her, "Look at me. Look right into my eyes!" She looked up, and our eyes were now locked on one another. I said a third time, "You are worthy," and she burst into uncontrollable tears. On Wednesday, when she went to the hospital to undergo the surgery, the cancer was gone, and it never returned, Praise the Lord!

Toward the end of April of 2019, I was feeling physically fine, with no problems at all, but when I went to the bathroom, there was blood in my urine. Because it was late in the evening, I went to the urgent care center near my house, and they said I probably had a urinary tract infection, gave me some antibiotics, and told me to see my primary physician on Monday. Before I left the urgent care center, however, they asked me to give them a urine sample. When I tried to urinate in the cup they had given me, it came out thick blood.

My primary doctor was not available, so I saw a nurse practitioner, someone I had seen on other occasions, and she was very concerned. She said, "This might be nothing, but it could be very serious. You need to see a doctor right away, and you need to be scoped."

"What is 'scoped?'" I asked.

She said, "I'm not going to tell you, but you need it."

Two days later I was in the office of a urologist getting scoped. I'll leave it to your imagination, but basically, they had to go inside me with a little camera and look at my bladder. The doctor left the room for a short time and then came back and sat down across from me. Just before he started to speak, a peace came over me like a heavy blanket, and then he said those words that put fear in everyone who hears them: "You have bladder cancer, and we need to operate as soon as possible."

I was completely at peace, and his words had no effect on me. I just said to him, "I need to be in Norway in three weeks for some meetings." He set the surgery for early the following week.

I went home and told Brenda what the doctor had said, then I got on Facebook, posted what was going on and asked for prayer. Hundreds of people responded to me on Facebook, and I expected that when the doctor went in, the cancer would be gone. But it really didn't

JEHOVAH-RAPHA, THE LORD WHO HEALS

matter what happened because the peace was staying with me, and it stayed with me for more than a month. I hadn't prayed for it, and I didn't ask God for it. He just sovereignly gave me His peace before I heard the doctor's words.

The doctor operated, and after I came out of the anesthesia, he came to give me a report of how the surgery had gone. He later told me, "I went into your bladder, and when I took hold of the cancer, it evaporated." As God is my witness, those were his exact words.

Yes, the cancer evaporated. It was gone, and it never came back. Jehovah-Rapha is still healing today. Two weeks later I was in Norway, preaching the Gospel and praying for the sick.

After that surgery, I shared my testimony in many meetings in several nations of the world. I told the people, "I don't know if God is going to heal you or not, but I can tell you for sure that His peace can come into your situation, so that you can go through anything victoriously!"

I had a friend named Jim Maloney. He was a great man of God. Jim went to Heaven in 2021. He had a ministry of praying for the sick. Because of his upbringing and the trauma he had gone through at the hands of a stepfather, he often prayed for emotional healing, with great success. I don't know if healing is the proper word in this situation. Perhaps a "creative miracle" would be a better phrase here. Jim was preaching at Christ for the Nations Institute in Dallas for a week, and on the final day, he made an altar call. He said, "If you're here today and you have some physical problems that have brought you emotional pain and distress, I'd like to pray for you." A few people went forward. One of them was a young lady in her twenties. She was very pretty, but one side of her face was totally deformed. Jim said it was hard to even look at her. When he reached out his hand to touch her, she backed away.

The young lady finally allowed him to touch her face, and as he did so, he felt another arm come over his arm and hand, and it began to move his hand as if it was manipulating her face. Then he heard the Lord say, "I am the Potter; you are the clay." He then felt the hand lift, so he lifted his hand and looked at the lady. She had a brand-new face. When she realized what had happened, she fell to her knees, weeping and proclaiming, "Now I know You love me, Lord. Now I know You love me!"

Just a few years ago, a pastor from Pakistan came to our home to share his testimony with a small group of us who had gathered. One evening in Pakistan, he heard a knock at his door, and when he answered the door, it was a Muslim man. The man asked if he was a Christian, and he said he was. Then he said, "Do you believe the Bible?"

"I do," the pastor said.

Then the man asked, "Do you believe Jesus healed in the Bible?"

He said, "Yes, I do."

Next the Muslim man asked, "Do you believe that Jesus heals today?"

The pastor answered, "Yes, I believe Jesus heals today."

The Muslim man said, "I'd like you to come to my home tomorrow and pray for my son. He is blind."

The next morning my Pakistani pastor friend went to the Muslim man's home to pray for his blind son. When he arrived, he was introduced to the man's five sons, all born blind. I would love to have been in that home and seen the Spirit realm open as he prayed. I can imagine there was a mighty war going on in the Spirit. Angels despatched from the throne of God were probably filling the room, standing with swords of fire, ready for battle. The demons of darkness that had spiritually blinded this Muslim man for years from knowing the true God and probably had physically blinded his five boys would soon be destroyed. Maybe I could have seen or heard the prayers of this humble Pakistani pastor ascending to the throne in Heaven, into the ears of the heavenly Father. Then He gave the command to His angelic army, the

JEHOVAH-RAPHA, THE LORD WHO HEALS

demons of darkness were slain, and a miracle was released from the voice of the heavenly Father through the Pakistani pastor's mouth. All five Muslim boys received their sight that day, and that entire Muslim family became followers of Jesus.

Jehovah-Rapha had seen the pain in the Muslim father's heart, and He saw the hope he had, thinking that just maybe Jesus would come to his house, like He had in the Bible. Jehovah-Rapha, moved with compassion toward the Muslim father and moved by the faith of the Christian pastor, had indeed come to that Muslim home.

This isn't just a story I heard somewhere. This pastor was in my home here in California. He was in the U.S. because the Taliban had put a reward out for his life, and the government of Pakistan encouraged him, for his own safety, to leave the country for a while. We were praying for this pastor one Sunday afternoon in my living room. I have a collection of swords and was led to bring one of them out. One of my friends took it during the prayer and began to swing it over the head of the pastor, and we all prayed the prayer of David in Psalm 143:12:

In Your mercy cut off my enemies,
And destroy all those who afflict my soul;
For I am Your servant.

I don't know what your theology is. I can only tell you that we prayed this prayer of David, and a few days later a U.S. drone fired a missile into the headquarters of the Taliban member who had put the reward out for the pastor's life. The headquarters was destroyed, and everyone there was killed. Soon the pastor was contacted by Pakistani officials telling him it was safe to come home.

Today the Lord is looking for people through whose hands He can touch the sick and suffering, through whose arms He can embrace men and women, boys and girls, and through whose mouths He can speak and release His healing power.

Several years later this same pastor and his wife started a school for girls in Pakistan, but the persecution became so severe from the Taliban that government officials advised them it would be better for their own safety if they left the country. They ended up moving to Spain, where other Pakistanis have also found refuge.

While in Spain, he was invited to speak at an interfaith conference held at an Islamic mosque. Present were representatives of the Catholic faith, the Jewish faith, and he represented the Pentecostal faith. It was not a time of teaching; it was just a time for sharing what your faith was about. The head of the mosque, the Imam, had a son who was blind, and he sat that day at the back of the auditorium and listened. There was no altar call or prayer for the sick, but the Lord sovereignly came, as my Pakistani pastor friend was speaking, and that Imam's son was healed of his blindness. The Muslims in attendance began to say that it was Allah who had healed the boy, but his father said, "No, this is not Allah. We have prayed for my son for many years, and Allah did not heal him. It was Jesus who healed him." Unfortunately, the next day the man was kicked out of the mosque. He is now following Jesus, along with his son who was once blind but now sees.

Paul is a man on staff at the hotel where I stay in Bangkok, and he has become a friend. Although he probably wouldn't classify himself as a believer like me, he's always open to talk about the Lord and has even brought others to me to talk about Jesus. I don't remember all the details, but I remember that he came to me with a cyst over his eye that he was going to have his doctor examine. In the lobby of the hotel, I laid hands on his eye, and when he got to the doctor there was no cyst.

Another time he had a shoulder problem, I prayed for him, and the pain went away. He was surprised and blessed and told everybody what had happened. I find that the Lord wants to heal people who don't really know Him so that they can experience His love for them.

JEHOVAH-RAPHA, THE LORD WHO HEALS

In my more than forty years of ministry, I have prayed for hundreds of people, possibly even thousands, not because I think I'm special, but because I believe with all my heart that the Lord wants to touch the sick and suffering through our hands. I would even say that we are the hands of Jesus to every person who needs healing. I wish I could say that everyone I prayed for was healed, but that has not been the case. Many were, and I continue to pray for the sick, believing that the Lord wants to touch them through me. Whether it's physical, emotional, or spiritual, Jehovah-Rapha is still healing people today, and most of the time it's through the hands of those of us who believe.

Many years ago, we had a young man visiting us in our apartment. Because the apartment was small, I left the bedroom doors open at night for circulation. However, I kept noticing that even though I would open the door before retiring, in the morning it would be closed. I asked the young man why he kept closing the door and explained my reason for wanting it to remain open. He couldn't think of any logical reason why he kept closing it.

One evening, after he returned to his home, he was lying on his bed and suddenly had an open vision. It reminded him that when he was young, he came home from school one day and found a pornographic magazine lying on top of his bed. In the magazine, his stepfather had written, "If you want to do these things with me, then take all your clothes off and leave your door unlocked tonight." Instead, the boy had closed and locked the door.

Somehow the stepfather still got into the room that night, and the boy couldn't believe what was happening. As his stepfather approached, he pulled the covers tightly around him. The stepfather kept trying to reach under the covers, and the boy kept resisting him. Finally, the man stopped, but he warned the boy never to tell his mother about this.

INHERITING THE NATIONS

That evening, after remembering what had happened in the past, my friend realized that his actions of closing the door when he was staying at our home was partially motivated by fear. He decided to fight that fear and leave the door open a little that evening. As he lay face down on his bed with one arm over his head, the spirit realm opened. He saw two dark objects, which appeared to be demons. One grabbed his arm and put it tightly on his side, while the other got on top of him in a seducing manner. He said, "I just kept calling on the name of Jesus."

At that moment an angel came up from the bottom of the bed. My friend described it this way, "The angel looked majestic and was covered with light, with light rays coming from it, and they were sparkling like crystals." When the demons saw the angel, they fled and never came back again. He was set free from the trauma and emotional bondage of that horrible experience and never had to close or lock his door again.

Since the day Adam and Eve disobeyed God's command in the garden, sin has overtaken man, and with it has come disease, sickness, and brokenness. But Jehovah-Rapha is still on the throne. Moved by compassion and love, His healing virtue is still available today. He hears our prayers and releases His glory through our hands, that He might be glorified. He uses His angelic hosts and His earthly host to heal and set free His sons and daughters, so that we might walk in an intimate relationship with Him as Adam and Eve had once done in the garden.

And Jesus went about all Galilee, teaching in their synagogues, preaching the gospel of the kingdom, and healing all kinds of sickness and all kinds of disease among the people. Then His fame went throughout all Syria; and they brought to Him all sick people who were afflicted with various diseases and torments, and those who were demon-possessed, epileptics, and paralytics; and He healed them. Matthew 4:23-24

Chapter 28

RELIGIOUS STRONGHOLDS

But when the fullness of time had come, God sent forth His Son, born of a woman, born under the law, to redeem those who were under the law, that we might receive the adoption as sons. And because you are sons, God sent forth the Spirit of His Son into your hearts, crying out, "Abba, Father!" Therefore you are no longer a slave but a son, and if a son, then an heir of God through Christ. Galatians 4:4-7

As noted in an earlier chapter, the first time I went to Thailand was on September 1, 1978. I arrived in Bangkok at 6:30 PM and left the next morning at 6:00 AM. I was coming from Hong Kong on my way to Nepal. I met with a few missionaries and talked about the future, but I had no idea that Thailand would become an important part of my life and ministry. It's not possible for me to remember how many times I've been there during my forty plus years of ministry.

In the late 1970s or early 80s, we rented a hotel room in Bangkok for five days. I taught about the Promise of the Father recorded in Acts chapters 1 and 2, and many were baptized in the Holy Spirit and spoke in tongues. My friend, Brother Sonny, believes those meetings were the first time there were charismatic meetings in Bangkok.

Thailand, Cambodia, and Burma are Buddhist countries, but Thailand and Cambodia particularly are known by foreigners for the sex trade that is carried on there. It is beyond comprehension how

INHERITING THE NATIONS

a country can be so religious and yet so perverse at the same time. Cambodia has entire villages that are unofficially protected by the police, where pedophiles from around the world come to live out their sick and perverse desires, while, the Cambodian people live in poverty, bound in the chains of darkness by Buddhism.

In Thailand, every Buddhist has displayed prominently in their front yard what they call a "spirit house." It looks like a little doll house. There, every morning, they make an offering to the gods that will protect them. It could be food, drink, or flowers. Then they bow down and pray. Commercial buildings and hotels have larger spirit houses, sometimes very elaborate, and each city has a spirit house the size of a small home where people worship every day. The Buddhists are very religious people.

It was only a few years ago that I noticed how large the ears were on the Buddha statues in Bangkok. Every day people are bowing down and praying to a statue made of stone or metal that has very big ears but does not hear. We serve a God who hears. He not only hears, but He comes and answers our prayers.

The curse of Buddhism has so permeated the societies of many Southeast Asian countries that most of the inhabitants consider it to be an integral part of their culture. They somehow cannot see that demonic forces are controlling many aspects of their lives. To them, it's normal.

I had a discussion with one young Thai lady about how Buddhist parents expect their children to financially support them. I let her know how wrong I thought that was. Her response to me was, "You don't understand the culture of Thailand." I thought a lot about those words. To me, it is not a culture, but a curse. The horrific curse of Buddhism is that parents sell their children, both boys and girls, to be defiled in the bars and massage parlors of the big cities, sold into prostitution to support the lifestyle of the parents. The few children who get a good

RELIGIOUS STRONGHOLDS

education are sometimes able to find a decent job in the city, but even then, most of their money goes back to support their family, sometimes at great sacrifice.

The reason I call this the curse of Buddhism is that I don't see any place in the Bible where it's the responsibility of Christian children to support their mother and father. On the contrary, the Bible seems to teach that parents should support their children and grandchildren:

> *He who loves father or mother more than Me is not worthy to follow Me.*
> Matthew 10:37

> *A good man leaves an inheritance to his children's children.*
> Proverbs 13:22

I have personally met young Thai men and women who really loved the Lord and desired with all their heart to follow His will for their life. The Lord had given them dreams and visions about their destiny, and yet this curse of Buddhism hindered them or detoured them from following their God-given dreams. Their gifts, talents, and God-given destiny were sacrificed for what they called "culture," but what I believe is part of the "curse" of Buddhism. As sad as this is, it is part of everyday life in many countries of Southeast Asia, where people live in the darkness and chains of Buddhism.

I know a young lady who is a missionary in Cambodia, and she lives from the support people give her. The organization she works under gives her a small monthly allowance, but she sends all her money to her parents in another country and lives herself in poor conditions in Cambodia.

In order for people to come out from under the stronghold of Buddhism, they must experience the Promise of the father. A few years ago, I was teaching a DTS class in Armenia. It was quite a large class, and many of the students were from Russia. Whenever I'm teaching in DTS, I always talk about the Promise of the Father in Acts 1 and 2, where Jesus told the disciples not to go out until they were baptized with the Holy Spirit. In every class, there are young people from many different denominations, and some have never even heard of the baptism with the Holy Spirit or the gifts of the Spirit. It is always a challenging time but also a very rewarding time.

In one particular class, there was a young lady from Uzbekistan named Linda. She and her two daughters now lived in Armenia. She had many questions about the filling of the Holy Spirit. I love to answer this type of questions, but she seemed to have a never-ending list of them. Finally, I had to say, "No more questions! It's time to pray." There comes a time in every class that teaching is not enough; the Holy Spirit must come to validate what I'm teaching, and there must be an encounter from Heaven.

Those who were seeking the Promise of the Father gathered in a small group, and the rest of us gathered around them and laid our hands on them and began to pray. I can honestly say that, with only a few exceptions, the Lord has been faithful to come and baptize people in the Holy Spirit and they begin to speak in tongues. The Lord heard our prayers that day. He heard Linda's prayer and saw her heart, and she, along with many others who were seeking, was baptized with the Holy Spirit and began to speak in tongues. There was no more need for questions.

In that group, however, as I said before, were several from Russia, and they appeared to be hungry and thirsty for the things of the Spirit. The Lord had touched them, and they had experienced His love. Sadly, however, as I tracked them on Facebook, I saw that they had returned to the pleasures of the world, not necessarily sin, but they were no longer pursuing their calling or destiny.

RELIGIOUS STRONGHOLDS

Now these are the ones sown among thorns; they are the ones who hear the word of God, and the cares of this world, the deceitfulness of riches, and the desires for other things entering in choke the word, and it becomes unfruitful.   Mark 4:18-19

I believe the Father hears our prayers, and I believe He heard our prayers that day, He saw our tears that day, and I'm trusting that He will rescue those who have wandered from His loving arms and from His plan for their lives. There are people in the nations of the world who are waiting for those students to obey their callings and bring the Gospel to their nations.

As I'm writing this chapter, I'm thinking about the many times I've spoken in churches about missions and becoming a missionary. It seems that after every service someone comes up to me and says, "I was called to be a missionary and was really excited about it, but then I got married and had children, and I abandoned my calling," and they ask me for prayer.

The Bible says, in Romans 11:29:

For the gifts and the calling of God are irrevocable.

I believe that no matter how far you have gone away from what the Lord has called you to do, there's always a way back, always a way to return to your calling. It is so important for you, and it is also important to the people who are waiting for you to be obedient to the Lord and come to them with the Good News.

Jesus said:

The thief does not come except to steal, and to kill, and to destroy. I have come that you might have life, and that you may have it more abundantly.   John 10:10

INHERITING THE NATIONS

Therefore if the Son makes you free, you shall be free indeed.
John 8:36

Jesus came so that we might be free, free to do His will for our life and free to be able to bless others. For those who are called to the nations of the world, we are free to be able to go to those nations and proclaim the freedoms He purchased for those who are bound with the chains of false beliefs and religions.

Once, we were in Northern Thailand, at the Thai/Laos border, for a conference with leaders of churches in Laos. Because Laos is a Communist country, it's very difficult to have Christian conferences there. So, we had brought many godly men and women across the border to a hotel for two separate three-day leadership conferences—one for women and the other for men. My wife and three other sisters were scheduled to minister to the women while we ministered to the men in another room.

We decided to take a night train from Bangkok to the border because we had a friend traveling with us for the first time. Her name was Vera, and we thought it would be interesting for her to see the countryside once the morning sun had come up. It was just a simple train, but the beds were comfortable, so we all got a good night's sleep. As the sun began to rise and people began to wake up, we made our way up to the dining car to have breakfast. It was just a plain car with metal tables, but it was interesting to see the rice fields of northern Thailand. When the conference was finally finished, we flew back to Bangkok.

Leadership conferences are always a wonderful time, no matter what country we're in. The people are always engaging and hungry for the Word of God, and it's a great time to impart to them the things that the Lord has imparted to us. One of my favorite verses in the Scriptures is Romans 1:11. There Paul said:

RELIGIOUS STRONGHOLDS

I long to see you, that I might impart some spiritual gift, so that you may be established.

Some versions say, *"so you may come into your destiny."*

After one of the lunch breaks, I was down in the lobby, and I noticed several of the women sitting in one area with a posture that seemed rather sad or defeated. I walked into the middle of them, almost like skipping, and proclaimed, "Praise the Lord! What a great day this is!" There was absolutely no response from the women. I then spoke to the leader and asked, "What's the problem? Why is everyone so sad or depressed?" I'll never forget what she said to me: "We have lived under a Communist stronghold for so many years that when we're out from under that spirit in another country, we don't even realize we're free." I could hardly believe my ears. What a horrible situation to live under! It made me think about elephants. When they're young, a chain is put on their leg so they don't run away. When they grow into such large and powerful animals that could easily break the chain that is on their leg, because it has been there for so many years, they don't realize the power they have to break free.

During an afternoon break Vera, Brenda, and I went to the local market. We bought a large, beautiful red rose for each of the women in attendance, and these were given out to show them how special they were to the Lord. That evening, I looked into the room where the women's meeting was being conducted, and it was easy to see that the Lord had done a miracle. Chains of depression and oppression had been broken, and the women were dancing and smiling in worship.

Once, on a flight from Hong Kong to Bangkok, I happened to look out the window and saw that we were coming to a coastline. Looking at a map later I realized that it was the coastline of Vietnam. We had been near the city of Hue, once called the Imperial City of Vietnam. As the plane crossed the coastline and we began to fly over Vietnam,

INHERITING THE NATIONS

the spirit realm opened to me, and I saw what looked like a silo. It was a large shaft that went from the ground into the heavens, and around it I saw demonic forces going up and down. It appeared that they had control of that area of Vietnam. Sometime later, Brother Sonny and I were in Vietnam, and there we visited a citadel that was known as the Walled City. We entered the main gate and then walked around praying in the entire area. The next time we had leadership training in Vietnam, I explained to those in attendance what I had seen in the spirit realm and challenged them to begin to join together and pray against this stronghold that was set up in central Vietnam by demonic forces.

As of these writings, I have been in some fifty countries of the world, and just crossing the borders into some countries you can feel an oppression, a heaviness that comes over you. Just a few weeks ago, a friend of mine from Armenia came back from Dagestan, a country that had been part of the old Soviet Union, but was now independent. She was there a week and said it felt oppressive and even evil. She only felt freedom when she came back across the border.

When I travel in America, many people tell me how they love San Francisco, but the truth is that San Francisco is controlled by spirits of lust and perversion. People who live there don't even realize how bad it is. They have lived under it for so long they think it's normal. The Bible is clear that there are territorial spirits over different cities or areas.

Daniel experienced this. He was fasting for twenty-one days:

In those days I, Daniel, was mourning three full weeks. I ate no [a] pleasant food, no meat or wine came into my mouth, nor did I anoint myself at all, till three whole weeks were fulfilled.   Daniel 10:2-3

Then an angel appeared to him.

RELIGIOUS STRONGHOLDS

Then he said to me, "Do not fear, Daniel, for from the first day that you set your heart to understand, and to humble yourself before your God, your words were heard; and I have come because of your words. But the prince of the kingdom of Persia withstood me twenty-one days; and behold, Michael, one of the chief princes, came to help me, for I had been left alone there with the kings of Persia.   Daniel 10:12-13

A word of caution here: It is not wise and is even dangerous to begin to pray against territorial spirits alone. My advice would be to gather a group of like-minded leaders together to first pray and see if the Lord wants you to begin this battle. Then ask for His wisdom and specific strategies to come against these strongholds.

Strongholds are real, and we, as Christians leaders, must pray and ask the Lord to give us strategies to break down these strongholds in the cities and nations of the world, so that people living in those areas might be set free and receive the glorious Gospel. Then people of every tongue and every nation can find the freedom that only comes from a personal relationship with Jesus.

Two warriors

CHAPTER 29

TSUNAMI IN ASIA

The floods have lifted up, O LORD,
The floods have lifted up their voice;
The floods lift up their waves.
The LORD on high is mightier
Than the noise of many waters,
Than the mighty waves of the sea.   Psalm 93:3-4

At 7:58 AM local time, the day after Christmas of 2004, an undersea megathrust earthquake measuring 9.1 on the Richter scale erupted off the coast of Sumatra, Indonesia. This began to send tsunami waves into the Indian Ocean, waves recorded as high as eighty to a hundred feet. Approximately two hours later, those waves were approaching Sir Lanka on the western shores of the Indian Ocean and, at the same time, Thailand on the eastern shore. The tsunami waves would eventually bring destruction to fourteen Asian countries, leaving in their wake more than 227,000 dead.

Pastor L is a Methodist minister who lives in Colombo, the capital of Sir Lanka. He heard some noise outside, so he told his wife he was going out to see what was going on. He walked a couple blocks to the main road, crossed over it and a railroad track that ran alongside the road, then he walked through a small community. It was about a half-mile walk.

INHERITING THE NATIONS

At the end of the community was a cliff that went down to the ocean, probably a fifty-foot drop. As he looked down at the ocean, he saw that the water was gone, and people were picking up fish that were lying on what had once been the ocean floor. Looking out further to the horizon, he saw a big dark object approaching. He realized that it was a wave, but it never occurred to him how dangerous it was. He had never even heard the word *tsunami*. Then he noticed that it was coming in at a very fast speed. He started yelling to the people below to run, but no one heard him. Then he turned and began to run for home. He had to pass the other community and cross over the railroad tracks and the main road before reaching his own community.

The wall of water was so powerful that when it hit the cliff, it came over it, and then wiped out all the houses between the cliff and the railroad tracks. Miraculously, the water stopped just before Pastor L's housing tract. In another area, where the railroad tracks came nearer to the ocean, an entire train was wiped out with hundreds of people on it. The death toll in Sir Lanka that day was more than 30,000.

Pastor L went to England, where he had attended college and had friends, to raise money among his old friends, his wife sold all her jewelry, and together they raised enough money to help build temporary housing for the community that had been wiped out from the cliff to the railroad tracks. The government promised to build homes for those affected by the tsunami, but, as of today, nineteen years later, they have done nothing for their people.

In 2009, Pastor L came to our yearly missions conference in Bangkok with his son. Because his son played the guitar and he played drums, they led the worship in one of the evening sessions. They were a great blessing and invited us to come to Sri Lanka to train some of their pastors. We scheduled to go there the following year.

We had a three-day church empowerment conference, it was well attended, and the people were very hungry for the Word of God. The meetings were held in a conference center built for some of the foreign corporations located there, so the facilities were first class and very comfortable. We even had a chef assigned to our team. Every day he would come and ask us what we would like to eat, giving us different options to choose from. It was amazing to be treated so special.

On the last day, I was scheduled to bring the final message, and then we would pray for people. As I was getting ready to wrap up my message, I noticed Pastor L motioning for me to keep going. He did that several times, and I ended up preaching for three and a half hours. Finally, it was time to pray for the people. We decided to have a fire tunnel, and those desiring prayer walked between us. As they walked slowly through, we laid hands on them and prayed for them. This is a wonderful way to pray for a lot of people in a short time, and they get the benefit if receiving the laying on of hands by many and even a prophetic word if the Lord speaks. After the fire tunnel, many of the pastors who had children with disabilities brought their children for special prayer.

One day, while we were there, we visited some of the homes that Pastor L and his wife built with their money. The people were so grateful that Pastor L is able to have prayer meetings in many of those homes during the week. They are just simple, two-room houses. They were only supposed to be temporary, but they have now served for many years. Whenever there is a prayer meeting or Bible study, each house is full, and people are literally standing outside the windows and door looking in to hear the message.

Sir Lanka, which once was named Ceylon, is famous for its tea. Usually, when we go to a country for a conference, we don't stay very long, so we don't have time to see the beautiful sites a country has to offer. On one of our trips to Sri Lanka, we actually scheduled a couple days in which we could drive up one of the mountains outside of Columbo and just enjoy the area.

INHERITING THE NATIONS

Colombo is very hot in the summer, so the wealthier people go up the mountains to another city where it is much cooler. The mountain road is very curvy, with steep cliffs, but on every available part of the mountains, were tea fields that stretch for many miles. Once in a while we would also see beautiful waterfalls pouring out crystal-clear cool water. At one point, we even exited our van and went down to one of the waterfalls. It was an amazing sight. At several locations along that curvy road were little fruit and vegetable stands literally hanging on the edge of the mountain road.

We also saw large tea factories that processed and packaged tea. They offered free tours of the factory and, of course, had a factory store where we could buy tea fresh from the factory.

After an hour or so ride, we reached the top of the mountain, which, among other things, had a horse racing track. This really surprised me. We visited an English Tudor style hotel that was old but majestic. When Pastor L was a young man, he used to play the piano in this hotel. For him, it was like a step back in time as we toured around that hotel. We inquired about the price for staying there, but it was not within our budget. We found another place to stay for the one evening we spent in that mountain city. Sadly, the next day we happened to look at that first hotel on the Internet and saw that we could have stayed there for a very reasonable price ... if we had booked on the Internet. Maybe next time.

The next day, as we travelled down the curvy mountain road, we decided to stop at one of the small stands that were hanging over the cliff, selling their fruits and vegetables. It seemed like we had passed dozens of them before we finally decided to stop. This shop was run by a man and his son. The wife of the family was a tea picker in the mountain tea fields. As we began to talk with them, we learned that they were Christians. Then we realized why the Lord had brought us to their stand, when there had been many others we could have stopped at.

TSUNAMI IN ASIA

The owner showed us the inside of his little shop. In it was a very small room with a single bed where the family lived. Out the back, the property dropped straight down the cliff. There was no real backyard, just mountains filled with tea trees. It was beautiful. The prices were good, so we bought many things at that shop. We were happy to bless a brother in the Lord.

Sir Lanka is a Buddhist country, and the people are sometimes violent toward Christians. Many believers have been beaten, and churches have been burned by those living in the neighborhoods around them. Sometimes the Buddhist monks actually lead the people down the streets to attack and destroy Christian churches.

Although Pastor L is a Methodist, he is also baptized with the Holy Spirit and operates in the gifts of the Spirit. I think I could say he has a strong evangelistic spirit and is always trying to reach out and share the Gospel everywhere he goes.

In 2012, we returned to Sri Lanka to teach in several churches and hold a conference in the northern city of Kilinichi. It was in this area that the final battle of Sri Lanka's twenty-five-year civil war took place. Government troops surrounded the opposing forces and killed them all. Brother Martin, a great Christian brother from Southern California and a great man of God was with us, and when we entered the border of the city, both he and I remarked about how heavy the atmosphere was. It felt like a spirit of death was still covering the area.

The people who attended our conference were hungry for the things of the Lord, and the times of praying for them were a blessing. On the final day of the conference, three of us who were ordained ministers officially ordained Brother Martin to the ministry. He has been traveling and ministering with the Bangkok team in many countries in Southeast Asia, sharing the Gospel.

Sri Lankan tea fields

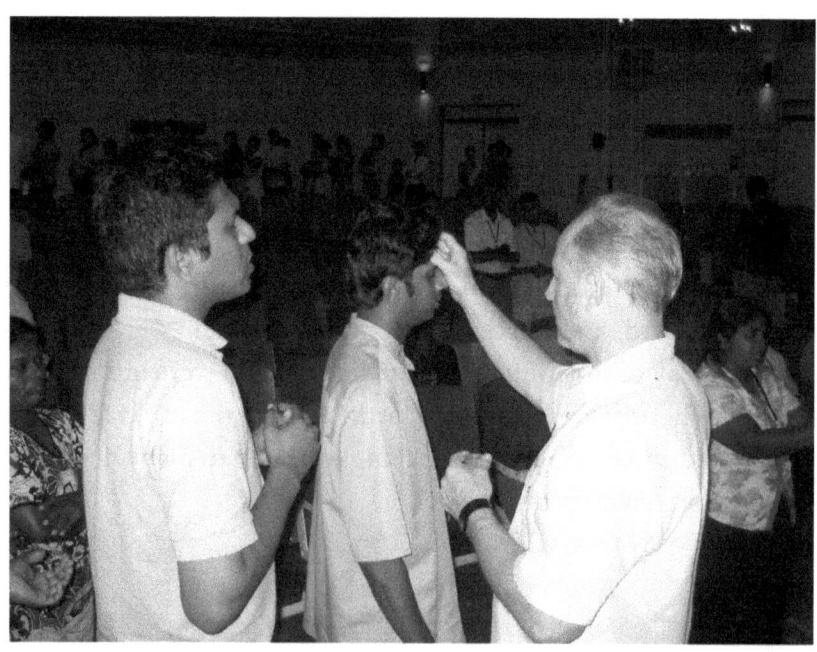
A Sri Lankan fire tunnel

In a Sri Lankan church

Chapter 30

TRAINING AND TRAVELING IN SOUTHEAST ASIA

For the word of God is living and powerful, and sharper than any two-edged sword, piercing even to the division of soul and spirit, and of joints and marrow, and is a discerner of the thoughts and intents of the heart.   Hebrews 4:12

From 1976 until 1997, most of the ministry I was involved with was concentrated in Thailand. However, in 1997 the vision of the base in Bangkok began to grow. The plan was to find leaders in other countries of Southeast Asia and to hold leadership conferences. These would be called CEP, Church Empowerment Program. If we could train other leaders, then they could pass down to their people what we had taught them. This would be better than trying to go to a church and minister to a larger group of people at different levels of their spiritual walk.

In the beginning, we reached out to the countries bordering Thailand, finding key leaders in Cambodia, Laos, Vietnam, and Burma. Each country had its own challenges, all had their history rooted in Buddhism, but some of them were now Communist, and they restricted the flow of Bibles and Christian teaching, and others were run by military-controlled governments. We began to classify these countries as access-restricted nations. The Lord had given us a vision to reach them. Now He had to give us strategies to do what

TRAINING AND TRAVELING IN SOUTHEAST ASIA

He had shown us would be necessary to build up and encourage the leaders there.

Bible delivery, Bible smuggling, or whatever word you are comfortable with, became a priority because access to the Bible was very limited in most of these countries. There are few experiences in the world equal to putting a Bible in the hands of a believer who has never owned one of his or her own.

Once, in Vietnam, the believers had acquired a large amount of Bibles in one home that would be given out to others. Then, however, one evening, they got a phone call from a believer who worked in the Police Department. He told them that the police had been informed about the Bibles in that home and were on their way. This would mean the Bibles would be confiscated, and the people in that home would go to jail.

Transportation in Vietnam, at that time, was by motor scooter. Everybody there began to load Bibles onto their motor scooters and to go off in different directions, to escape before the police arrived. One of the pastors turned down a road where there was a roadblock and was stopped by the police. He had Bibles piled high on the back of his bike and in a basket on the front. They were covered with a cloth and tied with a rope. The police officer asked him, "What do you have tied onto your bike?" He replied that they were "books." The officer said, "It looks like they're not very secure. They will probably fall off. Let me help you tie them more securely." Without looking under the cloth, the officer helped the pastor tighten the ropes, to secure the Bibles, so they wouldn't fall off. My friend said his heart had been beating so hard he thought it was going to come out of his chest. But, after the officer helped him, he sent him on his way safely with the Bibles.

Another time, my friends had a truck that was about half full of Bibles that they planned to deliver to Burma. At the Burma border, there is a river that divides Thailand from Burma, so there is a bridge

INHERITING THE NATIONS

you must cross. This bridge, because of political reasons, periodically gets closed. This particular evening, when my friends arrived, the border was closed.

They had planned to meet people inside Burma who would take delivery of the Bibles, and a time had been set for that connection. So, now they had a problem. Across the bridge there was a party going on. A military leader was celebrating something, and he had run out of alcohol. Some soldiers walked across the bridge to get beer and other drinks on the Thai side. Once they purchased everything they wanted, they realized it was too much to carry by hand across the bridge. Seeing my friend's truck, they asked him if he could carry their things across the bridge for them in his truck. He agreed, and the alcohol was piled onto the truck. Now the bed of the truck had Bibles in the front and alcohol in the back.

They crossed the border and delivered the alcohol to the military leader's party, and then, grateful to the Lord for Him opening the closed border, they continued on to deliver the Bibles to their contact inside Burma. As I have mentioned several times in the book, we have a saying: "It doesn't matter how the Lord delivers you, as long as He delivers you!"

Another time, on that same road, my friends had stopped at the border to have something to eat before crossing, and they heard that there were antigovernment people on the road robbing cars. Worried for their safety, they prayed and felt that the Lord would protect them, and so they crossed the border into Burma. After going only a short distance, the muffler fell off the truck, and they had no way to repair it, so they just kept driving with that very loud sound coming from their vehicle. They drove along the road without seeing any robbers at all and safely delivered the Bibles.

When they came back through, they again stopped at the same restaurant on the Thai side of the border to have something to eat and

TRAINING AND TRAVELING IN SOUTHEAST ASIA

heard people talking. Some of them were those who were robbing cars on that road. My friends heard them say that they had gone deeper into the forest that day because they heard a military vehicle coming. That was no military vehicle; it was the truck filed with Bibles and with no muffler. It only sounded like a military vehicle. The Lord had once again opened the way!

As I said before, through the Church Empowerment Program, we challenged the leaders to draw closer to the Lord in prayer, so that they could better comprehend His vision and strategies for the people who were under their care. Some of these leaders were responsible for many hundreds of people meeting in secret because of government restrictions and persecution. Brother Sonny had a unique gift of seeing the potential in leaders that they had not even yet seen in themselves, and he developed messages that would bring them to higher levels of empowerment, while, at the same time, challenging them to remain humble so that the Lord would be glorified.

I don't know if anyone has an accurate count of the growth of the CEP programs. They were so successful that soon leaders from other Christian groups in Southeast Asia began to request that Brother Sonny's team come to their countries too. Eventually the teams would teach multiple times in a total of thirteen countries in Asia. Over the years, I was part of these teams and enjoyed teaching in all those countries, some numerous times.

In 2008, a new vision for more concentrated schooling for leaders became known as MBS—Ministerial Bible School. This was mainly geared for leaders from the countries surrounding Thailand, but it was open to anyone who wanted to come. It was a twelve-week course that was broken up into four three-week classes; I taught about spiritual warfare there for the first nine years of the school ... until 2017.

One thing I always stress, as I talk about spiritual warfare: "This is not a picnic; it's a war! It's a war for the souls of men and women in the nations!"

INHERITING THE NATIONS

Another thing I always do in every class and in every church I have spoken in around the world is ask this question on my first visit, "Who would like to see Jesus tomorrow morning physically without having to die?" Of course, every hand goes up. "Well," I tell them, "it's simple." I hold up a mirror or something that looks like a mirror in my hand, and I tell them: "Tomorrow morning, when you get up, go into the bathroom, and look in the mirror, and you'll see Jesus. You are the Jesus the world sees. If they're going to see Jesus, it will be through you and me."

Next, I take the hands of someone in the room, raise it up and say, "These are the hands of Jesus. If people are going to feel the touch of Jesus, it will be through hands like these."

Then I embrace someone and say, "If people are going to feel the embrace of Jesus, it will be through our arms."

Then I touch the lips of one of the participants and say, "If people are going to hear the voice of Jesus, it will be through lips like these." And I finish by saying, "I would like for you to hold your hands up to the person next to you and say, 'These are the hands of Jesus.' Surely the Lord can physically reveal Himself to someone or do it in a dream. However, He most often touches people, He embraces people, and He speaks to people through us!"

In this way, I challenge my students and the members of the churches I minister in to touch people and believe that the touch of God will come through them. With all my heart, I believe it, and I've seen it in my own ministry hundreds of times.

On a short flight (thirty-five minutes) from Bhutan to Nepal, I had booked a seat on the right side of the plane so that I could see Mount Everest and the rest of the Himalayan mountain chain. As I got on the plane, I noticed a young lady sitting in my seat. I approached her and said, "Excuse me, but I think you're in my seat." She quickly got up and moved to the other side, apologizing.

TRAINING AND TRAVELING IN SOUTHEAST ASIA

Then, even before the plane took off, she came back over and said, "Excuse me, I wonder if I could sit next to you. I really wanted to see Mount Everest." She was a pretty lady, so I didn't mind, but I noticed that she had a husband across the aisle.

I said, "I don't mind if your husband doesn't."

She replied, "He doesn't care because he's not feeling well. He just wants to sleep."

As the plane took off and began its ascent, she began telling me she and her husband were from Paris. They had been married for nine years, but felt their marriage was getting stale, so they were on a spiritual search in Asia. As the plane climbed through the clouds and entered clear air, we realized that there was a solid cloud bank between us and the entire Himalayan mountain range. There would be no viewing Mount Everest or any of the other mountains that day. I turned to her and said, "You sitting next to me has nothing to do with those mountains. You're sitting next to me because I have the answer to what you and your husband are searching for. The answer is Jesus!"

The lady was listening, so I continued, "Pardon me for being so aggressive, but this is a very short flight." I told her about Jesus and how He had a plan for her and her husband. Then I asked if I could hold her hand and pray for her, and she said, "Yes." I looked over, just to make sure her husband was sleeping. I didn't want him looking across the aisle and seeing me holding his wife's hand. As we prayed, the presence of the Holy Spirit came upon her, and she said, "I've never felt anything like this in my life."

I said, "That's the Lord, and He has a plan for you and your husband's lives."

The following day a friend of mine and I were walking around the streets of Tamil, the area of the Nepali capital where all the shops are. It's like a mouse maze of streets, and occasionally they come together into a big square with a Hindu temple in the center. I've never counted them, but there are probably more than a dozen of these in that area of the city alone. The shops are amazing, and the owners are always ready to bargain. So, it's a shopper's paradise. But it is also a spiritual stronghold of Hinduism. The air is continually filled with the smell of incense from the temples, and many times the gutters alongside the streets are flowing with blood from the animal sacrifices that are made on the edge of the streets.

A friend of mine (Rudy from Australia) and I were walking along the streets, just window shopping, when we came across a lady who spoke perfect English. She was Nepali, and she was standing in front of her shop. We started a conversation with her and asked her how she knew such good English. She said her husband was from the UK, "But," she said, "he's in the hospital. Today I have visited ten temples praying for him."

I asked her if God had spoken to her in any of those temples, and she put her head down and replied, "No, he did not."

I told her that we were Christians and that we served a God who not only heard prayer, but who came and answered prayer. I asked her if we could pray for her, and she said yes. I took her by the hands, and Rudy put his hand on her shoulder. With blood flowing in the streets behind us and the smell of incense filling the air, we prayed to the God who sits on the throne of Heaven, the God who hears and answers the prayers of His children. As we prayed, the presence of the Lord came upon her, just as it had come upon the lady on the airplane. She also commented that she had never felt anything like it in her life. I told her it was Jesus, and that He was the only true God.

I believe with all my heart that the Lord wants to touch people with His presence through our hands. I always encourage my students to touch people when they pray for them. Jesus said:

They will lay hands on the sick, and they will recover.   Mark 16:18

TRAINING AND TRAVELING IN SOUTHEAST ASIA

When I'm teaching in a Bible school, another thing I encourage my students to do is to spend time in the morning listening to the Holy Spirit. When I start a class, I always ask for a testimony concerning what they have heard from the Holy Spirit in the last twenty-four hours, and it's amazing what happens. When anyone takes time to listen to the Holy Spirit, He comes and speaks with them.

I had a very funny thing happen one day, something that a young lady named Tisha, who was the president of the school at that time, reminded me of recently as I was writing this book. I always stayed in a hotel, and every day a motorcycle type vehicle that holds two passengers in the back (in Thailand, it's called a tuktuk) came to pick me up, and usually one of the students would come along with the driver. During one whole week, a student from Laos came.

On Friday, when we arrived at the school, this student got out his money to pay for the ride. I knew he didn't have much, so I said, "No, that's okay," and I gave him his money back and paid the driver. When I started the class that day, I asked for testimonies about what the Holy Spirit had said to them that morning. The student from Laos raised his hand and said, "I thought the Holy Spirit told me this morning to pay for your ride, but when you said no and paid yourself, I decided maybe it wasn't the Holy Spirit who spoke to me after all."

I couldn't believe what had just happened. I confessed to the class that I had not only robbed the brother from Laos of a financial blessing, but I had also robbed him of hearing the Holy Spirit. When I insisted on paying, he thought he hadn't heard the Holy Spirit. I literally got on my knees and crawled back to where he was sitting and received from him the money the Holy Spirit had told him to give. I asked his forgiveness for me missing the Holy Spirit. Of course, all the students were laughing as the Lord was humbling me. It was actually a great time of learning for us all.

Not long ago, I sent a text to Sister Tisha asking is she could think of anything else that happened at MBS that I should put in my book.

INHERITING THE NATIONS

As she read my text, she sensed a holy hand brushing her, confirming that my time with them had really been blessed. She became teary-eyed at this experience.

Something else that she said really touched my heart, and I quote: "I can vividly remember you reaching out to the students and giving them a hug to let them feel the love of God. I can still see the surprised look on many faces, especially among the simple village church workers from Laos, who were only acquainted to being harassed and maligned for their faith in Jesus. Some had been physically beaten and thrown into jail. When they felt the warmth of your hug, they softened and cried. What a glorious sight it was to see men who had been deprived of affection getting their soul touched by the tender embrace of the Lord."

Tisha went on to say, "Indeed, you have a message. But better than your teachings and animated delivery, it was your compassionate person expressing the love of God. The real Teacher Joe behind the image and aura of a tough man has made vivid marks of the steps you left behind among us."

Leaders began to come from Burma (now called Myanmar) for training at the school in northeast Thailand, so eventually the leadership decided to take a step of faith and build a school in Myanmar. It was in the city of Mandalay. This school was connected to a church led by Pastor John, a humble man of God who was always a great servant to me during my times of teaching at the school. In the evenings, he would pick me up, and we would look around town for a nice inexpensive restaurant. We found several that we returned to many times in my years of teaching at the school. Pastor John didn't speak a lot of English, but somehow we communicated, and I enjoyed the times of fellowship with him and his family.

For several years, we stayed in a hotel that was run by a Christian sister. It was small but comfortable and clean and had a restaurant attached to it, which was convenient. The only problem with the hotel

TRAINING AND TRAVELING IN SOUTHEAST ASIA

was its Internet connection. Most of the time it was very slow or not working at all, so I began to search for another hotel. Finally, I found one, the Wilson Hotel. It was very large, much more luxurious than the other hotel, had a free buffet breakfast, was closer to the school, and had great Internet service.

The first time I stayed at the Wilson, I went up to have breakfast, which was on the top floor, with a beautiful view of the city. I was looking over the food, trying to decide what to have, when a Burmese lady walked up to me and gave me a big hug. I was shocked. I said, "I'm sorry, do I know you?"

She said, "I'm the owner's wife."

A few seconds later a man who looked like he was a bouncer from a bar came up, shook my hand, and said, "Hi, I'm the owner of this hotel." They asked me to join them for breakfast. His name was Mr. Raymond, and he and his wife were both Christians. He had lived in California for quite some time, but when Myanmar began to open for business development, they came back to Mandalay and started the hotel. He told me that he also owned a gold mine. I said, "I would love to visit that mine sometime."

He said, "Sure! I can take you there anytime you're free." Unfortunately I never had enough free time to go. Meeting that couple, I was sure, was a divine appointment!

When it came time for graduation, we decided to have the ceremony at the Wilson Hotel. The leadership from Bangkok came, as well as ministers from other countries who had taught at the school. When several of them arrived from Bangkok, the owner came out, I introduced him to everyone, and we sat in the lobby to get to know one another. It turned out that he knew some of the people we were involved with in California.

Mr. Raymond had the workers change all our rooms to suites and didn't charge us. We had planned to use a room in the hotel for the graduation and to have a meal for everyone after the ceremony. He gave us both the room and the food for free.

During the graduation ceremony, several of us teachers spoke. When it was my turn, I introduced Mr. Raymond and told of his generosity toward us. He came up to the podium and shared a greeting with everyone. He had asked one of the staff from our office who the pastors were who had come from other countries and who the pastors from Myanmar were. At the end of the ceremony, he gave each of the pastors an envelope with $100, a sizable blessing for them. Every time I stayed there after that, if he was there, he would notify the staff in the lobby to let him know when I arrived so that he could personally greet me. I enjoyed many blessed times of fellowship and praying with him, and he was a great blessing to my friends and me.

Eventually we began to have Church Empowerment Programs, (CEP), in other countries of Southeast Asia—the Philippines, Burma (now Myanmar), Northeast India, Bangladesh, Nepal, Macau, and China in the beginning. Then we went to Bhutan, Pakistan, and Sri Lanka. In total, the CEP would be taught, alongside other teachings, in thirteen countries of Southeast Asia.

Since the late 1970s, working with Brother Sonny, I have travelled to these nations in Southeast Asia more times than I can count or remember. The Lord has been faithful to open many wonderful doors, and occasionally He has closed doors. It has been a journey complete with trials and tribulations, but also with great joy and satisfaction. I've tried my best to give God the glory, that Jesus might receive the reward of His suffering!

Bibles for Vietnam

Pilar with Vietnamese youth

Mr. Raymond of Myanmar

Asia

Chapter 31

BIBLES INTO CHINA

All Scripture is given by inspiration of God, and is profitable for doctrine, for reproof, for correction, for instruction in righteousness.

2 Timothy 3:16

Our trips into China have been too numerous for me to remember. We have traveled to many regions to deliver Bibles and encourage believers, many of whom have experienced severe persecution in the past and even now. Recently, percussion has again accelerated. Christians are being arrested, and churches are physically being torn down.

Chiang Kai-shek was the political and military leader of the Republic of China from 1928 to 1949. Then Mao Zedong overthrew him and formed the People's Republic of China. China was now Communist, and Chiang went into exile in Taiwan and continued there as head of the Republic of China until his death in 1975.

During Mao's leadership, it is estimated that between thirty and forty million farmers were killed, and a thousand forced-labor camps were built, where another twenty million reportedly died. In Mao's early rule, it is reported that forty-six thousand scholars were executed. Families were divided and sent to faraway locations around China. There is no official number, but among those families divided and relocated were multitudes of Christians.

One Christian family was split up, and the father and his thirteen-year-old daughter were sent to a labor camp in Manchuria in Northeast China. The father was assigned to work in a coal mine, but he soon got very sick and could not work, so there was no money for him and his daughter to buy food.

The daughter went to the owner of the mine and asked for a job, but because she was so young, she could not work in the mine. After much persistence on her part, the owner gave her a job manning a phone. If there was a problem in the mine, that phone would ring, and she was to activate a siren that would alert all the miners to quickly evacuate the mine. However, he gave her strict instructions never to activate the siren unless the phone rang.

The story that has been widely told is that one day the young girl felt the Lord was telling her to activate the siren. The phone was not ringing, but she felt so strongly that it was the Lord that she activated the siren anyway. When she did, four thousand miners came poring out of the mine.

The boss was understandably furious with the girl and reprimanded her. Then, a short time later, there was a massive cave-in in the mine. Because of this girl's actions, no miners were harmed. The little girl now was emboldened to tell her story of how the Lord she served had told her to activate the siren. Because of her testimony, thousands of miners turned to the Lord. This became one of the high points of a massive revival that shook Manchuria. Today it is estimated that there are a hundred million Christian believers in that area.

On one trip to China, I and another brother had filled our luggage with as many Bibles as we could safely carry on our short train ride from Hong Kong to Guangzhou. Later that first evening, we met some Chinese believers who came to receive the Bibles we had safely gotten across the border.

The next day I received a call from one of the leaders of the underground church who had heard that I was in town. He was hoping he could get some Bibles from me. He told me that a brother from a church in Manchuria had traveled for many days to Guangzhou, having heard that Bibles were available there. He had been at the pastor's house for almost two weeks, but they had only found two Bibles for him to take back to his people. Sadly, I had to inform him that all of our Bibles had already been delivered. Then I remembered that other believers were coming to Guangzhou that night by plane. I told him I would see if it would be possible to get Bibles from them and arranged for him to call me later that night. When he called, I was happy to inform him that I had some Bibles, and we made plans to meet at the local train station, a safe place because many people would be gathered waiting for their trains.

The pastor arrived on his bicycle and quickly began to tie the bag of Bibles I handed him onto the front carrier of the bike. As he did so, he shared with me the promise of Isaiah 65:24:

It shall come to pass
That before they call, I will answer;
And while they are still speaking, I will hear.

The Lord knew that the man would be coming down from Manchuria looking for Bibles, and He knew we would be coming in from Hong Kong bringing the needed Bibles.

After securing the Bibles, the pastor started to hug us and say goodbye, but I remembered there were more. I said, "Wait! This bag my friend is sitting on is also filled with Bibles for you!" My friend began to weep and quoted Ephesians 3:20:

Now to Him who is able to do exceedingly abundantly above all that
we ask or think, according to the power that works in us.

BIBLES INTO CHINA

With tears in his eyes, the pastor tied the second bag onto the back of his bike and rode off into the night. My friend and I stood there weeping, realizing that we just had been part of a great miracle. The next day those two bags of Bibles would begin their journey to Manchuria in Northeast China for the believers who were so hungry and thirsty for the Word of God.

As noted earlier, Mao had done everything he could to divide families and had sent them to difficult places to live, but God was actually moving an army of people into position, people empowered with His Word. Many of them had memorized the Scriptures prior to their Bibles being taken from them. The paper Bibles had been taken, but the living Bibles were inside of them, and everywhere they went they took the Word of God, and revival followed, as they shared and lived out the Word of God.

Three of us travelled from Bangkok to Jinghong in the Yunnan province of China to deliver some Bibles and plan for some future meetings in the area. One of the brothers with us, Brother N, was from Burma, and he had an amazing testimony and a burning desire to deliver Bibles into restricted areas.

Many years before, a mailman had delivered a Christian brochure to his home. He told the mailman, "This is not for me. I'm a Buddhist."

The mailman insisted, "This is your address, so it's yours."

Brother N took it, but he didn't open it for a long time. It just sat on his bedroom table. Then, one day, out of curiosity, he opened the envelope and began to read what was inside. It was a booklet that talked about a man named Jesus who had risen from the dead. He had never heard of anybody being raised from the dead, so he decided to attend a meeting that was advertised on the back of the booklet. The address was of a church. He slipped in the church and sat in the back row. Up front the pastor was preaching. Brother N said to the man sitting next to him, "Is that Jesus up there speaking?" He thought that if Jesus had

INHERITING THE NATIONS

been raised from the dead, that was probably him. At the close of the service, communion was served. As the bread and wine were passed, he did what he saw the man next to him doing.

Having concluded the service, the pastor greeted him with great enthusiasm and asked him how long he had been a Christian and what church he was from. He answered, "I'm not a Christian. I'm a Buddhist, and I don't even know what a church is."

Startled, the pastor said, "Why, then, did you take communion? It is only for Christians? You can't take communion here unless you're a believing Christian."

Completely ignorant about Christian things, Brother N told the pastor, "Okay, I'll just go someplace else where they'll receive me." The pastor talked to him for quite a while and encouraged him to come to other services, and eventually he became a believer.

After receiving the Lord in that church in Rangoon, Brother N wanted to start reading the Bible, but only three people in the entire congregation owned Bibles—the pastor, an elder, and a lady attorney. The attorney finally decided to allow him to borrow her Bible, but only for three months. Then he would have to return it to her. He agreed and was very happy to finally be able to read the Bible for himself.

Brother N read the Bible with great enthusiasm and made notes as he went along. He said in the end the notes were many times more pages than the Bible itself. In one month, he brought the Bible to church to give it back to the owner. She said, "I told you that you could keep it for three months." He said he had already finished reading it and had made many notes on it. She couldn't believe him. She said, "I can't believe you read this Bible in one month. This was my father's Bible. He gave it to me when he was dying, but I've never read it myself."

Another brother who joined us in Jinghong was Brother J. He is Chinese, but he works near the Burma/Tibet border ministering to the people of Tibet. He's a great brother with a big smile, and although he doesn't know any English, it's always great just to be with him. He really loves the Lord.

Brother J had travelled many days by bus from Tibet to get to us, and he was exhausted and needed a shower, but he didn't have any clean clothes to put on. I decided I would take him and Brother N the next morning to buy some new clothes. During the evening, we had a great time of fellowship and prayer and just had fun being with each other.

Brother J ministers in a very isolated area of Tibet to people who are mostly farmers. They must work in the fields almost every day, except during the winter. Before he left, he told them he would bring back Brother Sonny to meet them and share some Bible teachings with them, but Brother Sonny said, "I can't go. My schedule is full. I need to return to Bangkok, and Joe is scheduled to return to America. Neither of us can't go." Brother J was very disappointed, but there was no way for us to change our schedule. Finally, Brother N said he would go, and they should take Bibles for the believers.

Brother J said that would not be possible because there were too many checkpoints along the way. They could end up in jail if the border guards found the Bibles. Because of Brother N's history with the difficulty of getting a Bible, he was insistent that they must take Bibles. I distinctly remember him saying, "We are Bibles, and if we don't take Bibles, I don't go." With great reluctance, Brother J finally said, "Okay."

The next day I took them to a store to buy them some clothes. Brother J had only on one pair of shoes, and they were like hiking boots, so I bought him a nice pair of dress shoes. He told me, through the interpreter, that he had never owned a pair of dress shoes in his life.

When we got back to the hotel room, I told Brother N to take a shower and put on the new clothes because we were going out for lunch. He said, "I don't need a shower."

I said, "Oh, yes, you do and for two reasons. 1) I want you to try on these new clothes, and 2) You stink."

INHERITING THE NATIONS

He said, "When I was in the military, we lived in the jungle and didn't shower for weeks."

I said, "You're not in the military now, so go take a shower." He took his shower, and we all went to lunch, both brothers wearing their new clothes.

The plan for the two men was to take a bus to Kunming, the capital of the province. There would only be one checkpoint on that road. Then they would take an airplane, thus avoiding many more checkpoints and the long bus ride back to Tibet. We prayed before they left, asking the Lord to help them to get the Bibles safely to the believers in Tibet.

After lunch, we went back to the hotel to pack the suitcases and the Bibles for their journey, but while we were packing the Bibles, Brother N put his old, smelly clothes back on for the bus ride. On the bus, the two men would not sit next to each other, just in case one of them was caught with the Bibles. Although Brother N speaks Chinese, he only spoke Burmese on the bus.

They came to the one checkpoint, and two guards got on the bus. They were checking everyone's documents and were taking the suitcases in the overhead rack down to check the contents. When they got to Brother N, the one guard said to the other in Chinese, "Forget him! He smells too bad! Just move on."

Then they came to Brother J. They checked his documents, and then took his bag down from the overhead rack to open it and look inside. At that exact moment, a car was trying to drive around the bus on the wrong side of the road and ran head-on into another car right next to the bus. The guards hastily got off the bus to help with the accident and never checked the bag. The bus just drove away from the accident scene. Both brothers made it safely through to Tibet with their Bibles. Praise the Lord!

When we are smuggling Bibles in restricted areas, we have a saying: "It doesn't matter how the Lord delivers you; it just matters that He delivers you."

BIBLES INTO CHINA

On one of my last trips into China I had a very sad experience. In the early days, it was too dangerous to make personal contact with the leaders of the underground churches. However, as time went by, they felt more comfortable, and although we never went to their homes, one pastor, Brother L, would always meet us; then we would go to dinner together somewhere. It was very special to be with him, and I've talked about him in earlier chapters.

The last time I saw Brother L, the young Chinese lady we had met on my first trip and who had become a believer, took me to see him. We went to a small church building. She told me to wait in the back as she went up to the front and into what I assumed was an office. When she came out, Brother L was with her. But he didn't approach me. He just looked at me and then turned and went back into the room, and I never saw him again. I later learned that before that day, he had been arrested again and treated very harshly because of his contacts with outsiders such as myself. For him to be with me as before would have been too dangerous for him and could even have resulted in him going to prison. As he walked back into that room, my heart sank. I would never be able to put my arms around him or have dinner with him again.

We had enjoyed many wonderful times together, and thousands of Bibles had passed from me to him for the brothers and sisters of the Chinese underground churches. For him, life under the oppressive Communist government of China was hard, but he endured to serve his brothers and sisters. A few years ago, even though he was younger than I, Brother L went on to receive his eternal reward.

Hebrews 11:38 speaks of those who have suffered greatly for the Gospel and says of them, *"Of whom the world was not worthy."* Brother L was one of those people. The next time I see him we will be rejoicing together in the presence of Jesus!

With Brother L in China

With Brother L and other Chinese believers

Chapter 32

THE GOD WHO DELIVERS US

If this is the case, our God whom we serve is able to deliver us from the burning fiery furnace, and He will deliver us from your hand, O king. Then nebuchadnezzar said, "Praise be to the God of Shadrach, Meshach and Abednego, who has sent his angel and rescued his servants!"

Daniel 3:17 and 28

In the last chapter, I told the story of Brother N from Myanmar. As I noted, in the church where he received the Lord, only three people had a Bible—the pastor, an elder, and a lady attorney. The lady attorney let him borrow her Bible, and he read it and made many notes concerning it and then returned it to her. Now, however, he didn't have a Bible to read or study.

I imagine the Lord looking down from Heaven and seeing the hunger in Brother N's heart for the Word of God. Because there was no Christian bookstore where to could buy a Bible, the Lord decided to deliver a Bible to him in a very unusual way.

He was a member of the Burmese military and was in charge of a group of soldiers stationed at one of the many checkpoints around the country. Their usual duty was to make sure people were not moving drugs and other illegal items along the roadways.

One day one of his men stopped a man that was carrying a bag, The man looked very suspicious and nervous, so they brought him into the office of Brother N and reported to him, "We think that he's smuggling some thing; it may be books."

Brother N dismissed the other officers and was now alone with the man who was suspected of smuggling Bibles. He could see that the man was very fearful what might happen to him now. As soon as they were alone, he said to the man, "Relax, I'm a Christian brother also. All I want is some of your Bibles." When the man turned over some of his contraband, Brother N was overjoyed. Now he had his own Bible, and he had extra Bibles to share with others. In time, he, too, became a Bible smuggler!

As I have noted, when we are smuggling Bibles in restricted areas, we have a saying: "It doesn't matter how the Lord delivers you; it just matters that He delivers you!"

Sometime in the late 1980s, Shawn, a friend of mine from Albany, New York, was traveling with me in Romania. It was my second time and his first, and we were driving. At one point, we were getting very low on gas, and there were no gas stations to be found on the country roads we were on. Somehow we met a young Romanian man, and he offered to help us with gasoline if we would pay him in U.S. dollars. This would be very inexpensive for us, so we agreed and followed him to a private home.

While we were getting the gas, some policemen arrived. They searched the car and found my video camera. It had a tape in it of some meetings with believers we had taken in another Romanian city. These men didn't speak English, so the young man was trying to translate for us, but his English was also quite limited. They wanted me to show them what was on the camera, and I kept trying to explain that it had to be plugged into a TV, and I didn't have an accessory with me that would allow me to plug it in.

Eventually, the policemen had us follow them to a hotel where they got a room with a television and again wanted us to play the video. I explained to them again that I didn't have the accessory with me that would allow me to connect to the TV set. One of them kept pointing the camera at the television, thinking that it was like a projector. The country was still very backward at the time, and they couldn't understand this new technology. The truth is he could have simply looked in the viewfinder and played the whole video, but I wasn't about to tell him that and compromise our Christian friends.

After a lot of frustrating back and forth, the policemen made us pay for the room and told us they would be back in the morning. When they left, we got in the car and left, heading deeper into Romania and our destination with other Christian brothers.

When it was finally time to leave Romania, we had to go back through that same town where the police had stopped us. I said to Shawn, "Put on your seat-belt because if we see those policemen again and they come after us, we're going to make a run for the border." Praise the Lord, we drove through that town without seeing any police.

Crossing international borders and going through immigration can be a very stressful experience. It almost seems like there's a spirit of intimidation operating when you're talking to an immigration officer. Even though you have a visa, they can still deny you access into their country if they want to.

I normally travel on a tourist visa because it's easier to get, not nearly as complicated as trying to get a business visa. However, in 2018, I successfully acquired a religious visa to enter Russia and teach at the YWAM base in Rostov. I was one of the first ones off the plane and quickly went to one of the three immigration stations. The officer didn't know any English, and he spent a lot of time looking through my passport, which had dozens of visas from other countries. Finally, he called another officer over who knew some English, and he questioned me about why I was there in Russia. I told him that it was stated right there in the visa why I was there. I surely didn't want to start talking to him about Christianity because he could have easily rejected my entry. He had a conversation with the other officer at the counter and finally told me to go back and get at the end of the line.

Now, I was standing in line again, with hundreds of people who had just arrived by plane. Most of them were going through immigration without a problem. Eventually, everyone ahead of me had cleared immigration, and two of the officers had left. I was the only one standing there. Finally, the remaining immigration officer called me back to his counter. Again the other officer was called over to question me about why I was there. I just kept saying that it was fully explained in my visa and all they had to do was read it. I wasn't quite sure why they were holding me up. It was very possible that they wanted money from me. I was now the only one who had not cleared, and they continued to intimidate me.

Finally, they asked who I was staying with. I told them that I had a friend who was going be picking me up at the airport and that I would be staying in his home. With that, they stamped my passport, and I made my way out of the immigration area to the main lobby of the airport where my friend would pick me up. I was finally in Russia for the first time and excited about teaching at the YWAM base. Thank You, Lord!

CHAPTER 33

ENCOUNTERING THE MASTER

Then I turned to see the voice that spoke with me. And having turned I saw seven golden lampstands, and in the midst of the seven lampstands One like the Son of Man, clothed with a garment down to the feet and girded about the chest with a golden band.   Revelation 1:12-13

The book of Revelation was written by the apostle John. In the first chapter we discover that he was writing from the island of Patmos, where he had been exiled for the Word of God and the testimony of Jesus. In verse 10, John said:

I was in the Spirit on the Lord's Day, and I heard behind me a loud voice, as of a trumpet.

Then, in Revelation 4:2, John said:

Immediately I was in the Spirit; and behold, a throne set in heaven and One sat on the throne.

Whenever I read these verses, I have to wonder, "What does it really mean to be 'in the Spirit'?"

As I said before, many times, when you go to a church meeting, people talk about the presence of the Holy Spirit. They say things like, "Did you feel the Spirit? It was so strong tonight?" In the case of the apostle John, when he was "in the Spirit," he heard a literal voice, and he saw Jesus standing among the golden candlesticks. Then, in chapter 4, he was taken up into Heaven. Again, I have a feeling that there is much more to being "in the Spirit" than most of us have yet experienced.

In chapters 1 through 3, John was told to write to the angels of the seven churches, informing them of their spiritual condition and the blessing that would follow if they obeyed the Lord. Then we have Revelation 4:1:

After these things I looked, and behold, a door standing open in heaven. And the first voice which I heard was like a trumpet speaking with me, saying, "Come up here, and I will show you things which must take place after this."

John was taken up into Heaven, and there he saw the throne of God in all its glory, with the living creatures and elders around it worshipping. They proclaimed:

Holy, holy, holy,
Lord God Almighty,
Who was and is and is to come! Revelation 4:8

Paul wrote:

I know a man in Christ who fourteen years ago—whether in the body I do not know, or whether out of the body I do not know, God knows—such a one was caught up to the third heaven. 2 Corinthians 12:2

I wonder what it would be like to be taken up into Heaven to see the things that John and Paul saw? If they experienced it and it's in the

INHERITING THE NATIONS

Bible, is it possible for us today? As of this writing, I cannot testify that I have ever been taken up into Heaven. However, I've heard testimony by many people who have been taken up in a time of prayer or worship, so I certainly believe it's possible!

I have a pastor friend from the Philippines, Pastor Emmanuel. He's a great man of God and has many missionary stories that could fill a book like this one. I'd like to share here just one of his stories.

Pastor Emmanuel was planning a trip to one of their islands for ministry. He was to be away for several weeks, so he and his wife decided to do something special together before he left. They decided to go bowling. He said he was trying really hard to beat her, but the truth is she was a professional, and he could never beat her. As they were playing, he started to feel weak. He sat down, put his head on his arm, and was gone. Just like that, he was taken up!

He saw his spirit leave his body, then he passed through a thin veil about the thickness of a movie film and quickly entered another realm. He saw his body, but he lost all desire for physical things. As he turned, he was attracted to the beauty, and the awesomeness of his surroundings. He experienced unspeakable joy and peace. It was like a place of deep sleep, and he wanted to go there.

His spirit was drawn to this place. It seemed that he could not resist it. He was helpless, because the place was so desirable. But, at the same time, he could feel something trying to pull him back to the physical world he had left.

He heard the Lord speaking and felt like melting because the voice was so powerful, and yet it was so soft and filled with love. It was more than his spirit could contain.

The voice was coming from outside of him but also from within him. He felt it was a confirmation that since he had accepted Christ as his personal Savior, the Lord was actually living in him.

Then the Lord showed him pictures of his life, like moving screens revealing various intervals. On the screens were scriptures that related to these particular times. He felt that this showed him that our life will be judged by the Word of God, and there will be no excuses. It will be a fair judgment, or assessment, of our life.

The interesting thing was that these movie screens, as he called them, were not in a room. They were suspended in the spiritual realm, and all around it he could see the galaxies. He felt that the Lord was trying to make it clear to him how important his life was. The Lord told him that before he was created He had already known him. The Lord said, "Before you were born, I counseled Myself about your future because I would be putting in you My highest dreams, your purpose for life." The Lord said that He gave him all the potential and all the opportunities to fulfill his destiny.

At certain points in the presentation he was seeing on the screens, there were leaves and branches that sort of fell through the picture. He was thinking to himself, "What's this garbage?" Before he could ask, "What is this?", the Lord said, "These things are the garbage of life. They are opportunities that I gave people, and they missed these opportunities that would have helped them to fulfill My plan for their life."

The Lord was showing Pastor Emmanuel many things, and his ability to comprehend these things was expanding because he was out of his physical body and now in a different realm. There are no real words to fully explain it, but as the Lord was speaking, he understood everything clearly.

What really caught his spirit was when the Lord said, "At the end of the journey of life, there will be just two things you will have to answer for at the gate of Heaven. 1). What have you done with the Lordship of My Son, Jesus Christ? and 2). What have you done with the gifts and talents I have put in you for My glory?"

INHERITING THE NATIONS

Pastor Emmanuel couldn't comment because there was such authority in the Lord's words, and when he made that statement "the Lordship of My Son, Jesus Christ," it brought conviction to his heart. He realized that the word *lordship* was more encompassing than most of us realize. He thought in his heart, "Is He really Lord of everything in my life?" It was a very sobering moment. He said, "I realized that I must live purposefully, not just for myself, but for the Lord's glory. I also realized that part of that is attending to my physical health, taking care of my body. Sickness is not God's will for my life, so I have a part to play in keeping myself healthy."

Eventually, Pastor Emmanuel woke up, only to find that he was in a hospital. It felt as if he had been with the Lord for just a few minutes, but it had been nearly two days. He was in a hospital bed with all sorts of tubes and machines hooked up to him. When the doctor came in, he had the reports of the tests that had been taken, and there was nothing wrong. Every test had come back negative, and Emmanuel was released to go home. Physically he was healthy; he had just been on a journey with his heavenly Father!

As he tried to explain to his wife where he had been and what he had seen, he realized what the pull was that was trying to draw him back to the physical realm. His wife had been sitting at his bedside pulling on his arm and weeping, saying, "Don't leave us! Don't leave us!" What she was doing in the physical realm he was feeling in the spiritual realm.

The apostle John, it appears, was taken up into Heaven and saw things and heard things to bring back to the early Church that would bring correction and affirmation to them in their condition, but also to encourage them during the coming persecution. In the case of Pastor Emmanuel, it appears the Lord was trying to reassure him of his salvation, and also the importance of his calling, for him and for others.

Many Christians love the Lord, read the Bible, pray daily, and go to church, but they never come to the realization that God has a specific plan and purpose for their life.

ENCOUNTERING THE MASTER

As noted in an earlier chapter, several years ago, Pastor Rick Warren wrote a book called *The Purpose Driven Life*,[1] and it sold millions of copies. Why? Because people are hungry for a purpose and meaning in life. Most people don't realize that there is nobody like them, there never was, and there never will be. We are the only ones who can fulfill our calling and, ultimately, our destiny. The eternal destination of people and nations are in our hands. Obedience to the Lord's calling on your life is a serious thing. We must obey the Master's call, for our own benefit and also the benefit of others. May the Lord give us the grace to follow Him, even in challenging times, that He might receive the glory and that Jesus will receive the reward of His suffering through us!

---

1. (Grand Rapids, MI, Zondervan Publishing: 2012)

With Pastor Emmanuel, 2nd from left

Chapter 34

THE HEALING POWER OF JOY

*A merry heart [a]does good, like medicine,
But a broken spirit dries the bones.*   Proverbs 17:22

As I noted in an earlier chapter, one thing I and my great friend in Rio de Janeiro, Brazil, Pastor Paulo, have in common is that we like a good joke. It might be a practical joke, or it might be a joke we heard and decide to retell to others. Whatever the case, something happens when you laugh. Sometimes you laugh so hard it hurts your stomach, but it's always great fun. Many times, in the foreign fields, after long days of meetings, we just sit around having some nonalcoholic drink and talking, and I tell some joke I've heard. In this way, everyone ends the evening with a good laugh.

If you have known me for any length of time, you know I love to tell jokes. I can be serious, and I love the Lord with all my heart, but you don't have to be with me for many days before you'll hear some jokes. I like to laugh.

Some people think that if you're a Christian, you have to be serious all the time, but I don't see it that way. I think God anoints our personalities for His purposes and glory. Some people are serious, some are quiet, and some are loud. Then some are like me—humorous.

When I was still a very young Christian, we had a guest speaker one Sunday in the Community Church I was attending. As I observed him sitting in a chair behind the pulpit waiting to speak, he looked like a very serious guy, and I thought his message would probably be very boring. He had a little mustache and what looked like a frown on his face. When he finally got up to preach, he said, "I want to talk to you this morning about the humor of Jesus." I couldn't believe my ears. Because it has been so many years, I don't remember his message, but I do remember being shocked when he announced the title. It was totally different from what I had expected.

I have always appreciated good humor and tried to use it in my messages. On two specific occasions, after I had preached, people came to me afterward and said, "You missed your calling. You should have been a comedian." I don't know if they really didn't like my message or if they just liked my jokes, but it was an interesting comment.

Some think I take humor too far. After working in Asia for many years, I was invited to be part of the International Board of Ethnos Asia Ministries in Bangkok. When my friend, Sonny, spoke to the other board members about wanting to invite me to be a member, one of the older members of the board, a man from England, commented, "Sonny, do you think Joe can ever be serious about anything?"

His wife quickly rebuked him: "John, we love Joe."

John replied, "Yes, I love him, but I just don't know if he can be a serious board member."

Ultimately, I was allowed to be on the board and enjoyed great times of fellowship with all of the other members, and I didn't have to leave my joy and sense of humor at the door.

When talking about joy and laughter, the subject that always comes up is what has come to be known as "holy laughter." I had never heard of it or seen it until one night some friends and I visited a small Pentecostal church in the high desert of Southern California. Everyone, including us, had suits and ties on, and the women were also dressed very nicely. We had gone there because a friend was speaking that night.

INHERITING THE NATIONS

At a certain point in the service, a lady at the end of our row began to laugh quietly. One of my friends whispered to me, "Don't look at her." When she began to laugh a little louder, he turned and looked her way. As he did this, he started laughing, and then he fell off his seat onto the floor and lay there laughing his head off.

By this time, others in the church had started laughing too. It then hit my other friend. He, too, fell to the floor, and both of them were still there laughing when the service finally came to an end. I had to drive them home that night because they were both totally intoxicated with laughter.

When we finally got to the house of one of my friends, the two of them were still laughing. We sat in the living room for a very long time. I was just looking at them, and they were just laughing. Somehow, I wasn't feeling a thing. I did sense that there was something real about this experience, but it hadn't affected me yet.

After that, there were meetings Brenda and I went to where some would break into this thing called holy laughter, and now Brenda started laughing. I still didn't feel anything. At one of those meetings, Brenda was still laughing when the service ended, so I had to carry her out to the car, and physically put her into it. She couldn't walk because she was laughing so hard. She later explained to me that the laughter brought her great peace, enjoyment, and a lightness to her soul and spirit. "It seemed," she said, "like the cares of the world were just washed away."

In all my years of ministry, I have usually traveled alone, with Brenda, or with a friend. Then, when I reached some foreign country, I became part of a team. The first time I took a team myself it was Brenda and I and four other women. We were scheduled to go to Thailand, Burma, and Vietnam. The responsibility of being in charge of a team was something I had never experienced before, and I was a little unsure of myself.

THE HEALING POWER OF JOY

Our flight to Bangkok was eighteen hours long, which leaves you exhausted, but the next morning we were up and went to a church camp where we started several days of teaching. The activities were nonstop. There were some personality clashes within our small group, and that also affected me, to the point that I was experiencing some stress. Leading my own team was a very new experience for me.

When the camp meetings were finally ended, our team got into a rented van with a few of my friends to go back to Bangkok. It was early evening, and we hadn't eaten our evening meal, so we decided to go to a seafood restaurant near the sea. While riding in the van, everyone was talking to each other, but I was sitting alone, trying to relax. Then something began to stir in my spirit, and, for no apparent reason, I began to laugh. As my laughter grew louder, others in the group heard it and began to pray, "Give him more, Lord! Give him more!"

I don't know if there are words that can fully explain this experience. It seems that you really have to experience it in order to understand it. That evening, in the van, as we traveled toward the restaurant, holy laughter continued to pour forth from my spirit. This went on for a good fifteen to twenty minutes before we arrived at the restaurant.

As we were arriving at the restaurant, I felt a relief from the stress and a freedom from the cares of the world. My soul and spirit had a lightness to them. Maybe another phrase for it would be *a refreshing*. For years I had seen this in other people. Now I had experienced it myself, and it was wonderful.

Several years later, in 2011, I was at Sonny's house in Bangkok. Ed, a friend of mine from California, and I, along with Sonny's son and his girlfriend, had just returned from having meetings in Bhutan, a country high in the Himalayan Mountains. We were sitting around the dining room table, and Ed began to talk about holy laughter. He shared how sometimes in prayer meetings with friends, they would hold up an imaginary bowl that was filled with water from the Lord. As they would hold it to their lips and pretend to drink it, holy laughter would come upon them. It sounds kind of crazy, and I can't give you a Bible verse for it, but I can only say that as he was sharing this, he put this imaginary bowl up to his mouth and begin to drink, and holy laughter spilled over onto me, and I began to laugh there at the dining room table. Ed put his hands on me and started praying, "More, Lord! More, Lord!"

I was saying, "Stop," but the laughter kept coming.

Sonny's wife, Dahlia, was sitting across the table from me, and now she started laughing. I was laughing so hard that I finally got up, in an attempt to get control of the laughter, and I fell on the floor and continued to laugh, while Ed continued to pray, "Give him more, Lord! Give him more."

I heard Sonny say, "Well, this is what it's all about!"

To me, it was like a refreshing washing over me after a week of ministry in the Buddhist stronghold of Bhutan.

Another time, when we had a meeting in Bangkok with many of the leaders who were working with Sonny in Southeast Asia, he had invited a brother from England to speak. On the final night of the meeting, there was a time to go forward and receive prayer for any need you might have or just for a fresh touch from the Lord. The speaker was standing in the middle, and two other people lined up on both sides of him, so there could be five lines for people to get prayer. I decided I was going to get all the prayer I could, so I wanted to go through all five lines.

It was a very encouraging time, especially for the leaders who had come from countries under strong spiritual oppression. Meetings like these allow them to be in an atmosphere of real freedom where the Holy Spirit can come and bring a genuine refreshing to their souls. Many received encouraging prayers, and some were falling in the presence of the Lord.

THE HEALING POWER OF JOY

I went through the prayer lines, one after the other. When I went to get prayer from the fifth person, it was actually a couple, and it seemed that they were hooked up to an electrical cord, as they were praying with an amazing anointing. As they prayed for me, I really felt the presence of the Lord. It was precious.

Because everyone in the room was in an attitude of prayer, I decided to have other leaders lay hands on me and pray for me. Finally, a group of about five of them laid hands on me together and began to pray. As they were praying, I began to experience holy laughter. At the same time, someone was calling me over the microphone to come and pray the final prayer. I slowly moved toward the front, staggering like a drunken person and laughing the entire time.

I got near the front of the room, but I could hardly stand up. I leaned against the wall, and someone brought me the microphone to close in prayer. The problem was I was still laughing, I'm sure some of the leaders thought, "What is going on with Joe?" Some of them may never have seen holy laughter before. I finally was able to give the closing prayer.

Late in November of every year we have a conference for leaders of churches in Thailand. I have had the opportunity to be one of the speakers at several of these conferences. On the final night of one of the conferences, my friend, Pastor Rene from the Philippines, was scheduled to give the final message. He's a great man of God, and the Lord uses him in many precious ways to bless people.

Because there had already been a lot of Bible teaching by other speakers, Rene's plan was just to encourage everyone and to have a time of prayer. However, from the very beginning it seemed like the translator couldn't stay focused on what Pastor Rene was trying to say. He was trying to translate, but it appeared he was on the edge of starting to laugh, and he seemed physically unstable, leaning on Pastor Rene many times.

INHERITING THE NATIONS

At some point, both the translator and Pastor Rene started laughing and eventually collapsed on the floor, laughing joyfully. As they lay there laughing, several people began to move around to get a better look at them and to try to understand what was going on. I realized there would be no speaking that night because the Holy Spirit had come and wanted to release holy laughter to many of those leaders who labored in difficult situations around Thailand. They needed a release. They needed a refreshing that cannot be taught; it can only be experienced. I got up from my seat and knelt down next to the two of them and laid my hands on the translator. As I did, it was like I touched a 220 volt electrical line. I began to laugh and fell next to them. Now the three of us were on the floor laughing.

They remained on the floor a while laughing, but I got up and started touching other people, and they began to laugh. All around the room, people were experiencing holy laughter, some for the first time in their life. Everyone was refreshed in body, soul, and spirit and would return home, most to small churches scattered around northeast Thailand. A majority of them made their living as farmers, but they were also pastoring churches and caring for the spiritual needs of their people. It's not easy being a leader, and in places like Thailand, it can be even more difficult and challenging. We need times when the Holy Spirit breaks through and touches our emotions in a way that brings a release of the burdens of everyday life and fills us with joy and rejoicing.

There are many passages in the Scriptures that talk about laughter, rejoicing, and joy. However, it's my personal opinion that some of these things cannot be understood completely by the human mind. Holy laughter is a spiritual experience, and, because of that, until it is experienced, you cannot realize the spiritual benefits of it.

Armenian laughter

Pastor Rene on the right with his Thai translator

Chapter 35

THE ROAR OF THE LION OF THE TRIBE OF JUDAH

But one of the elders said to me, "Do not weep. Behold, the Lion of the tribe of Judah, the Root of David, has prevailed to open the scroll and [a]to loose its seven seals."   Revelation 5:5

In the early 1990s, Brenda and I, along with a friend named Jeff Bennett, decided to visit a church in Toronto, Canada. It was called the Toronto Airport Vineyard Church, and it was widely reported that a true revival was happening there. We wanted to see what the Lord was doing, and it turned out to be a very powerful and blessed time for us.

In many of the revivals in church history, there were manifestations that seemed strange, and many people did not believe they were from God. When the Holy Spirit comes upon human flesh, there can be many different reactions. Some revivals have a strong message about repentance, which is followed by a lot of new people coming to know the Lord. In Toronto, it was more like joy and blessing was being poured out upon the people from all over the world, and they were taking this joy back to their churches. One of the rather strange physical manifestations was people roaring like a lion. This seemed to bring about a very strong presence of the Holy Spirit.

INHERITING THE NATIONS

When it was time for prayer, there were lines drawn on the floor at the back of the church where you were to stand. Someone would come and pray for you there. Of course, there were hundreds of people lined up on these lines waiting for prayer. One of the things I noticed in Toronto was that no one on the ministry team seemed in a hurry. They would continue to pray until there was a move of the Holy Spirit. I went for prayer because I was having a lot of pain in my shoulders. I assumed it was from all the driving I had been doing. After praying for quite a while, with no apparent results, the brother praying for me asked if I was feeling burdened about anything. I thought about it and told him I would be visiting my oldest son, whom I hadn't seen in a very long time. He had me confess that I was worried about seeing my son, and immediately the pain in my shoulders went away.

One of the pastors from my home church in California had visited Toronto and decided to have meetings three days a week following the format of the Toronto Vineyard Church. It was pretty much a lot of worship, with a short teaching, and then a long time of prayer, with some people just lying on the floor experiencing the presence of the Lord. One evening I was there lying on the floor, relaxing, as worship music was being played. About ten feet away was a young lady who was also lying on the floor. Suddenly, she began to roar like a lion, and when she did, it felt like a strong presence of the Holy Spirit covered me like a blanket. After several months of these special meetings at my church, they finally ended, and I never again experienced anyone roaring in the Spirit until 2020 during a great time of darkness in my life.

One day, during an intense time of praying in English and in other tongues, I could feel something coming up from deep within me. In my mind, I remembered the time I first saw someone roaring in the Spirit like a lion, and for the first time in my life I began to roar a very aggressive and load roar. As I did this, I could see chains coming off of me. Darkness was turning to light, and I could see myself preaching in

THE ROAR OF THE LION OF THE TRIBE OF JUDAH

Armenia. (You can read the full story in Chapter 40, "Descending into Darkness."

Many believe and the Bible makes it clear that when Jesus first came, He came like a lamb prepared for the slaughter. He came in submission to the Father, to pay, with His own blood, the debt that was owed for our sin. On the cross of Calvary, the Lamb of God was slain for the sins of the world, for my sins and yours.

John 1:29 records the words of John the Baptist as he saw Jesus coming toward him:

"Behold! The Lamb of God who takes away the sin of the world!"

In the last few years, there have been many prophetic words about the Lion of the tribe of Judah (Jesus), and many have had visions of Him in this role. The prophet Amos said:

A lion has roared!
Who will not fear?
The LORD God has spoken!
Who can but prophesy?   Amos 3:8
Hosea foretold:

They shall walk after the LORD.
He will roar like a lion.
When He roars,
Then His sons shall come trembling from the west.   Hosea 11:10

Throughout the world there have been many recent visitations of the Lord. Sometimes this is just a powerful visitation of the Holy Spirit during a church service or a prayer meeting. At other times, it turns into a revival that may last for weeks or months. Sometimes it affects only

INHERITING THE NATIONS

a particular church, but at other times, it becomes global and changes Church history as we know it. In all of these times of visitations, there are manifestations which some accept but others don't believe are from God. One thing is for sure: when the Holy Spirit comes upon human flesh, manifestations do occur.

On Father's Day, June 18, 1995, in the Brownsville Assembly of God Church in Pensacola, Florida, there began a visitation of the Holy Spirit which resulted in great repentance and a call to holiness. Over the next five years, it is reported that more than four million people attended those services. One of them was my close friend, Pastor Chuck.

When you first meet Pastor Chuck, you would think that he is a very hard guy, very unemotional. He was a bull rider and a construction worker, a real tough guy, prior to becoming a pastor. He said that when he first walked into the church in Pensacola, out in the foyer, even before he got into the sanctuary, the presence of the Lord came on him so strongly that he began to cry, and he never cries. In an effort to stop crying, he went back outside and was able to stop. But he was there at the church for several days, and every day he did a lot of crying.

When Pastor Chuck came back to California and tried to share his testimony, every time he said the name of Jesus, he began to cry. The Lord was doing something really deep in his spirit. It was as if he was experiencing a deeper love for Jesus.

One of my friends, Brother T from Kyrgyzstan, took a group of DTS students to Karakol City, near the Kazakhstan-China border. He had been praying for this city for a long time and felt the Lord wanted him to start a work there among the existing churches. His desire was to help them all grow and to bring them encouraging teaching. When he got there, however, all the doors seemed to be closed to him.

Karakol is a Muslim city, and when people learned that he and his team were Christians, no one was willing to rent them a place to hold their meetings.

THE ROAR OF THE LION OF THE TRIBE OF JUDAH

Then Brother T had a vision of a lion roaring in four directions. Believing that this was from the Lord, he went up to a high place and began to roar in the Spirit over the area, facing the North, the South, the East, and then the West. As he did this, he felt there was a breakthrough in the spirit realm. Within only about five minutes of him roaring like that, he received two calls from pastors offering him their churches to use for doing the YWAM training. It appears that roaring in the physical realm, at the direction of the Lord, does something in the spiritual realm, something that then affects the physical realm and brings a breakthrough.

Recently, in a home church that I belong to, a brother came and asked for prayer because he had been having dreams of demonic visitations that were keeping him up most of the night. Several people prayed for him, and then I felt that I should put my face on his chest and roar. I roared into his chest three times, and he later testified that he felt something leave his mind when I roared.

A Vietnamese girl who had a strong occultic background came to Dina, the leader of the home church, asking for prayer because she was hearing voices in her mind. While Dina was leading her in prayer to renounce her occultic past, the Vietnamese girl suddenly lost the ability to speak and couldn't say the name of Jesus. Finally, Dina stood behind her and roared into her back. Immediately the Vietnamese lady was set free and was able to proclaim that Jesus is Lord. She is now reading God's Word with great hunger.

In May of 2023, I was invited to attend a small meeting of seasoned pastors in California. We spent two and a half days together sharing the Word and praying for one another. When we were praying for one brother, I felt led to roar into his spirit. The roar came with such force that two of the other pastors later said they had felt the power of the roar in their spirits.

In Ezekiel 37, the Lord brought Ezekiel to a valley of dry bones and then spoke to him to prophesy to those bones. Verses 5 and 6 record:

INHERITING THE NATIONS

Thus says the Lord God to these bones: "Surely I will cause breath to enter into you, and you shall live. I will put sinews on you and bring flesh upon you, cover you with skin and put breath in you; and you shall live. Then you shall know that I am the Lord.""

Verses 7 and 8 record the result:

So I prophesied as I was commanded; and as I prophesied, there was a noise, and suddenly a rattling; and the bones came together, bone to bone. Indeed, as I looked, the sinews and the flesh came upon them, and the skin covered them over; but there was no breath in them.

Then, in verses 9 and 10, God spoke to Ezekiel again:

"Prophesy to the breath, prophesy, son of man, and say to the breath, 'Thus says the Lord God: "Come from the four winds, O breath, and breathe on these slain, that they may live."'" So I prophesied as He commanded me, and breath came into them, and they lived, and stood upon their feet, an exceedingly great army.

Ezekiel and many others of God's people did what we might consider strange things. They heard from God, and then they did what He said to do, no matter how strange or challenging it was. They obeyed and moved by faith. They did something in the physical realm that released God to move in the spiritual realm, and this, in turn, caused change in the physical realm. In Ezekiel's case, his obedience in proclaiming what the Lord told him to say caused a valley of dry bones to become an exceedingly great army.

Sometimes, when the Lord speaks, we don't understand what He's about to do, but that's okay. We're not called to understand everything, just to obey what God is saying and move in faith, trusting that His desire will be accomplished, because of our obedience.

THE ROAR OF THE LION OF THE TRIBE OF JUDAH

A member of our home group is a sister named Maritza. Two years ago Maritza had a stroke caused by an aneurism in her brain, and the doctors told her she would either die or be a vegetable because of the size of the aneurism. However, the Lord is the God of restoration, and He is restoring her.

What is going on in Maritza's life is a real miracle. Just recently we were praying for her because she somehow fractured her foot. Half of her foot was a deep black and blue. As we gathered around her and prayed, the pain she was having started to lessen, and she was able to walk more freely. She stood there with one hand on her heart and the other in the air, praising the Lord, and I heard her say, "The Lion of Judah is coming." I felt that this was a sign from the Lord to roar over her.

I waited a little, as people continued to pray, and she continued to thank the Lord for what He was doing in her foot. Then, I looked over at Dina and she asked, "Do you want to roar over her?" I then stepped forward, told Maritza to put her other hand on her heart and that I wanted to roar into her spirit. Not wanting her to fall, I put my arm around her and a couple of other people came behind her to support her. Then, I put my face into her hand and roared as loud as I could three times. It shook both her spirit and her body, and she testified that she felt the Holy Spirit come and bring a major release to the nerves in the entire left side of her body, nerves that had been damaged by the stroke.

I can't say that I fully understand what's going on. I can only say that when I feel the Lord leading me to roar into people, I obey Him, and leave the results to Him. I believe that the Lion of the tribe of Judah is rising up for His people and His Church. He is tired of seeing people defeated, and He wants His Church back. Therefore, there is a roar coming from Heaven as the Lion of the tribe of Judah is setting people free!

Chapter 36

SEASONS OF CHANGE

To everything there is a season,
A time for every purpose under heaven.   Ecclesiastes 3:1

Both life and ministries have seasons of change. Sometimes the change has global effects, and other times it just affects us personally. In my international travels, I've seen global change and changes that have affected my personal life and ministry.

Global change came when Brother Sonny and I were in Hong Kong on July 1, 1997, the evening that the British government's ninety-nine-year lease was ending, and China would take political control of the territory. The television showed Communist Chinese troops in trucks sitting at the border, so that many in Hong Kong feared that the night would end with people being killed for their Christian faith. Christians were praying.

Our plan was to attend an all-night prayer meeting at the church that had supplied us with Bibles through the years. Before the prayer meeting, we planned to visit Brother L outside of the city in what is known as the New Territories. He and I had made many trips together into China smuggling Bibles. We took the train out and then got a taxi from the station to his apartment. When I had last seen Brother L, he was single. Now he was married and had a daughter. We had a great time together, praying and fellowshipping. The family was very frightened about what could happen next.

While we were there praying, I felt the Lord say to me, "Wash their feet." I knew foot-washing was in the Bible, but I had never personally seen it done and had no idea how to go about it. I thought to myself, "I am *not* going to wash their feet."

Sonny and I left and caught our train back to town. While we are on the train, I confessed to Sonny that I had missed the Lord. He had told me to wash the feet of these precious people, and I hadn't done it. Sonny said, "Well, let's go back."

"No," I said, "we should go on to the all-night prayer meeting. That's important."

Looking back on it, I'm not sure what kind of logic this was. Going to an all-night prayer meeting was more important to me than doing what the Lord had clearly told me to do, wash the feet of His servants. We went to the overnight prayer meeting, and the troops that were amassed at the border never did come into the city that night.

Sonny and I had planned to go on into China for a few days afterward to see what was happening there. Then we would return to Hong Kong, he would immediately take a flight to Bangkok, but I planned to stay one more day in Hong Kong and then meet him in Bangkok the next day. The entire time we were in China the Holy Spirit kept speaking to me, "I told you to wash their feet! I told you to wash their feet!" It was relentless.

I finally said, "Lord, I confess that I didn't do it, but it's over!" But the Holy Spirit kept speaking during those few days, "I told you to wash their feet!"

We had a funny thing happen while we were in China. Late one evening, Sonny and I were both looking for something to snack on. We went to the hotel restaurant, looked over the dessert menu, and both decided the best thing was to have some apple pie ala mode. We could envision a big piece of apple pie, like Grandma used to make, and a huge pile of vanilla ice cream on top of it. Sonny also wanted a

INHERITING THE NATIONS

Coke in a can, but unfortunately our waitress knew very little English. Finally, Sonny very slowly said, "Coca-Cola," then said, "No glass." As he said it, he was taking off his glasses and setting them on the table. Then he said, "No ice," as he pretended to pull out his eyes. We both laughed, but somehow the lady understood and brought him a can of Coca-Cola.

We were still waiting for this wonderful piece of apple pie piled with vanilla ice cream. When it finally came, we looked at it in unbelief. It looked like a small flat pancake with a very small scoop of vanilla ice cream on top. We started laughing. The waitress just looked at us, wondering what was so funny.

A couple of days later we returned to Hong Kong, Sonny caught the next flight back to Bangkok, and I went to my hotel to spend the night. As planned, I was to join him the next day. However, I still couldn't get out of my mind what the Holy Spirit had been saying to me in China: "I told you to wash their feet." Now Sonny was gone, and I was alone. However, just like in China, the Lord continued to speak to me in my hotel room in Hong Kong. Now I had no excuse. I had to obey.

I called Brother L and told him I'd like to come back out and see him again, then I boarded the train for the short ride out to the New Territories. At the train station, I bought a small cake for the family. Maybe it was some sort of peace offering. Then I took a taxi to their home.

Brother L, his wife, and his daughter sat on a couch, and I sat across from them in a chair and began to explain why I had returned. I had disobeyed the Lord, and now I had come back to wash their feet. The daughter and wife immediately covered their mouth and started to giggle quietly. Brother L, in a very scholarly way, said, "Well, it's in the Bible, so, if the Lord told you to do it, you have to do it."

The daughter went and got a large basin and filled it with water and set it in front of her father. Then she and her mother started to giggle again. It was apparent to me that they expected me to wash his feet but not theirs. I said, "No, the Lord wants me to wash all your feet, not just your father." With that, they stopped giggling.

I'd never seen a foot washing, so I didn't really know how to do it, but I did my best. There was no felt presence of the Lord, no miraculous manifestation. I just washed their feet, and that was it.

When the evening ended, Brother L walked me out to the taxi. On the way, he said, "When we got married, we were still involved with Bible smuggling, but we were caught on three separate occasions, and each time we gave false information. Then, when we had our daughter, we were really scared about what would happen to her if we got caught again. So, we stopped smuggling Bibles and stopped ministry completely. When you and Sonny came a few days ago to be with us, it meant so much to us. We were filled with such fear of what might happen that night. Now that you came back and washed our feet, I know how much God loves us, and I know we must return to ministry."

I took the taxi to the train station and boarded the train to return to the city. On the way I heard the Lord's voice clearly. He said, "Joe, you've been a Christian a long time now. I shouldn't have to speak to you the second time!" Our obedience to the Lord is important, not just for our own sake, but also for the sake of others. Brother L returned to working in China and eventually established a work in Cambodia.

Sometime in the late 1990s, I stopped full-time international ministry and started a contracting business. I spoke about it more detail in Chapter 24, "Betrayal, the Making of a Leader." During that time, I didn't need financial supporters because I was making a lot of money with my business. This allowed me to travel at least three times a year overseas. At least twice a year I would go to Southeast Asia, and once a year I would go to Brazil.

In 2009 things changed dramatically. I was in Bangkok, trying to help a brother from India change some money, and it started raining very heavily, so we started to run to avoid getting wet. I slipped, trying to run into a shopping center, and my kneecap came down on the edge of a granite steep. Immediately, I felt some pain, but I thought maybe I had just dislocated something. I slapped on the kneecap hoping to bring it back into place. Then, however, my knee began to swell up, so I got in a taxi and went to the Christian hospital which was only a couple blocks away.

After an examination, the doctor informed me that my kneecap was broken, and they would have to do surgery immediately. Within a short time, I was lying on an operating table with three nurses and an anesthesiologist preparing me for surgery.

There was an announcement over the loudspeaker, and the anesthesiologist told me that the doctor was running late. Then, a short time later, another announcement came saying that he would even be later. The nurses all left the room and only the anesthesiologist stayed with me.

The anesthesiologist apologized for the doctor being late, but I said, "No problem. I'm not going anyplace anyway." Then, as I was lying there on the operating table, we started a conversation. I told her I was a missionary and shared the Gospel with her. It was a God-ordained encounter. A few days later I had one of the girls from our office bring a Bible to her.

The doctor finally came. As it turned out, he was an elder in the Presbyterian Church, and we prayed together before he began the surgery. He put some metal wires into the kneecap that would have to be removed a year later. The doctor said that I would have to stay in the hospital for several days, but I told him that I had to leave in two days to teach in our Bible school in the northeast of Thailand. He said, "They will have to get someone else."

"No," I replied, "they're not going to get anybody else. I'm going to be there."

SEASONS OF CHANGE

I've already mentioned someplace in the book that faithfulness is very important to me. If I give my word and say I'm going to do something, you can be sure I will do it. The only exception would be if I died.

Two days later, Alma, one of the ladies from the office, came to help me check out. The total bill for surgery, medication, and my room was $1,500. I thought to myself, "I need to pay for this quickly and get out of here before they realize I'm robbing them."

I flew to the northeast of Thailand and began teaching the next morning at the Bible school using crutches to stand. Brother P stayed with me in my hotel room and was a real servant to me. Every day, after standing for long periods of time, my knee would swell up. I finally decided to use the cold beer cans in the hotel refrigerator to help bring the swelling down. I put a picture of it up on Facebook, joking about how I don't drink but had finally found a use for beer. One of my friends saw the post and put a comment there, "You should have drunk it; you would have felt better."

When I finally returned home, I realized I wouldn't be able to continue my contracting business. I closed the business and made plans to return to full-time international ministry. I had been ministering in Southeast Asia since the late 1970s and also traveling to Brazil at least once a year when Brother Andrey, a Russian who was the leader of Youth With A Mission in Armenia, invited me to come there and teach in 2012. This opened doors for me to return to Armenia once a year to teach about Spiritual Warfare at the YWAM base and to minister in local churches. Every year I went, I had opportunity to minister in new churches, the people were always friendly and hungry for the things of the Holy Spirit, and the food in Armenia was amazing.

People at other YWAM bases heard about my teachings and invited me to come and teach them. First, it was Kyrgyzstan through Zoom over the Internet in 2016. Then, in 2017, I went to Kyrgyzstan and to Uzbekistan. The Lord was giving me a vision

INHERITING THE NATIONS

for Central Asia. Amazingly, prior to this I had never even heard of these countries.

The Lord had given me a fresh vision for Armenia, and now that began to expand to Russia and Central Asia. The Bible school in Mandalay, Burma was desiring to have more local teachers, so in 2017, I taught my last class on Spiritual Warfare there. I had always enjoyed going there to teach, but also I enjoyed the wonderful times of fellowship with many of the brothers. I miss those brothers and our times of fellowship and having dinner together in Mandalay.

Shortly after that, the new leadership at the MBS in Khon Kean, Thailand changed, and they now desired to bring in different teachers from other countries. Until that time, I had been traveling to Southeast Asia at least four times a year. Now, as things were changing, I was trying to discern what the Lord wanted me to do. Brother Sonny, being a close friend, said he would speak with the leaders in the Thailand school on my behalf, but I felt it wouldn't be right to have me teaching there just because he wanted me to. I wanted to give the leadership at the school the liberty to do what they felt the Lord was directing them to do. At the same time, I believed that when one door closes, the Lord opens another door or other doors.

In 2011, I was invited to become a director on the California Board of Ethnos Asia. I had been invited several times in the past, but I felt now was the time. Shortly after that, I also became a director on their International Board, which met in Bangkok for its yearly meetings. For me, board meetings were important, but what was more important was the fellowship with my friends and to be able to strategize with them for the vision Ethnos Asia was carrying for the nations of Southeast Asia.

After being on the board in California for almost six years, I began to question my worth to them. Except for attending the board meetings and voting on various issues, I didn't feel that I had much to offer. I have always been a doer, and I didn't think I was *doing* all that much. I began to think about resigning from the board. I remember talking to Pastor David, the president of the board and voicing my frustrations. He said, "Joe, it's not what you do; it's who you are. You have history with EA, and we need you." It was true that I had been involved longer than anyone else on the board, but I continued to struggle with not being able to make any more practical contribution. It appeared that others on the board were doing those practical things.

In late 2017, we were voting on helping a ministry outreach at a refugee camp at the Burmese border. We had already sent a lot of money to this camp for evangelism, so I voted against sending more money for blankets. As it turned out, one other brother voted against it also, feeling that our focus should be more on evangelism. When I left the meeting that day, I felt sad in my spirit. For the first time, as a board member, I had voted against a proposed project. For me, it was the final straw that made me decide it was time to resign. Because of the long history with Brother Sonny, I wrote him a letter telling him of my plan to resign. He wrote me back and asked me to give him some time to pray about it before I officially announced my resignation.

In January of 2018, I was planning a trip to Armenia and then to Kyrgyzstan, and I needed more money than I had. I was trusting the Lord to bring in what I needed before my scheduled departure. I had not heard from Brother Sonny for quite some time, so at the following board meeting, I intended to submit my resignation.

As I was driving to that meeting, I was praying about my upcoming trip and telling the Lord I needed more money for my expenses. At the meeting, I gave my resignation letter. After trying to convince me not to resign, the board finally accepted my resignation and told me if I ever wanted to return, the door would always be open. They handed me an envelope, thanking me for my service and wanting to bless me. In it was a check for $2,000, just what I needed to complete the budget for my trip to Armenia and Kyrgyzstan. I felt that this was a confirmation from the Lord that I had done the right thing.

One of the board members jokingly said that if I decided to return to the board, I would have to give the $2,000 back. I miss the fellowship of those wonderful brothers.

Although I resigned from the Ethnos Asia Board in California, I had no intention of leaving the International Board. The members on that board were from boards in other nations, but there was also a brother who didn't belong to any board. I assumed there was no reason for me to resign. However, at the following meeting, it was decided that I had to resign. I was surprised and even a little disappointed, but again I had to trust my future involvement with Ethnos Asia into the Lord's hands. I now set my focus on Armenia and Central Asia.

Brother L and his family in Hong Kong

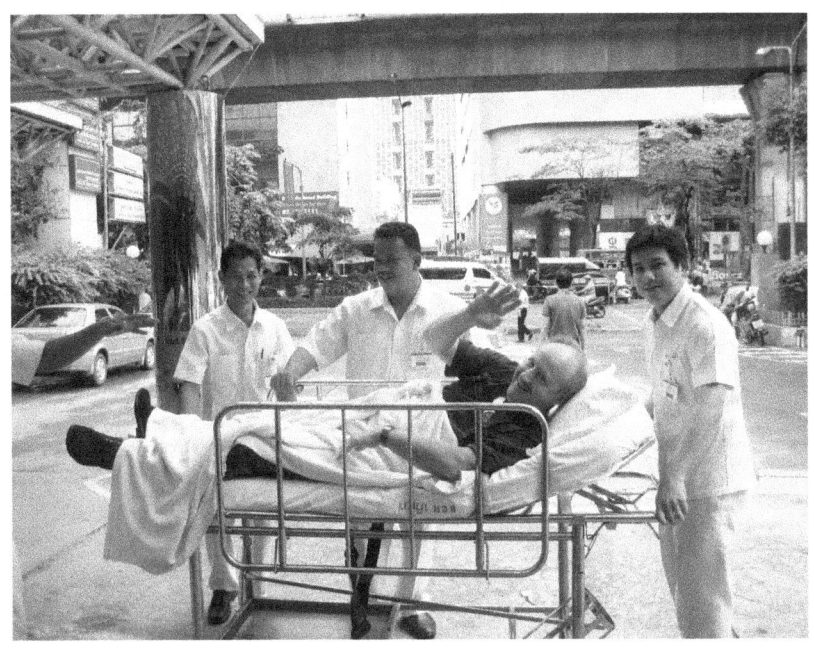

In the hospital in Bangkok

Alma from the EA Office

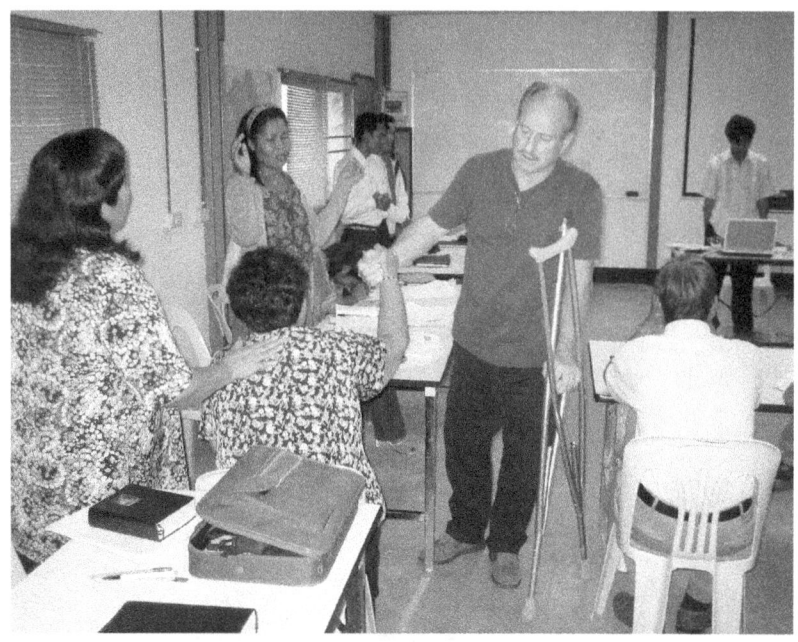

Ministering on crutches in Thailand

Teaching on crutches

Apple Pie in China

CHAPTER 37

A VISION FOR CENTRAL ASIA

So continuing daily with one accord in the temple, and breaking bread from house to house, they ate their food with gladness and simplicity of heart, praising God and having favor with all the people. And the Lord added to the church daily those who were being saved. Acts 2:46-47

Central Asia is made up of five countries—Kazakhstan, Kyrgyzstan, Tajikistan, Uzbekistan, and Turkmenistan—all part of the former Soviet Union. All of these are Muslim countries with limited freedom for Christians. Some permit church buildings, but it appears that the real anointing of the Holy Spirit is found in the home groups or home churches. Turkmenistan is the most restrictive of these countries.

Several years ago, a couple from there came to an Ethnos Asia Missions Conference we were having in Bangkok. I was scheduled to speak in the evening service, so I gave them some of my time to share about their country and their faith. Later, Brother Sonny had some time to talk with them when he took them to the airport. He expressed his desire for the two of us to go to Turkmenistan to encourage and teach the believers they knew there. They, however, said that although they would love to have us come, it would be too dangerous for everyone involved. To date, we have not traveled there.

From my first trip to Armenia in 2012, I continued to return every year to teach about Spiritual Warfare at the YWAM base and teach in local churches. In 2016 I taught over the Internet through Zoom in YWAM bases of Kyrgyzstan, Rostov, in the western area of Russia, and Vladivostok on the East Coast of Russia, but soon I would be standing on the soil of these countries.

Many times, before I go to a country, I have visions of myself being there and ministering to the people. My vision was growing, and my heart was expanding.

In May of 2017, I boarded a Turkish Airlines flight for my first trip to Central Asia. After a layover in Istanbul, Turkey, I flew to Bishkek, the capital of Kyrgyzstan and was met there by Brother T. We had seen and talked to each other many times over the Internet, but now we were physically face to face, and I was standing on the soil of Kyrgyzstan.

Brother T is the base leader of YWAM Kyrgyzstan, and he has an incredible testimony. His parents were basically farmers, his mom and dad divorced, and his father became an alcoholic and eventually became homeless, wandering the streets of their small town. As a young man, he grew up working the fields, harvesting sugar beets, to support his mom and sisters. It was hard work, with little reward. He used to wonder if there was a living God and, if so, why He didn't see their situation and help them.

Kyrgyzstan is a Muslim country, and so he decided to go to a mosque to find God. After two or three months of attendance there, he realized that it was just a place for rules. There was no real God in the mosque.

Then some Jehovah Witnesses came to their house one day, and for two months, he went to the Jehovah Witness meetings. Again, he was not able to find God.

Then one day a friend of theirs who was not a Christian told them that she had attended a Christian home church just out of curiosity, and even though she wasn't a Christian, she said, "I think if you go to this meeting, you'll find the God you're looking for." A short time later, he and his mom visited that home church. When they first entered the home, they were greeted by very friendly people and addressed by their names. Brother T asked them, "How do you know our names?"

They answered, "A friend of yours was here recently and told us about you, and we have been praying for you since then."

The worship that day touched Brother T's heart, and he began to weep. This was strange, for at the same time, he felt very happy. After the meeting, the pastor and his wife invited them to stay for some tea, and during the tea, they shared the Gospel with them.

Brother T said, "If He is the living God, I want to receive Him." He received the Lord that day, and his mom received the Lord about a year later. He said his heart felt like it was burning and overflowing with love, an unlimited love. He began to see color in a different way. He said, "It was as if I had been seeing a black and white world, and suddenly everything was colorful." Brother T was so hungry for the things of the Lord that whenever there was a church services, he was there, and he would stay after everyone else had left. He just wanted to be around the pastor and hear more about Jesus.

Sometimes the pastor would have to say to him, "T, don't you think you need to get home now?" Then one day, the pastor said to him, "T, you need more than I can give you, and I think I have a place where you should go." He took him to the Youth With A Mission base and suggested that he should pray about going to their DTS program. Brother T was excited about the opportunity and came home and told his mother. She said that wouldn't be possible because he had to work in the fields to support the family. He was very discouraged, but he continued to pray, and the Lord showed him a way they could earn more money.

He took his mother to the city where she would buy things, and he built a little roadside stand where she could sell her products. It turned out she was making more money than they had been making

A VISION FOR CENTRAL ASIA

harvesting sugar beets. His mother and sister would now have the money necessary to live on, and he could enroll in the YWAM school. The Lord had seen his hungry heart and provided a way for him to learn more about the Bible and about this God who had filled his heart with an overflowing love.

A teacher came from Norway, teaching a course entitled "The Father Heart of God." Brother T now had a problem. He had received Jesus and understood who the Holy Spirit was, but he could not see God as a Father. The father he knew was a drunken homeless man. One day, after the class, he and a young lady were standing on the balcony of the school talking. They were both having difficulty seeing God as their Father because of the way they saw their earthly fathers. Finally, T prayed, "Lord, if You set my father free from alcohol and bring him and my mother back together, I'll serve You the rest of my life." The next day someone came to T and said, "Your mother and father and another man are at the front gate, and they want to talk with you. He thought they must be joking, but they said, "No, it's true. They're at the front gate." He went to the gate and standing there were his mother, the pastor, and his father. He embraced his father.

As I mentioned earlier in the chapter, his father had become an alcoholic and was living on the streets as a homeless man. Occasionally he had come back home, but usually his wife would not allow him to come in. The night before, he had come totally drunk wanting to come in. This time, she said to him, "Look, I'm going to let you come in and sleep, but you have to go see the pastor tomorrow. You need to get saved." He slept there that night, and the next day she took him to see the pastor. He, too, prayed to receive the Lord. Afterward, the pastor said to him, "You need to get into rehab." They had been on their way to the rehab center to check him in when they stopped at the YWAM base. The Lord had heard the cry of T's heart and was beginning the process of setting his father free.

INHERITING THE NATIONS

The Lord had done His part; now it was up to T to serve the Lord the rest of his life. Part of that service meant becoming the director of YWAM for Kyrgyzstan. As of this writing, he is Director of Youth With a Mission for three central Asian countries.

Everybody in YWAM lives by faith and must raise their own support so they can contribute to the food and the maintenance of the base. This is true whether you are a director, a staff member, or a student. You must contribute.

The first day I arrived there, Brother T wanted to take me to a Uyghur Muslim restaurant that apparently had amazing noodles that he wanted me to try. After our food came and we were enjoying the meal, he said to me, "Brother, could I borrow some money to pay for this meal. I'll pay you back later." We both started laughing.

I said, "No problem! Let me pay today."

I don't completely understand the structure in that country in relationship to Christian churches. It's a Muslim country, but apparently some churches are allowed to have services. Brother T wanted to take me to one of those churches, one where some foreigners attend on Sundays. During the worship I noticed that there were only a couple elderly ladies raising their hands. One of them seemed to be very engaged with the Lord during the worship. After the service, I asked Brother T if we could talk to that lady. We approached her, and he translated for me. It turned out that she was having a women's meeting that afternoon, and she invited us to come and share. It was a group of ten ladies, mostly elderly, but very friendly and hungry for the Lord. I shared a bit, and then the Lord graciously gave me a prophetic word for every single one of them. They were very blessed, and so were we that the Lord had come in this way.

As a result of that meeting, they wanted me to come and speak at their church. However, when they spoke with the pastor, he said he didn't want anybody speaking at his church that he didn't know personally. It was sad that the pastor had that attitude, but at least we got to sow God's Word into those ten women.

I taught for a week, as usual, about Spiritual Warfare, and it was a good time. The students were engaged and hungry. During the classes, I noticed one young lady named Sister A. Sister A had two brothers, but she was the only Christian in the family. She was short and thin, but somehow I saw great potential in her. She had a prophetic gifting, but she needed a mentor.

When I wasn't teaching in the class, T and I would go and visit people in need and to pray for them. We took Sister A with us and encouraged her to use her prophetic gift and give a word to the people. She was growing quickly in her gifting and was a blessing to everyone she gave a word to. Plus, she was gaining confidence in herself. Unfortunately, Sister A's life had a sad ending.

Sister A's mother became ill, so she had to return home to care for her. Then, however, when her mother had gotten better, she didn't want Sister A to go back to the YWAM base because it was a Christian organization. She wanted her to stay in her city and marry a Muslim man. Sister A ran away from home, found a local Christian pastor and told him what had happened. He took her to the home of one of his members to spend the night. The lady of the house promised to put her on a bus the next morning so that she could get away from her Muslim family and live at the YWAM base and continue growing in the Lord. No one knows why, but this lady called Sister A's brothers and told them when she would be taking Sister A to the bus station. The brothers arrived there and forced her to accompany them back home. Sometime later, Brother T received word from someone in that town that Sister A's family had forced her to marry a Muslim man, and we never heard from her again. I think of her often. It brings pain to my heart, and I pray that the Lord would somehow rescue her.

When I was in Kyrgyzstan last year, Brother T said had he received a phone call from Sister A informing him that she has a deep desire to return to the base for more teaching and to bring her husband with her. Hopefully, that will happen, and he will become a believer.

While in Kyrgyzstan, I met a brother named Roman. He is from the Ukraine, and his wife is from Korea. They attend a Korean church in Bishkek. Roman's heart is for the homeless and the poor, and he works in two major places. One of them is the city dump, where many homeless people live (maybe a better word for it would be "exist"). At least once a week he prepares enough food to take a hot meal to every person living under those horrible conditions. I went with him once. It was near the end of the winter, so it was still quite cold, with ice on the ground in some places, and the rest of the area was all mud and smelly trash. This was home to many men and women and some entire families. Roman and other volunteers bring food and some dignity to these people. They feed their bodies and, at the same time, feed their spirits with the Word of God and prayer. On Saturdays, they open the fellowship hall of their church for the poor people living in the city to come and get a meal and prayer.

I travelled with Roman one day by car to a small village outside of the capital to visit some families and pray for them in their homes. The streets of the village were just dirt, but at this time of the year it was thick mud, and there were large potholes. I thought for sure we were going to get stuck. Although the people had homes, they were still very poor. In several of the homes, even though it was winter, there was no heat, so it was very cold inside.

After visiting and praying for many people, we went to a building that Roman had bought and was making into a community center that would have activities for the people of that village — after school classes that would help school children with their studies, and a soccer field where kids could play, a center where their personal needs could be met, but also where they would encounter the Word of God and, hopefully, come to know the God of Heaven.

A VISION FOR CENTRAL ASIA

As I'm writing this chapter, it's September of 2022, and bombs are falling on the Ukrainian city where Roman's mother lives, She is old and must use a wheelchair. He flew home in the hope that she would come to live with him in the safety and peace of Kyrgyzstan, but she didn't want to go that far away from her city and country. She was hoping she could soon return to her own home.

Because many of the people in that area of the Ukraine were fleeing to Poland for safety, one day, with sadness in his heart, Roman pushed his mother in her wheelchair across the border of Ukraine and into Poland. From there, strangers, refugees themselves, took her to a safe place where she would be cared for. Roman returned to his wife and child and a land that is not his own, to fulfill his calling, by helping and sharing the Gospel with the poor of Kyrgyzstan. He was trusting the Lord to protect and provide for his mother in a land that was not her own.

Jesus said in Matthew 25:34-36 and 40:

"Come, you blessed of My Father, inherit the kingdom prepared for you from the foundation of the world: for I was hungry and you gave Me food; I was thirsty and you gave Me drink; I was a stranger and you took Me in; I was naked and you clothed Me; I was sick and you visited Me; I was in prison and you came to Me."

"Assuredly, I say to you, inasmuch as you did it to one of the least of these My brethren, you did it to Me."

On the western border of Kyrgyzstan is Uzbekistan. Brother T knew one of the leaders with YWAM who lived in the capital, Tashkent, so I decided to go to the Uzbekistan Embassy to see about the possibility of getting a visa to go there. It was a little complicated, but in the end, I got a one-week visa. I was excited about the opportunity to visit one more of the five countries of Central Asia.

INHERITING THE NATIONS

Brother M met me at the airport, and then we passed by his house to get his wife and go to lunch, one of the best *shaurma* I had ever eaten. It was a very simple place, almost like a fast-food place in America, but the food was so delicious that I asked to be taken there again on the day I left. For those of you who have never had a *shaurma*, the one I prefer is prepared with honey bread known as *lavash*. It's very thin, similar to a burrito wrap, and inside can be various types of meats. I prefer the beef, which has onions, cheese, and garlic sauce. Other things can be added, but that's all I like on mine. Wrap it all up, and it looks like a giant burrito, but it's much more tasty.

After lunch, another couple picked me up to go to the YWAM base about an hour outside of the capital. Once we got outside of the capital, the countryside was covered with strawberry fields, and there were fruit stands set up alongside the road, selling fresh strawberries just picked from the field. Of course, we had to stop and buy some. They were delicious.

The students at the base had already finished their twelve weeks of practical teaching and were leaving the next day to go on their outreach. The leader had brought me there because he wanted me to talk to them about Spiritual Warfare, I did my best to put a week of teaching into a couple hours, and then I laid hands on each one and prayed for them. The Lord was gracious, and I had a prophetic word for several of them, as we were praying.

After praying, the leader brought me back to the capital, where I checked into a hotel. This was necessary because it would be too dangerous for them, as believers, and for me, as a foreigner, to stay at any of their homes. At that time, in fact, foreigners were required to stay in hotels.

The next day was probably one of the strangest days I've had in all my travels around the world. One of the leaders of YWAM picked me up at my hotel. When we met in the lobby, I greeted him with a typical

A VISION FOR CENTRAL ASIA

Christian greeting, "Praise the Lord, Brother! It's going to be a great day!" He quickly motioned to me to be quiet and then, when we got out to the car, he rebuked me very harshly. He said we couldn't do that in public. It was too dangerous in that Muslim country. I apologized and told him I hadn't known, but inwardly, I was very disturbed at how strongly he had spoken to me.

He didn't tell me what the plan was or where we were going, but there were a few other people in the car. We drove outside of the city, but then we came to a dead end, and there was a river flowing very swiftly. The pastor got out and looked at the river for a while, and then got back in the car. During the whole ride, he was speaking to the others in his own language, so I didn't understand anything that was going on.

At this point, the strangest thing happened. Somehow I got it in my mind that he was so mad at me that they were going to put me in that river and drown me. I became very fearful. Thankfully, we soon drove away from the river.

Then we came to another dead end. As before, they were all talking in their own language and not telling me what was going on. Finally, we got on a freeway and drove for what seemed like a long time, eventually arriving at a village area. Just at the end of the village there was a massive quarry. Now I thought, "They're going to kill me and bury me in this quarry." I decided I would jump out of the car, but then I realized that I had no idea how to get back to my hotel, and no one would be able to understand me and help me. Again, no one spoke to me in English, and no one translated what was being said. But I was in escape mode.

A little past the quarry, we stopped in front of a house that had double metal doors at the driveway. We drove in and parked the car. Then I saw a familiar face, an old student of mine from Armenia, and I was finally at peace.

INHERITING THE NATIONS

A very long table was being set up for dinner. The tables are usually very low because the people sit on the floor. The host asked me to sit at the middle of the table, where my back would be against the wall, and as we started to eat, he asked me to share my testimony. For me, where I was sitting was very uncomfortable and didn't give me the opportunity to get up without asking several people to move too. Still, I shared for quite a while.

Then one lady said, "I'm sorry, but I must leave early."

I took the opportunity to say, "Wait, I'd like to pray for you." When I said this, everyone sitting against the wall moved so that I could get up and lay my hands on her to pray. As I laid hands on her, I had a prophetic word for her. While I was giving it, everyone else came up and wanted me to pray for them. The lady left, but I said to the others, "No problem! We have plenty of time. I can pray for everyone." I talked a little bit about prophecy before I began to pray for the others and read to them from the Scriptures:

He who prophesies speaks edification and exhortation and comfort to men.   1 Corinthians 14:3

We finished eating and then began to pray, and just as the day before, the Lord graciously came and gave me a prophetic word for every person. It was really a blessing. By the time we finally left there, it was 1:00 o'clock in the morning.

A young lady who had been at the meeting asked if we could give her a ride home. When she got home, her mother was waiting up for her, to hear how the meeting went. As she began to share with her mother, the presence of the Lord came mightily upon them both.

Her mother belonged to a home group, so the next morning she called the leader and told her what had happened and encourage her to invite me to their meeting. I should add here that when I say "home group," in Uzbekistan, a "home group" is a secret meeting, like the underground groups of China. As I have noted, in all of Central Asia, the religion is Muslim, and there are different degrees of persecution according to the country. In Uzbekistan, the believers must be very careful when they meet.

The next day I was having lunch with one of the brothers who had been at the meeting the night before and another brother. While we were eating, he got a phone call. It was someone wanting to know if we could come that night to the home group the young lady's mother attended. We accepted the invitation.

When we got there, it was like the other places. A table of food was set up where we would sit down together and talk and pray. This group really touched my heart. There were only nine people, but they were hungry for the Lord, and they were very loving, the food was fabulous, and the fellowship was precious. Then the Lord came, as He had in the other meetings, and I had a prophetic word for each and every person.

When I finished praying, someone said, "We have been praying for two months for direction from the Lord for our lives and for our group, and you spoke to every one of us what the Lord wanted us to hear. We are amazed!"

I said to them, "You're amazed? I'm even more amazed."

I returned to Uzbekistan on two other occasions and I made it a priority to visit that group of precious brothers and sisters. I visited this group in 2023, and they confirmed to me that some of those prophetic words had already come true.

In my more than forty years of ministry, I've had the honor to speak in some very large churches, but there is something special about a small group of people who are hungry for the Lord. The love and the warmth they exude captivates your heart, and you would rather be in those small groups than in a large church.

INHERITING THE NATIONS

When I got my visa to go to Uzbekistan, I didn't know anybody in the country, and no one had heard of me, but the Lord knew my heart. I wanted to visit the underground churches and bless them in any way I could. He entrusted me with the responsibility and privilege of bringing His words of encouragement to brothers and sisters who live under the oppressive spirit of Islam, and through me, through my arms, He was embracing them.

The following day, we were invited to share with a group of women who normally met for Bible study. Again, there was a long, low table, just like in the other homes. It was filled with food, and sitting around it were daughters of the living God who were hungry for the things of the Spirit. They had heard about my other meetings and were hoping that the Lord would give them a word. Once again, the Lord came and gave me a word of encouragement for each of them personally.

On Sunday afternoon, we were invited to attend a youth gathering that met in secret in a home. During worship, the windows were all closed, and we couldn't sing loud, but the Lord hears, and He heard our worship that day. This would be my final meeting because I would be leaving in the evening to return to Kyrgyzstan. Again, the Lord was faithful. He saw the hungry hearts of these young people, and He came and gave me a personal word for each one if them. I laid hands on them, gave the word, and then prayed for them.

This was my first trip to Uzbekistan, and it was a precious and rewarding time. I returned the following year to teach Spiritual Warfare at the YWAM base and then revisited some of the home groups that I had been in the year before. It is my hope and desire that the Lord will continue to open doors in other cities of this country and in other countries of Central Asia that live in the darkness of the Muslim world, that I may bring encouragement to brothers and sisters in other home groups who are desiring to hear God's Word and experience a visitation of His presence.

Brother T and his wife in Kyrgyzstan

A Kyrgyzstani women's group

With Sister A and a friend in Kyrgyzstan

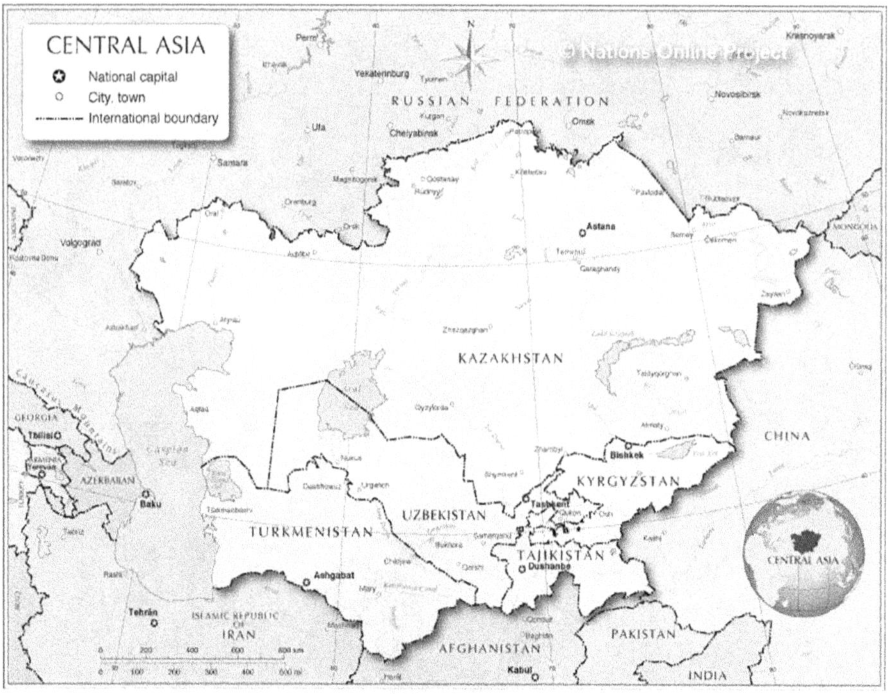

CENTRAL ASIA
National capital
City, town
International boundary
© Nations Online Project
RUSSIAN FEDERATION
Yekaterinburg
Chelyabinsk
Samara
Omsk
Novosibirsk
Volgograd
Astana
KAZAKHSTAN
CHINA
Bishkek
KYRGYZSTAN
Tashkent
UZBEKISTAN
TURKMENISTAN
TAJIKISTAN
Dushanbe
Ashgabat
Baku
AZERBAIJAN
GEORGIA
Tbilisi
Tehran
ISLAMIC REPUBLIC OF IRAN
AFGHANISTAN
Kabul
PAKISTAN
INDIA
CENTRAL ASIA

Belgorod
Kharkiv
UKRAINE
Dnipropetrovsk
DONBASS
Donetsk
Rostov
Don
Volgograd
KAZAKHSTAN
Tsimlyansk Reservoir
Volga
RUSSIA
Astrakhan
Sea of Azov
CRIMEA
Sevastapol
Kuban
Krasnodar
Stavropol
Caspian Sea
Sochi
Nalchik
Groznyy
Black Sea
GEORGIA
Tbilisi
Samsun
WWW.FREEWORLDMAPS.NET

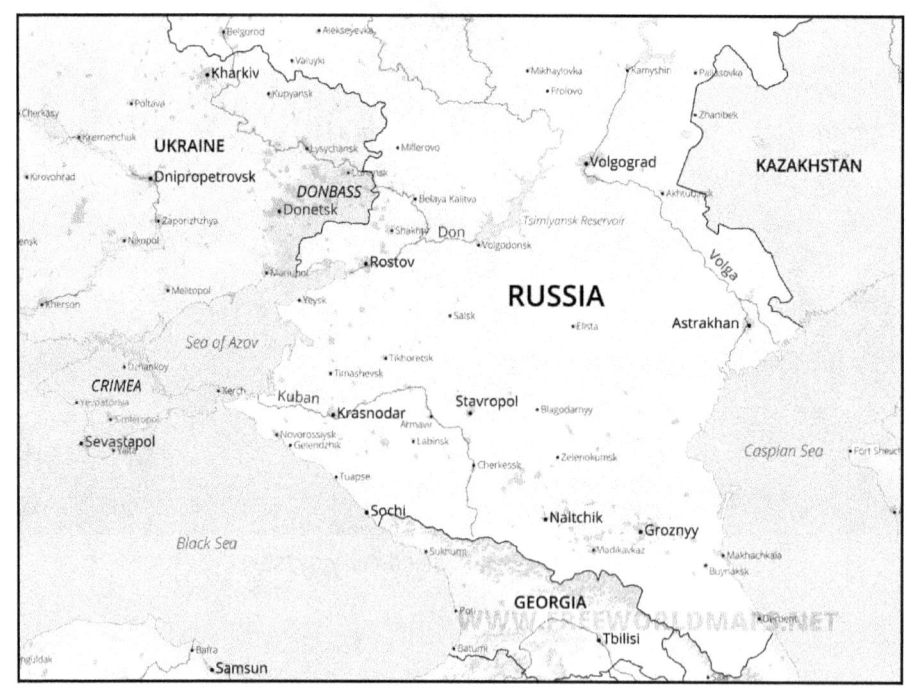

Chapter 38

EXPRESSIONS OF HEAVEN IN RUSSIA

After these things I looked, and behold, a great multitude which no one could number, of all nations, tribes, peoples, and tongues, standing before the throne and before the Lamb, clothed with white robes, with palm branches in their hands, and crying with a loud voice, saying, "Salvation belongs to our God who sits on the throne, and to the Lamb!"

Revelation 7:9-10

I've already spoken of my first trip to Russia, but it took me many years to finally get there. In the early part of 1986 I met a brother who was doing work with the underground churches of the Soviet Union, and the desire came to my heart to go there and share what I could with those believers who lived under the heavy spirit of persecution. Two friends, Tim and Jeff, joined me in planning a trip to that part of the world.

We acquired the necessary visa for the travel, and my missionary friend gave us several connections in places where he thought we could bless the people. We knew that it wouldn't be an easy trip, and that it could possibly be dangerous for us and even more dangerous for the people we would be visiting, but we were ready for whatever came and excited about the possibilities of visiting for the first time an area controlled by Communism.

INHERITING THE NATIONS

We were scheduled to enter the USSR in early May of 1986. We would be concentrating on the western part of the country, the Ukrainian and Polish areas that had been taken over after World War II. Then, in late April, the unthinkable happened: the Chernobyl nuclear plant outside of Kiev, Ukraine had a meltdown and a subsequent explosion, sending clouds of nuclear radiation into the air for many miles around. At the time I had no idea how massive the destruction had been, so I didn't think there was any need for us to change our plans. Tim and Jeff, however, were adamant that it was too dangerous for us to go there. So, our trip was canceled. We didn't go to the USSR.

Several years later, in 1991, the USSR collapsed, with fifteen countries becoming independent. One of them became what we now know today as Russia. Sometime in the 90s a friend of mine named Dave formed a ministry that was working with refugees in that area of the world, and he invited me to come to Moscow to teach at a conference about spiritual warfare. I was excited about the possibilities. Finally, I was going to be able to minister in Russia, which was still under the spirit of Communism.

With my airline ticket and visa in hand, I boarded a flight to Moscow with a layover in Munich, Germany. When I arrived in Moscow and approached the Immigration desk, I handed my passport and visa to an immigration officer. She looked at them; then, without a word, she handed them right back to me. I wasn't sure what was happening, but the travel agency I had used to plan the trip had secured the visa and assured me that all was in order, so I just pushed the passport back to her. She pushed it back to me. This happened several times before she called another immigration officer over. He took my passport from her and, without saying a word, motioned for me to follow him.

The man ordered me to sit down outside an office, and he entered and handed my passport to an officer sitting behind a desk. This man began to copy something from my passport into a book. After waiting there a while, I got up and went into the office and asked, "Is there a problem? Do I need to pay something?" The man didn't answer.

More time went by, and finally, my passport was given back to the officer who had brought me there, and he again motioned for me to follow him. He took me down a long hallway with a maze of offices. I assumed he was taking me to someone higher up in the immigration process, someone who could help with whatever problem they were seeing with my passport and visa.

At the end of the hallway, the guard opened a door to another hallway. Straight across that hallway was a door that led to the plane I had arrived on. The stewardess was standing there. He handed her my passport and walked away as I shouted, "Hey, wait a minute! What's going on?" He kept walking and didn't respond.

The airline stewardess politely said, "Could you please quickly board Mr. Zeyak. We have been waiting for you, and we are late for takeoff." I sat down in one of the seats, not understanding what was going on, just knowing that I was being returned to Munich, while my luggage went around and around on a Moscow baggage belt.

My friend Dave, who was waiting for me at the airport, had begun to inquire about me when I didn't arrive, and he was finally informed by immigration officers that there had been a problem with my visa so they were not able to allow me to enter the country. It turned out that I had arrived in November, but my visa said that I would not be arriving until December. In most countries of the world, once you have a visa, you can enter at any time within a thirty- or sixty-day period. With Russia, the visa had to indicate the exact date that I was arriving. Of course, I hadn't known this.

To get another visa while I was still in Europe would be very difficult. There was no Russian Embassy in Munich, so I would have to travel to Frankfurt to apply and then wait for approval. It would all be very challenging because of the language barrier and also very expensive. I decided to just stay in Munich that night in a hotel and then return to California the next day. My luggage would be delivered to my home several days later. This was my second attempt to visit that part of the world, and again the doors had closed.

On the return flight from Germany to California, I sat next to a couple who were from Egypt, but they also had a home in California. We struck up a conversation, and the man told me he was a Coptic Christian. When I told him I, too, was a Christian, he asked me, "What's the difference between a Christian and a Catholic?" Having been raised in the Catholic Church I had more than enough information to answer his questions, and so for much of our ten-hour flight to Los Angeles we talked about the Lord.

Although our conversation was going very well, I didn't see that it was leading to a conclusion in which the man would pray with me and accept Jesus as his personal Savior, so I finally posed a question to him: "Do you suppose that the Lord brought me on this trip and then had the officials in Russia reject my visa, so that I would have to return to Germany, and then be on this flight sitting next to you for these many hours, just to share with you how much God loves you and wants to come into your life in a personal way?"

After thinking for a while, he said, "I guess that's a possibility." But he still wasn't ready to pray. I had done my best, and the rest was in the Lord's hands.

After returning to America, I talked to the travel agency that had sold me my airline ticket and secured my visa. They should have known that the ticket was for a certain day and the visa for another. They agreed and refunded me all the money I had spent on the ticket and the visa and offered me a free visa for any future travel. The other plus side of all of this was that my flights enabled me to achieve, for the first time, Gold Status with United Airlines and their partners, and this would allow me to carry extra luggage without additional charges and have access to the Business Class lounges around the world. I was able to maintain that status for several years. Just a few years ago I finally accomplished traveling on United Airlines for a million miles. This gave me and Brenda Gold Status for life.

Finally, in 2018, I was again invited to go to Russia, this time through Brother Andrey, to teach about spiritual warfare at the YWAM base in Rostov. He had left Armenia, and he and his family were now living in Rostov, which was his hometown, and he was now leading the YWAM base there. I was very excited about going there and also to be able to once again be with him and his family.

Normally, I get a tourist visa, no matter where I go, but this time I applied for and received a religious visa, which would allow me to legally teach about religion in Russia.

When I arrived at Moscow's Immigration, an officer began to question why I was there, and no matter what I said to him, he wasn't happy about it. As before, he eventually brought another immigration officer in on the discussion. After a while, they told me to go to the back of the line. I had to wait while everybody else on the plane cleared Immigration. Then, finally, he called me up, another officer was brought in, and they questioned me and questioned me. It seemed to be a form of intimidation.

When I protested that someone was waiting for me, they finally let me through. Then, however, when I finally got out to the area where people pick you after you have arrived, no one was there to meet me. As it turned out, the young man who had been assigned to pick me up was still in bed. Now the immigration officer who had questioned me was out walking around in that area, and I became very concerned that he might question me again and ask why there was no one there to pick me up when I had told them someone was waiting for me. I walked around, a little fearful, trying to avoid him. Then I went out to the parking lot, to wait for whoever was coming to pick me up. Eventually, the young man came, and I was on my way to the safety of the YWAM base.

It had been thirty-two years since I had first planned to go to the USSR, borders had changed, and in general, people had more religious freedom, but the spirit world had not changed. The oppressive and intimidating spirit of Communism and also Islam still ruled the land, controlling the culture and the people.

The Russian city of Rostov-on-Don is in the southwestern part of the country. It is about seven hundred miles south of Moscow and four hundred miles east of the Ukraine. It's a beautiful city with an amazing history, and if you are blessed to have a friend such as Brother Andrey, you will surely have an incredible time visiting the historical sites.

One day Andrey took me to a small city outside of Rostov and explained to me that it was from that area that armies coming from Mongolia had gone out and conquered all the way to the Pacific Ocean. As the armies conquered an area, others would come behind them to bring political and economic growth and set up cities. This happened across what we know as Russia today.

Being at the YWAM base in Rostov was a great joy. Both the students and staff are all hungry for the things of the Lord, so teaching there is always very rewarding. The Holy Spirit always comes where people are hungry. Students who are not baptized in the Holy Spirit are always rewarded when the Spirit comes and meets the desires of their hearts. And when the last day finally comes, and I bring out my sword, to allow them to make their declaration to the Lord and to everyone present that they are now a warrior for the Lord, even staff members (who were once students themselves) are desirous to again hold up the sword and renew their declarations. It's a very moving and momentous time for everyone.

Shortly after I arrived at the base, there was a meeting of local pastors, so I got to meet several pastors and share a bit about my testimony.

EXPRESSIONS OF HEAVEN IN RUSSIA

As a result of that, several pastors wanted me to come to their churches. When my schedule permitted, Brother Andrey set up meetings in four different churches. This turned out to be one of the most interesting times of my more than forty years in ministry.

My first meeting was with a Messianic congregation. The pastor, or maybe rabbi (I'm not sure what they called him), had come to a couple of my Spiritual Warfare classes, and so he was really excited about me teaching his people. It was a small group, probably only about thirty people, but they were engaged, the worship with the Jewish flavor was very wonderful, and everyone was giving their best to it.

Brother Andrey translated for me as I spoke about spiritual warfare, and when it was time for me to bring out my sword, which we had brought in secretly under a jacket, the people were astonished. Even the pastor hadn't seen my sword when he was at the base. As always, I told the story of Gideon and read from the book of judges how the battle cry became *"the sword of the Lord and the sword of Gideon."* Then, I decided, rather than invite each one to come up and hold the sword, to ask the pastor to hold the sword up to the Lord and make a declaration for his entire congregation. I prayed as he stood there holding the sword up, and when I finished, he began to pray and committed himself and his people to be warriors for the Lord, prepared for battle. It was a great and moving time.

Afterward, several people came up to me and asked for personal prayer, so Andrey and I laid hands on them and prayed for the desires of their hearts. That pastor was a precious brother. I hope that someday, if Russia opens again for me, I can once again enjoy fellowship with him and his people.

Before I went to another church, a group from the YWAM base in Armenia came to Russia for the outreach phase of their training. One of the staff that was leading them was a young lady named Anya. She was from Kazakhstan and had overseen the DTS program in Armenia

INHERITING THE NATIONS

for many years. She had usually translated for me in Armenia, both in the school and in the churches we would visit. The two of us worked seamlessly together, and I helped her develop her prophetic mantle. She always encouraged people with her prophetic words.

All of my teachings on Spiritual Warfare have been translated into Russian, and Anya helped me to make some necessary revisions to my syllabus. She is a great sister, has always been a servant to me, and is always joyfully ready to minister.

Interestingly, Anya had been a student of mine in the early days of my ministry in Armenia. After her schooling, she had returned to the small town she was born in near the Russian border in northern Kazakhstan. One day, when she was ministering to the Lord, He spoke to her heart to return to Armenia. She left family, friends, and country to obey the Lord's calling on her life, so that Jesus might receive the reward of His suffering through her obedience. Because Anya was now in Rostov, she and some of the students accompanied me while I was speaking in three more churches.

The next church I went to was an Assembly of God church and was the church that Brother Andrey attended when he wasn't traveling to other bases in Russia. This was a very large church, and even though this was a week-day meeting, the attendance was still rather large. When we arrived the pastor joyfully came up to us and gave me a great big hug, greeting me and saying how happy he was that I was able to come to his church. Andrey told me that he had never seen his pastor greet anybody with a hug like that, and he was very surprised. The worship was great, and they even had a few young ladies doing expressive dance with worship flags. It was very beautiful and well done. I don't remember what I spoke about that night, but I do remember that I gave a few prophetic words and then laid my hands on and prayed for the members of the worship team. I also remember that while I was speaking a lady passed out. I was about to go down and pray for her, but several of the leaders gathered around her quickly and prayed. As I remember it, she was just dehydrated and they had to get some liquids into her.

Prior to my speaking, the pastor had given me free reign to share whatever I wanted. When I had finished, he got up and said, "Well, we're not used to this type of teaching, but it was very interesting and very anointed. Thank you, Brother Joe, for coming." Probably their structure was more expository teaching, whereas most of my teaching is topical and is based on my life experiences or even what I'm going through at the moment. That church is open to me returning at any time.

The third church I went to was a Russian Charismatic church. Brother Andrey had a previous commitment, and so Anya would be my interpreter. We entered the church and introduced ourselves to the leaders. The pastor himself was out of town because of a previous engagement, so his wife oversaw the service. They invited us to sit on the front row, but I asked if I could sit in the back so that I could get a better feel of the service, and they said that was okay.

The service was electrifying, as in most charismatic churches. Some people were dancing. Others waved worship flags. One man had a worship flag that was probably seven feet tall, and he kept waving it during worship. One lady played an accordion, and there were other instruments. All the instruments were loud, the people were singing with all their hearts, and the presence of the Holy Spirit was wonderful.

While the worship was still going on, a lady came in and sat in the seat next to me. Then she stood up and laid her hands on the person in front of her, and it looked like she was giving her a prophetic word. Then she left our row and went over to the other side of the church and did the same thing to several other people. I believe in prophecy and have, many times, given prophetic words to people, but I didn't really appreciate her giving prophetic words during the worship time when

INHERITING THE NATIONS

people we're trying to focus on the Lord. That's sometimes the way it is in a charismatic churches.

I finally got up to speak, Anya was my interpreter, and, as always, she did a great job. The people were hungry, and later we prayed for many. Unfortunately, we had to speak at another church, so we could not stay and enjoy fellowship with these people after the service.

As we were getting ready to go, someone said, "Wait a minute! We have something for you!" And they gave me an offering. Andrey told me later he had never heard of a Russian church giving an offering to a foreigner. In fact, he said, they don't usually give an offering to any of their special speakers.

On Sunday evening, I was invited to speak at a traditional Pentecostal church. The pastor had been at the pastors' meeting at the YWAM base and was excited to have me come to his church. I called it a traditional Pentecostal church because all the men were in suits and ties, and all the women had on long dresses, most of them with their hair up.

The pastor greeted me with great enthusiasm, and I introduced him to Anya and some of the students who were with us. He invited us all to sit up on the front row, although some of the students moved back a couple rows to feel more comfortable. When we sat down, Anya turned to me and said, "I can't interpret here. I have jeans on, and all the women are wearing dresses."

I turned to her, probably with a little arrogance (I'm sorry to say), and said, "Anya, we are the speakers, and we can wear whatever we want." She didn't protest further.

The worship was very good, but I noticed that between every song the pastor, who had a microphone in his hand, made a comment, and whatever he said seemed to break up the flow of the worship. Then they had communion. The pastor put on a pair of white gloves, and the elders did the same. Then he gave the elements to them, and they served the people.

EXPRESSIONS OF HEAVEN IN RUSSIA

After that, I was invited up to speak, and Anya interpreted. I gave several testimonies about my life and ministry because this was my first time at that church. Then I spoke from Hebrews 11, Living by Faith. The beginning of the chapter talks about all the great things people did by faith. They heard the voice of the Lord and then did what He told them to do and received the reward of their obedience to His Word. But then, in verse 35, there is a shift. In the first part of the verse it says:

Women received back their dead raised to life again.

Then it says:

Others were tortured, not accepting deliverance, that they might obtain a better resurrection.

The chapter continues with verses 36 and 37:

Still others had trial of mockings and scourgings, yes, and of chains and imprisonment. They were stoned, they were sawn in two, were tempted, were slain with the sword. They wandered about in sheepskins and goatskins, being destitute, afflicted, tormented.

Then in verse 38, it makes an amazing observation:

Of whom the world was not worthy. They wandered in deserts and mountains, in dens and caves of the earth.

In my more than forty years of ministry, as I noted in a previous chapter, I have met some people like those mentioned in the second part of Hebrews 11. They have spent horrific times in prison, they have been beaten and put in solitary confinement for many days. Others, some of whom were students of mine at one time, have paid the ultimate price and been killed for their faith.

I have had the privilege, during my years of ministry, to know these people about whom the Bible says, *"of whom the world was not worthy."* I have had the honor to teach them, hug them, pray for them, and love them, during their time here on their earthly journey with the Lord.

And all these, having obtained a good testimony through faith, did not receive the promise, God having provided something better for us, that they should not be made perfect apart from us. Hebrews 11:39-40

I have read these last two verses many times, but I have to admit that I don't have the complete revelation of it yet. I just know that there is some kind of connection, maybe a spiritual connection, between those who did not receive the promise and us. I don't know if this is theologically correct, but it's possible that the Lord is waiting for us to do something so that they who came before us can receive their promise. I'm still looking to the Lord for revelation about these two verses.

That day in the traditional Pentecostal church in Russia, I wrapped up the message by telling the people that this chapter ends with what I consider one of the most amazing verses in the Bible—Hebrews 11:41. The man operating the video screen couldn't find it in the Russian Bible, and no one in the congregation could find it in their Bibles either. Even the pastor, who had a phone with the Bible on it, couldn't find it in his electronic Bible. I went down to the pastor and said, "Let me see your phone." I looked at it and then asked, "What version do you have here? You should throw this phone away because it doesn't have verse 41."

Then I returned to the pulpit, which had a huge Bible sitting on it. It was probably about four inches thick, very decorative and very heavy. I picked it up and opened it to Hebrews, and then I said, "Let me read verse 41 to you from your own pulpit Bible."

EXPRESSIONS OF HEAVEN IN RUSSIA

I walked toward the pastor, who was sitting on the front row, and said, "Are you ready to hear it?" Of course, he was ready, and everyone else was ready to hear this verse that they couldn't find.

I turned to a brother a couple seats from the pastor and said, "What is your name?"

He said, "Andrew."

I began to read an imaginary verse 41, but I substituted Andrew's name. It read, "By faith Andrew obeyed God and went out and did a great work for Him."

I turned to someone else in another row and said, "Now, verse 42 is what you did by faith for the Lord."

I continued walking around the congregation quoting verse after verse, adding the names and saying what they did by faith. By now, everyone was shouting and praising the Lord.

I returned to the pulpit and told them all: "This chapter is not complete. It is waiting for your name. It is waiting to write your verse with your name, recording what *you* did by faith in obedience to the Lord's word to you."

When we finally finished, we prayed for a few people and got ready to leave, but the pastor wouldn't let us go until he took many pictures of us with him. He must have hugged me a dozen times before we finally got out the door. It was an honor to share the Word with these noble people and a great blessing to receive such love from their pastor.

I have often thought about those four churches in Rostov-on-Don, Russia. Each one of them was unique, each one was totally different than the other, and I realized that they were just four expressions of what Heaven must be like. Heaven will be filled with people from many different cultures and languages, all of them united in worshiping the Father who sits upon the Throne. I don't know exactly what Heaven will look like, but I believe that when I was in those four churches in Russia, I got a small glimpse of what it will be.

Anya of Kyrgyzstan

In a Russian Charismatic church

In a Russian Pentecostal church

Chapter 39

THE SWORD OF THE LORD

Proclaim this among the nations: prepare for war! Wake up the mighty men, let all the men of war draw near, let them come up. Beat your plowshares into swords and your pruning hooks into spears; let the weak say, I am strong.   Joel 3:9-10

    Whenever I am preaching or teaching, I like to do things that are dramatic, things that will leave an impression on those I'm teaching, something that will stick with them, something that will leave a memory. I'm always, as the phrase goes, "pushing the envelope," doing something that I have never done.

    I had been teaching about spiritual warfare for some years when my son sent me a tape series entitled, "Go Buy a Sword." A short time later, I was at a computer show one Saturday, walking through a maze of different booths where people were selling computers and computer parts, when I came upon a vendor with a booth selling all kinds of swords and medieval weaponry. Most of these things always have dragons and other evil symbols on them, but there was one beautiful sword. It had a handle made from light and dark wood, and it had a big symbol of a lion at the end of the handle where the blade began. I fell in love with it and bought it.

    Sometime later I went to a gun store and bought a case that could carry a rifle. This would be the perfect case for me to use for carrying my sword to the nations. I wanted to use it when I was teaching Spiritual Warfare. I never told people in advance what was in the case. Most thought it was just some type of musical instrument. I would only bring it out at the very end of my five days of teaching.

As I was searching for scriptures about swords, I came across the story of Gideon in the book of Judges. In chapter 6, it tells how the children of Israel had been disobeyed the Lord, and so, for seven years, whenever it was time for harvest, the Midianites would come and steal the harvest and the animals, leaving the children of Israel in fear and poverty. Thankfully, the children of Israel eventually cried out to the Lord because of their situation, and God heard their cry.

Gideon was just a young man who was gathering wheat to hide from the Midianites when an angel appeared to him. The angel said, *"The Lord is with you, you mighty man of valor!"* Some versions translate this as *mighty warrior*. The truth, however, was that Gideon was not a mighty warrior. He was little more than a fearful farm boy. The angel had seen him as the Lord saw him. The angel knew what Gideon would become and what he would do for the Lord.

Many people are like Gideon. They don't see themselves the way the Lord sees them. They are satisfied with the normal Christian life. Those of us in America seem to easily get detoured away from God's call on our life because of all the comforts that surround us.

I'm on a mission to raise up an army of men and women, boys and girls who will pay the price and make the sacrifices necessary to come into the fullness of their calling, to become spiritual warriors. I'm looking for men and women who will go forth into the nations of the world and set people free.

I often use a saying I read many years ago:

"Never forget that you are a miracle, that you are unique, possessing talents, experiences, and opportunities that no one else has ever

INHERITING THE NATIONS

had, or will ever have. It's your responsibility to become everything that you are, not only for your benefit but also for everyone else's."[1]

If you know the story of Gideon in Judges chapter 7, he gathered 32,000 men to go to war against the Midianites and the Amalekites, who were themselves too numerous to number. The Lord, however, told him he had too many. If they had conquered the enemy with numbers, they would have thought they had done it on their own. The group was pared down to ten thousand, but still the Lord said it was too many. After a test, Gideon ended up with only three hundred men to go to war against many thousands of Midianites:

> *Then the three companies blew the trumpets and broke the pitchers — they held the torches in their left hands and the trumpets in their right hands for blowing — and they cried, "The sword of the LORD and of Gideon!"*　　　　　　　　　　　　　　　　　　Judges 7:20

This battle cry is very interesting: *"the sword of the LORD, and of Gideon."* It wasn't just the Lord's sword, and it wasn't just Gideon's sword. It was the Lord and Gideon working together to bring a great victory for the children of Israel and for the glory of God.

The course I have developed over the years on Spiritual Warfare has fourteen lessons. There is never enough time to teach all of them, so I must prayerfully consider what teachings are needful for the specific group I'm addressing. Usually, over a period of five days, I give seven lessons. The final teaching is always about Weapons of Warfare.

I start with an introduction to spiritual warfare, going over stories in the Old Testament and New Testament. In the Old Testament, it was a physical war for the Promised Land; in the New Testament it's a spiritual war to expand God's Kingdom in the nations of the world.

---
1. Author unknown

THE SWORD OF THE LORD

Then I teach about the cross, which I believe is God's ultimate weapon. Next, I teach about the Promise of the Father, the baptism of the Holy Spirit, the gifts of the Spirit, the armor of God, and the fruits of the Spirit.

When teaching times are over, the students, whether they be young people in YWAM or church leaders in Southeast Asia, always have questions. I do my best to answer their questions, mixing biblical truth with my personal experiences in ministry. I also give liberty in each class for the Holy Spirit to come, and He is faithful to speak to the hearts of His people.

In most of the classes, I go around the room and lay hands on people as the Lord leads me and pray for them or maybe even give them a short prophetic word. It is my belief that what the Holy Spirit imparts to the hearts of others is more important than filling their heads with biblical knowledge. They need a divine encounter with the God of Heaven during their teaching times.

As we have seen, Paul wrote to the Roman believers:

For I long to see you, that I may impart to you some spiritual gift, so that you may be established. Romans 1:11

People, especially those who are in ministry, need an impartation from Heaven.

Now, with all teaching completed and the notebooks closed, I tell the story of Gideon, a poor, fearful farm boy whom God made into a warrior and who brought deliverance to the children of Israel. I tell them about the battle cry that was used when they went to war against the Midianites:

THE SWORD OF THE LORD AND OF GIDEON!

INHERITING THE NATIONS

At this moment, I bring out my sword. For some, it will be the first time they have seen a real sword. I ask them to come up one at a time, hold up the sword in front of the whole group, and proclaim, THE SWORD OF THE LORD AND OF THEIR OWN NAME. For example, if a student's name was Aram, he would proclaim: THE SWORD OF THE LORD AND OF ARAM. Then the whole class will loudly repeat this proclamation: THE SWORD OF THE LORD AND OF ARAM! You would have to be there to understand what is going on in the spiritual realm as they make these proclamations in the physical realm.

Just before they give their proclamation, I anoint them with oil on their forehead and pray a short prayer. Some people, when they hold the sword, start to weep even before giving their proclamation. Some fall on their knees and then give their proclamation. Once, in Armenia, a young man took the sword, I anointed him, and then he stood there very quiet for some moments. Then he began to weep, and all the other students came up, gathered around him, laid hands on him, and began to pray. It was a powerful time.

Some give their proclamation with a lot of energy in a loud voice, and others just quietly hold the sword high in the air and make their proclamation. Whether it's loud or quiet is not important. What is important is that there's a God in Heaven who hears and sees the heart of the one holding the sword, and that day He accepts them as a mighty warrior, prepared for battle. I like to believe that a mantle of war is imparted to them in that moment. They are now ready to go into the nations of the world, proclaiming the Gospel with power, breaking the chains of the enemy that have bound people for years, and setting the captives free. It is all done so that the Lord who sits on the Throne in Heaven might be glorified, and that Jesus might receive the reward of His suffering.

The sword itself is just a piece of metal. My sword has a wooden handle, but of itself, it has no power. What counts is what a person does

THE SWORD OF THE LORD

and says when they hold that sword up to the Lord, and it's what He does when He sees them holding it up.

In the book of Exodus chapter 4 is the story of Moses and his encounter with God. In verse 2, the Lord said to Moses, *"What is in your hand?"*

Moses answered, *"A rod."* The Lord told him to throw it down, and when he did, it became a serpent. The rod itself was just a piece of wood, but for Moses it was more. Before God's touch, it was the thing that held him up when he was tired and possibly the tool that he used to fight off animals when he was tending sheep. It was Moses' security.

In the end of verse 20, it says:

And Moses took the rod of God in his hand.

It had been Moses' rod, but it was now God's rod. After God's touch, it became a weapon that opened the Red Sea when the children of Israel were fleeing from Egypt. Because it was now God's rod, it would be used by Moses to do many miraculous works as the children of Israel wandered in the wilderness. What the Lord does with your gifts and talents is what makes the difference. When we give Him what we have, He anoints it for His glory.

The first time I took my sword overseas was in 2001 to a missions conference in Bangkok. I don't remember what I spoke about, but I'm sure it was something to do with spiritual warfare. Then I brought out the sword and challenged the people to make a proclamation to the God of Heaven. One pastor from Vietnam came to me later and said he had known he was called to spiritual warfare many years before. Then he got a big smile on his face and with real enthusiasm said, "But today I held a real sword."

In 2003, I stood in the land of Nepal looking up at the majestic mountain chain of the Himalayas, held up my sword and proclaimed the Lord's victory for the people of that land. This and other swords I have used in my teachings have been held up by many hundreds of people in dozens of nations around the world, and now those people are part of the army the Lord has called me to raise up, men and women, boys and girls changed into warriors by an impartation of the Holy Spirit.

In the book of Joel chapter 3, it talks about preparing for war and that we need to wake up the mighty men. It doesn't say anything about women, so one day I said, "Lord, what about the women?"

I felt the Lord say, "Joe, the women are already awake. It's the men who are sleeping and must be awakened." I had to admit that in most of the churches of the world it seems like the women were the workers.

Once, when I was with a pastor who had a two-thousand-member church in the capitol of Mongolia, he showed me a photo of the leaders of his fifty-two home groups. As I looked at the photo, I couldn't see any men. I said, "These are all women. Where are the men?"

Sadness crossed his face as he replied, "In Mongolia, most of the men are alcoholics. It's the women who are doing the work of the ministry." Pastor Cho of Korea had one of the largest churches in the world. He famously said that his best men were women.

We must pray for the men, to call them in the Spirit, to wake up, to come into the Church, and to become the warriors God has called them to be. Men, it's time to prepare for war!

With Russian students in DTS class

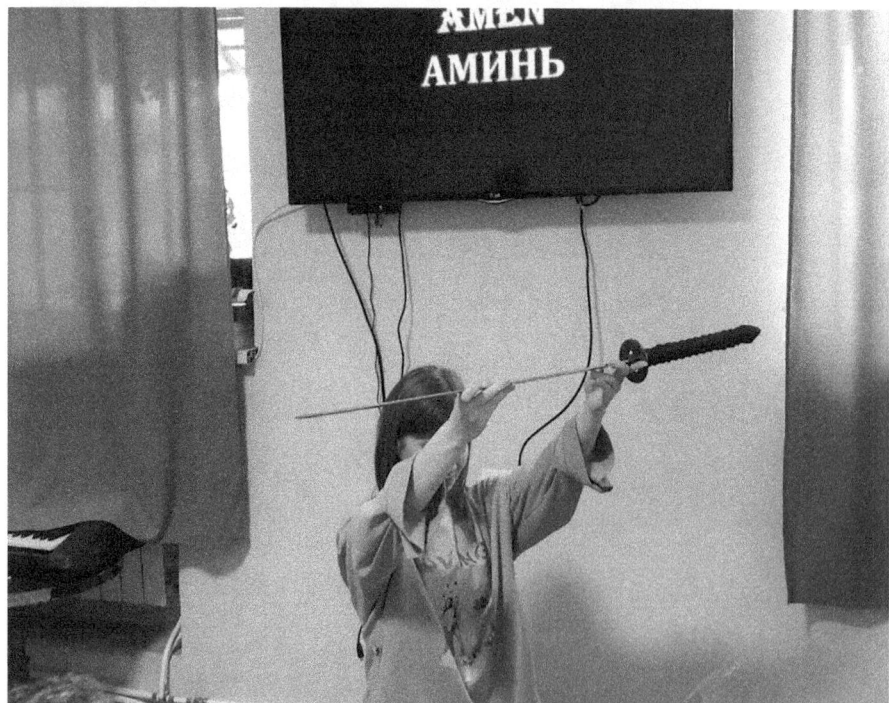

CHAPTER 40

DESCENDING INTO DARKNESS

I waited patiently for the LORD;
And He inclined to me,
And heard my cry.
He also brought me up out of a horrible pit,
Out of the miry clay,
And set my feet upon a rock,
And established my steps.
He has put a new song in my mouth—
Praise to our God;
Many will see it and fear,
And will trust in the LORD.   Psalm 40:103

In studying church history, many times you run across the phrase "The dark night of the soul." Between 1577 and 1579, a Spanish Christian who came to be known as Saint John of the Cross, wrote a poem entitled "Dark Night of the Soul."[1] In that poem, he talked about his journey through darkness. A light guided him and eventually brought him to his Beloved, to a place of forgetting the cares of this world and abandoning himself to the Lord Jesus. Many others throughout church history have experienced and written about this "Dark Night."

---
1. Public domain

INHERITING THE NATIONS

What is a dark night? It's like a journey in which the Holy Spirit does a deep work in us, to purify our soul and bring us into greater intimacy with the Lord. In the darkness, there is confusion, helplessness, and a withdrawal of the conscious presence of God. It's a place of total surrender to the purposes and perfect will of God for our life. In this journey, self is finally crucified, we are drawn closer to the Lord, and are finally free to live for Him and not for ourselves. Revelation comes, bringing us to a deeper level and drawing us into His love, a place where we feel the embrace and the kiss of the heavenly Father.

Paul said in Galatians 2:20:

I have been crucified with Christ; it is no longer I who live, but Christ lives in me; and the life which I now live in the flesh I live by faith in the Son of God, who loved me and gave Himself for me.

I have been in ministry now for a little over forty years, and I have been teaching Spiritual Warfare for about half of that time. I always tell my students, "This is not a picnic; it's a war!" It's a war for the souls of men and women in the nations of the world, and the enemy is forever planning how to take you out of this war. He doesn't care if you go to church. He just doesn't want you to follow your calling and complete your destiny, for that will glorify the Lord.

In late 2020, I received some discouraging news about a young Asian lady I had met six years before while on a flight in Thailand. We became Facebook friends, and on a later trip to Bangkok, I invited her to dinner with another lady from the mission office. I told her that I believed Jesus had a plan for her life and then Goi, the lady from the office, shared the Gospel with her. A short time later, there in the restaurant, the two of them bowed their heads and were praying. I looked across the table in amazement. This young woman, who had been a Buddhist for twenty-seven years and never heard the name of Jesus, was beginning to open her heart to the heavenly Father. Her life would never be the same again.

She eventually become a believer, after seeing how the Lord was moving in Goi's life. She attended Alpha Discipleship Course in English at an Anglican church and in Thai at a Thailand church, and she was water baptized in the Anglican church.

I saw that she had a real heart for worship. She had a ukulele, but I knew the Lord was giving her a gift to bring healing and encouragement to others through songs that the Lord would give her, so I took her to the music store in Bangkok and bought her a guitar. She began to get up every morning at 5:00 AM to sing to the Lord, pray, and read the Word. With a heart of worship, she applied to attend the Bethel School of Worship for two weeks. She attended a church camp in Thailand, and there she was overwhelmed with the Lord's presence, baptized in the Holy Spirit, and received all the money needed to fly to California the following week.

Twice she traveled to Canada by faith to work with a Christian ministry. The first time she left Thailand with only $100, but the Lord honored her faith and supplied all her needs. She traveled to several other countries sharing her testimony.

The Lord had put in her heart, even before she was a believer, the desire to go to Turkey. She saved her money and found a cheap ticket to Turkey, put on two backpacks, and traveled there to several places mentioned in the Bible, and she did it all by herself.

I had arranged a Christian guesthouse for her first night, but the rest of the trip it was just her and her backpacks. I worried a lot about her when I saw Facebook posts of her alone. At the time, I also made a connection for her to go to Armenia to visit the Youth With A Mission base there and meet some of my friends. It was there that she met the base leader Andrey, who, within a short time, moved to Russia to become the base leader in Rostov.

INHERITING THE NATIONS

One afternoon he took her to a mountain in Armenia that still had snow, and for the first time in her life, she experienced snow and had a snowball fight with him.

Coming from a Buddhist background, this young lady didn't know much about the Bible. Even though she was reading it every day with a hungry heart, she wanted more. After much prayer, she applied to go to Rostov to attend the YWAM discipleship training school. Because Andrey had met her several months before in Armenia, he was delighted that she wanted to come to Russia, so he gave the approval for her to attend the school.

In the outreach phase of the school, she would be traveling to Turkey, so her dream would become reality, and she would be able to go deeper into the things of the Spirit at the YWAM base. She was happy.

She finished her DTS course in Rostov in 2019 and then returned to Bangkok in 2020 to work with a ministry that was reaching out to prostitutes and bar girls. She poured her heart and soul into that ministry and into the lives of the girls they were trying to pull out of darkness.

All the things she had accomplished for the Lord and how He used her for His glory in the first six years of her Christian life are too numerous to mention in this chapter. Her life was sold out to God, and this was reflected in her dedication to prayer, Bible reading, and worship.

When she contacted me in late 2020 with some discouraging news,. I decided to start fasting for her. I fasted and prayed for her for twelve weeks. There was a war going on for her calling and her spiritual gifts, and for some reason she wasn't able to see the danger. I encouraged her to return to Rostov. Andrey was looking for graduates who could work as staff members. She was officially invited by Andrey, and it would be perfect for her. She would be near the country of her destiny, Turkey, and she would be in a safe place with people who loved her and believed in her.

DESCENDING INTO DARKNESS

Because of things that were happening in the natural, 2021 started out for me to be a very difficult year, and I failed to see that a spiritual attack was now coming at me.

The results of the U.S. elections had gone in a different direction that most Christians had expected, and Americans had voted for Socialism instead of Democracy. This was a real attack on my mind. My body was also under attack, with severe pain in my shoulder and leg. Then I got a text from this young friend. She was now calling me Father, and I was calling her Daughter. She informed me that she was in America, and I sensed that this would end in a detour from her destiny.

This felt like a massive attack on my heart and spirit, and the attack was now affecting every part of my being. For some reason, although I teach a lot on spiritual warfare, I didn't see this as coming from the devil. The result was that I descended into a place of darkness that cannot be described with words.

I suddenly felt complete hopelessness, depression, fear, and desperation. All vision was sucked out of me, and this resulted in hours of weeping. It was all so overpowering that I didn't know how to pray, and I couldn't explain to others what was happening to ask them for prayer. How could I explain it to them when I didn't fully understand it myself?

I was scheduled to go to Armenia to teach the Russian DTS group, but I was in such terrible condition that Brenda encouraged me to cancel the trip. I knew I couldn't do that. I had made a commitment, and I would fulfil that commitment. I must be honest: I felt like this might be my final trip.

Two weeks before I was scheduled to travel, I had to go to the airport to check about my covid requirements. I was like a zombie driving on the freeway, my mind and soul consumed with total darkness. Then something started to stir deep in my spirit, and I started to speak in tongues very softly. Then it got louder and louder ... until I was screaming in tongues and in English and weeping uncontrollably at the same time.

I remembered the verses in the book of Revelation that talked about the Lion of the Tribe of Judah who prevailed to open the books in Heaven, and I began to roar like a lion. As noted in an earlier chapter, this was one of the many manifestations that had been in evidence in the revival in Toronto, and it seemed to bring a spiritual release to people's lives. For the first time in my life, I began to roar like a lion as loud as I could.

As I was doing all these things and crying deeply, I could see chains coming off my body, darkness was lifting, vision was coming back, and I saw myself preaching in Armenia. I continued this for an hour and then another half hour on the way home. The next day I did the same thing for an hour and felt a lot of freedom, but it was not total. That night Pastor Dina asked me to share what was going on in our home group over Zoom. I did, and felt about ninety percent free, but it was still as if my heart was bleeding.

My flight to Armenia was very challenging. It required three stops and twenty-six hours of travel, and the pain in my knee was excruciating. When the plane was dark, and everyone else was sleeping, I cried from the pain. Eventually a stewardess gave me some aspirin, and I finally got some relief.

My time in Armenia was the most powerful and anointed time I have ever experienced in all my years of ministry. Maybe it was the weeks of fasting, or maybe it was my brokenness, or a combination of both. For sure, El Roi, the God who sees, had seen my brokenness and had come to minister to the people of Armenia in their time of brokenness through me.

There was a physical war with Azerbaijan going on in the south of Armenia. Houses were being bombed and people were being killed. It was a horrible time for the Armenian people.

DESCENDING INTO DARKNESS

One of the young ladies at the base had heard me teach Spiritual Warfare on three separate occasions, and she commented that she had never seen me minister under such a powerful anointing as this time. Many times, in the classes and during the times I was preaching in churches around Armenia, I had to pause because my heart was breaking, and my eyes were filling with tears. For those who knew me, tears had never been part of my life. There was a breaking going on inside me, maybe an emptying or a cleansing by the Holy Spirit.

Armenia had just gone through a war and betrayal by their government leaders. I could feel their pain, and they could fell mine. Most meetings were filled with tears during prayer time. Once there was a mixture of great joy and weeping.

I also had the opportunity to be on Christian TV for four sessions. This was an appointed time for me in Armenia. Because of the grief and pain of war, the Armenian people didn't need some flowery Gospel message. What they needed was someone who could feel their pain, relate to their brokenness, weep with them, and hug them with the hug of the Father in Heaven. I did my best to fulfill that need. I opened my heart and was as transparent as possible as I stood before the people in the churches and home groups of Armenia. I tried my best to share with them the love of Jesus, the love that compelled Him to go to the cross so that we might be free from sin and its consequences, so we could experience the love of the heavenly Father.

All the time I was in Armenia I continued to fast and pray for my spiritual daughter and asked others who knew her to join me in prayer. I was expecting a great victory for her.

Whenever I'm at a YWAM base, I always make it a point to hug everyone in the morning and sometimes during the day, for I understand the power of a hug. Without words, it communicates acceptance, approval, and love. It says that someone cares. It wasn't until I had returned to California that I realized how much the hugs from the students and staff had meant to me. My heart was still bleeding inside, but as I thought back on the many hugs I had received, I believed they were hugs from the Father through my brothers and sisters, and they really sustained me emotionally and mentally during my time in Armenia.

I particularly remembered the hugs of two young ladies. One was Dina. She was from Russia, and she was in her early twenties and full of life and enthusiasm. In Russia, she was always out on the streets sharing the Gospel with anybody who came near. She was amazing. Her hugs always came with a big smile and great laughter that made you laugh. They made you feel like you had just drunk a double energy drink. One time she even started singing to me. I miss her hugs. Her father was one of my students in 2019 and is now a missionary in South Africa.

Lucine, also Russian, is another great hugger. Before I met her, she had been on an outreach to the Belgian Congo in Africa working with the pygmies. While she was there, the Lord gave her a burden for these people, so she made a commitment to return there for two years. The pygmies are a people group that are very short. Lucine is also very short, so I always joked with her that maybe she would find a husband while she was working with the pygmies. She works in an orphanage, a women's prison, and in a pygmy village.

The last time I was in Armenia, Lucine was part of the staff and was assigned to help me with any practical needs. She prepared my breakfast, did my laundry, and was there whenever I needed anything. Many times, I would sneak up behind her and hug her around the neck, and she would let out a crazy laugh that was contagious.

Lucine returned to the Congo, and I stayed in touch with her through the Internet. I try to talk to her once a week. The conditions she was living under were challenging. The facility she lived in was very substandard. The electricity was turned off every day at a certain time, and she had suffered from malaria and covid. To be honest, there are not many people who would want to serve where she does, but it's her calling, it was her dream, and her dream became reality in the Belgian Congo.

I can no longer receive physical hugs from Lucine, but her laughter and her smile make my heart smile whenever I am able to talk with her.

There was a male student at the base named Klim. Klim was also Russian. He had been a basketball player, but because of a physical problem, he had to give up that dream. He was very tall, with beautiful blonde hair, and the ladies liked him. One day, when the class was on a break, Klim came up and hugged me with a big tight hug and then raised me up over his shoulder. All the students started cheering. He was a great young man.

I hadn't fully realized how emotionally drained I had been from the spiritual battle that had begun long before I got to Armenia, and I didn't realize it at the time, but every hug from every student and every other person on that trip was refilling my emotional tank. The Lord has many ways of filling us and touching the deep needs of our heart and soul. On this trip He was filling me with the power of a hug from His arms through the arms of the brothers and sisters of Russia and Armenia.

I read this quote somewhere:

I walked in the desert.
I heard a voice from Heaven say,
"Spend time with Me, because I have appointed you to be My messenger."

Chapter 41

THE ROOMS OF MY HEART

Create in me a clean heart, O God,
And renew a steadfast spirit within me.   Psalm 51:10

For what man knows the things of a man except the spirit of the man which is in him? Even so no one knows the things of God except the Spirit of God.   1 Corinthians 2:11

This is another hard chapter for me to write, but I felt from the beginning that if I was going to write my story, I needed to be honest and tell the whole truth. As I write this chapter, I need to say, as I have already said several times, this is not a theological book. It's about my life, my experiences, and my walk with the Lord through the nations of the world. In trying to be honest. It is my desire that I will help others avoid some of the mistakes I've made and encourage everyone that, despite our mistakes, shortcomings, and disobediences, the Lord, through His grace and mercy, will restore us and bring us into the fullness of our calling and walk with Him. The great thing about restoration is that when He restores us, He makes us better than we were before. The anointing increases, our faith grows, and our intimacy with God becomes deeper. He is an amazing God, overflowing with love.

THE ROOMS OF MY HEART

Blessed be the God and Father of our Lord Jesus Christ, the Father of mercies and God of all comfort, who comforts us in all our tribulation, that we may be able to comfort those who are in any trouble, with the comfort with which we ourselves are comforted by God.
2 Corinthians 1:3-4

As we are on this journey called *life*, we experience many emotions—joy and sadness, laughter and grief, feelings of abandonment and disappointment, rejection and acceptance, betrayal and hopelessness. Sometimes we have great faith; at other times, unbelief. All these feelings and how we process them and react to them make us into the person we are today.

On October 14, 1971, I became a believer, a few weeks short of my twenty-fifth birthday. The person I am today is not the person I was in my younger years. I recently turned seventy-six, and I have walked with the Lord for more than fifty years now. On this journey, I have experienced all of these emotions. Some of them I have handled in a healthy way, but others in an unhealthy way. I hope and believe that day by day I'm becoming more like Jesus.

A few years after I became a believer, I was working at an engineering firm as a draftsman, and I was very verbal about my faith. As I said early on, I saw many people come to the Lord because of my testimony. On this particular job, one of my coworkers happened to meet an old friend of mine from my prior days before I became a believer and was telling him all about me. I don't know exactly what he told him, but at some point in the conversation, my old friend said, "That must be a different Joe Zeyak. That's not the Joe I knew years ago."

Therefore, if anyone is in Christ, he is a new creation; old things have passed away; behold, all things have become new. Now all things are of God, who has reconciled us to Himself through Jesus Christ, and has

INHERITING THE NATIONS

given us the ministry of reconciliation, that is, that God was in Christ reconciling the world to Himself, not imputing their trespasses to them, and has committed to us the word of reconciliation.
2 Corinthians 5:17-19

Because of Jesus and His crucifixion and resurrection, our sins are paid for. So now we can come into relationship with the Father. We are a new creation. We're not the same anymore. He didn't just repair us; He made us completely new. Now, through us, other people can feel the touch of Jesus, they can feel the embrace of the Father, and they can hear the voice of the Father calling them to come into an intimate relationship with Him.

As I said in an early chapter, as I was growing up, we attended a Catholic Church, but even though I knew all about Jesus, I didn't know Him personally until 1971.

Until I was five, we lived with my father's parents. They had a two-hundred-acre farm, and I can vividly remember the day we moved to the suburbs. My uncle was a truck driver and came with a very big moving van. I was sitting between two big oak trees next to the truck crying at the thought of leaving the only security I had known. My father reached down, picked me up and put me up in the front seat of the moving van between him and my uncle and tried to comfort me as we drove away from the farm. It's interesting that for most of my life, every time I had a dream, no matter what the dream was about, it was always at that farm or somehow related to that farm. Looking back now, it was almost as if the little boy in me wanted to return to that place of security.

Life in the suburbs was actually pretty good. There were only two streets of a new development with fifty houses on each, and all around us was woods, two ponds, and a massive sandlot at the end of the street. The ponds were great for ice skating and hockey playing in the winter, and the sandlots became our baseball and football fields in the summer. Life was simple but good for me and my two brothers.

At an early age, I became interested in comic books, and once a month my dad would take me to the pharmacy, which was also an ice cream bar and magazine stand at the end of the street. He would give me a dollar and that would buy ten comic books. I wish I had those comic books now. I would probably be a millionaire because of their value to collectors.

When I became a teenager, we were allowed to go to the movies by ourselves. For a dollar we could take the bus to the city and back, buy a movie ticket, and get soda and popcorn. Sometimes I would work around the neighborhood, weeding gardens, washing windows, and painting the parts of houses where neighbors couldn't reach. That would give me extra money because we never received an allowance. That was never in Dad's budget.

During the summers my brother and I would take turns going to our grandparent's farm to work. They had beef cows and milk cows, racehorses, pigs, and chickens, which all had to be fed. This meant collecting thousands of bales of hay to put up in super-hot barns on the hot and humid days of upstate New York, combining oats and lifting hundred-pound sacks of grain, and plowing fields for new crops. It was hard work but great for the soul and great for building the physical body of a teenager.

My grandmother would take us to the store and buy us a few pairs of jeans, a jean jacket, and some steel-toed leather boots so we didn't get hurt working around the heavy equipment. I thought it was great going there every summer, and it did help me to appreciate hard work and taught me how to do a good job.

My uncle, who was only a few years older, also lived on the farm, and he was in charge of the work. It would never have succeeded without his wisdom and hard work. I was a teenager and just

INHERITING THE NATIONS

getting interested in girls, and my uncle became my mentor in this regard, teaching me most of what I learned about how to treat girls. Unfortunately, this ended in many broken relationships.

In looking back, I can't remember any time when I was growing up that my mother or father told me they loved me, so I came to believe that giving things to us was their way of saying, "I love you." We weren't rich, so we never had anything fancy. Our neighborhood was made up of middle-class people, and we all knew one another and helped one another. Every year we had a weekend picnic in the sandlot at the end of the street, and every neighbor came. At Christmas time, we had a large Christmas tree decorated on the only empty lot on the street. Santa Claus would come on the fire truck and have presents for all the kids.

Even after I had become a Christian, it was easier for me to do something for someone else than to look them in the eyes and say, "I love you." Giving had become the love language I learned, without realizing it, from my parents. I mentioned in an earlier chapter that it was only after I had met Pastor Paulo in Brazil that I began to understand love.

All through high school I had one goal—to become an Air Force pilot. That was the dream of my heart. In high school I stayed physically fit and was involved in track and cross-country running. My real strength was short runs in track. I remember the first time we had a cross-country race against another school. Being a sprinter, I started the race very fast and was quickly far out in front of everybody else. But this was a three-mile race, and I began to lose energy. In the end, I was next to the last person to cross the finish line.

After the race, in the locker room, the coach was evaluating everyone. When it came my turn, he said, "And then there was Zeyak ... out like a lion and in like a lamb." I soon learned to pace myself better. I never won a cross-country race, but trying kept me in good physical condition during track season.

THE ROOMS OF MY HEART

Prior to graduation, I had already taken all the tests necessary for the Air Force, so now I went down to take the physical and officially enrol in the force. To my deep sorrow, I failed the physical. I couldn't hear one tone in one ear. They told me it was quite common to lose some tones, especially if you were around guns or loud noises. We always had guns on the farm, and I belonged to a rifle team. At the time, we were never issued safety gear for our ears as is common today.

After being rejected by the Air Force, I went down to the Army recruiter, hoping I could at least get into the Army, but the recruiting officer had my Air Force folder. He said, "I'm sorry, but we can't take you."

The war in Vietnam was ramping up, and all my close friends were joining the military. Thank God they all came back in one piece. For myself, I'd had no other plan but the military, and now those doors had closed. I didn't know the Lord at the time, so I couldn't look to Him for direction for my life. I got a job working in a factory for General Electric and turned to car racing, partying, and girls.

Eventually, my girlfriend, who had physical problems and had been told she could never get pregnant, started gaining weight. When I took her to a doctor, he informed her that she was four months pregnant. We got married, and two month later, our first son, Joseph Daniel Zeyak, III was born. He was three months premature. Two years later, our second son, Kenneth Michael, was born. I was a terrible father and a worse husband, and my wife finally left me. Chapter 1 tells the sad story.

While my wife was pregnant with our second son, my father had a heart attack and died. He was only forty-two. I couldn't ever remember him being sick. He was physically fit. His only vice was that he was a heavy smoker, which was true of many people at the time. Looking back, it was probably stress that killed him. Many things in his life took a turn for the worse, and it drove him into depression. I can only

INHERITING THE NATIONS

believe that he did his best as a father with the tools he had and the wisdom that had been imparted to him from others. Unfortunately, even though we were religious people, we didn't know the life-giving power of a personal relationship with the Father through Jesus.

As I thought about what I would write in this chapter, I realized the title had to be "The Rooms of My Heart." Even though physically I know there are not rooms, someplace in this magnificent thing we call the human body, there are places where we store things that we experience in life—both good and bad. Many of us learn to compartmentalize things. We can somehow separate emotions and experiences into what I have chosen to call the rooms of my heart.

All through my life, feelings of disappointment, rejection, betrayal, grief, and others were never dealt with correctly. They were all stuffed into what I think of now as a large room in my heart, a place that I had long forgotten about. Even after I had become a believer, if there were negative things that happened, things that brought pain, they were automatically stored in that room.

There are other rooms. If I had to put labels on them, I would label them: Work, Ministry, Friendships, Family, Visions, Dreams, Our Relationship with the Lord, Our Christian Experiences—and there could be others. Each is separate, but all are important in forming us into the unique person we are today. I never had a daughter, so when the Lord gave me a daughter from Asia, it seemed like there was a room in my heart just for her. That room was right next to the one that was filled with the pains of life.

In my chapter, "Descending into Darkness," I shared about the spiritual attacks I had been going through and how, just prior to me leaving for Armenia, the Lord had given me a great victory. However, upon returning, I didn't see what I was hoping for regarding my spiritual daughter. Instead of achieving the expected spiritual victory, she was continuing down a path that would eventually lead to her losing her calling and the faith that she had walked in for six years. For me, it was all about her calling, her destiny, and the people she was called to share God's love with. She had a clear calling to the country of Turkey and had been making plans to go there when the enemy detoured her.

She had called me her father, and I had called her my daughter. I felt that she was a gift from the Lord to teach me how to love a daughter I never had and to bring me into deeper levels of His love that I could take to the nations of the world. I had given her my best, but in the end, I failed her. I couldn't help her in her hour of temptation. The enemy had captured her heart. I returned from Armenia on a spiritual high after the powerful times of ministry there, but now I again found myself in a spiritual battle for my own life and calling.

There are two important points about the room in my heart that was filled to the point where it was about to overflow: 1). The Lord wanted to empty that room so He could fill it with the things of the Spirit, things that would bring me deeper into my intimacy with Him, further equipping me for my calling and destiny. 2). I didn't even know the room was there. Our mind has an incredible ability to block out emotional pain and trauma, to the point that it takes a ministry of the Spirit to reveal the things the Lord wants to deliver and heal us from, so that we can be whole—body, soul, and spirit.

Several things happen that caused the relationship between me and my spiritual daughter to become fractured, and when she left that place in my heart, it was extremely painful. When she was leaving, she put that pain into the room and didn't close the door securely. I don't blame her for what was about to happen. It could have been anyone. She just happened to be the one.

I know this talk of rooms in our heart may sound strange to some, but it's the only way I can explain it. I can only testify to what I experienced. The door was not securely shut, so all the unresolved pain of more than seventy years came rushing out into my mind and emotions, eventually affecting my physical body. I didn't know what to do or how to resolve what was going on within me. I believe that some of it was a spiritual attack, but I also believe the Lord wanted me to clean out that room. To this day, I don't know how to separate the two. I only know that I don't have the proper words to explain how deep I had sunk into darkness.

Some advised me not to put these things in the book, but I feel that being honest and truthful is something I must do. Hopefully, the book will be read by some who have also stored up years of pain, and in reading my story they, too, can become whole—body, soul, and spirit.

In the DTS classes, there was one entitled "The Father Heart of God." Jim, a brother who lives in Oregon, travels around the world teaching this class. I had come to know Jim because sometimes our classes were connected. I called Jim, and we set up a time that we could pray over the phone together. We finally connected one evening over FaceTime, and after talking for a little while, Jim began to pray. As he prayed, the Holy Spirit began to show me the things that needed healing in my heart and mind. The details of what the Lord revealed are probably not important because each of us has different experiences and different things in our hearts and minds that don't allow us to come into the fullness of what the Lord has for us. It's a personal relationship we have with the Lord.

Jim and I prayed for three and a half hours, as the Holy Spirit revealed things that I needed to be healed from so that I would no longer carry the burden that was hindering me from coming into God's fullness for my life. The Lord wanted that room in my heart to be cleaned out, so He could fill it with Himself.

During this journey, I heard a song by Elevation Worship & Maverick City called "Come Again." Part of it says:

> It's not a building You wanna fill, it's my heart.
> This empty space is what You wanted all along.[1]

---
1 Songwriters: Steven Furtick, Chandler Moore, Brandon Lake, and Dante Bowe. Come Again lyrics

THE ROOMS OF MY HEART

The Lord Himself, through the Holy Spirit, was beginning a deep work in me that probably should have been done a long time before, but I had not seen the need of it. Sadly, it took me losing my spiritual daughter for me to finally discover it. The Bible says, in Romans 8:28:

And we know that all things work together for good to those who love God, to those who are the called according to His purpose.

After praying with Jim, I laid my head down and had a good rest for the first time in many months. The following night, as I laid my head on the bed, the Holy Spirit peaceably and gently began to show me pictures of people I had hurt or who had hurt me. One by one, I forgave them or asked them in prayer to forgive me. There were many, dozens of people, some I had long forgotten, but the Holy Spirit brought them to my mind. Finally, after a long time, I fell into a deep and restful sleep. The Divine Surgeon had removed negative things from that room in my heart. To Him be all the glory!

I have rewritten this chapter several times, but I realize that it can never be perfectly written. I do know that God is the God of the second chance. He is the God of redemption, and no matter what decisions we make in life—good or bad—He can turn them around for our good and His glory. For sure, we all make bad decisions that allow the enemy to detour us from the perfect will of the Father.

The way back to the heart of the Father, into His perfect will, is through repentance, the tearing of our hearts, not our garments, a turning away from sin by the power of the Holy Spirit through His grace. True repentance will lead us into a deeper understanding and an experience of God's amazing mercy and power to restore us. We can experience the kiss of Heaven and the embrace of the Father filled with pure love.

---

copyright © Be Essential Songs, Bethel Music Publishing, Bethel Worship Publishing, Maverick City Publishing, Maverick City Publishing Worldwide, Brandon Lake Music, and Dante Bowe Music

INHERITING THE NATIONS

Surely there are consequences when we leave God's perfect will for whatever reason. People will be hurt, and for those of us that are in ministry, those of us who are called to the nations, there can also be eternal losses to the people who we were called to reach.

During one of my trips to Armenia I had a discouraging time. One of my close friends had a very powerful and fruitful ministry with children. She had been in the ministry for a long time and even traveled to several other countries to teach others about children's ministry. Because of her maturity in the ministry and in the Lord, she was also involved with counseling other leaders. She was a very anointed and loving person. She left the ministry to marry a man who was a new believer, and my heart was very heavy when I learned of her decision. I felt that somehow the enemy had detoured her from God's plan for her life.

At the same time, a precious pastor friend of mine made the decision to leave pastoring a wonderful church. Every time I went to Armenia, I had ministered in his church and later had a wonderful time of fellowship. It was always a time of joy and rejoicing when I was with him and some of his friends. I invited him to dinner when I heard he was having some challenges. I'll never forget the look on his face when he and his friend entered the restaurant. It was almost like a cloud of despair and gloom had settled over him. My heart was saddened just seeing his physical presence.

After talking for a while, I began to pray for him while weeping. My heart was overwhelmed with grief. As I was praying, I looked up and saw that he was just checking his phone. My prayers could not penetrate what was going on in his heart.

When I went home that night to my room at the YWAM base in Armenia, I thought of those two and others who had amazing giftings and a call to the ministry, but for some reason, got detoured and settled for the pleasures of the world. My heart was so heavy as I lay in bed that night overwhelmed with sadness and crying from deep within.

Since that night in Armenia, I've thought a lot about how the enemy detours those of us who are trying to fulfill our calling to the ministry. First, let me say that we are called to follow God personally, to have a daily, intimate relationship with a loving and compassionate Father. He is more interested in us than in our ministry.

Having said that, it's also very important to fulfill what the Lord is calling us to do for His glory. It's not just about us; it's more about others, other people, other nations. It's about people living in darkness without hope and without the ability to dream. It's about people living under the strongholds of Buddhism, Hinduism, and Islam. They are all waiting for us, to hear the Good News of a loving Father and how His Son, Jesus, died to pay the penalty for our sin so that we can be free. It's about fulfilling the Great Commission:

And He said to them, "Go into all the world and preach the gospel to every creature." Mark 16:15

As I noted earlier, almost every time I speak in a church about missions, after my message someone comes up and says, "The Lord called me to the mission field when I was younger, but I didn't go. Now I have a job, a wife, and children, and I can't go." They are enjoying the pleasures of this world, but one day they'll stand before the Father, and He will ask, "What have you done with the gifts and talents I put in you to glorify Me." That will be a very sad day.

But just as important is the question: What about the people that we didn't go to? We had a call and got detoured. What about the people we were supposed to reach? Where will those people spend eternity? The Lord wanted to touch through us and speak through us, but we did not go. Or maybe we were fulfilling our calling and then we gave up. There can be many reasons or excuses. However, none will be adequate when we stand before the Judge of All the Earth.

What does the enemy's detour look like? For Eve, it fulfilled all the desires of her heart:

> *So when the woman saw that the tree was good for food, that it was [a]pleasant to the eyes, and a tree desirable to make one wise, she took of its fruit and ate. She also gave to her husband with her, and he ate.*
> Genesis 4:6

John wrote to the early churches:

> *Do not love the world or the things in the world. If anyone loves the world, the love of the Father is not in him. For all that is in the world—the lust of the flesh, the lust of the eyes, and the pride of life—is not of the Father but is of the world. And the world is passing away, and the lust of it; but he who does the will of God abides forever.*
> 1 John 2:15-17

If you're not free to do the will of God (to fulfill your calling or destiny), the enemy has detoured you, and you are deceived and trapped. You have settled for the pleasures of the world. But God said:

> *For the gifts and the calling of God are irrevocable.*   Romans 11:29

Luke 15:20-24 tells the story of the prodigal son:

> *And he arose and came to his father. But when he was still a great way off, his father saw him and had compassion, and ran and fell on his neck and kissed him. And the son said to him, "Father, I have sinned*

against heaven and in your sight, and am no longer worthy to be called your son."
But the father said to his servants, "Bring out the best robe and put it on him, and put a ring on his hand and sandals on his feet. And bring the fatted calf here and kill it, and let us eat and be merry; for this my son was dead and is alive again; he was lost and is found." And they began to be merry.

Many people who teach about the prodigal son put the emphasis on the son's sin and repentance, but there is another story—the story of the father. He must have been waiting daily on the front porch, wishing, hoping, and praying that his son would return from the pleasures of sin. His heart must have longed to embrace his son. If his son returned, there would be no condemnation, no judgment, just love and mercy.

Behold what manner of love the Father has bestowed on us, that we should be called the children of God!   1 John 3:1

Chapter 42

PASSING THE MANTLE OF WAR

Yet who knows whether you have come to the kingdom for such a time as this? Esther 4:14

The early part of 2022 was to be a busy time. I would be traveling to Kyrgyzstan, Armenia, and Russia to teach Spiritual Warfare at the YWAM bases. It would be a challenging schedule for me because I was still having my own spiritual battles, and these were compounded by a physical attack on my sciatic nerve, creating excruciating pain in my back and left knee. I had been to four different doctors and spent a lot of money, with only partial release from the pain. However, the ministry trip must be made, commitments must be fulfilled, and I felt that a combination of prayer and medication would get me through the several weeks of ministry I had scheduled.

As I was preparing my flight schedules, I had no idea things would be changing dramatically. First, several students at the school in Kyrgyzstan had to cancel coming for various reasons, to the point that there were only four students left. It wouldn't be financially and physically feasible to make that long trip for just four students, so I made the offer to teach over the Internet, which I had done on other occasions. The leadership decided to replace the class with another subject.

Next, I began to work on my Russian visa, which is always a long and expensive process. The paperwork is extensive, and the visa with postage ends up costing $500 for a single entry into Russia. I had been there in 2018 to teach at the Rostov-on-Don base and was looking forward with great joy to returning there and reuniting with many of the brothers and sisters I knew who were working at the base. There would be the added benefit of being with Brother Andrey again, always a great blessing.

Then, on February 24, Russia began special operations on the Ukraine border, and eventual entered Ukraine. Rostov-on-Don, where the YWAM base is located, is the closest major city to the Ukraine border, so the leadership was uncertain what might happen with their base so close to the border. Two other teachers and I decided it would be too dangerous to travel there at that time, and there would be a good possibility that our visas would be denied. When that happens, the Russian Consulate keeps your visa fee.

I called two of my former students, who were on the base at that time, to encourage and pray for them—Parvina from Tajikistan and Kristina from Russia. Kristina had been a roommate and classmate of my spiritual daughter in 2019. They had come to Armenia for the final few weeks of their class. Because it was a large class, I hadn't gotten to know Kristina personally then. Later, when my spiritual daughter would call me, she would connect Kristina on the line for a three-way conversation.

After graduation, Kristina went on to Brazil to work with the YWAM base in the southern part of that country, and her schedule there got changed because of covid. She made the best of it, learning Portuguese and making many Brazilian friends, before returning to Russia and the corporate world.

Kristina told me that while working in the corporate world, she was making good money, and her boss had even offered her a promotion that would result in more money. She finally had to say to him, "I can't do this anymore. My heart is not in it. I need to return to the ministry." She had returned to the Rostov base, and then Russia had entered the Ukraine, so uncertainty was now on her doorstep.

I had been led to tell Kristina and Parvina that the Lord had brought them to the base for this time, that this was their hour to shine for Jesus. They would be needed to encourage their fellow workers, but also to minister to the refugees who were now beginning to pour across the border.

I spoke with the two leaders, Egor and Dasha. They decided that because of the war and the uncertainty of the future for foreign teachers coming into Russia, they needed to pray about raising up teachers inside the country. I shared with them the essence of my conversation with Kristina and that I personally felt that the depth of her commitment and anointing had prepared her to teach Spiritual Warfare, and that I would pass my notes to her and help her in any way possible.

On March 12, I got a text from Kristina telling me that Egor and Dasha had spoken to her about this. She said, "I talked with them yesterday. I had already received a word from God that I would teach about spiritual warfare one day. I am surprised, but I understand that this is exactly God's plan and His blessing. Of course, I will be very glad if you can help me."

When I read her text, I began to weep. God had already been speaking to her heart, so this was a confirmation of the Lord's perfect will for her life. I emailed her all my teaching notes, but I also told her the Lord would be giving her strategies and wisdom He had not given me as she prepared herself to teach.

The staff and students at the YWAM Rostov base began to have other problems, this time involving finances. They all lived by faith, and people from around the world, myself included, would send money to them through different Internet apps. Now, because of the war, none of the apps would allow us to send money to Russian accounts. At the same time, the expenses at the base began to grow because of the flow of refugees coming out of Ukraine.

PASSING THE MANTLE OF WAR

Many of those who arrived at the base had nothing but the clothes on their back, and they were looking just to pass through Rostov and then go on to some European country where they could be safe and start a new life. We had to figure out a way to get the necessary finances to the YWAM base.

I finally decided to invite Kristina, accompanied by Dasha, to meet me in Armenia. I felt that if she was going to teach my classes, it would be best if I could lay hands on her and pray for her personally. I'm a strong believer in praying for people for impartation of giftings and callings. In Romans 1:11, Paul said:

For I long to see you that I might impart to you some spiritual gift, so that you may be established.

He admonished Timothy:

Therefore I remind you to stir up the gift of God which is in you through the laying on of my hands. For God has not given us a spirit of fear, but of power and of love and of a sound mind.   2 Timothy 1:6-7

I was at a service at the Eagles Nest Ministries in Costa Mesa one evening, and there was a spacial speaker from New Zealand. An altar call was given at the end. Because I knew this speaker was a very anointed brother, I went up for prayer. People stood in two lines across the front of the altar on the left and the right, and I got on the end of one of those lines. He came along praying for people, and many were being touched by the Holy Spirit. But just when he got to me, he stopped and went to the other line.

I walked over and got on the end of that line, and he came through praying for people. Then, just as he got to me again, he moved to another area to pray, without praying for me. I was a little discouraged, so I just went back to my seat.

INHERITING THE NATIONS

I sat there praying. I said, "Lord, You know what I need." At that moment, I looked up and he was coming down the main aisle of the church praying for people at the end of each aisle. This was my chance. I jumped out into the aisle, knowing now he could not get by me without praying for me. But, just before he got to me, he started to run, and when he ran by me, he touched my arm lightly and said, "Receive."

Even though he had touched me very lightly, it felt like my whole skeletal frame shook violently, and I believe at that moment a spirit of war was imparted to me. I had been teaching about spiritual warfare for a long time, but after that touch, I began to teach with much more power and authority.

I was confident that when Kristina came to Armenia, and we laid hands on her and prayed, the Lord would impart something to her that would be dramatic and would equip her with the giftings necessary for her calling. This fresh anointing on her life would set her apart from others and would give her favor with God and man. I told her that this was her time. She had been born for this hour! At the same time, I would be able to put cash in the girl's hands that they could carry back into Russia.

Most of the airports were closed because of the war, so they would have to take a ten-hour train ride to get to an open airport from which they could fly to Armenia. The schedule was set. They would meet me in late March in Yerevan, Armenia.

My flight to Armenia was, by far, one of the worst flights I've ever taken in my life. At the airport near my home, they told me I needed a second covid vaccine and that I needed a return ticket out of Armenia before I could board the plane in California. I hadn't purchased a return ticket because I wasn't sure how long I would stay in Armenia. Also, I had been there eleven times before, and I knew I didn't need a return ticket in order to enter Armenia. They kept insisting I did and said they could not allow me onto the flight without it.

PASSING THE MANTLE OF WAR

I insisted that I didn't need a second covid shot because the shot I had gotten was a Johnson & Johnson one-shot-fully-vaccinated vaccine. Eventually, I told the agent to forget the flight and to re-book me for the next day. She went to another computer, to reschedule me, and then she said, "Wait a minute. I think I can get you on." The plane was already boarding. In the end, I was finally on the plane headed to Texas for a connecting flight to Germany.

Then, in Texas, I again had a problem over the covid vaccine, but I finally got on my flight to Germany, which would be an eleven-hour flight. After dinner, the lights were turned down and most everyone was sleeping. Now that sciatic pain in my knee became excruciating, so bad that I cried.

I had a six-hour layover in Germany before my next flight to Austria. Because of my flying status, I could stay in the business lounges for free. The pain was so bad that I ordered a wheelchair to take me to the business lounge. The chair never arrived at the gate, so I had to walk to the business lounge, which probably was the best thing for me after having to sit for so long.

At the lounge, they again questioned my vaccine status. They had just passed a new law in Germany that required everyone to have two vaccines to enter a restaurant, and the lounge was considered a restaurant. Finally, the attendant at the lounge told me that if I got a negative test at the nearby covid testing center, I could come into the lounge. I would have to exit the airport, use a bridge that went over the freeway, go to an office building to find the testing center, get tested, then walk back. All of that took an hour and a half, but finally I was in the business lounge, where I could eat and relax during my long layover.

Eventually, I boarded another flight, this one to Austria, where I would have a two-hour layover before getting on my way to my final destination—Yerevan, Armenia.

INHERITING THE NATIONS

I knew the ladies would want to meet me at the airport, but I specifically told them, "Please don't come. My plane won't be landing until 3 AM. I'll see you in the morning."

After twenty-six hours of travel, I arrived at the YWAM base at 5 AM on Sunday morning, and the ladies were waiting in the living room to greet me. We stayed up another hour, talking and laughing. It was great to see them and receive their hugs. The business lounge in Germany had offered big pretzels, some covered with salt and others with cheese. I had put six of them in my carry-on bag for these ladies.

The Lord had given me great favor in many Armenian churches. I had asked Aram, the leader of the base, if he would set up a meeting for us in a small church that is special to my heart. This church is like my family, where I can open my heart, I can laugh, and I can cry, and they laugh and cry with me. He made the arrangements.

I was standing in the back of the church as worship was starting, and one brother came in the door. When he saw me, he just hugged me for the longest time and started to cry because he was so happy to see me. This is family in Armenia.

I gave the congregation an update of what was going on in my life and shared the Word with them. Then I asked Dasha and Kristina to also share what was on their hearts. When Kristina finished speaking, I shared with everyone the fact that I had decided to pass my mantle on to her, to teach Spiritual Warfare in Russia, and I asked if anyone felt led to come up and lay hands on her and pray for her. Three ladies came up and gracefully laid hands on her and prophesied over her. It was a special time—for them and for Kristina.

Aram told me later that he didn't remember ever having someone ask the normal members to come up and pray for someone like that. They told him that it was a real blessing to be used by the Lord to pray for Kristina.

PASSING THE MANTLE OF WAR

After church, we went to the training base where the girls had been in 2019. I'd had a vision of the base several weeks prior, so it was in my heart to go there and pray for my spiritual daughter and the other students who had trained there but had lost their vision and calling.

Kristina began to reminisce about the great times there when everyone dreamed together, prayed together, and heard and wrote songs from Heaven together. Because there was limited internet, there had been a lot of interpersonal relationships that developed. As we were praying, she now began to cry, remembering so many who had left there with dreams but had abandoned their dreams for the things of the world. It was a very emotional time of prayer and weeping—for them and for me.

Later the girls thanked me for taking them there. They thought they were just going to ride along with me because I wanted to go there and pray, but it was an amazing time for them to be there, to remember what was born there in their hearts and in the hearts of others and to be able to stand there on the same ground and cry out to the Father for those who had been detoured from their callings. It was a God-ordained time for all of us.

I had known Dasha and her husband for a few years, but my times with Kristina had been basically over the Internet, so it was great just to be with them for a few days before we prayed for her. We walked around the city, went to my favorite restaurant, and just spent time talking. The way Kristina carried herself as we walked impressed me. To me, she seemed like a woman of integrity and confidence, even though she was only twenty-seven. Soon the weight of the mantle that I carried would be placed upon her, and she would become a woman of war.

I had told her in our conversations, prior to meeting in Armenia, that the girl that came from Russia would not be the same one that would be going back there. She would be forever changed, and the anointing and authority upon her would be increased for God's glory.

The time finally came to pray for Kristina and to impart to her the things the Lord had imparted to me and some of my friends. We were joined in prayer by Aram, who runs the base, Rosanna his wife, Dasha, from Russia, Pastor Dina, from California (over FaceTime), and Karina, from Rostov (also over FaceTime), who would partner with Kristina when she returned to Russia.

Before we prayed, I read some scriptures about Elijah and Elisha recorded in the book of 2 Kings. The time of Elijah's departure to be with the heavenly Father was near, and Elisha, in his heart, wanted the anointing that was upon Elijah. He even asked for a double portion of it:

*Then he took the mantle of Elijah that had fallen from him, and struck the water, and said, "Where is the L*ORD *God of Elijah?" And when he also had struck the water, it was divided this way and that; and Elisha crossed over. Now when the sons of the prophets who were from Jericho saw him, they said, "The spirit of Elijah rests on Elisha." And they came to meet him, and bowed to the ground before him.* 2 Kings 2:14-15

I also read the scripture that motivates me to lay hands on people and pray for them, where the apostle Paul said:

I long to see you that I might impart to you some spiritual gifts, so that you miay be established. Romans 1:11

I had Kristina sit in a large soft chair, we gathered around her, and our two friends on FaceTime watched online. We prayed for a long time. I don't remember all the prayers. I think that Dasha recorded everything, and I know the Lord recorded it in Heaven. He had ordained this time and these prayers for His daughter, Kristina.

PASSING THE MANTLE OF WAR

Pastor Dina, online from California, prayed for Kristina and prophesied over her. Then Aram laid a sword upon her head and prophesied over her, and we anointed her for war.

Dasha and Rosanna also laid hands on Kristina and prayed over her. I hugged her and prayed that the Spirit that was upon me would come upon her.

Kristina is not me; she is Kristina, a young, twenty-seven-year-old Russian lady, but God has called her to be a warrior for Himself and to raise up an army prepared for spiritual battle that will go out and set people free for the Lord in the nations of the world. This is her time. She was born for this hour, and just like Elisha did more than Elijah, I believe Kristina will do more than I have done. She will do things that I have never done, and the Lord will impart things from His heart to her heart that He has not given to me. The Lord believes in her, He trusts her, and He will continue to walk with her in the nations of the world. She will raise up other warriors who will be strong in spiritual battle and will break down strongholds and set the captive free, that the Lord in Heaven will be glorified, that Jesus might receive the reward of His suffering.

I have said repeatedly that this is not a theology book. I know that some reading it will not agree with everything in it, but it has not been written to correct or even change the theology of anyone. This is my story, my experiences, as I have walked with the Lord to the best of my ability in the nations of the world.

Praying for Kristina was a special and sacred time for all of us involved in that holy moment. There are people in Russia whom the Lord wants to raise up to be mighty warriors for Him, and He needs a teacher to prepare them and call them to war. Because of the physical war going on in Ukraine, it is impossible for me to go to that region at this time, and only the Lord knows what the future will be. I may never return to Russia. Therefore, the Lord needed someone else who could carry the spirit I carry, to teach spiritual warfare, and He chose Kristina.

In praying and prophesying over Kristina, we were only agreeing with what the Lord had already told her in her heart and what I felt the Lord was showing me about her. Some may question our methods of praying for her. The methods are not as important as what the Lord was doing in the spirit realm for her, and I'm confident that her fruit will validate the anointing upon her life and her anointing for war, to raise up an army ready for spiritual battle in the nations of the world.

Those of us who prayed for Kristina there in Armenia and, over the Internet, and for Karina, who would teach with her, had done our part. We could do no more. It was now up to the Lord to continue to speak to Kristina's heart as she returned to Rostov to teach.

The following day the two ladies would begin their travel back to Russia, to the base, where there would be spiritual warfare. Also, a physical war was still raging, and refugees were still coming through Rostov to find a way to freedom in a new country. The students and staff at the YWAM base would reach out to them, meeting their physical needs, but also sharing with them the Gospel. Some would be hearing it for the first time.

Before the ladies left, we were able to gather from my friends in America several thousands of dollars that they could physically carry back. Some of it would be used for the needs of the refugees, and some would be used by the students and staff, who no longer had any way to get support from the West because of the war.

Because Kristina would be teaching Spiritual Warfare, I felt it would be important for her to have a real sword to use in her class. So, before she left Armenia, I gave her $100 and told her to use it to buy her own sword. When she got back home, she searched many places but was having difficulty finding a sword that did not have demonic symbols on it. Then she found a man who made swords, and he made

PASSING THE MANTLE OF WAR

one specifically for her. That was an answer to prayer.

With the two ladies, I sent a birthday card to my friend, Dina. I had talked to her after the war broke out and asked about her finances. She told me she now had no income because there was no way to receive money through the Internet. I asked her how much she needed to live on, and she said she needed $200 a month to pay for her room and food.

I told Dina that I would send her a little money for her birthday. She probably thought I was going to send her $50, but I had it in my heart to send her $100. Brenda heard me talking about it and gave me another $100 to put in the birthday card, and people at the home church we attend gave $400. So, in that birthday card, was $600, enough to support Dina for several months. It was a great blessing to her.

Dina doesn't speak any English, but after she received the card, Dasha called me on FaceTime with Dina on the line and translated her words of gratitude to us all, and then I prayed for her.

Dasha and Kristina were scheduled to leave the following evening, so the next morning when I was teaching my class to the Armenia group, I gave part of the time to Kristina to speak to the students and to pray for everyone personally before she left.

We drove the ladies to the airport, and I had mixed feelings. I'd had some special days with them, I had felt their love and experienced their physical hugs. I knew I would miss them greatly. I reached my arm over to the back seat and took their hands and prayed for them as Aram was driving. When I finally finished praying, I released their hands, but Kristina held on to my hand for a while longer. As she did, the Lord touched my heart that was still needing some healing from the spiritual warfare I had been experiencing the past two years, and her touch meant a lot to me.

After the ladies were gone, I continued teaching Spiritual Warfare in the DTS class at the base, then spent two more weeks, sharing in local churches, and recorded four teachings that would be broadcast on Christian Internet television to the Armenian world at a later date. On April 11, 2022, Kristina and Karina began to teach the DTS class on Spiritual Warfare in Rostov. A spiritual warrior had become a teacher of war.

After the two ladies returned to Russia, I received this text from Kristina:

> Joe, thank you very much for the trip. It was really a very important and special time for Dasha and for me personally. Thank you for inviting me, convincing me of the need to go, investing and sharing financially, and letting me enjoy every minute. It was a great honor to pray with you and experience the presence of the Holy Spirit and your parental care and love. Every prophecy, every prayer, and every word of blessing is now written on my heart.
>
> With these prayers, and spiritual and financial blessings, we are happy to return to continue to serve and fight spiritually, to stand firm in what we do and in the promises that God has for us. Thank you very much to each of your friends who donated finances and have been praying for us. We are deeply grateful to absolutely everyone for their open and warm hearts and for every dollar which will be a huge blessing for the ministry here. Thanks for the opportunities we now have because of these gifts.
>
> Joe, you know you told me before we even came to Armenia that it would be a special

time, and I would come back another person, not the same Kristina. Well, it is like that. Right now I feel God's power and His trust in me, His presence is in my heart and on me and my ministry partner, Karina. This is truly a special time!

Sometimes I speak in small churches and sometimes in large churches, but there are special times when you touch just one person with the hands, arms, and words of Jesus. This was one of those times. Kristina, a young Russian lady, was that one person Jesus touched through me during our prayer time. She drew a picture of the words I tell her often.

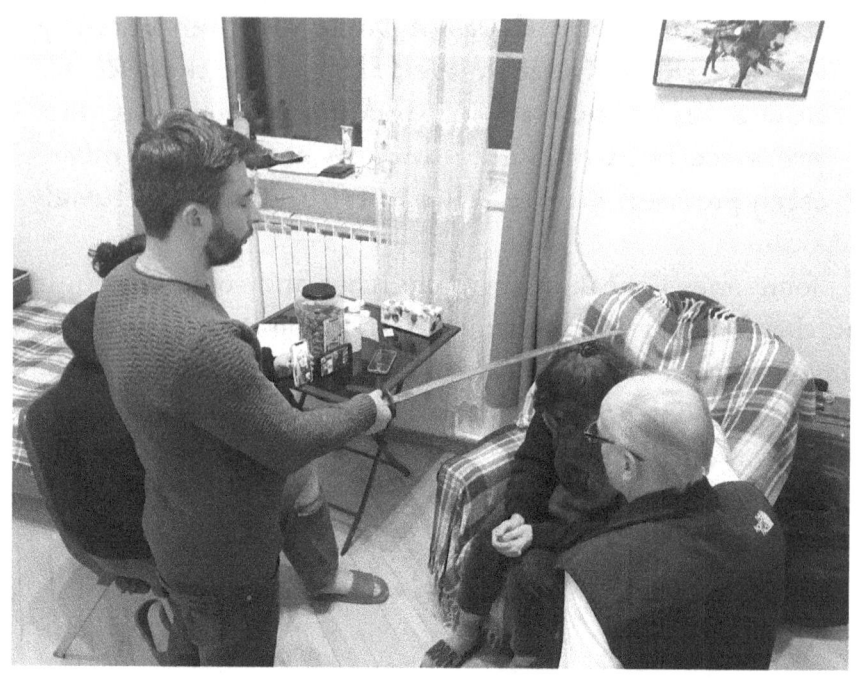

Passing the mantle to Kristina

WHEN'S GOD'S WARRIORS GO DOWN ON THEIR KNEES, THE BATTLE IS NOT OVER. **IT HAS JUST BEGUN**.

Kristina and Karina in Russia

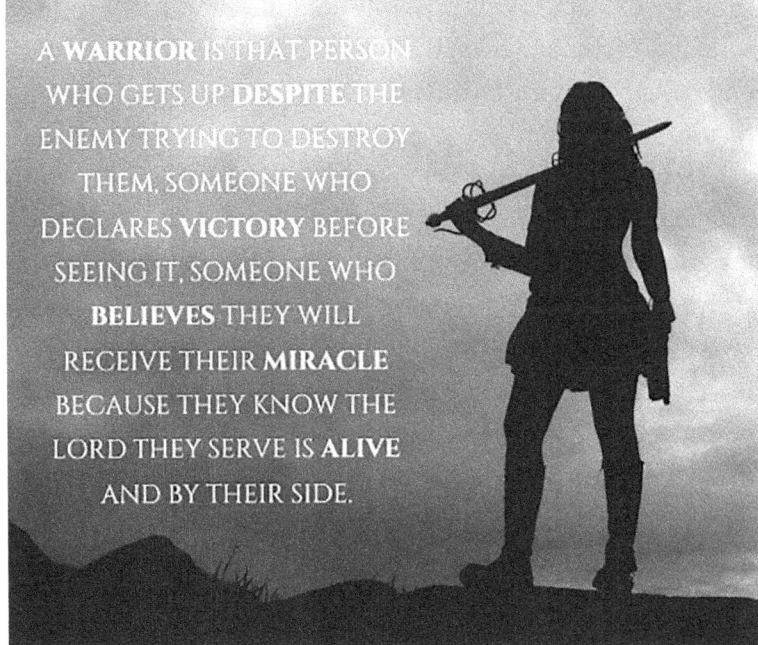

CHAPTER 43

THEY CALLED ME FATHER

And he arose and came to his father. But when he was still a great way off, his father saw him and had compassion, and he ran and fell on his neck and kissed him.   Luke 15:20

As I said in the very first chapter of the book, I came to the Lord shortly after the experience of coming home one day from work and finding that my wife and two sons were gone. She stayed in the area for a while, and I put my sons in a Christian School and tried to spend time with them when possible. Then, one day they didn't arrive at school, so someone from the school called me. I went by where my wife and sons had been living, and it was empty. They had mysteriously disappeared,

Unable to discover where my family was, I went to California to visit some friends for Christmas. During that trip, I felt the Lord telling me to move to California to attend seminary. Eventually, I began to travel to several nations in the world, sharing the Gospel.

I was visiting China one year not too long before Christmas. I have been to China so many times that I don't remember the actual year this happened, but I remember that it was in wintertime, prior to Christmas, and I was in my hotel in Hong Kong opening a package from my brother who had forwarded a lot of mail to me. There were many letters, but there was one that particularly touched my heart. It was from my youngest son. He was asking if I could send him money to buy a bicycle for Christmas. Sadly, I didn't have the money at the time, and so I was unable to buy him the bike he desired. Even today, more than fifty years later, he still brings that up to me sometimes. The good thing was that I now had the address in Pennsylvania where my family was living, and I was finally able to start communication with him and his brother. Eventually, I was able to start seeing them again when I could get to the East Coast.

Unfortunately, I had never developed the skills of a father, so I was never able to be the father my boys needed at that time in their life. My ex-wife had remarried, but, sadly, that marriage also ended in a divorce after many years of abuse, to her and even to my sons, according to one of them.

Not many years after my wife's second divorce, I was in Cambodia, and an urgent email from Brenda telling me to call my youngest son. There was no phone service where I was, so I went into the city and called. My son relayed a tragic scene to me. His mother had fired a man from work on Friday, and he had come back on Monday, shot and killed her, and then gone home and killed himself. It had been twenty-five years since I had seen her, but when my son's words came into my ear, it was as if someone had punched me with great force right in my chest. It nearly took the breath out of me.

I finished my meetings in Cambodia, flew to Bangkok, then home to California and caught the first possible flight to Pennsylvania. I arrived a couple days after the funeral, which was probably best because I didn't need to see any of the old relatives. It was just important to be with my sons at that devastating time. We went to the cemetery and together bowed at their mother's grave. That was a sad day!

That was many years ago. Both of my sons are now married and have started families, and I never got the opportunity to be the father they needed. Some years ago, when I met that young lady on a plane in

INHERITING THE NATIONS

Thailand, who eventually became a Christian, I felt that she was a gift from the Lord, a daughter I never had. He would use her to teach me how to love a daughter. She had a deep need in her heart for a father's unconditional love. I saw her pain, but for some reason, I couldn't reach in and heal that pain. I did my best, but in the end, it wasn't enough. I failed her.

Because our God is the Lord of redemption, He uses all things to bring us into the image of His Son. We become His sons and daughters, and each day, as we yield to the Holy Spirit, we become more like Jesus. He loves us with a love that we don't fully understand, and He gives us the ability to love other people, people who are broken, who are in pain, who just need someone to wrap their arms around them, that they might feel the embrace of the heavenly Father.

A few years ago, when I was feeling very sad and the enemy was telling me that I was a failure because I felt I didn't have the ability to be a father to my spiritual daughter, my friend, Aram, the leader of the YWAM base in Armenia, called me and said, "I know you miss your spiritual daughter, but you have many sons and daughters here in Armenia. You are not just our teacher; you're our friend, you're our father, and we need you." I just cried hearing his kind words.

I was recently in Armenia for my thirteenth trip, to teach at the YWAM base about Spiritual Warfare. My students were to be many Armenians and Iranians, some coming from Iran and others who had moved to Armenia. Just prior to my arrival, Russian President Putin announced that he would be calling up men for the conflict in the Ukraine. Because of this, twenty-nine students and staff from the Rostov base fled to Armenia. I would now be teaching Armenians and Iranians in one class, and Russians in a few other classes. It was fun, challenging, and a great blessing. The base would now have to house more than fifty people, but thankfully, there was a special bedroom just for guest speakers such as myself.

Every day, sometimes more than once a day, I would hug each student personally. One morning, when I walked into the kitchen, there were several people there, and I began to hug each one. One was a very tall, thin Russian young man. I asked if he was a basketball player, but he said no. Then I gave him a big, long hug. As I walked away, he said something I'll never forget: "Thanks for noticing me!" In that moment, I realized once again the importance of a heartfelt hug.

There was another young Russian man. He didn't speak any English, so we always had to talk through a translator, usually a former student of mine from Tajikistan. She was now living in Russia and was part of the YWAM staff. He kept asking me what my gifting was? I never answered him directly, but I knew what he meant. He wanted to know what spiritual gift I was operating in. Usually, when that happens, a person wants you to use your gift to bless them. I decided to just play with him a little. I told him I was like Jesus. Then he asked his question again. I told him, "I have the hands of Jesus, so I lay hands on and pray for the sick." That didn't satisfy his curiosity, but it gave the three of us a good laugh.

The next morning, when I woke up, his question was on my mind, and I thought to myself, "Well, what is my gifting?" When I had begun traveling to the nations in the late 1970s, my strength was evangelism, and many people were coming to the Lord. So, I was then called an evangelist. Later, I even had a business card made that said Missionary Evangelist on it. But when I went to Brazil, they called me Pastor, and in many parts of Southeast Asia, they call me Teacher. When I went to Central Asia, the Lord used me to give prophetic words to people. In India, I taught a large group of Baptist leaders how to receive a prophetic word from the Lord and to give a prophetic word to someone else. So, sometimes I'm called Prophet. There have been some occasions in these later years of my life and ministry that people say I have an apostolic ministry, probably because my ministry has been mainly to leadership and those being trained to be leaders.

INHERITING THE NATIONS

As I thought about the different titles I've had over the years, I began to think: "What about now? What are the deep desires of my heart? What are my priorities? What has the Lord been trying to teach me in this season of my journey with Him?" It has been during these years that many have started to call me Father, and one of my priorities is to hug people, young and old, every opportunity I get. Some cry, some hold on tight for a long time, and somehow, in some miraculous way, the Lord uses my arms to love people. I believe with all my heart that people are hungry for real love. It's almost as if we have a generation of orphans who are looking for a father to love them, to accept them, to notice them, and to believe in them.

In May of 2023, I was in Armenia speaking at a church about the gifts of the Holy Spirit. After the service, many people came up for prayer, but one lady came up to share what the Lord had told her about me. She said, "The Lord showed me that you have the aroma of a father." I was amazed at this revelation. I had not said anything about feeling that the Lord was calling me to be a father, but she saw it in the spirit realm. I asked her to pray for me. She was quite shocked that I would ask her to pray for me, but she did.

Even though I failed many times at being a good earthly father, for some reason, the Lord continues to use me to raise up spiritual sons and daughters in the nations of the world and to be a father to them. What a miracle of His grace!

Egor and Dasha, YWAM in Russia

YWAM friends

Brother Aram and family, YWAM in Armenia

Chapter 44

Preparing for War

Proclaim this among the nations:
"Prepare for war!
Wake up the mighty men,
Let all the men of war draw near,
Let them come up."   Joel 3:9

Many people believe that this is a prophetic verse referring to the end-times, when God will judge the nations. However, I believe it is also a word for the Church today, a cry from the heart of God for His people to rise up. Much of the Church in this present day is asleep, with little or no understanding of the reality of the spiritual war that is going on all around us in the nations of the world.

Because of my schedule and desires, I usually don't watch much television. However, recently I was watching a program on a Christian channel. The host said, "My father taught me that because of the cross there is no longer any spiritual warfare going on in the earth." I couldn't believe my ears. I thought to myself, "What planet does this guy live on?"

I'm not a person who believes there's a demon behind every corner or that everything comes from the devil. The truth is that many wrong things are from our human flesh and desires. The old nature has not been crucified, and Jesus is not Lord of many areas of believers' lives.

INHERITING THE NATIONS

In 2006, I was involved in developing the teaching on Spiritual Warfare for the leadership training school we were starting in northeast Thailand. Over time, I developed the fourteen lessons for the class. I don't focus on the enemy, but I also want to make it clear that there is a spiritual war going on for the souls of men and women in the nations of the world. I believe that one of the reasons missionaries are having little success in seeing people turn to Jesus and become Christians is because they fail to understand the reality of spiritual warfare.

Many slaves from Africa were brought to Brazil, and along with them, these slaves brought their different practices of worshipping demonic spirits. The first missionaries who went to Brazil were Catholics. When the slaves converted to Catholicism, they continued to worship their demon spirits. When the missionaries taught them that this was wrong according to the Bible, the slaves simply took the names of saints, put it on their demons, and continued to worship them.

There's a theological term called "syncretism," where two religious beliefs are formed into one. If you go to Brazil today and ask a person, "What religion are you?" they will say they're Catholic, but the truth is that when they need a healing or need a miracle, they go to a spirit store where they are told what kind of sacrifices they must make in order to get answers to their prayers. They are Catholic in name but spiritist in practice.

I've been in many services in Brazil where an altar call was given to receive Jesus or pray for healing, and I can testify that many times, when a person tries to pray, a demon will scream out, as they are delivered and receive Jesus.

In one meeting, the pastor was preaching about addictions. When he finished, he asked if anyone wanted prayer for addiction. Many people went forward, but I noticed one young man who happened to be standing near me. He had been living on the streets of Rio, his clothes were filthy, and his hair was set in dreadlocks. His shoes were worn through to his socks, and his socks were worn through to his bare feet. He smelled horrible. I found out later that he was from Argentina.

The pulpit area had a few steps up to it, and the people who had come for prayer were standing on a level below it. This young man took a pack of cigarettes out of his pocket and put them on the altar. When the pastor started to pray a general prayer to break addictions, this man began to scream. It was a noise that came from the depths of Hell. Because I was standing near him, I saw that his mouth was open so far I thought his jaw would break as this blood-curdling sound came from him.

This scream was so loud that it drew the attention of everyone and disturbed the prayer time. A pastor and I, along with two deacons, took the man into a private room to pray for him. We sat him in a chair, and the four of us gathered around him and began to pray in the Spirit. His head was leaning to the side, and liquid was oozing out of his mouth. He appeared to be unconscious. Then my pastor friend said, "Everybody stop praying." Then he said, "Come out of him in the name of Jesus!" With that, the young man came to life, leaped off of the chair and into the arms of the pastor.

At the same moment, the pastor again said, "Come out of him in the name of Jesus!" The young man fell to the floor and began to move around like a snake. Within a very short time, he sat up and said, "Where am I? What's going on?" He was completely delivered, without a long deliverance session, just by the simple words, "Come out of him in the name of Jesus," uttered by a pastor who knew his authority.

The New Age movement across the world has many people involved with crystals, yoga, and other spiritual practices that give Satan legal rights to enter their life. Spiritual war is a reality that we, as Christians, must understand if we are going to see people turn their lives to Jesus.

Just a few days after I started writing this chapter, I was at church and met a young lady who is a missionary to Japan. We were talking

INHERITING THE NATIONS

about the spiritual forces at work there, and she told me that prior to boarding the airplane to fly back to America, she got an extreme pain in her back. It felt like metal bands were being placed on her back, and she could almost hear them locking like a metal brace that was going to bind her up. Fortunately, she realized it was a spiritual attack and prayed against it. The spiritual bands came off, the pain left, and she boarded her flight to America. It was wonderful that she recognized it as a spiritual attack and didn't just think it was back pain. Then, with spiritual wisdom and authority, she was able to stop this attack with prayer.

We had a youth conference in a small mountain village outside of Kathmandu, Nepal, and, at the same time, had a women's conference. The women used the church that was available, and for the youth, we used a large community building that would accommodate the approximate three hundred we were able to gather.

The first couple sessions we had seemed like absolute chaos. The young people were talking and appeared uninterested in what we were teaching. It was very frustrating. During the break, I noticed that on top of the building were Tibetan prayer flags. These are colorful pieces of cloth that prayers are written on and then hung in the trees, on the bridges, or on wires over buildings. Buddhists believe that when the wind blows these cloths, the prayers written on them ascend up to God. I learned that the building was built by Tibetan workers and had been dedicated to Tibetan gods. That was why the prayer flags were flying overhead.

I remembered the story of the Lord speaking to Joshua, giving him a strategy to break down the walls of Jericho. I decided that a similar act would be a form of spiritual warfare against these Tibetan spirits that controlled the atmosphere over and in the community building.

When break was finished, I informed everyone that we would line up two-by-two and march around the building, remaining totally silent as we marched, and then come back to our seats. Then, once we were back in our seats, we would give a shout of victory unto the Lord. The march around the building was a physical thing we could do in the natural realm, and that would allow God to move in the spiritual realm, which would affect the natural realm.

The march went very well. Everyone remained silent. Then, when we returned to our seats, we all gave a great shout of victory to the Lord. The Buddhist strongholds were broken, and the atmosphere changed. The Lord's presence now came, bringing a total change to the meeting. For the next two and a half days that community center became a place where the young people could meet the Lord who hears and answers prayer.

As I mentioned earlier in this book, spiritual warfare is not a picnic or a Sunday school game we play for fun; it's a war for the souls of men and women, a reality that we must be aware of every single day. We must stay focused on Jesus and walk in the authority that He has given us to take the Gospel to the nations. We must also be ready at all times to engage the enemy, as the Lord directs us, so that through us His Kingdom may expand in the earth, bringing glory to God!

When I first started teaching about spiritual warfare, I realized there needed to be a balance. We were made to enjoy fellowship with the Lord through the Holy Spirit, to daily experience His presence, while, at the same time, being ready, through the authority of Jesus, to encounter the enemy whenever he tries to assault or deceive us or others. During this daily journey with the Lord, we must be ready to share the reason for our faith with other people we may encounter, and as the Lord would direct us, help them to come to know this loving God.

During my travels in the nations of the world, I have experienced varying degrees of oppression and bondages that control the people. An understanding of spiritual warfare is vital if we are to see people set free and become a productive part of the family of God.

INHERITING THE NATIONS

In developing my teachings on spiritual warfare, I saw that there were at least three levels of warfare. First, is the personal level. Although salvation is a onetime experience, when the Holy Spirit comes into our life, there is an everyday walking out of our salvation. Some call this sanctification. It's a daily battle in which we lay down the flesh and choose to follow the Lord, and in the process, become more and more like Jesus.

... work out your own salvation with fear and trembling.
Philippians 2:12

Then there is a level of spiritual warfare that is outward to others. This is when the Lord uses us, by His direction, to help others get free of the demonic forces that are controlling and binding them.

And these signs will follow those who believe: In My name they will cast out demons; they will speak with new tongues. Mark 16:17

Then there is the level of spiritual warfare that is outward to the nations of the world. It is here that we encounter strongholds over large areas, such as villages, cities, and even entire countries. This warfare, again, must be conducted at the clear direction of the Holy Spirit.

And they went out and preached everywhere, the Lord working with them and confirming the word through the accompanying signs.
Mark 16:20

In writing this chapter and thinking about the many times I've taught on spiritual warfare to young people in Youth With A Mission classes and to pastors and leaders in the Bible schools of Thailand and Burma, I realize that this teaching could be a book in itself. I probably should consider, with all the material I have already accumulated, writing a book just on spiritual warfare.

In all my teachings, I try to be sensitive to whatever the Holy Spirit may want me to do, other than just teaching. Often I'm led to go around the room, lay hands on the people, and pray for them. Sometimes I even anoint them with oil before I pray. Many years ago, I was teaching in Armenia on spiritual warfare, and in the class was a girl named Anya. She wrote me a beautiful letter. In part, she said:

> "During the time you were praying for us, I felt the wounds of Christ on my hands. I physically felt the wounds. I didn't see the actual holes of crucifixions, but I felt that they were there. At that moment, I experienced the presence of Jesus. I prayed, cried, and thanked Him for everything. It was wonderful! Until now, when there are difficulties in my life, I look at my hands and, in my mind, I see His wounds. This has incredible power. Each time I understand and experience the value of His decision to go to the cross for my salvation, yours, and everyone else's. How incredible!" Anya of Kazakhstan

As I noted earlier, Anya returned to Armenia to become a missionary, and for a long time was the leader of the DTS classes there for Youth With A Mission.

One time there in Armenia a brother was having a celebration because his son had just come out of the military. He invited me and some others and said that Anya could come also to translate for me. I thought the celebration was at his house, with just family members, but it turned out to be in a massive party house with hundreds of people,

INHERITING THE NATIONS

Christian and non-Christian alike. He introduced me, telling the people I was a missionary and asking me to open the celebration with prayer.

The celebration started and the food started coming. I've never seen so much food in my entire life. It just kept coming and coming. It was an incredible feast. As people were enjoying the evening, and because they knew I was a missionary, Anya and I started to go around to the different tables where I felt the Lord was directing us to pray for people. With everyone we prayed for, Anya had a prophetic word that was very accurate. She blessed many people that night.

I have a friend named Pedro who lives in the slums of Rio. He got saved and went to Europe to study the Bible at a Youth With A Mission base. He finished school, met a girl, got married, and they went back to live in the slums, to bring the Gospel to the people he had grown up with.

He had it in his heart to visit Israel and walk in Jerusalem where Jesus walked. My other friend, Pastor Paulo, who lives in Rio, was taking many tour groups to Israel. Pedro was praying fervently to the Lord for Pastor Paulo to invite him to go on one of those tours. After a long time of his praying in this way, the Lord finally spoke to Pedro and said, "I know it would be wonderful for you to walk in places that I walked in Jerusalem, but what would be more wonderful would be for me to walk in you, places I've never walked."

There are still people in the nations of the world, and even in North America, who have never heard the Gospel. They are broken-hearted, held captive by the enemy, blinded from the truth of the Gospel, enslaved to the lusts of this world. The Father's heart cries out for us to wake up and to go out as mighty warriors into our neighborhoods, our cities, and the nations of the world, with His love and power to set people free, so that Jesus might receive the reward of His suffering!

My grandsons, young warriors

Dasha of Belarus painted this for me

Chapter 45

RELIGION OR RELATIONSHIP

No longer do I call you servants, for the servant does not know what his master is doing; but I have called you friends, for all things that I heard from My Father I have made known to you.   John 15:15

As I was growing up in a Catholic home, all the religious symbols were around our house. My parents had a beautiful blue glass cross with Jesus on it over their bed. It was probably more than a foot tall. We had a large family Bible that was always on our living room coffee table. There were salesmen who went door to door selling those Bibles back in the 1950s. We had a medal of Saint Christopher pinned to the headliner of our car for protection. And, after our first Holy Communion, each of us three boys received a daily missile. In those days, we didn't read the Bible because our understanding was that only the priests could interpret the Bible.

We went to church every Sunday and on special holy days, but aside from those days, religion didn't play a major part in our life. It was for Sunday, not for the rest of the week.

Although I never read a Bible in all those years, the religious instructions we received helped us to understand that we were sinners, and Jesus died for our sins. In order to receive communion on Sunday, we would have to go to confession on Saturday night. I can still remember that even as a teenager, when I went into the confessional booth and knelt down waiting for the priest to slide open the wooden door with a screen in front of it, I would be so nervous that I would wet my pants a little.

After what seemed like an eternity, the screen would finally open, and you would ask for the priest's blessing and tell him how long it had been since your last confession and then confess your sins. When you were finished, he would give you some kind of penance to do, different prayers like the Hail Mary or the Our Father. Once those prayers were said, you were clean, and we would try our best not to sin on Saturday night before Sunday church.

I remember one time my father went into the opposite side of the booth ahead of me, the priest heard his confession first, and I heard him say, "It has been one year since my last confession." I almost laughed out loud, but I didn't, and I didn't overhear any more of his confession.

I think I can honestly say that I knew all about Jesus, maybe not in detail like I do now, but I knew about Him as most good religious people would know about Him. But looking back on it now, even though we had all the religious symbols, went to church, and went to confession, I didn't know Jesus as my personal Savior. I knew *about* Him, but I didn't really know Him.

I think I could say it's like reading an autobiography of someone. Then, after reading the autobiography and knowing everything about a person, you have the opportunity to meet that person personally. That's the difference between religion and relationship. It's the difference between going to church on Sunday and the holy days and walking in a daily relationship with the living God.

When I was eighteen, I got my first full-time job working at the General Electric company in their factory. I bought my first car, a 1964 Chevrolet Malibu SS. At work, I met another young man named Mike Hall. He had just come out of the Air Force, and he was really into car racing. He invited me to go to the drag strip with him on Sunday. I had to make a choice. Which was the most important thing? Going to church or drag racing? As an eighteen-year-old with a new car, the choice was a no-brainer. I started going to the drag strip every Sunday. That first Sunday I won two trophies and never went to church again for many years. You can read the results of my wrong decisions and the consequences of those decisions in Chapter 1.

In that chapter you can also meet the woman I call my spiritual mother, Joan. I think I can honestly say that if I had not spoken to her on October 14, 1971 at 6:30 in the evening, I would probably be dead or in jail right now. Why? Because of the lifestyle I was leading.

What Joan said next created a major shift in my religious thinking. She said, "Tell God that you believe His Son, Jesus Christ, died for you personally." She ended by saying, "Ask Him to come into your life." After I prayed that simple prayer, I left religion, and I came into a personal relationship with God the Father through Jesus, His Son.

It was no longer a religious duty to go to church on Sunday and holidays. Now it was a daily intimate walk with the Creator of the Universe, because of what Jesus did on the cross for me personally. I now had a deep desire to read the Bible and have the joy of hearing the voice of the Holy Spirit speaking personally to me through that Bible.

While working for General Electric in their drafting department, I met a man named Joe Corolla. He was a believer and attended a Presbyterian Church. During Lent, they had what they called Lenten Luncheons on Friday afternoons, so I went with him. The church also had a bookstore, and Joe took me in there one day and bought me my first full Bible. It was a hard cover King James Version. In the beginning, it was hard to read because it was written in Old English, but with time, I read it with great joy and memorized some of the scriptures.

Three years later, on my third spiritual birthday, one of my neighbors, Peggy Sherman, who was also a believer, bought me my first leather-bound Bible. It was the right size for travel, so it became my main Bible as I traveled and taught in the nations of the world. Over the years the cover of that Bible took a real beating from all the use. Just recently I had it rebound in a beautiful blue leather.

I heard someone talking about reading the Bible every day, and they said, "The Bible will keep you from sin, or sin will keep you from the Bible." Here are some verses in the Bible that give us reason to read it every single day:

The Bible builds our faith:

So then faith comes by hearing, and hearing by the word of God.
Romans 10:17

The Bible gives us direction:

Your word is a lamp to my feet
And a light to my path. Psalm 119:105

The Bible gives us life:

But He answered and said, "It is written, 'Man shall not live by bread alone, but by every word that proceeds from the mouth of God.' "
Matthew 4:4

The Bible instructs us in the ways of God:

All Scripture is given by inspiration of God, and is profitable for doctrine, for reproof, for correction, for [a]instruction in righteousness.
2 Timothy 3:16

The Bible helps us to test the motives of our heart:

RELIGION OR RELATIONSHIP

For the word of God is living and powerful, and sharper than any two-edged sword, piercing even to the division of soul and spirit, and of joints and marrow, and is a discerner of the thoughts and intents of the heart. Hebrews 4:12

When I was growing up, the only Bible I knew was the big family Bible that lay on our coffee table. The only time we ever opened it was to look at the beautiful colored pictures that were in it. We never read it. After my encounter with the Lord, my attitude toward the Bible changed. It was now my daily bread.

My attitude toward prayer also changed. Prayer was no longer reciting prayers I had learned in church; it became a conversation between me and the Father in Heaven who loved me.

A friend of mine, also a new Christian, went away on a personal retreat to seek the Lord for her life. She later texted me and said, "I have a plan for my life." I assumed it was some elaborate dream or vision, but she only sent a picture. It was a picture of her holding a Bible. I was so blessed and proud of her.

Praying Matthew 6:9-13, better known as the Our Father, now is a joy. Why? Because He is my Father, He loves me, and I know He hears my prayers.

Our Father in heaven,
Hallowed be Your name.
Your kingdom come.
Your will be done
On earth as it is in heaven.
Give us this day our daily bread.
And forgive us our debts,
As we forgive our debtors.

INHERITING THE NATIONS

And do not lead us into temptation,
But deliver us from the evil one.
For Yours is the kingdom and the power and the glory forever. Amen.
Matthew 6:9-13

I now have confidence in my prayers:

Now this is the confidence that we have in Him, that if we ask anything according to His will, He hears us. And if we know that He hears us, whatever we ask, we know that we have the petitions that we asked of Him.
1 John 5:14-15

In the beginning of this personal relationship with God, even though I enjoyed praying, most of my prayers were in private. I did *not* enjoy praying in public or out loud where other people were present. When someone would ask me to pray for them, I would say, "I'll pray for you later in my prayer time." I never prayed at that moment with them. Maybe I was embarrassed or maybe I thought my prayers were not going to be grammatically correct. Whatever the reason, I didn't pray with people personally, but I remember when all that changed.

I had dated a girl named Linda for a short time prior to my marriage. Then, when I got married, I lost track of her. When my wife left me, a friend of mine ran into Linda and gave her my phone number. One day she called me, asking if I would give her and her sister a ride home. I hadn't seen her in many years, and I was curious about what she had been doing all those years, so I agreed to drive them home. When I picked them up, Linda had a baby with her. She informed me that she was married to a drug dealer. He was in the hospital very sick with hepatitis from a bad needle. She and all her friends were doing drugs, and their life was miserable.

RELIGION OR RELATIONSHIP

When we had dated, we were not Christians, but now I was an on-fire Christian. During most of the forty-five-minute drive to her home I told her and her sister about Jesus and what He was doing in my life. When I dropped them off, I gave her a little red booklet. It was filled with nothing but Bible verses. Linda called me a few days later to tell me that when she was listening to me tell my story about Jesus, she thought I was crazy and couldn't believe what had happened to me. That week, while she was in the hospital waiting room reading the Bible verses in the little red book, a nurse came to inform her that her husband had just died. She was only in her twenties, and yet here she was a widow with a young baby and a drug addiction.

It was clear that Linda needed help, so I started to hang out with her and some of her friends. I shared my story with them, took them to church and Bible study with me, and yet I never prayed with them privately. I clearly remember one of her friends saying to me one evening with tears in her eyes, "We have to get off these drugs. We have to have something better."

One afternoon, Linda, with her baby and her sister, came by my house. It's been so long ago that I don't remember what else happened that day, but I do remember that as they were leaving, she stepped onto my front porch, turned around, and said, "Will you pray for me now?" I can see it even now, as if it were happening this moment, and cannot forget the desperation in her eyes.

I said to her, "I'll pray for you when I go to bed tonight."

As she turned and walked away, I felt like a total failure. I had led her to the Lord, but I couldn't pray with her out loud. That night, as I lay in bed, I made a conscious decision that I would never let that happen again. I had to start praying publicly with people who needed my prayers. Since that day, I have traveled the world and prayed for thousands of people. When I pray, I know the Lord hears my prayers; He not only hears; He answers.

INHERITING THE NATIONS

I have dozens of books about prayer, but when I teach about prayer, I tell everyone that they can throw all the books away. There's only one secret to prayer, and that is to actually pray. The devil will do everything he can to stop us from praying.

When I'm teaching, I love demonstrations, and so when I'm at the Youth With A Mission bases around the world teaching about spiritual warfare, one of my lessons is about prayer. I choose a girl from the class, and I say to the students, "This is only a demonstration. I am a happily married man, but today this is my girlfriend." She comes up, and we hold hands, and we're on our way to a prayer meeting. On the way, however, we see an ice cream store, and we both love ice cream. We have plenty of time to get to the prayer meeting, so we get an ice cream cone, and we share it as we look into each other's eyes, because we're boyfriend and girlfriend. Everyone can relate to this, especially the young people in the class.

We finish our ice cream and continue on our way to the prayer meeting. Along the way, we encounter some Christian friends. So, we stop to fellowship with them for a little while. It's always great to talk with Christian friends and share what the Lord is doing in our lives. Then, I look down at my watch. "What time is it? Oh my, the prayer meeting is over already, and we didn't get there to pray." I use this demonstration to show that many times we are caught up in doing good things that are used by the enemy to stop us from praying.

I read an article one time that said the average American pastor prays less than ten minutes a day. In this day, when almost everyone is carrying a smartphone, we spend more time on social media then we do praying. I can imagine that the heart of the Father in Heaven is breaking. He loves to hear the voice of His sons and daughters communicating with Him.

When I'm teaching about prayer, I tell people that God is a collector, and then I ask them, "What do you think God collects. He created all things, so what would He want to collect?"

RELIGION OR RELATIONSHIP

When I was a teenager, I collected stamps for a while. The books the stamps were in were very luxurious, but the value was not in the book. The valuable things were the stamps inside the book. But what God collects He puts in golden bowls. What could possibly be more valuable than bowls made of gold? Then I read to them from Revelation 5:

Now when He had taken the scroll, the four living creatures and the twenty-four elders fell down before the Lamb, each having a harp, and golden bowls full of incense, which are the prayers of the saints.
Revelation 5:8

Imagine, God saves your prayers and puts them in golden bowls. Our prayers are precious to Him. Why? Because He enjoys hearing our voice.

Many years ago, I decided to close my construction company and return to full-time ministry. That would mean a major shift in my finances and would require me to find people who were interested in investing in what the Lord was showing me to do in the nations of the world. I decided to form a nonprofit religious corporation so that people in America could give financial gifts and receive a tax deduction for their gifts from the government.

Forming such a corporation was complicated, but a friend of mine who was a lawyer walked me through the process. I had to have a name for the corporation, and this became a challenge. Everything I decided on my wife didn't like. Months went by, and we couldn't come to an agreement. Finally, a friend of mine who had a nonprofit organization told me to just choose any name, and I could change it later. At least I could get the process going. I thought about this verse in Revelation 5:8 and decided to call the organization Golden Bowl Ministries International. I filed the required paperwork, and it was quickly approved. In the end, there was only one small glitch; my wife

INHERITING THE NATIONS

still didn't like the name I chose. She said it sounded like a Chinese restaurant. Personally, I can't think of anything more wonderful, amazing, encouraging, and comforting than the fact that the Lord has heard our prayers and keeps them in golden bowls.

You pray about stress and anxiety, and peace comes. You pray for direction, and the Lord shows you a way. You see a spiritual battle coming, you pray, and the Lord gives you a strategy for victory. You pray about your financial needs, and the Lord brings to you exactly what you need. You pray for a person who doesn't know the Lord and who's addicted to drugs, and the Lord saves them and delivers them. You pray for healing, and God brings you healing to show His love. When we pray, the possibilities are endless. God is a loving Father who is just waiting to hear the prayers of His precious children.

Jesus had many followers and, from among them, many became His disciples. But the day was coming when He would have to choose a smaller group whom He would call apostles. He would send them out to represent Him in the cities and nations of the world. They would do the miracles He had done. This would be a great responsibility for those He would choose, so He must choose the correct ones. He must talk to the Father about this important task. He must pray!

> *Now it came to pass in those days that He went out to the mountain to pray, and continued all night in prayer to God. And when it was day, He called His disciples to Himself; and from them He chose twelve whom He also named apostles*   Luke 6:12-13

The Father loved us, so He sent His Son to pay for our sin:

> *For God so loved the world that He gave His only begotten Son, that whoever believes in Him should not perish but have everlasting life.*

RELIGION OR RELATIONSHIP

For God did not send his Son into the world to condemn the world, but that the world through Him might be saved.   John 3:16-17

But when the fullness of the time had come, God sent forth His Son, born[a] of a woman, born under the law, to redeem those who were under the law, that we might receive the adoption as sons.
And because you are sons, God has sent forth the Spirit of His Son into your hearts, crying out, "Abba, Father!" Therefore you are no longer a slave but a son, and if a son, then an heir of God through Christ.
     Galatians 4:4-7

Jesus came because He had a destiny to fulfill. He came to lead a sinless life, so that He could qualify to pay for your sins and mine. Before Him was the cross, where He would experience a horrible death. He would be the ultimate sacrifice standing between a holy God and sinful man.

I have not come to call the righteous, but sinners, to repentance.
     Luke 5:32

This is a faithful saying and worthy of all acceptance, that Jesus Christ came into the world to save sinners, of whom I am chief.
     1 Timothy 1:15

Many churches in America in this present time have become what we would call "seeker-friendly." The church is now a place to go and meet other people, hear Bible teachings, and enjoy fellowship with others. If you're single, you might even find your future husband or wife. However, there are no messages about sin or repentance. Nothing is taught that would make people uncomfortable.

Charles Finney was a twenty-nine-year-old lawyer who decided he must settle the question of his soul's salvation. So, on October 10, 1821, he went into the woods near his house in Adams, New York to find God. He said, "I will give my heart to God, or I will never come down from there." There in the woods he had an encounter that changed his life. He later wrote, "The Holy Spirit seemed to go through me, body and soul. I could feel the impression, like a wave of electricity, going through and through me. Indeed, it seemed to come in waves of liquid love, for I could not express it in any other way."

Charles Finney became one of the leading revivalists in the nineteenth century and was called by many the Father of American Revivalism. He said, "Revival is a renewed conviction of sin and repentance, followed by an intense desire to live in obedience to God. It is giving up one's will to God in deep humility."

I heard it said that eighty-five percent of people who became believers under Finney's ministry remained true to the Lord. This is the exact opposite of many American evangelist today. The difference was that Finney preached about sin. He also said, "Sin is the most expensive thing in the universe. Nothing else can cause so much harm."

When we talk about sin and the human heart, there's an amazing thing that happens in our mind. We can always justify our sin. We look at other people who we believe are worse than us, and we think our lifestyle is "okay." As I mentioned earlier in the book, if I hadn't experienced the Lord when I was twenty-five, I probably would be in jail or dead. Without elaborating too much, the reason I said that was because I was involved in a lot of robberies. In my mind, I always justified this because whatever I stole I sold to have money for my family. So, in my mind that was "okay." But when I received the Lord, the Holy Spirit began to convict me and show me that I needed to make restitution.

After doing all the restitution I could, I wrote down a list of robberies that I had committed. Then I called a detective from the local police department whom I knew personally. He also knew that my life had been changed because of Jesus. I asked him to come to my house, and when he arrived, I handed him a three-page list of robberies that I had committed, all still unsolved. He looked over the list and said, "What is this?"

I told him that these were robberies I had committed, and the Lord wanted me to make restitution. I must admit I was nervous and somewhat fearful of what could happen, but I had no choice. I had given my life to the Lord, and I had to obey the Holy Spirit. This man wasn't a believer, but he knew of my conversion. After looking over the list for a while, he finally looked up and said to me, "Well, I guess ten or twenty years in prison will probably take care of this."

After a period of stressful silence, he added, "Joe, the truth is most of these robberies happened a long time ago and have already been covered by insurance companies, so just leave this up to me and the Lord."

When the policeman had left, I breathed a sigh of relief. I learned that day that I simply had to obey the Holy Spirit.

Jesus came to pay for our sin and to set us free from sin, so we could have a personal relationship with a loving Father. Jesus is the only way to the Father.

> *Jesus said to him, "I am the way, the truth, and the life. No one comes to the Father except through me."*   John 14:6

> *If you love Me, keep my commandments. And I will pray to the Father, and he will give you another Helper, that He may abide with you forever-the Spirit of truth, whom the world cannot receive, because it neither sees Him nor knows Him; but you know Him, for He dwells with you and will be in you.*   John 14:15-17

I mentioned earlier that my parents had that beautiful blue glass crucifix in their bedroom. Probably most of my neighbors in our middle-class neighborhood in Albany, New York had crucifixes in their home too. However, after my encounter with the Lord, the crucifix took on a new meaning. I realized that Jesus was no longer there. The payment for my sin was over. He paid the full price that day on Calvary, and because the sacrifice was accepted by the Father, Jesus is no longer on the cross. He has risen from the dead and now sits at the right hand of the Father making intercession for us.

I took my spiritual daughter, who was a new Christian, to a bookstore one day in Bangkok. The store was connected to a local church and had a lot of Christian things. I purchased her first Bible, and she wanted to buy a cross. While I was talking to one of the workers, she looked around the store to find a cross she liked for her apartment. After a short time, she came to me and said, "I can't find a cross I like. I'm looking for one with Jesus on it." I had to explain to her that, as Christians, we don't believe that Jesus is on the cross anymore. He is risen. Maybe she didn't understand everything, being a new Christian, but she accepted my explanation and bought a nice wooden cross.

There probably is not a picture in the world that can really portray what Jesus went through on the cross to pay for our sin—the torture, the exhaustion, His blood pouring out, blood pouring down His face from the crown of thorns, and the worst thing, separation from His Father. There was a movie some years ago called "The Passion of the Christ" produced by Mel Gibson. I didn't see the movie, but those who did said that the crucifixion of Jesus looked so real and so horrible that it was very difficult to watch it.

The prophet Isaiah foretold the suffering of Jesus on the cross:

He is despised and rejected by men,
A Man of sorrows and acquainted with grief.
And we hid, as it were, our faces from Him;
He was despised, and we did not esteem Him.

RELIGION OR RELATIONSHIP

Surely He has borne our griefs
And carried our sorrows;
Yet we esteemed Him stricken,
Smitten by God, and afflicted.
But He was wounded for our transgressions,
He was bruised for our iniquities;
The chastisement for our peace was upon Him,
And by His stripes we are healed.   Isaiah 53:3-5

Matthew was a tax collector before he met Jesus, but then he became a disciple, and eventually Jesus called him to be an apostle. He wrote what we know as the first book of the New Testament, and he gives a first-person account of that day when Jesus was crucified.

And when they had come to a place called Golgotha, that is to say, Place of a Skull, they gave Him sour wine mingled with gall to drink. But when He had tasted it, He would not drink.
Then they crucified Him, and divided His garments, casting lots, that it might be fulfilled which was spoken by the prophet:

> *"They divided My garments among them,*
> *And for My clothing they cast lots."*

Sitting down, they kept watch over Him there. And they put up over His head the accusation written against Him:

> THIS IS JESUS THE KING OF THE JEWS.
>   Matthew 27:33-37

Jesus experienced separation from His Father:

INHERITING THE NATIONS

Now from the sixth hour until the ninth hour there was darkness over all the land. And about the ninth hour Jesus cried out with a loud voice, saying, "Eli, Eli, lama sabachthani?" that is, "My God, My God, why have You forsaken Me?"
Some of those who stood there, when they heard that, said, "This Man is calling for Elijah!" Immediately one of them ran and took a sponge, filled it with sour wine and put it on a reed, and offered it to Him to drink. The rest said, "Let Him alone; let us see if Elijah will come to save Him."
Matthew 27:45-49

Jesus willingly gave up His life in payment for our sin:

And Jesus cried out again with a loud voice, and yielded up His spirit. Then, behold, the veil of the temple was torn in two from top to bottom; and the earth quaked, and the rocks were split, and the graves were opened; and many bodies of the saints who had fallen asleep were raised; and coming out of the graves after His resurrection, they went into the holy city and appeared to many.
So when the centurion and those with him, who were guarding Jesus, saw the earthquake and the things that had happened, they feared greatly, saying, "Truly this was the Son of God!"   Matthew 27:50-54

Think about this: Jesus, because the Father loved us, went to the cross in obedience to His Father, so that we, sinful men and women, might be reconciled to a holy God.

After He had paid the price for our sin, the body of Jesus was placed in a tomb:

Now when evening had come, there came a rich man from Arimathea, named Joseph, who himself had also become a disciple of Jesus. This man went to Pilate and asked for the body of Jesus. Then Pilate commanded the body to be given to him. When Joseph had taken the body, he wrapped it in a clean linen cloth, and laid it in his new tomb which he had hewn out of the rock; and he rolled a large stone against the door of the tomb, and departed. Matthew 27:57-60

But death could not hold Jesus:

Now after the Sabbath, as the first day of the week began to dawn, Mary Magdalene and the other Mary came to see the tomb. And behold, there was a great earthquake; for an angel of the Lord descended from heaven and came and rolled back the stone from the door, and sat on it. Matthew 28:1-2

The angel announced the good news:

But the Angel answered and said to the women, "do not be afraid, for I know that you seek Jesus who was crucified. He is not here; for he is risen, as he said. Come, see the place where the Lord lay. Matthew 28:5-6

Jesus appeared to His disciples:

And Jesus came and spoke to them, saying, "All authority has been given to Me in heaven and on earth. Go therefore and make disciples of all the nations, baptizing them in the name of the Father and of the Son and of the Holy Spirit, teaching them to observe all things that I have commanded you; and lo, I am with you always, even to the end of the age." Amen. Matthew 28:18-20

This year, I will turn seventy-seven. When I was young, growing up in Albany, life was different. Children respected adults, and we honored all those in authority. Life was simple and fun. But things have changed dramatically. I now live in California, where sin, according to the Bible, has become a normal way of life. Across America, it seems like our world gets more wicked every day. Billy Graham once said, "Even in this modern age, the wages of sin is still death." All humanity is following the wickedness of their hearts. They are fatherless, and they wander without a purpose. Why? Because they don't know the heavenly Father, who gives meaning and purpose to life, a life filled with joy and content, a life filled with Him and His presence.

Only an encounter with Jesus can change us and bring us back to God's original plan in the garden to have a son and a daughter who would walk with Him. He's looking for a family.

Jesus did not come just to set us free from drugs, alcohol, or other addictions. He came to set us free from ourselves and our sinful ways, to break the chains of wickedness and doing our own thing, instead of pursuing the things of our heavenly Father. His will is not that we walk so as to fulfill religious duties, but walk in a relationship with our Father, just like Adam and Eve did before they sinned.

Because Jesus paid the price for your sin and my sin, we can once again walk with God. We can feel His presence. We can hear His voice. We can experience the embrace of the heavenly Father. It's not about going to church or fulfilling religious duties. It's not religion; it's a relationship with a loving Father because of the sacrifice of Jesus. It's not about going to church on Sunday or religious holidays; it's about a daily intimate walk with Jesus. It's about the Holy Spirit living within us and speaking to us and through us. It's time to throw off the shackles of religion and enter into a relationship with the Father that will fulfill the deep desires of our hearts. We can experience real, unconditional love that will transform every part of our lives.

When You meet someone from the underground church in China who hasn't had a real Bible in more than thirty years and you hand them one, they draw it up to their chest and they begin to cry. You can never be the same after you see that, and you will always think of the Bible in a different way. When you meet someone who has been in prison for a long time because of their faith and they lay hands on you and pray for you, prayer takes on a whole new meaning in your life. When you walk the streets of Bangkok, Thailand and Phnom Penh, Cambodia in the night, you see how sin is destroying the people. It robs them of their innocence and never allows them to experience true love. Then you realize what it cost Jesus to go to the cross. You know the only way they will ever be free is by having an experience with Jesus, the Savior. Only He has the power to deliver and heal them. His blood was poured out on the cross to give them hope for a better life, an eternal life.

When you pray for a friend who is scheduled for breast cancer surgery in a few days, and the Lord totally heals them, you know that Jehovah-Rapha, the God who heals, is still healing today. Then you realize the Lord wants to use your prayers and your hands to bring healing to others.

When you meet someone who has been a worshipper of Buddha all their life and you tell them that Jesus has a plan for them, then you see them become a disciple of Jesus, sharing the good news wherever they go, you understand the transforming power of the cross. You see that the words of Jesus are true, when He said:

> *The thief does not come except to steal, and to kill, and to destroy. I have come that they may have life, and that they may have it more abundantly.* John 10:10

All of these things are so the Father might be glorified through us, and that Jesus might receive the reward of His suffering! This is the story of my journey with Jesus, and this is the difference between religion and relationship.

A Christian's tools of intimacy

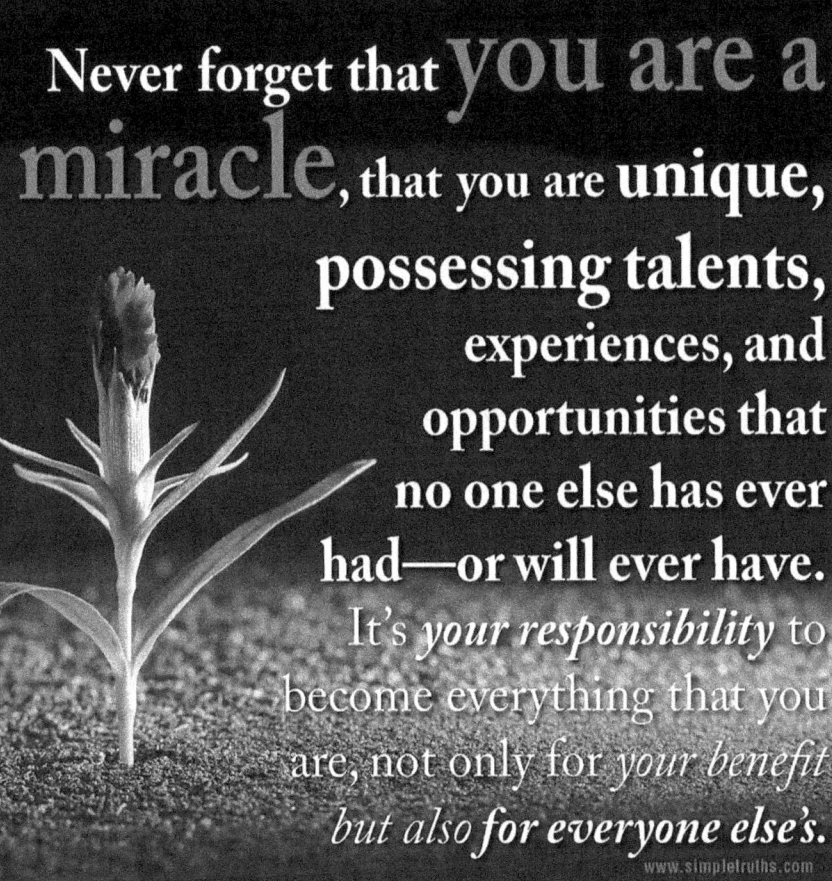

SUGGESTED READING

Believe and Be Love by Caitlan Ann, Self Published: 2013

Why Speak in Tongues by Hobart Freeman. Faith Ministries & Publications

Intercessory Prayer by Dutch Sheets-Regal Books

To Golden Shore-The Life of Adoniram Judson by Courtney Anderson-Judson Press

The Beauty of Spiritual Language by Jack Hayford. Thomas Nelson Publishers

Blood Brothers in Christ by Malcolm Smith-Fleming H. Revell Company

The Heavenly Man: the Remarkable True Story of Chinese Christian Brother Yun by Paul Hattaway

Son of the Underground: the Story of Issac Liu, Son of Brother Yun By Albrecht Karl

AUTHOR CONTACT PAGE

You may contact Joseph Zeyak, Jr. in the following ways:

Mail:
Joseph Zeyak, Jr.
PO Box 394
Tustin, CA 92781

Telephone: 714.747.2216

Email: Zeyak2@gmail.com
GoldenBowlMinistries@gmail.com

Facebook: Joseph Zeyak Jr.

Instagram: JosephZeyak

GOLDEN BOWL MINISTRIES

If you have been blessed by the testimonies of Joseph Zeyak Jr. in this book and would like to have a part in the outreach of Golden Bowl Ministries, whether as a financial contributor or to invite Joseph to come and share with your church or home group, please contact him at any of the addresses on the previous page. All contributions are tax deductible and will fund this vision for the unreached nations.

Joseph at Victory Church, Albany, New York

www.ingramcontent.com/pod-product-compliance
Lightning Source LLC
Chambersburg PA
CBHW050708160426
43194CB00010B/2051